HOW **DEMOCRACY** WORKS

Political Institutions, Actors, and Arenas in Latin American Policymaking

Carlos Scartascini
Ernesto Stein
Mariano Tommasi

Editors

Inter-American Development Bank

David Rockefeller Center for Latin American Studies
Harvard University

Co-published by
David Rockefeller Center for Latin American Studies
Harvard University
1730 Cambridge Street
Cambridge, MA 02138

Produced by the IDB Office of External Relations

The views and opinions expressed in this publication are those of the authors and do not necessarily reflect the official position of the Inter-American Development Bank.

**Cataloging-in-Publication data provided by the
Inter-American Development Bank
Felipe Herrera Library**

How democracy works : political institutions, actors, and arenas in Latin American policymaking / Carlos Scartascini, Ernesto Stein, Mariano Tommasi, editors.

p. cm.
Includes bibliographical references.
ISBN: 978-1-59782-109-4

1. Latin America—Politics and government. 2. Policy Sciences—Latin America. 3. Political planning—Latin America. 4. Politics, Practical—Latin America. 5. Public Administration—Latin America. 6. Political science—Latin America. I. Scartascini, Carlos G., 1971-. II. Stein, Ernesto. III. Tommasi, Mariano, 1964-. IV. Inter-American Development Bank.

JL959.5.P64 H69 2010
320.98 H830—dc22   LCCN: 2010928756

To order this book, contact:
Pórtico Bookstore
1350 New York Ave., N.W.
Washington, D.C. 20005
Tel.: (202) 312-4186
Fax: (202) 312-4188
E-mail: portico.sales@fceusa.com

Contents

TABLES

FIGURES

Acknowledgments

The initial inspiration for this project came from the work on Argentina by two of the editors of this book, Pablo Spiller and Mariano Tommasi, reflected in their book, *The Institutional Foundations of Public Policy in Argentina* (Cambridge University Press, 2007). In that work, Spiller and Tommasi developed a methodology that, with some refinements and adaptations, became the basis for the conceptual framework used in the related volume *Policymaking in Latin America: How Politics Shapes Policies*, published in this series in 2008. While that volume focuses on country cases, this one looks at the role of specific institutions and actors in the policymaking process.

The book is part of a larger agenda on political institutions and policy outcomes in Latin America being carried out by the Research Department of the Inter-American Development Bank (IDB), which includes the 2006 Report on Economic and Social Progress in Latin America, *The Politics of Policies*.

The chapters in this book were written by well-known experts under the auspices of the IDB Research Department, and the coordination of Ernesto Stein and Mariano Tommasi. Luis Estanislao (Koldo) Echebarría, and, in particular, Mark Payne, also helped coordinate part of the work. Carlos Scartascini joined this project at a later stage and was instrumental in transforming a collection of working papers into the cohesive set of chapters that follow.

The process of writing the book was highly interactive, with ample opportunities for cross-fertilization among the authors of the chapters, as well as frequent give and take (in both directions) between these authors and the project coordinators. A seminar organized by the IDB in Washington, D.C. in March 2005 was a very important focal point in this interactive process. For their help in organizing this seminar, as well as for their invaluable support during the whole process, we want to thank Norelis Betancourt and Raquel Gómez of the IDB.

We would also like to recognize our colleagues at the Research Department of the IDB and at the Universidad de San Andrés for their support, encouragement, and feedback. Within the IDB, we especially want to recognize the support received from Guillermo Calvo, Santiago Levy, and Eduardo Lora, Chief Economists and Managers of the Research Department at different stages of progress of this project. Without their support, this project would not have been possible. Mariano Tommasi acknowledges the support of the John Simon Guggenheim Memorial Foundation and the Inter-American Development Bank.

Apart from the authors of the chapters and those already recognized above, many others deserve recognition for their valuable comments at different stages of the process. These include Pablo Alonso, Mauricio Cárdenas, Fernando Carrillo-Flórez, Juan Carlos Cortázar Velarde, Rafael de la Cruz, Ariel Fiszbein, Phil Keefer, Fabrice Lehoucq, Andrés Mejía Acosta, Bernardo Mueller, Juan Carlos Navarro, Michael Penfold, Carlos Pereira, Javier Santiso, and an anonymous referee. Participants at various seminars in which some of the papers were presented should be recognized as well. The chapter authors are also grateful to the various workshop participants and interviewees who gave generously of their time and knowledge. Barbara Murphy and Maria Florencia Guerzovich provided valuable research assistance to Ben Ross Schneider. A revised version of Ben Ross Schneider's chapter appears in *The Oxford Handbook of Business and Government*, edited by David Coen, Wyn Grant, and Graham Wilson and published by Oxford University Press.

Ideas become successful books thanks to capable editorial and administrative support. For their invaluable support in this area, we would like to acknowledge Rita Funaro, María Helena Melasecca, Mariela Semidey, and John Smith. For pulling everything together, we are most grateful to the main editor, Nancy Morrison, as well as the publications team at the IDB, led by Gerardo Giannoni and Rita Funaro, with the support of John Dunn Smith and Elisabeth Schmitt. Finally, Melisa Iorianni assisted in the final stages of the process, and Cesar Rodriguez Mosquera provided valuable inputs for the drafting of Chapter 1.

Foreword

The restoration of democracy in Latin America in the 1980s was expected to bring with it a new era of progress. Most people across the region agreed at the time that democracy—albeit imperfect—was preferable to any other form of government. Today, however, the situation has changed. Public opinion polls reveal that support for the democratic system has waned as citizens have realized that democracy alone does not assure prosperity and equality.

Of course, opinions vary from country to country because results, too, have varied. Countries that have managed to pursue better policies have enjoyed better development outcomes. Political results have varied too: some countries have transitioned smoothly from one administration to the next with little political conflict, while others have been mired in corruption scandals and political unrest.

For decades, unstable democracies were blamed for the region's slow development and inequality, and much of the academic discussion was focused on the alleged limitations of presidentialism, particularly in the context of minority governments. Once democracy had reestablished itself as the rule of the game, the political economy literature rapidly switched its focus to the issues related to the timing, sequencing, and implementation of economic reforms. Neither approach proved sufficient to explain the differences in development and political stability across a region where all countries are presidential democracies but only a few have persevered with a program of structural reforms coherent and sustained enough to reap significant economic and social benefits. Clearly, at least part of the explanation lies somewhere else.

The Inter-American Development Bank (IDB) launched a search for answers in the political process itself. In 2005, it published *The Politics of Policies,* which proved to be the first step in a journey to understand how democracies work in Latin America. Looking at the characteristics of public policies and the political institutions that shaped them appeared to provide important clues about countries' paths of development. A subsequent volume, *Policymaking in Latin America: How Politics Shapes*

Policies, delved deeper into the process with country studies that showed how the diversity of actors, their identities, incentives, and the arenas in which they interact help explain political decisions and the outcomes of those decisions.

How Democracy Works is the latest book in the policymaking series, but instead of viewing the process country by country, it explores the institutions, actors, and arenas across Latin America. Each chapter looks at one of these aspects and provides comparative evidence on how it works across the region and its impact on the policymaking process and the resulting policies. This comparative perspective highlights differences in the institutions, actors, and arenas that help explain how presidential systems in a relatively culturally homogeneous region can produce such different results. For example, dissecting the structure of the executive branch reveals differences across countries in the role of cabinets and the capacity of the civil service. Other chapters study the role of legislatures and courts in the policymaking process. In addition to traditional political actors, the book delves deeply into the characteristics of political parties and how they mobilize candidates, proposals, and interests that play a part in the policymaking process. How political decentralization has restructured political incentives and the roles of non-state actors such as business, labor, and the media are also addressed.

How Democracy Works caters to a large and varied audience. The breadth of data provided by the country chapters provides a wealth of information for academics to use in their own research and raises many questions for future study.

For policymakers, it provides a benchmark to compare their own countries with the rest of the region. How does my legislature fare in comparison to others? How does the relative power of the president and legislature in my country compare with that of my neighbors? How active and independent is the judiciary in my country? Does my country suffer more or less turnover among ministers and other public officials than other countries? Do these facts explain the quality of public policies? Can labor policies be explained by alternative union strategies and structures? Is the media as important as in other countries in shaping opinions? These questions and more can be answered with the material in this book and may provide policymakers with ideas for directing their efforts and investments to improve policymaking.

The development community can also benefit from this book as it provides evidence for understanding how politics in the region affects policies and how institutions, actors, and arenas affect their development efforts. Those who wonder why certain countries have a harder time passing loans through the legislature or executing projects may find clues in this volume. Even more interestingly, they may discover where and how to focus their efforts in order to increase government capabilities and foster economic development while pursuing social and political inclusion.

I believe the IDB's investment in this line of research has been well worth the time and resources spent. This book is a significant addition to the stock of knowledge about **how democracy works** in Latin America and by shining a light on the process rather than simply the policies, may very well mark a new path for promoting development in the region.

Eduardo Lora
Manager of the Research Department and
Chief Economist a.i.
Inter-American Development Bank

CHAPTER 1

Political Institutions, Actors, and Arenas in Latin American Policymaking

Carlos Scartascini, Ernesto Stein, and Mariano Tommasi

In the past thirty years, democratic freedom and competitive electoral processes have taken hold as never before in Latin America. This book zeroes in on the intricate workings of democratic institutions, the actors that participate in democratic systems, and the arenas in which political and policy interactions take place in Latin America. The focus is on how those institutions, actors, and arenas affect the policymaking processes (PMP) of Latin American countries for better or worse.

In its scope and complexity, the volume moves well beyond two stylized views of the political systems in Latin America. One view, associated with the notion of hyperpresidentialism, emphasizes personalization of power, disdain for institutions, and confrontational political style. Another view emphasizes the difficulties faced by reform-minded presidents who have had to deal with recalcitrant and parochial legislatures while trying to advance their own modernizing agendas. Between the stylized views of hyperpresidentialism and of the stalemate of divided government, a recent wave of analysis has delved deeper into the workings of Latin American democratic institutions. This book is a contribution to that endeavor.

The chapters of this book take a detailed look at each of the main actors in the PMP of Latin America, as well as the arenas in which they interact. *Actors* that are central to policymaking include official state *actors* and professional politicians (presidents, party leaders, legislators, judges, governors, cabinet members, bureaucrats), as well as other members of civil society (such as business groups, labor unions, the media, and public opinion leaders). These actors interact in a variety of *arenas*, which may be formal (such as the legislature or the cabinet), or informal (such as "the street," or the proverbial smoke-filled rooms where powerful actors meet to close deals), and may be more or less transparent. The relevance of some of the actors, their specific role in the PMP, and the way they play the game varies from country to country, as does the importance of alternative arenas. While in some countries (Chile, for example) the central loci of policymaking are the legislature and the cabinet, in others (such as Bolivia or Ecuador) the street plays a much bigger role.

The complex interaction among actors—and thus the policy outcomes—is influenced by a wide range of *political and institutional factors*. These include the nature of the political party system, the structure and functioning of the legislature, the constraints and incentives facing presidents, the federal structure of the country, the autonomy and capacity of the bureaucracy, and the role and independence of the judiciary. These factors affect the roles and incentives of each of the actors, the characteristics of the arenas in which they interact, and the nature of the transactions in which they engage.

For each set of actors, the chapters look at their formal roles, incentives, and capabilities, as well as the way in which they actually engage in the policymaking game, against the backdrop of each country's political and institutional factors. The chapters show, in rich detail, how these political institutions, actors, and arenas matter for policymaking in Latin America, and how they affect—and are affected by—both the policy process and the resulting policies. The analysis pays special attention to the extent to which political institutions facilitate or hinder political cooperation and compromise over time, and thus help or harm the quality of public policies.[1]

Each chapter has been written by a well-known expert on the subject, who presents comparative indicators of the characteristics of

---

[1] This volume refers to a number of policy features, including stability, adaptability, coordination, enforcement, and orientation toward the general interest ("public regardedness"). Stein and Tommasi (2007) and Scartascini, Stein, and Tommasi (2008) show a positive correlation between these features and development outcomes such as GDP per capita growth and the advancement in the Human Development Index. For a complete discussion of these policy features, see IDB (2005, 2008); Spiller and Tommasi (2007); Stein and Tommasi (2007); Spiller, Stein, and Tommasi (2008); and Scartascini, Stein, and Tommasi (2008).

these actors and arenas across most countries in the region. Using these indicators, readers may compare the performance of specific countries in a particular institutional domain and compare how countries fare across domains. The authors supplement these general measures with attention to the richness and complexity of each case, drawing from detailed country studies, which are presented in a separate volume (Stein et al., 2008). These country studies allow readers to understand how the individual institutions, actors, and arenas examined in this volume come together and frame policymaking in each country.

The chapters that follow are not a random collection of studies of political and democratic institutions, actors, and arenas. They are the outcome of an integrated research project and an interactive process among all the authors based on a common conceptual framework for studying the PMP.

Analytical Context and Conceptual Framework

The nine studies commissioned for the research project upon which this book is based are heirs to a number of currents in political science and political economy: currents that reflect the main research concerns that have arisen during each stage of political and economic development in Latin America in the last several decades.

For much of the twentieth century, most Latin American countries followed a pattern of state-led development based on import substitution strategies. This era was characterized by the importance of the role of the state, mainly through its bureaucracies and enterprises, mass mobilization, political polarization and instability, democratic breakdowns, military coups, and repression. The most notable streams of politico-economic research at the time (and of those times) focused on various structural conditions as well as on the impact of foreign economic pressure and interest groups, trying to understand the relationship between economic modernization and its impact on the political regime and its stability.[2]

The late 1970s and 1980s were the time of democratization in Latin America. By the time of the 1989 democratic elections in Brazil and Chile, all Latin American countries, with the exception of Cuba, had elected constitutional governments, marking a significant transformation in the

---

[2] Classic works include Lipset (1960); Cardoso and Falleto (1968); and O'Donnell (1972).

region away from long periods dominated by military authoritarianism. Not surprisingly, scholarly research on the workings of Latin American polities at the time focused on understanding the processes of the transition to democracy, on the likelihood of democratic consolidation, and on the type of institutional regimes (presidential or parliamentary) more likely to facilitate governability in such polities in transition.[3]

Once democratic governments had been established, economic and social crises soon arose, ending mainly in high deficits, debt crisis, and social commotion. The effectiveness of the new regimes was called into question and the size and efficacy of state machinery seriously challenged. This opportunity paved the way for the implementation of a number of "market-oriented reforms." At that time, policymakers and governments were markedly preoccupied with the strategies and conditions leading to different reform sequences and outcomes in the various countries.[4]

Much of the reform literature—at least the economics literature—worked on the premise that the reforms that countries needed to undertake were technically obvious for any half-competent economist, and that it was just a matter of figuring out the way to implement those reforms in the context of some collective action problems that arose because losers from reform were concentrated, whereas beneficiaries were diffuse.

Those waves of political and economic liberalization have left a mixed terrain of successes and failures. Moreover, ideas and approaches have continued to evolve. The intellectual perspective guiding the studies in this volume reflects some strands of recent thinking about the political economy of Latin America.

On the one hand, economists have started to move away from the conviction that there are policy recipes that can be universally applied to all countries. A universal set of "right" policies does not exist. Policies are contingent responses to underlying states of the world. What might work at one point in time in a given country might not work in a different place or in the same place at another time. In some cases, some particular characteristics of policies or the details of their implementation

---

[3] Classic works include O'Donnell, Schmitter, and Whitehead (1986); Karl (1990); Huntington (1992); Mainwaring, O'Donnell, and Valenzuela (1992); and Linz and Stepan (1996). See also Hagopian and Mainwaring (2005).

[4] See, for instance, Stallings and Kaufman (1989); Nelson (1990); Bates and Krueger (1993); Acuña and Smith (1994); Haggard and Webb (1994); Geddes (1995); Rodrik (1996); Tommasi and Velasco (1996); Sturzenegger and Tommasi (1998); and Stokes (2001).

might matter as much as the broad type of policy.[5] Thus economists and development practitioners more generally are paying more attention to the democratic processes behind policies.

At the same time, the analysis of democratic processes has gained from the incorporation of microanalytical perspectives drawing from institutional economics and rational choice political science. Drawing from the insights of recent generations of institutional scholars,[6] a new breed of researchers is deploying some of the tools originally developed to study U.S. politics (and, later, European politics) to study the details of the workings of political institutions in Latin America.[7] The chapters of this book are in part a reflection and elaboration on what has been learned about various actors and institutional arenas.

Twenty years or more have elapsed for most Latin American countries since the return to democracy. The discussion about the consolidation of democracy has given way to new questions relating to the quality of the democracy and to the ability of democratic systems of government to deliver in the face of various societal demands. Over these two decades, actors and institutions that were almost irrelevant in previous eras have gained center stage, including political party systems, legislatures, subnational authorities, and the media. These are precisely some of the actors and arenas upon which this book focuses.

These actors and arenas are studied from a perspective that is now common in comparative politics and political economy, emphasizing the

---

[5] For instance, Dani Rodrik analyzed six countries that implemented a set of policies that shared the same generic title—"export subsidization"—but had widely different degrees of success. Rodrik relates their success to such features as the consistency with which the policy was implemented, which office was in charge, how the policy was bundled (or not) with other policy objectives, and how predictable the future of the policy was (Rodrik, 1995; see also Tommasi, 2004).

[6] The revolution of institutional analysis in economics and in politics is too vast to be summarized here. The Nobel Prize in Economics has been awarded in the last several decades to scholars who have examined this approach, including R. Coase, D. North, O. Williamson, and E. Ostrom. Rational choice institutional analysis in politics has tended to focus initially on U.S. institutions, but has been expanded into the comparative politics domain by scholars such as A. Lijphart, M. Levi, and G. Tsebelis. Some excellent books focusing on institutional features of Latin American polities are Shugart and Carey (1992) on presidents and assemblies; Mainwaring and Scully (1995) on party systems; Mainwaring and Shugart (1997) on constitutional and partisan powers of the president; Carey and Shugart (1998) on the executive decree authority; and Morgenstern and Nacif (2002) on legislative politics.

[7] See Geddes (2002) for some reflections on the transformation in the study of politics in developing countries.

way in which the institutions and political practices of each country affect the roles and incentives of each actor, the characteristics of the arenas in which they interact, and the nature of the transactions in which they engage. The focus is on the PMP, with special attention paid to the way in which the PMP affects the qualities and characteristics of resulting public policies.

Within the PMP framework, public policies are seen as the outcome of the interaction among a variety of political *actors*. These actors, each with its own preferences and incentives—and within the constraints of the rules that frame its engagement—meet in different arenas to define public policies. The complex interaction among these actors—and thus the policy outcomes—is influenced by a wide range of *political and institutional factors*, examined in detail in this volume.

Predecessors to this volume have emphasized that good policy-making can be facilitated if political actors have strong capabilities and relatively long horizons, and the arenas for the discussion, negotiation, and enforcement of political and policy agreements are relatively encompassing and well institutionalized.[8] These features tend to enhance the ability of political actors to cooperate, and to reach and enforce agreements over time (*intertemporal agreements*). In political environments that facilitate such agreements, public policies will tend to be of higher quality, less sensitive to political shocks, and more adaptable to changing economic and social conditions. In contrast, in settings that hinder cooperation, policies may be either too unstable (subject to political swings) or too inflexible (unable to adapt to socioeconomic shocks); they may be poorly coordinated; and investments in state capabilities may be lower.[9] Consequently, when looking at the impact of institutions or configuration of actors on the PMP—and through the workings of the PMP—on the features of policies, the individual chapters show how the different institutional configurations affect various policy features such as *stability* (the ability of countries to sustain policy over time), *adaptability* (the ability of countries to change policy when needed), and *public regardedness* (the ability of countries to reach, with

[8] See IDB (2005); Spiller and Tommasi (2007); Spiller, Stein, and Tommasi (2008); and Stein and Tommasi (2008).

[9] These links are discussed in Spiller and Tommasi (2003); IDB (2005); and Stein and Tommasi (2007).

their policies, broad constituencies in society instead of narrow interest groups).[10]

Each of the remaining chapters in this book focuses on a different set of actors that participate in the PMP, as well as on the arenas in which these actors play the game. In each case, the authors characterize the key dimensions that affect their role, their power, and the way they affect (and are affected by) the PMP. They also show how differences across countries with regard to these key characteristics lead to differing roles, and the way in which these roles can affect the quality of policies and policy outcomes. While the approach in the chapters is eclectic and varies from case to case, each of them, to a greater or lesser extent, picks up on the discussion of intertemporal cooperation outlined above, which becomes a unifying theme for the volume.

Actors and Arenas: Highlights of the Next Nine Chapters

Political Parties. In Chapter 2, Mark Jones discusses the role of political parties and party systems in Latin America. Political parties are a vital component of a democracy, with broader relevance beyond crucial tasks such as recruiting candidates, mobilizing electorates, and creating, presenting, and implementing policies. Outside the electoral arena, parties are also active participants in a host of other areas of modern democratic life such as forming governments and coalitions; organizing the legislature; and aggregating and articulating the interests and preferences of the citizenry, from within government as well as from the opposition.

Viewed this way, the aspects of political parties and party systems that matter for the PMP can be summarized as a set of characteristics, such as the degree of institutionalization, nationalization, polarization, fragmentation, and the relevance of programmatic versus clientelist politics. These characteristics do not operate in a vacuum; in varying combinations and degrees, they define the extent and nature of intertemporal agreements in which political parties engage. Considering the joint influence exercised by other institutions such as the presidency, cabinet, judiciary, bureaucracy, and subnational leaders, Jones concludes that democracies with more institutionalized party systems tend to have

---

[10] Other features introduced in IDB (2005) and related works include *efficiency, coordination and coherence,* and *the quality of implementation and enforcement.*

more programmatic politics. Parties that tend to compete on the basis of policy proposals also have greater consistency in public policy, and higher levels of accountability than their less institutionalized counterparts.[11]

The degree of nationalization of political parties and party systems also has several important effects on the functioning of a democracy. It is relevant for legislative careers and for executive–legislative relations, for instance; in highly nationalized party systems, national issues are likely to play a central role in legislators' careers. Jones' findings imply that in a nationalized party system, public policy is likely to be more oriented toward working for the national common good. Country examples of this type are Bolivia, Costa Rica, Paraguay, and Uruguay, where the design and functioning of the countries' political institutions should be expected to produce a highly nationalized party system. In contrast, in a weakly nationalized party system, public policy is likely to be directed far more toward the satisfaction of particularized local interests, often to the detriment of the national common good. For example, in countries such as Argentina, Brazil, and Colombia, each country's institutional framework provides incentives favoring more weakly nationalized party systems.

The party system plays a distinctive and central role for policy-making through its influence on executive–legislative relations. Chapter 2 suggests that low legislative fragmentation and/or a large contingent in the legislature that is aligned with the president enables presidents to implement their policy agenda effectively, regardless of the level of ideological polarization.[12] El Salvador features an especially complicated combination of modest presidential legislative contingents and high levels of polarization.

Jones highlights an alternative form of interparty interaction: political competition among parties based not on programmatic policies, but on clientelistic concerns. Voters do not necessarily select candidates according to their policy platforms and the potential impact of the candidates' policies on the general welfare; rather, voters may also look at

---

[11] In contrast, in weakly institutionalized party systems, interparty competition is based primarily on the candidate's personal appeal or short-term populist promises. These systems tend to produce inconsistent policies and have low levels of accountability and party identification.

[12] While low levels of polarization may have some positive attributes, they are not necessary for effective and efficient governance in these situations.

the particular and individual resources they get from candidates, such as government-sponsored jobs. Of course, no political party system falls exclusively into a purely programmatic or purely clientelist category. Even in the most programmatic party systems, parties engage in some forms of clientelist practices. Thus Jones identifies clientelism (broadly construed) as one of the dominant linkage mechanisms between parties and voters. He finds that only two countries have parties that are more programmatic than clientelistic: Chile and Uruguay.

Legislatures. In Chapter 3, Sebastian Saiegh evaluates the main factors that affect the role of legislatures in the PMP in Latin America. The role of the legislature in the PMP can have an important effect on the nature of policy outcomes. If the legislature is a marginal actor, the executive will have considerable discretion to pursue the policies it sees fit. But the lack of legislative deliberation and the weakness of oversight might mean that the policies adopted are poorly conceived in technical terms, poorly adjusted to the real needs or demands of citizens, and lacking in consensus—and thus politically unsustainable.

Comparing eighteen Latin American legislatures to identify the main differences in their organizational structures, institutional features, and membership characteristics, Saiegh identifies four types of legislatures according to two dimensions: their technical capabilities, and the degree to which they act in a more reactive or proactive manner. Legislatures that have more legitimacy, more experienced legislators, and well-developed committee systems will tend to be more constructive and/or proactive. Legislatures with weaker capabilities will tend either to play a limited policymaking role or to be active, but only in a fairly obstructionist way, rather than a constructive one.

The evidence found by Saiegh—using a multidimensional scaling technique—confirms that legislatures with greater capabilities play more constructive roles in the PMP, facilitating intertemporal agreements and policies with long time horizons. As expected, the extent and nature of the role of each legislature in the PMP vary greatly from country to country. At the more constructive end of the spectrum, legislatures such as those in Brazil and Chile have the potential to become active and effective players capable of participating in setting the policy agenda and overseeing policy implementation. On the other hand, legislatures (such as those in Nicaragua and Paraguay) lacking the organizational resources and experienced members and staff to serve as a mature and autonomous point of deliberation in the PMP, operate more as veto players.

The Judiciary. In Chapter 4, Mariana Magaldi de Sousa analyzes the role of the judiciary as a central actor in the PMP: one that can maintain checks and balances to help enforce public-regarding policy choices. How courts engage in the PMP and how such engagement varies across countries is inevitably conditioned by the degree of judicial independence from the executive in power. The chapter provides a typology for categorizing and comparatively assessing the extent of courts' involvement in the PMPs of specific Latin American countries.

Magaldi de Sousa identifies four main characteristics and roles of the courts: the extent to which the judiciary can veto new legislation; shape legislative content; enforce the implementation of existing rules as an impartial referee; and act as an alternative representative of society in the PMP. In particular, when judiciaries are active as veto players, policies are likely to be more stable, since policy changes must be consistent with the preferences of another institutional actor. As an impartial referee, the judiciary can help ensure the effectiveness of the implementation and enforcement of policies, thus facilitating intertemporal political transactions and encouraging policy stability. Moreover, by performing their role as societal representative—such as when courts rule according to the requirements of broad public welfare rather than according to the strict letter of the law—courts can help make policies more public-regarding.

The evidence presented by Magaldi de Sousa supports the argument that courts are increasing their impact on the PMP in Latin America. Furthermore, while countries with broad judicial activism seem to produce rather stable and adaptable public policies, the democracies with narrower levels of judicial activism are characterized by more volatile and rigid policies. The chapter argues that it is the structure and characteristics of judicial institutions that ultimately pave the way for courts to veto laws, shape their content, enforce other public policies, or act as an alternative representative of society.

Cabinets. In Chapter 5, Cecilia Martínez-Gallardo analyzes the role of cabinets in the PMP by focusing on their characteristics—the process through which they are formed, the ways they organize their work, and their stability—and on the mechanisms through which these character-istics affect the prospects for cooperation and better policy outcomes. Cabinet ministers play key roles in every stage of policymaking. Together with the bureaucracies they head, ministers nearly have a monopoly on the design of policy, with occasional input from political parties and/or interest groups.

Martínez-Gallardo identifies three main features of the institutional arrangements of cabinets that determine ministers' ability to coordinate and cooperate with one another and with other political actors in ways that make better policies more likely: cabinet formation; cabinet struc-ture and decision-making rules; and cabinet stability. The way these features interrelate determines the extent of cooperation, coordination, and flexibility—among cabinet members and between them and other institutions—that facilitate the intertemporal agreements that are central to making more stable and better policies.

When cabinet decision making is more fragmented and cabinets are more unstable, policymaking and intertemporal cooperation tend to suffer, Martínez-Gallardo finds. While cabinets across the region dif-fer in many ways, there are two common trends: a predominant role of finance ministers in policymaking, and a relatively low level of cabinet stability. About one-fifth (22 percent) of all ministers in Latin America remain in the same portfolio less than six months, and one-third have tenures of less than two years. Rapid turnover shortens the time horizon of policymakers, who tend to favor policies that have benefits they can capitalize on in the short run, regardless of their potential future costs. For instance, countries with unusually large and unstable cabinets, such as Ecuador, Peru, and Venezuela, are usually below the mean level of policy performance, while countries with rather stable or small cabinets, such as Chile, Costa Rica, and Mexico tend to perform better.[13]

Ministers and political actors in general must rely heavily on the bureaucracy to convert policy ideas and laws into specific acts of government. A strong and capable bureaucracy is likely to improve the quality of implementation of public policies. The role of bureaucracies goes beyond implementing policies: they also play an important role in preparing, executing, controlling, and evaluating public policies. Having a technically competent and independent bureaucracy to which some

---

[13] Causality is clearly a complex issue in some of these associations.

policy decision making and implementation may be delegated can facilitate intertemporal agreements, particularly in policy areas that are prone to politicization and political opportunism.

Bureaucracies. In Chapter 6, Laura Zuvanic and Mercedes Iacoviello discuss some characteristics of Latin American bureaucracies, their role in the PMP, and their capacity to carry forward long-lasting agreements. Zuvanic and Iacoviello's characterization is based on a model of strategic human resources management in which two dimensions are considered: autonomy of political power, and technical capacity. The authors group bureaucracies into four types: patronage, administrative, meritocratic, and parallel. Depending on the predominance of the types in each country, the role of the bureaucracy can range from informal veto player to an active player that can provide not only leadership but also facilitate collaboration and cooperation to maintain or improve a specific policy.

Only a few countries stand out in the region because of the higher level of development of their civil services, including Brazil, Chile, and Costa Rica. The rest tend to have relatively poorly developed civil services, according to the evidence presented by Zuvanic and Iacoviello. In terms of classifications, some are meritocratic bureaucracies such as those of Brazil and Chile; some are administrative, such as those of Argentina, Costa Rica, and Ecuador, and the rest tend to fall in the category of patronage bureaucracies. Zuvanic and Iacoviello emphasize the strength and professionalism of the bureaucracy as an important feature leading to better public policy, and note that the weakness of bureaucracies has contributed to the weakness of the state in Latin American countries, particularly in its relations with other political actors. The transformation of civil service systems requires—above all—consensus building, with clear and transparent rules accepted by all actors, the authors also stress.

Subnational Governments. In Chapter 7, Francisco Monaldi evaluates the role played by governors, regional party leaders, and other regional players in the national PMP of Latin America's democracies. This view is relatively novel. So far, most of the literature has focused on the role they play at the local level. Yet Monaldi finds that the degree of autonomy of subnational authorities (governors) is a central element that can influence the workings of the national polity. Subnational actors can influence the implementation stage of the national PMP by obstructing, delaying, or reshaping national policies. Under certain circumstances, governors and other subnational authorities can introduce problematic features into the nationwide PMP, as they pursue a strategy to accumulate power at the expense of the national political party system and policymaking arena. This can weaken state capacities, favor clientelistic practices over programmatic linkages, and even increase macroeconomic instability as states or regions encourage overspending, overborrowing, or both.

The exact role that governors play in the national PMP depends on particular configurations of institutions in each country. Key institutional determinants include the method of selecting regional authorities, the federal or unitary constitutional structure, federal fiscal arrangements, and the electoral system and party structure. Governors will tend to have relatively little influence on the national political stage if they are appointed by the president; if the electoral system promotes presidential coattails and nationalized parties; if the country has a unitary political structure, with no territorial legislative chamber; and if the country has a low level of decentralization of public expenditures and low vertical fiscal imbalances.

On the other hand, the influence of governors in national politics will be higher when subnational authorities have strong incentives to be responsive to their constituencies; when the fiscal structure allows loose subnational fiscal policy (soft budget constraints); when the federal structure includes a territorial chamber with a malapportioned legislature; and when the party structure is not nationalized, and the electoral system gives governors control over nominations to the national congress and encourages the existence of regional parties that end up playing a pivotal role in national elections. The combination of several of these conditions favors an environment where pork-barrel politics, a tendency to divert resources to the states or provinces at the expense of the nation as a whole (the *commons problem*, with respect to national fiscal resources), and unstable macroeconomic policies prevail.

In order to understand the specific role that governors play, the full institutional context should be analyzed, since some individual factors could have different effects, depending on how they are combined with other factors. For that reason, Monaldi takes an integrated look at the role of subnational forces in national policymaking in a number of Latin American cases.

Official political actors like the executive, the legislature, political parties, the judiciary, the cabinet, the bureaucracy, and governors also interact in the PMP with a wide range of actors from civil society, such as business groups, unions, the media, social movements, and international organizations. These groups seek to influence the policy agenda in various ways; these different forms of influence affect the characteristics of public policies. For instance, behind-the-scenes networking or payoffs to corrupt politicians may yield private advantages to particular businesses at the expense of the public welfare, while broader consultations with a wider group of businesses improve economic policymaking.

Business. In Chapter 8, Ben Ross Schneider analyzes the role of domestic business groups in the PMP of Latin American countries. Despite the prominence of business in policymaking, patterns of business participation vary widely across countries, across policy areas, and over time. Business participation can be organized and collective, or dispersed and individual.[14] It can be open and formal, as in the form of business associations, or it can be closed and informal, as in the form of corruption. Opportunities for business influence in Latin America are many, ranging from offering bribes to public officials to the appointment of business executives to positions in the government. Most countries in Latin America seem to have a little of everything when it comes to business influence: corruption, advice, pressure, and direct involvement in government.

To analyze the variations in business participation in politics, Schneider introduces a general framework, viewing business influence as a portfolio of political investments made by businesses. Business-people can invest in a range of different political activities—such as participating in business associations, lobbying, contributing to electoral campaigns, networking, and engaging in corrupt practices—according to the expected returns on each investment.[15] Where they concentrate their investments will depend, in large part, on their perceptions of the opportunities for influence offered by the political system. For instance,

---

[14] For example, business tends to be a more organized political actor in northern Europe and Japan than in the United States.

[15] To take advantage of evolving opportunities, they can balance their portfolio of political investments by shifting political investments to activities that generate the greatest return.

in countries like Argentina and Brazil, policymakers pay less attention to associations; thus businesses tend not to invest much time or money in them. On the other hand, in Chile, Colombia, and Mexico, where the governments have drawn on associations for business input, business-people have strong incentives to invest in associations and build up their institutional capacity for the long term.

Using this conceptual framework, and verifying it with interviews with key actors, Schneider presents evidence supporting the argument that the more encompassing the organization representing business is, and the more transparent the policy process, the more business influence in politics will result in public-regarding policies.[16] A feature that favors longer intertemporal commitments among policymakers and businesspeople is the representation of business on policy councils. Both policymakers and business representatives have incentives to develop reputations and not to renege on agreements reached in the policy council. An example of this type of arrangement is found in export promotion policies in Brazil, Chile, and Mexico.

Labor. Another actor from civil society that has played a fundamental role in the history of Latin American policymaking is the labor movement. In Chapter 9, Victoria Murillo and Andrew Schrank examine organized labor's role in the PMP from a historical and theoretical standpoint. Labor unions were crucial actors in the establishment of the postwar party systems of many Latin American countries and have traditionally been key participants in the PMP, although their influence has declined over the last two decades. Murillo and Schrank argue that organized labor can be understood as both a producer and a product of the PMP, and highlight two crucial determinants of organized labor's role: goals and resources. Labor unions organize to defend their members' interests through collective action (collective bargaining, strikes); political strategies (lobbying, general strikes); and social services (cooperatives, health insurance, pensions). All these strategies involve delegation of representation from union members to labor leaders as they work for a common goal. These leaders organize workers' behavior in exchange for

---

[16] On the other hand, business influences that favor private-regarding policies are likely to arise when policies are narrow, and when business representation occurs predominantly through channels that are less transparent and that involve small numbers of firms or individuals.

concessions to improve their lot, as well as payoffs to union leaders for their representation. The payoffs can include material or policy benefits of different types. In terms of resources, union members constitute a well-organized voting bloc capable of rewarding and punishing politicians in electoral democracies. For instance, in Latin America, electoral strategies often involve forging alliances with labor-based parties.

Based on a historical cross-national analysis of the region, Murillo and Schrank find that the nature of unions is corporatist rather than liberal and conclude that they have played and will continue to play an active part in the Latin American PMP. Latin American unions have a number of valuable assets at their disposal and continue to use their assets to defend the interests of their members, taking advantage of alliances with political parties, social movements, and their fellow unions abroad. For instance, organized labor formed the backbone of the movements that brought Presidents Lula (Brazil), Néstor and Cristina Fernández de Kirchner (Argentina), and Evo Morales (Bolivia) to power. Furthermore, they have been key actors in the impeachment and/or ouster of Presidents Fernando Collor de Mello (Brazil), Gonzalo Sánchez de Lozada (Bolivia), and Carlos Mesa (Bolivia).

The News Media. Finally, in Chapter 10, Sallie Hughes presents a first approximation of the role of the news media in the PMP in Latin America, based on empirical comparative literature on media and policymaking, and observations of media behavior in Latin America. The effect of the media on the political system depends on the degree of influence of the media on the policy agenda, the symbolic or substantive nature of policy responses to the media by the political system, the incentives for rent-seeking by both politicians and the media, the legitimacy of the policy options considered, and the criteria for policy evaluation.

By mapping the distinctive stages of the PMP and hypothesizing about the media influence in each step, Hughes characterizes conditions where the media exerts influence in the PMP and affects the possibility of reaching intertemporal cooperation. For instance, media can bring to light issues that policymakers had not considered or did not view as urgent, playing the role of agenda setter. Conversely, demands by the media for quick, high-profile responses to events framed as crises can lead policymakers to pursue symbolic actions or poorly designed policy.

News coverage can expose secret actors or moves during policy negotiations and implementation, including who benefits and what motives they have, increasing the visibility of players' moves and decreasing payoffs for secrecy. On the one hand, positive coverage focusing on policy benefits, beneficiaries, or proponents increases incentives for long-term cooperation. On the other hand, negative news coverage focusing on corruption, conflict, or future losers may affect cooperation and decrease the likelihood of intertemporal agreements.

The power of the media has become increasingly important—to the extent that media-fueled scandals have been the origin of numerous presidential crises across Latin America in the past decade. Hughes concludes that the media can also influence the process of adoption of a policy by playing a role as an interest group; in these circumstances, media outlets openly support coalitions. This seems to be especially the case when policy issues that directly affect the media business or professional interests are discussed by political actors, such as when legislatures take up telecommunications reform or issues related to journalism professionalization.

The Need for a Systemic Approach

This chapter has presented a brief overview of the content of the chapters ahead, which highlight the characteristics of the institutions, actors, and arenas that are important within the context of the guiding framework. Each chapter points out several characteristics of the institutions, actors, and arenas studied and stresses how they affect the number of actors, their incentives, their discount factors, and the arenas where transactions take place. Because of their impact on the PMP, particularly through their impact on the ability of reaching intertemporal cooperation, these institutions and actors determine the features of policies—which are good predictors of development outcomes.

The framework that has guided the work for this book stresses the need for a systemic approach: one that emphasizes configurations of institutions and interactive effects. The country cases in a previous volume (Stein et al., 2008) examine these configurations and interactions in great detail, offering a general equilibrium perspective on the workings of political institutions, PMP, and policy outcomes in Latin America. Yet to understand these interactions among multiple institutional dimensions, it is important to first understand each of them individually, focusing on the variety of rules and constraints in place in Latin America, and the way that these rules and constraints affect the incentives of political actors and the way they play the political and policymaking game. For this reason, this book focuses on a number of distinct institutional dimensions of democratic systems and studies them one at a time. We hope that the chapters that follow will provide the reader with some of the tools necessary to embark on the fascinating exploration of how democracy works in Latin America.

CHAPTER 2

Beyond the Electoral Connection: The Effect of Political Parties on the Policymaking Process

Mark P. Jones

Political parties exercise an important degree of influence on the policymaking process (Stein et al., 2006) and are a vital component of a democracy. Parties perform crucial tasks such as recruiting candidates, mobilizing the electorate, and creating, presenting, and implementing policy. Outside the electoral arena, parties are also active participants in a host of other areas of modern democratic life, such as forming governments and coalitions, organizing the legislature, and aggregating and articulating the interests and preferences of the citizenry, both from within government and from the opposition (Norris, 2004).

Other characteristics of parties and the party system affect the policymaking process somewhat more indirectly, influencing the nature of executive–legislative relations, the possibilities for interparty and intraparty coordination in the national legislature, and the incentives of elected officials to cater to narrower or broader sets of societal interests, for example (Norris, 2004; Stein et al., 2006; Payne, Zovatto, and Mateo Díaz, 2007). Finally, not only do the different components of a country's party system interact with one another, but they also interact with other democratic institutions and political actors, such as the presidency, the legislature, and the judiciary. Thus the expected effects of the principal components of a party system will depend greatly on their interaction with other key institutional actors in a country.

This chapter describes the characteristics and workings of political parties and party systems by focusing on four distinct characteristics that have been shown to affect the policymaking process in Latin America:

political party and party system institutionalization; political party and party system nationalization; partisan polarization, fragmentation, and presidential legislative support; and the relevance of programmatic versus clientelist politics for the functioning of the political system. Included in this analysis are all Latin American democracies with 3 million or more inhabitants: Argentina, Bolivia, Brazil, Chile, Colombia, Costa Rica, the Dominican Republic, Ecuador, El Salvador, Guatemala, Honduras, Mexico, Nicaragua, Panama, Paraguay, Peru, Uruguay, and Venezuela.

Political Party and Party System Institutionalization

A crucial characteristic of party systems is their level of institutionalization. While too much institutionalization can potentially have a deleterious effect on the functioning of a democracy—with the pre-1993 Venezuelan party system a classic example (Crisp, 2000)—party institutionalization generally is seen as a positive trait for a democracy (Mainwaring, 1998, 1999; Mainwaring and Scully, 1995).

The more institutionalized a party system is, the greater the likelihood that it will have programmatic parties: that is, parties that compete electorally primarily based on their established policy reputations regarding key policy issues and concrete policy proposals.[1] In a party system dominated by programmatic parties, interparty competition is based primarily on competing policy programs (hence the use of the term "programmatic") (Kitschelt et al., forthcoming). Furthermore, the parties' policy orientations tend to be relatively stable, allowing for higher levels of democratic (voter) accountability and voter identification than in weakly institutionalized party systems (Shugart and Mainwaring, 1997; Mainwaring, 1998). Institutionalized party systems also help ensure greater policy consistency because of the strong role played by parties in political recruitment and the concerted efforts made by elites to promote and protect the value of the party label (which implies maintaining relatively consistent policy positions over time, with dramatic changes in policy stances made only infrequently).

In weakly institutionalized party systems, interparty competition is based primarily on personal appeals or short-term populist policy

---

[1] It is possible, however, to have high levels of party institutionalization within political parties that have a clientelist, nonprogrammatic base (Taylor, 1996; Kitschelt, 2000).

proposals designed to win over voters and then be forgotten once the election takes place (Mainwaring, 1998). Parties also play a much less prominent role in the political recruitment process. In weakly institutionalized party systems, political parties often are short-lived, and their policy positions on specific issues tend to be highly malleable.

It is much more difficult for voters in weakly institutionalized party systems to hold political parties accountable than in institutionalized party systems. It is also much less easy to identify how one's vote will translate into a governance option, and what that governance option will be once the party is in power (Shugart and Mainwaring, 1997).[2] Furthermore, since parties play a weak role in the recruiting process, are often short-lived, and place less importance on the policy brand name and value of their party label, policy consistency is much lower in weakly institutionalized party systems than in their institutionalized counterparts. Lastly, given the comparative lack of commitment of political elites to their parties in particular and to the party system in general, weakly institutionalized party systems are more conducive breeding grounds for anti-system politics (that is, the establishment and rise of political groups—especially political parties—whose goal is the overthrow or radical transformation of the existing democratic regime).

Four key components together influence the level of party system institutionalization in a country: *stability in patterns of interparty competition; party roots in society; the legitimacy of parties and elections*; and *party organization* (Mainwaring and Scully, 1995; Mainwaring, 1998, 1999). The discussion that follows briefly examines each of these components, first discussing the conceptual base for each component, then operationalizing it as a set of empirical indicators, and finally providing values for these indicators.[3] The discussion concludes with the presentation of a party institutionalization index (see Table 2.1).

Stability in Patterns of Intraparty Competition

In institutionalized party systems, the relevant parties tend to be the same year in, year out, and to garner relatively similar shares of votes

---

[2] Government options include such considerations as which elected officials will be part of a government coalition.

[3] For a complete description of these components as well as the data utilized, see Jones (2005).

TABLE 2.1	Party Institutionalization Index, Latin American Democracies				
Country	Institutionalization Index	Electoral Volatility	Party Roots	Party and Election Legitimacy	Party Organization
Uruguay	76	84	73	51	97
Dominican Republic	74	75	75	50	98
Nicaragua	70	84	62	34	98
Honduras	68	94	66	40	74
Mexico	67	88	62	33	85
Panama	67	77	66	41	83
El Salvador	66	90	62	35	78
Chile	65	95	49	40	77
Paraguay	64	79	82	32	65
Argentina	62	74	46	34	94
Costa Rica	61	77	62	40	67
Colombia	60	89	49	30	73
Brazil	59	80	49	40	66
Bolivia	56	66	60	26	72
Venezuela	55	60	47	42	73
Peru	53	51	54	34	75
Ecuador	50	63	53	23	62
Guatemala	48	58	45	34	58

Source: Author's calculations based on vote and election data for each election; legislative delegation seat data; Latinobarometer (2003, 2004); and Proyecto de Elites Latinoamericanas (PELA) (2005).

and seats over time. In weakly institutionalized party systems, parties that are relevant in one year often are irrelevant a few years later. Furthermore, the percentages of the vote and seats that parties win in these weakly institutionalized systems tend to vary considerably from one election to the next.

The stability of interparty competition is measured using the average of two indicators: *vote volatility,* the level of vote (percentage of the valid vote) volatility in the two most recent lower house/single house elections; and *seat volatility,* the level of seat (percentage of the seats) volatility in the same elections (Pedersen, 1983). Latin America presents a wide range of volatility, with countries such as Chile, Honduras, and El Salvador possessing volatility levels comparable to those found in Western Europe (Bartolini and Mair, 1990). In these democracies the same parties tend to win comparable vote and seat shares over time. In contrast, the region is home to other countries with extremely high levels of volatility, such as Peru, Guatemala, and Venezuela. Here, parties that had been among the most relevant in the country either ceased to exist or saw their popular support plummet over a very short time period. At the same time, parties that either did not exist, or were inconsequential players only a few years earlier, were among the most prominent in the country a few years later.

Party Roots in Society

In institutionalized party systems, parties have strong roots in society (Mainwaring, 1998). Voters tend to cast their ballots for the same party in election after election, and the parties possess a high level of linkage with society. In weakly institutionalized party systems, parties are rooted only loosely in society. Voters commonly lack loyalty to parties, and instead cast their votes based more on the traits and characteristics of the individual candidates or their electoral campaign messages. In addition, parties possess relatively weak and ephemeral ties with society.

The extent of party roots in society (*party roots*) is measured by employing two indicators. The first is the percentage of the population that possessed some form of identification with a party in a 2003 Latinobarometer (LB) public opinion poll. The second is calculated by subtracting from 100 the percentage of legislators (lower house/single house) who believe parties are distant from society in their country, based on the Proyecto de Elites Latinoamericanas (PELA, 2005).[4]

In terms of overall party roots in society, one extreme is represented by Paraguay, the Dominican Republic, and Uruguay, all of which have parties with deeply entrenched roots in society. In contrast, party roots in society are quite shallow at the other extreme of this measure, such as in Guatemala, Argentina, and Venezuela.

---

[4] PELA is run by the Instituto de Iberoamérica of the Universidad de Salamanca. Since 1994, PELA has conducted representative surveys of the members (national legislators) of each legislative class in the region's national lower/unicameral chambers (with some exceptions, which are detailed in the sources cited next). For additional details on PELA, see Alcántara Sáez (2008) and the Instituto de Iberoamérica's Web site (iberoame.usal.es). For Brazil and Panama, proxies are used in many instances when the PELA data are employed. See Jones (2005) for more details.

The Legitimacy of Political Parties and Elections

A basic prerequisite for an institutionalized party system is that both parties, as well as the elections in which they compete, are viewed as legitimate by the population (Mainwaring, 1998; Norris, 2004). Furthermore, for an institutionalized party system to exist, parties must be viewed as institutions that are vital to the functioning of the democratic system. In contrast, in weakly institutionalized party systems, both parties and elections do not enjoy a high level of legitimacy. Furthermore, a significant proportion of citizens are skeptical of the usefulness of parties as institutions.

Political party legitimacy and election legitimacy are measured using two separate indicators, respectively. The averages of each of these legitimacy measures are combined, then summed, and then divided by two to provide an overall measure of *party and election (P&E) legitimacy.*

Two aspects of political party legitimacy are examined. The first is the percentage of citizens who stated that parties were indispensable for the functioning of the country (LB, 2003). The second is the percentage of the population that had a great deal or some confidence in parties. The average of these two is the *party legitimacy* measure.

Election legitimacy is assessed using two measures. The first asked respondents to rate elections in their country on a scale of 1 (clean) to 5 (not clean) (LB, 2000). The second asked respondents the extent to which they agreed with the statement that elections offer voters a real choice between parties and candidates, on a scale of 1 (strongly agree) to four (strongly disagree). In each case, the average score (1 to 5, and 1 to 4, respectively) for all valid responses is calculated. This result is then divided by the high score for the scale (5 and 4, respectively). Finally, this resulting percentage is subtracted from 100 to produce the two measures.

P&E legitimacy is an aggregate measure of *political party legitimacy* and *election legitimacy.* One extreme on this aggregate measure is represented by Uruguay and the Dominican Republic, where both political parties and elections enjoy considerable legitimacy among the population. At the other extreme, represented by Ecuador and Bolivia, both elections and political parties suffer from a serious crisis of legitimacy.

Party Organization

In institutionalized party systems, the parties possess a noteworthy level of material and human resources, intraparty processes are predictable and routinized, and the party as an institution prevails over individual party leaders (Mainwaring, 1998). In weakly institutionalized party systems, parties have limited resources, internal processes are unpredictable, and individual leaders dominate the parties, with the party as an institution weak to nonexistent.

Party organization is measured using two variables: political party age (Mainwaring, 1998), and the opinion of elites that their party is a continuously functioning organization and not primarily an electoral vehicle. The party age variable is itself the average of two variables. The first is the percentage of parties (those that held at least 10 percent of the seats in the lower house/single house) that as of 2004 had been in existence for at least 10 years. The second is the percentage of the same parties that as of 2004 had been in existence for at least 25 years. The second measure of party organization is based on a PELA (2005) question that asked legislators if they considered their party organization to be continuous or if they thought the party organization was merely an electoral vehicle.

Party organization is the strongest in the Dominican Republic, Nicaragua, and Uruguay. It is the weakest in Guatemala, Ecuador, and Paraguay.

Party Institutionalization Index

In Table 2.1, the four aggregate measures discussed above are presented, and then aggregated, to create a *party institutionalization index*. According to this index, countries such as Uruguay, the Dominican Republic, and Nicaragua possess well institutionalized party systems, while countries such as Guatemala, Ecuador, and Peru possess weakly institutionalized party systems. Overall, and ceteris paribus, democracies with more institutionalized party systems should have more programmatic politics, parties that tend to compete based on policy proposals, greater consistency in public policy, and higher levels of accountability and identifiability than their less institutionalized counterparts. In these latter systems, personalistic politics—in which the personality and charisma of the leader carry more weight than his or her positions on issues—campaigns focused on candidate characteristics or short-term populist promises, policy inconsistency, and low levels of accountability and identifiability will tend to be more common.

Party and Party System Nationalization

The degree of nationalization of political parties and party systems has several important effects on the functioning of a democracy (Jones and Mainwaring, 2003). Schattschneider (1960) linked the nationalization of the party system to voters' orientations. He argued that in highly nationalized party systems, national factors may be more important in forging bonds between voters and parties. Conversely, in less nationalized party systems, subnational factors may be more salient in creating such bonds.

The degree of nationalization is relevant for legislative careers and for executive–legislative relations (Jones and Mainwaring, 2003). In highly nationalized party systems, national issues are likely to be central in legislators' careers. Executives may have greater ability to broker legislative coalitions on the basis of national issues and to negotiate with a few key national party leaders. In a weakly nationalized party system, subnational issues are likely to be more important in legislative careers. Under weak party nationalization, the central party leadership may be less able to speak for the entire party and to deliver its legislative support.

Differences in nationalization also are likely to have public policy consequences (Jones and Mainwaring, 2003). Decisions related to national transfers to subnational units, administrative reform, and subsidies may be strongly influenced by the degree of party system nationalization. Where a party's base of support is relatively constant across geographic units, it may be more likely to treat all units equally. In contrast, where its support varies widely across geographic units, the party may tend to base its decisions in part on the degree of support it receives in specific geographic units. Finally, in young democracies where pronounced ethnic or religious cleavages coincide with territory, the nationalization of some major parties may be a key factor in preserving democracy (Jones and Mainwaring, 2003). While this factor has historically not been a major concern in Latin America, current events in Bolivia highlight the potential pitfalls of the relative absence of national-based parties in that country.

In sum, under a nationalized party system, public policy is likely to be more oriented toward working for the national common good, ceteris paribus. In contrast, in a weakly nationalized party system, public policy may tend to be directed far more toward the satisfaction of particularized local interests, often to the detriment of the national common good.

This section examines the concept of party system nationalization from two perspectives. The first analyzes the effect of the country's electoral and political institutions on the incentives for a national versus locally oriented party system. The second evaluates the extent to which the vote in a country is nationalized.

Political Institutions and Incentives for Party System Nationalization

The extent to which a country's electoral and political institutions provide incentives for the nationalization of the party system, and indirectly influence the approach to public policy taken by a country's parties, is measured through an assessment of five institutional factors: control over the nomination of legislative candidates (*candidate nomination*), the electoral system for legislative elections (*electoral system*), the timing of presidential and legislative elections (*presidential elections*), the extent of autonomy enjoyed by governors (*autonomous governors*), and the autonomy possessed by municipal governments (*municipal autonomy*). These five measures are then combined to create an aggregate *nationalization index* (see Table 2.2).

Candidate Nomination. At one extreme of the spectrum for nominating legislative candidates are instances where national party leaders play a preeminent role in determining who runs as a party's candidates (and their location on the list of candidates, in closed list systems) (Norris, 2004). At the other extreme, the individual candidates are primarily the ones who determine whether or not they are going to run as the party's legislative candidates, and obtain election primarily on their own (without the direct assistance of their party). Intermediate between these two extremes are systems where regional party leaders (those whose territory encompasses at least one of the multi-member legislative districts)

TABLE 2.2	Nationalization Index, Latin American Democracies					
Country	Nationalization Index	Candidate Nomination	Electoral System	Presidential Elections	Autonomous Governors	Municipal Autonomy
Uruguay	14.0	3	3.0	3	2	3
Costa Rica	14.0	3	2.0	3	3	3
Paraguay	13.5	3	2.5	3	2	3
Bolivia	13.5	3	2.5	3	3	2
Panama	13.0	3	1.0	3	3	3
Honduras	13.0	3	2.0	3	3	2
Nicaragua	12.5	3	2.5	3	3	1
Guatemala	12.5	3	2.5	3	3	1
El Salvador	12.5	3	2.5	1	3	3
Ecuador	12.0	3	1.0	3	2	3
Dominican Republic	11.5	3	1.5	1	3	3
Peru	11.0	3	1.0	3	2	2
Mexico	10.5	2	2.5	2	1	3
Venezuela	9.5	3	1.5	1	2	2
Chile	9.0	3	1.0	1	3	1
Argentina	8.0	2	2.0	2	1	1
Colombia	7.3	1	1.3	2	2	1
Brazil	7.0	1	1.0	3	1	1

Source: Author's calculations based on Alcántara Sáez and Freidenberg (2001); Nickson (1995); and party system and legislative data for each country.

dominate the candidate nomination process. Reflecting these options, and based on Alcántara Sáez and Freidenberg (2001), countries are coded on a three-point scale: from 3 (the nomination decision is made principally by the national party leaders), to 2 (the nomination decision is made principally by regional party leaders), to 1 (the nomination decision is made principally by the individual candidates).[5]

Electoral System. The design of a country's electoral system can work to enhance or diminish the prospects for party system nationalization. A country's electoral system (the one used in the most recent legislative election as of 2005) is coded based on the type of electoral districts (national, regional, single-member, or some mixture thereof) it uses, as well as the presence or absence of preference voting.[5] One extreme on this dimension is a single national district in which a closed list is employed (this arrangement is coded as a 3.0). The other extreme is represented by either single-member plurality districts or the use of open lists within regional multi-member districts (under proportional representation), which is coded as a 1.0. Intermediate categories include systems that combine a national closed party list and regional closed party lists (coded 2.5); that employ regional closed party lists (2.0); that utilize a single national district and open lists (1.5); and that use a mixture of regional closed party lists and single-member districts (1.5). For bicameral systems, the average of the two houses is employed. Added to this resulting number is 0.5 in those cases where a fused vote is utilized for the election of the president and the legislature, as well as in those cases where a party must cross a national vote threshold in order to obtain either some or all legislative seats.

Presidential Elections. In Latin America, the timing of presidential and legislative elections has several important effects on the party system (Mainwaring and Shugart, 1997; Payne, Zovatto, and Mateo Díaz, 2007; Hicken and Stoll, forthcoming). First, when presidential elections are held concurrently with legislative contests, they exercise a strong influence over the vote decision, generally leading to a significant coattail vote in which legislative candidates or lists of the more popular (competitive)

---

[5] Preference voting is a type of ballot structure in which voters rank a list or group of candidates in order of preference.

presidential candidates benefit from their coattails. Second, concurrent elections result in larger presidential legislative contingents than is the case when presidential and legislative elections are held separately, ceteris paribus. Third, given the coattail effect, the president's influence over his/her legislative contingent is likely to be greater when the presidential and legislative contests are held concurrently, and hence where at least some of the legislators owe their election to the president's coattails.

Systems where the presidential and legislative elections are concurrent are coded 3. Systems where half the legislative elections are held concurrently with the presidential contest and half are held separately are coded 2. Systems in which less than one-third of the presidential and legislative elections are concurrent are coded 1.

Autonomous Governors. Autonomous regional officials influence the level of party system nationalization. The greater the autonomy and power of local-level officials, the more decentralized the party system is likely to be. The most prominent regional officials are directly elected governors whose territory corresponds to the electoral districts employed in the legislative elections (or contains multiple single member or multi-member districts). These governors, however, vary in terms of their political and administrative autonomy. Systems in which governors are directly elected and possess an important degree of political and administrative autonomy are coded 1, while systems in which these directly elected governors possess limited political and administrative autonomy are coded 2.[6] Systems in which there are no directly elected governors are coded 3.

Municipal Autonomy. In the past two decades, municipal governments in Latin America have become increasingly important political units (Nickson, 1995). Nonetheless, these municipalities vary considerably in terms of their political and administrative autonomy. Autonomy is measured by the municipal government's percentage share of total government expenditures (Nickson, 1995). Countries where this share ranges from 0–5 percent are coded 3; from 6–10 percent are coded 2; and those with 11 percent or more are coded 1.

---

[6] For additional information on this and other measures discussed in this chapter, see Jones (2005).

The five measures are combined to create a nationalization index that ranges in potential value from 5.0 to 15.0 (see Table 2.2). The actual values range from 7.0 to 14.0. At the nationalized extreme are countries such as Uruguay, Costa Rica, Paraguay, and Bolivia, where the design and functioning of the country's political institutions should be expected to contribute to a highly nationalized party system, ceteris paribus. At the other extreme are countries such as Brazil, Colombia, and Argentina, where the country's institutional framework should, ceteris paribus, be expected to provide incentives for a more weakly nationalized party system (incentives that can be counteracted by the other institutions and political arrangements).

Party System Nationalization in the Popular Vote

A second way to assess the level of party system nationalization in a country is to examine the distribution of the popular vote. Following Jones and Mainwaring (2003), the Gini coefficient for the distribution of the party vote in the most recent lower house/single house election was calculated, and this coefficient was then subtracted from 1. This inverted Gini coefficient is the *party nationalization score* (PNS), which measures variance in a party's electoral performance across electoral districts. Building on the nationalization score for individual parties, Jones and Mainwaring (2003) develop a measure of the nationalization of party systems. To create this measure, the PNS for every political party is multiplied by its share of the national valid vote, with all of these values then summed to create the *party system nationalization score* (PSNS). The contribution of every party to the PSNS is thus proportionate to its share of the vote.

Table 2.3 provides the party system nationalization score for all of the Latin American countries for the lower house/single house election held closest to the year 2002. The table also provides the party nationalization score for all parties that won at least 10 percent of the vote in the election. Countries with high PSNS values include Honduras, Chile, and Uruguay. In these countries, the percentage of the vote won by the parties does not vary a great deal across the departments, regions, or provinces in the country. At the opposite extreme are countries with much lower PSNS values, such as Peru, Ecuador, and Argentina. In these countries, the political parties tend to win widely varying percentages of the vote across the country's departments, provinces, or states.

TABLE 2.3	Party System Nationalization Scores and Major Party Nationalization Scores					
Country[a]	Election Year	PSNS	Party 1	Party 2	Party 3	Party 4
Honduras	2001	0.91	PN (.95)	PL (.94)	—	—
Chile	2001	0.90	CONCERT (.94)	ALIANZA (.92)	—	—
Uruguay	2004	0.89	PN (.92)	FA (.89)	PC (.85)	—
Nicaragua	2001	0.88	PLC (.89)	FSLN (.89)	—	—
Costa Rica	2002	0.85	PUSC (.91)	PLN (.91)	PAC (.81)	—
Dominican Republic	2002	0.84	PRD (.92)	PLD (.81)	PRSC (.79)	—
El Salvador	2003	0.83	ARENA (.93)	FMLN (.90)	PCN (.81)	—
Mexico	2003	0.78	PRI (.89)	PAN (.78)	PRD (.58)	—
Panama	2004	0.78	PRD (.94)	PA (.79)	SOL (.69)	—
Guatemala	2003	0.76	PAN (.84)	GANA (.83)	UNE (.83)	FRG (.81)
Paraguay	2003	0.73	ANR (.89)	PLRA (.75)	UNACE (.72)	MPQ (.61)
Bolivia	2002	0.71	MNR (.82)	NFR (.82)	MIR (.76)	MAS (.61)
Brazil	2002	0.64	PMDB (.76)	PT (.73)	PSDB (.69)	PFL (.61)
Venezuela	2000	0.61	MVR (.86)	AD (.66)	—	—
Argentina	2001	0.59	PJ (.83)	ALIANZA (.76)	—	—
Ecuador	2002	0.59	PRIAN (.75)	ID (.67)	PRE (.65)	PSC (.65)
Peru	2001	0.50	PP (.67)	UN (.63)	FIM (.59)	PAP (.49)

Source: Author's calculations based on Jones and Mainwaring (2003).
— not available.
[a] Data not available for Colombia.

Fragmentation, Contingents, and Polarization

Perhaps nowhere is the party system more consequential for policymaking than through its influence on executive–legislative relations (Payne, Zovatto, and Mateo Díaz, 2007). As this topic is analyzed in detail elsewhere in this volume, the discussion here focuses on four key party and party system variables that affect this relationship: the level of legislative fragmentation; the size of the presidential legislative contingent (which is influenced by the level of fragmentation); the level of polarization that exists among the parties; and the extent to which the members of the president's legislative delegation are responsive to the party leadership and/or president.

Legislative Fragmentation and the Presidential Legislative Contingent

The level of fragmentation in the legislature directly influences the size of the presidential legislative contingent as well as the number of partners with whom the president must form some type of legislative coalition or structure piecemeal alliances specific to a particular legislative initiative to implement his/her policy agenda. Table 2.4 reports on these factors.

The *effective number of legislative parties* uses the measure devised by Laakso and Taagepera (1979) and corresponds to the two most recent legislative elections. Table 2.4 also provides the average percentage of seats held by the president's party (*presidential party's chamber contingent, presidential party's senate contingent*) in the legislature following the two most recent legislative elections. (The discussion that follows uses data for only the lower house/single house.)

Ideological Polarization

There is considerable debate in the scholarly literature regarding the consequences of presidential legislative contingents that have less than majority status, particularly those that drop below one-third or one-quarter of the legislative body (Foweraker, 1998; Payne, Zovatto, and Mateo Díaz, 2007). While some observers consider small presidential contingents (especially those that are around 33 percent and below) to be problematic for governance, others do not. However, there is substantial agreement that in instances where the president's party lacks a majority

TABLE 2.4   Fragmentation, Legislative Contingents, and Polarization

Country	Effective Number of Legislative Parties	Presidential Party's Chamber Contingent	Presidential Party's Senate Contingent	Overall Polarization	Party in the Electorate	Party in Congress
Argentina	3.18	48	58	1.00	0.28	1.71
Bolivia	5.21	27	41	1.08	0.89	1.26
Brazil	7.81	19	16	2.84	1.04	4.63
Chile	2.02	55	45	4.61	3.40	5.82
Colombia	5.00	20	20	0.60	0.06	1.14
Costa Rica	3.12	40	—	0.70	0.12	1.27
Dominican Republic	2.52	41	52	0.72	0.07	1.37
Ecuador	6.71	25	—	1.56	1.33	1.78
El Salvador	3.50	34	—	10.00	7.67	12.33
Guatemala	3.46	43	—	1.52	0.13	2.90
Honduras	2.30	50	—	0.75	0.07	1.42
Mexico	2.79	37	48	1.74	0.10	3.38
Nicaragua	2.39	54	—	5.66	2.72	8.61
Panama	3.09	39	—	0.86	0.17	1.55
Paraguay	2.73	51	45	0.52	0.46	0.58
Peru	4.24	41	—	2.06	0.10	4.03
Uruguay	2.73	43	46	4.92	5.80	4.05
Venezuela	4.75	34	—	1.32	0.29	2.35

Source: Author's calculations based on Laakso and Taagepera (1979); Latinobarometer (2002, 2003, 2004); and PELA (2005).
— not available.

of the seats of the legislature (or does not at least approach a majority, with, for instance at least 40–45 percent of the seats), that in order to be able to govern effectively the president must form some type of legislative coalition. Where these coalitions are not formed, governance problems are likely to emerge (Chasquetti, 2001).

The formation of coalitions is most feasible when there are low levels of ideological polarization in the party system (Foweraker, 1998). Where high levels of ideological polarization exist, the barriers to forming coalitions are more extensive, and the costs (in terms of payoffs/side-payments) much greater. As a consequence, to adequately understand the relationship between the size of a presidential legislative contingent and governance, one also must have some knowledge of the level of ideological polarization in the party system in general and in the legislature in particular.

Ideological polarization is measured among voters (using LB data for 2002–04) and legislators (using PELA data) employing a ten-point, left–right scale. A strong advantage of the left–right measure is that it almost universally taps a salient cleavage in a polity (Knutsen, 1998) and is available in a comparable format for a large number of countries. Furthermore, many hold the opinion, succinctly expressed by Thomassen (1999, p. 54), that "Political cleavages in western societies have become more and more one-dimensional in the sense that the left–right dimension has gradually absorbed other conflict dimensions." Thus while the left–right measure does not tap all salient cleavages in a polity, it is vastly superior to any other single measure of cleavages. The extent of the ideological cleavage in a country is measured using the Taylor and Herman (1971) measure of *ideological polarization,* which "is the most frequently used measure to tap left–right polarization in the party system" (Knutsen, 1998, p. 15).

Two LB questions (2002–04) are used to calculate the level of ideological polarization in the electorate (*party in the electorate*). The first asked respondents if an election was held the next day, which political party would they vote for. Only parties supported by at least 5 percent of the survey population (LB, 2002–04) are analyzed. The second question asked respondents to place themselves on an eleven-point left–right scale.

Two PELA items are used to develop two measures of ideological polarization. One asked legislators to place all parties other than their own on a ten-point left–right scale. The other, separately, asked legislators to place their own party on a ten-point left–right scale.

These results are then utilized to calculate one measure of ideological polarization for the party in the electorate and two for the party in congress. For each measure, the calculation involved subtracting every party's mean left–right score from the overall mean, squaring this value, and then multiplying it by the percentage of the respondents who expressed a vote preference for the party (*party in the electorate*) or by the percentage of the seats (of those held by parties with at least 10 percent of the seats) held by the party in the lower house/single house (*party in congress*). These two congress measures are averaged to calculate an aggregate level of polarization in the congress (*party in congress*). Finally, the *party in the electorate* and *party in congress* measures are averaged to provide an overall measure of ideological polarization (*overall polarization*), which, along with its main subcomponents, is presented in detail in Table 2.4.

Fragmentation, Presidential Contingents, and Ideological Polarization

Where there is low fragmentation and/or a large presidential legislative contingent, presidents should be able to implement their policy agenda effectively regardless of the level of ideological polarization. While low levels of polarization may have some positive attributes, they are not necessary for effective and efficient governance in these situations. When levels of legislative fragmentation are moderate to high, and where the president lacks a legislative majority or near majority, however, the level of ideological polarization becomes much more important. Where ideological polarization is low, presidents should be more likely to form, and then successfully maintain, legislative coalitions. Where polarization is high, presidents will find it much more difficult to form and maintain coalitions, and it will be more costly in terms of payoffs (such as inefficient pork expenditures, bribes, and excess patronage positions). In sum, the presence of high levels of legislative fragmentation and moderate to small presidential legislative contingents, when combined with moderate to high levels of ideological polarization, should be expected to inhibit effective and efficient policymaking by the president.[7]

---

[7] This does not imply that the president will be unable to govern, but simply that the president will be unable to govern in the most effective, efficient, and optimal manner.

FIGURE 2.1	Ideological Polarization and the President's Legislative Contingent

Ideological Polarization

		Very Low (0–1.0)	Low (1.1–2.0)	Moderate (2.1–4.0)	High (4.1–6.0)	Very High (6.1–10.0)
	Very High (55+)	Colombia			Chile	
	High (50–54)	Honduras Paraguay			Nicaragua	
Presidential Contingent	Moderate (40–49)	Argentina Costa Rica Dom. Rep.	Guatemala	Peru	Uruguay	
	Low (34–39)	Panama	Mexico Venezuela			**El Salvador**
	Very Low (0–33)		*Bolivia Ecuador*	*Brazil*		

Bold: Countries in the "Danger Zone".
Italics: Countries potentially in the "Danger Zone".

Source: Author's calculations.

Figure 2.1 displays the location of the individual countries on a five-by-five scale in terms of the size of the presidential legislative contingent (lower house/single house) and the level of ideological polarization. Areas considered to be potentially problematic by all scholars (moderate to very low presidential legislative contingents combined with high to very high levels of polarization) are highlighted in bold, while those considered potentially problematic by only some scholars (very low presidential legislative contingents combined with moderate to very low polarization) are highlighted in italics. The country that appears to possess the most complicated mixture is El Salvador, which combines modest presidential legislative contingents with high levels of polarization. At the same time, it is likely, though less certain, that countries such as Bolivia, Ecuador, and Brazil may be experiencing governance problems because of the very small size of their presidents' legislative contingents.

The Centralization of Power

A comment is warranted on the responsiveness or discipline of the president's legislative contingent. This level of responsiveness can vary considerably across countries, thereby influencing the extent to which a president can count on the support of his or her co-partisans in the legislature. This level of responsiveness to the president (and to the central party leadership) can also influence the nature of legislative coalitions, particularly the individuals with whom a president negotiates the formation and maintenance of the legislative coalitions (such as the national party leadership versus intraparty faction/regional leaders versus individual legislators).

The *party centralization index* values are located in Table 2.5. The level of party centralization is measured using six indicators: the locus of nomination authority for the selection of legislative candidates (*candidate nomination*); the electoral system employed for the election of legislative candidates (*electoral system*); the timing of presidential and legislative elections (*presidential elections*); the presence of autonomous regional leaders (*autonomous governors*); the extent of intraparty democracy vis-à-vis the party faithful (*intraparty democracy*), and the degree of intraparty democracy vis-à-vis the public (*presidential primaries*). Three of these six indicators (*electoral system, presidential election, autonomous governors*) are identical to those employed for the party nationalization index. A fourth variable (*candidate nomination*) is nearly identical, except that instances where national-level faction leaders predominate in the candidate nomination process are coded 2 (and not 3, as in the party nationalization index calculations).

The fifth variable (*intraparty democracy*) measures the involvement of the party's members in the decision-making process. Legislators (PELA, 2005) were asked to evaluate the extent of internal democracy in their party (related to decision making), with possible responses ranging from very high (1) to very low (5). The actual mean values ranged from 2.4 to 3.2. For this centralization measure all values 3.0 and higher are coded 3; values 2.6 to 2.9 are coded 2; and values less than 2.6 are coded 1.

As a proxy for intraparty democracy, the sixth variable (*presidential primaries*) measures the extent to which direct primary elections were employed to choose the major parties' candidates in recent presidential elections (Carey and Polga-Hecimovich, 2004; Freidenberg and Sánchez López, 2002). Instances where all major parties have employed primaries to choose their candidates for recent elections are coded 1. Where less than all but at least two-thirds of the major parties have selected their

TABLE 2.5	Centralization of Power in the Political Parties						
Country	Centralization Index	Candidate Nomination	Electoral System	Presidential Elections	Autonomous Governors	Intraparty Democracy	Presidential Primaries
Bolivia	17.0	3	2.50	3	3	3	2.50
Guatemala	16.5	3	2.50	3	3	2	3.00
Nicaragua	15.5	3	2.50	3	3	2	2.00
Honduras	15.0	3	2.00	3	3	3	1.00
Costa Rica	14.5	3	2.00	3	3	2	1.50
Peru	14.0	3	1.00	3	2	2	3.00
El Salvador	14.0	3	2.50	1	3	3	2.50
Ecuador	14.0	3	1.00	3	2	2	3.00
Panama	14.0	3	1.00	3	3	2	2.00
Venezuela	13.5	3	1.50	1	2	3	3.00
Paraguay	13.0	2	2.50	3	2	2	1.50
Uruguay	12.0	2	3.00	3	2	1	1.00
Mexico	12.0	2	2.50	2	1	2	2.50
Colombia	11.8	1	1.25	2	2	3	2.50
Dominican Republic	11.0	3	1.50	1	3	1	1.50
Chile	11.0	2	1.00	1	3	2	2.00
Brazil	10.5	1	1.00	3	1	2	2.50
Argentina	10.0	2	2.00	2	1	1	2.00

Source: Author's calculations based on Alcántara Sáez and Freidenberg (2001); PELA (2005); Carey and Polga-Hecimovich (2004); Freidenberg and Sánchez López (2002); and party system and legislative data for each country.

candidates via primaries, a score of 1.5 is given. Where between two-thirds and one-third of the parties used primaries, a score of 2 is given. Countries where less than one-third (but at least one) of the parties used primaries are coded 2.5. Countries where none of the major parties held presidential primaries are coded 3.

Countries in which the president should expect the most responsive co-partisan legislators and where coalitions will be formed primarily via negotiation with the national leaders of the opposition parties include Bolivia, Guatemala, and Nicaragua. Countries in which the president should not expect especially reliable legislators and where coalitions would be formed primarily via negotiation with regional/factional party leaders or individual legislators include Argentina and Brazil.

Programmatic Politics versus Clientelist Politics

The previous discussion highlighted the important impact of the presence, or absence, of a party system in which parties compete primarily on the basis of programmatic policy appeals and public policy achievements (Kitschelt, 2000; Norris, 2004; Kitschelt et al., forthcoming). An alternative form of interpartisan interaction, however, involves political competition among parties based not on programmatic policy, but rather on clientelism (Calvo and Murillo, 2005; Lyne, 2008; Taylor-Robinson, 2009). While in programmatic systems, political parties compete based on policy and are judged by voters primarily based on policy outcomes, in clientelist systems, political parties compete based on the distribution of selective incentives to voters, and are judged by voters primarily based on their ability to distribute/deliver these incentives. Of course, no political party system falls exclusively into a purely programmatic or purely clientelist category. Even in the most programmatic party systems, parties employ some forms of clientelist practices. And even in the most clientelist party systems, parties are evaluated in part based on policy. However, these nuances aside, it is possible to locate parties along a programmatic–clientelist continuum.

A summary measure of the extent of programmatic politics in a country was developed, followed by a summary measure of the extent of clientelist politics in a country. Finally, the two measures were combined to locate the 18 Latin American democracies on a programmatic versus clientelist continuum.

Programmatic Politics

The extent of programmatic politics in a country is measured using an index that in turn is based on three components: the level of programmatic politics among party supporters in the electorate; the level of programmatic politics among the party elite (legislators); and the extent of electoral volatility in the country. These three components are combined to create the *programmatic politics index* for each country.

The extent of programmatic politics in the electorate is measured using two measures. The first (*electorate ideological polarization*) is the measure of *ideological polarization* in the electorate presented in the previous section. Values of 0 to 0.99 are coded 0; values of 1.0 to 2.5 are coded 1; and values of 2.6 and above are coded 2 (see Table 2.6).

The second measure (*electorate ideological cleavage*) is drawn from Jones (2005). Countries are scored based on the salience of the left–right partisan cleavage in the electorate. Where this cleavage is low, the countries are scored 0. Where the cleavage is medium or high, the countries are scored 1 and 2, respectively.

The two above measures are combined to create the *programmatic electorate* component of this index. Table 2.6 indicates this measure ranges from a high of 4 (four countries) to a low of zero (seven countries).

The degree of elite programmatic politics (*programmatic elite*) is calculated using two measures (see Table 2.6). The first measure (*elite economic cleavage*) examines the presence or absence of significant relevant party differences regarding the role of the state versus the market in the regulation of the economy (a relevant party is one that occupies at least 10 percent of the legislative seats). First, relevant party means and standard deviations are calculated based on legislator responses (PELA, 2005) to a question that asked their preference regarding who should regulate the economy on a scale of 1 (maximum role for the state) to 5 (maximum role for the market). Mean party scores whose 95 percent confidence intervals did not overlap are considered to be significantly different. The percentage of the relevant dyads for which there existed significant differences was then calculated. Countries for which this percentage is less than 34 percent are coded 0; those between 34 percent and 66 percent are coded 1; and those above 66 percent are coded 2 (see Table 2.6).

The second measure (*elite ideological polarization*) is based on the congress ideological polarization score discussed previously. Countries

TABLE 2.6 | **Extent of Programmatic Politics in Latin American Democracies**

Country	Programmatic Politics	Volatility Reduction	Programmatic Subtotal	Programmatic Electorate	Electorate Ideological Cleavage	Electorate Ideological Polarization	Programmatic Elite	Elite Economic Cleavage	Elite Ideological Polarization
Chile	8	0	8	4	2	2	4	2	2
Nicaragua	8	0	8	4	2	2	4	2	2
El Salvador	7	0	7	4	2	2	3	1	2
Uruguay	7	0	7	4	2	2	3	2	1
Argentina	2	1	3	1	1	0	2	2	0
Brazil	2	1	3	1	0	1	2	1	1
Honduras	2	0	2	2	2	0	0	0	0
Mexico	2	0	2	0	0	0	2	1	1
Costa Rica	1	1	2	0	0	0	2	2	0
Ecuador	1	1	2	2	1	1	0	0	0
Paraguay	1	1	2	2	2	0	0	0	0
Bolivia	0	2	2	2	2	0	0	0	0
Colombia	0	0	0	0	0	0	0	0	0
Dominican Republic	0	0	0	0	0	0	0	0	0
Guatemala	0	3	1	0	0	0	1	0	1
Panama	0	1	0	0	0	0	0	0	0
Peru	0	4	3	1	1	0	2	1	1
Venezuela	0	3	1	0	0	0	1	0	1

Source: Author's calculations based on Latinobarometer (2002, 2003, 2004); and PELA (2005).

with *party in congress* polarization scores between 0 and 2.0 are coded 0; those between 2.1 and 5.0 are coded 1; and those 5.1 and above are coded 2.

The two measures are combined to create the *programmatic elite* component of this index. As Table 2.6 details, this component ranges from a high of 4 (Chile, Nicaragua) to a low of 0 (seven countries).

The *programmatic elite* and *programmatic electorate* measures are summed together to create a *programmatic subtotal*. This programmatic subtotal was then adjusted using information on the level of stability in interparty competition drawn from the first section of this chapter. Because of current data limitations, the stability of programmatic cleavages in the 18 Latin American democracies cannot be assessed directly. It is apparent, however, that for a viable programmatic party system to exist, considerable party system stability must also exist. In particular, where parties win major percentages of the votes and seats in one election, but win only a handful of votes and seats in the next or cease to exist, it is difficult to consider that party system to be highly programmatic, even in the presence of strong programmatic cleavages, since the relevant parties in one election are generally not the relevant parties in the next. Based on the above logic, a country's programmatic subtotal is reduced (*volatility reduction*) based on its average level of volatility (see Table 2.1). A reduction of 4 is made if the average level of volatility is between 50 and 59; of 3 (between 40 and 49); of 2 (between 30 and 39); of 1 (between 20 and 29); and of 0 (between 0 and 19). If the *volatility reduction* value is greater than the programmatic subtotal, a value of 0 is assigned for the final programmatic politics index.

Table 2.6 provides the final index of the extent of programmatic politics in a country. Its value ranges from high values of 8 (Chile, Nicaragua) and 7 (El Salvador, Uruguay), to low values of 2 (four countries), 1 (three), and 0 (seven).

Clientelist Politics

The analysis of the extent of clientelism is handicapped by the lack of valid cross-national empirical measures of this concept (Kitschelt, 2000). Here, however, a proxy measure of clientelism (corruption) recommended by Kitschelt (2000) is employed.

The extent of corruption is measured using data from the World Bank (Kaufmann, Kraay, and Mastruzzi, 2003). Specifically, the average percentile ranking of the countries for 2000 and 2002 (among a group of 195 countries) in terms of their ability to control corruption (*control of corruption*) is used.

Programmatic versus Clientelist Politics

According to Kitschelt (2000, p. 871), "It is pretty safe to conclude that clientelism prevails in a polity if we find that parties are programmatically incohesive and that experts also attribute high scores of corruption to that country." Extending Kitschelt's logic, in the presence of programmatic parties, and in the absence of high levels of corruption, it is reasonably safe to assume that programmatic politics prevails in a country.

Using the measures highlighted in the previous two subsections, the extent of programmatic versus clientelist party politics in a country was evaluated. Figure 2.2 arranges the 18 countries on two dimensions: *extent of programmatic politics* and *level of corruption* (as a proxy for clientelism). For the former dimension, programmatic politics scores (see Table 2.6) are categorized as follows: very high (7–8); high (5–6); moderate (3–4); low (1–2); and very low (0). For the latter dimension, average corruption scores are categorized as follows: 75–100 (low); 51–74 (moderate); 34–50 (high); 20–33 (very high); and 0–19 (endemic).

The resulting figure reveals four general clusters of countries: programmatic, clientelist, programmatic and clientelist, and nonprogram-

| FIGURE 2.2 | Programmatic versus Clientelist Politics, Latin American Democracies |

		Level of Corruption				
		Low	Moderate	High	Very High	Endemic
	Very High	Chile Uruguay		El Salvador	Nicaragua	
	High					
Extent of Programmatic Politics	Moderate					
	Low	Costa Rica	Brazil	Argentina Mexico	Honduras	Ecuador Paraguay
	Very Low		Peru	Dom. Rep. Colombia Panama	Bolivia Guatemala Venezuela	

Source: Authors' calculations.

matic and nonclientelist. The largest group of countries (a total of 14) is located in the clientelist politics cluster. While there is some variation in terms of the extent of programmatic politics in these countries (for example, Brazil versus Paraguay), the dominant linkage mechanism between parties and voters is based on clientelism (broadly construed). Only two countries are located in the programmatic cluster (Chile and Uruguay).

Finally, two countries do not fall into these two clusters. The party systems in El Salvador and Nicaragua combine programmatic politics with high levels of clientelism.[8] This unique combination is most likely explained by the political history of each country, which involved extensive and violent civil conflict during the latter quarter of the twentieth century. In the post-conflict period, politics is still heavily conditioned by this historical legacy—particularly since the main actors from the conflict period coalesced into opposing political parties within the respective electoral democracy (especially in El Salvador). Since the strong ideological cleavages in these countries trace their origins in large part to the civil conflict, as the distance between the present and the conflict years grows, the level of programmatic politics in each country should decrease (a process that is occurring more rapidly in Nicaragua than in El Salvador).

Conclusion

Party institutionalization, party and party system nationalization, the interaction of legislative fragmentation/size of the presidential legislative contingent and ideological polarization, and the extent of programmatic versus clientelist politics all exert a profound effect on the policymaking process. For example, factors related to political parties and the party system determine the degree to which voters are able to hold elected officials and policymakers accountable, as well as the ability of voters to make the most efficient and effective use of their suffrage rights. They also have a profound impact on the extent to which public policies are universal or particularistic in scope and content, as well as on the speed in which public policies are designed, approved, and implemented.

---

[8] The third outlier is Costa Rica. See Lehoucq (2005) for a discussion of this case.

More generally, the features of a country's political parties and party system help determine the quality of its public policies, the degree of policy stability, and the ability of the country to adapt its public policies in the face of external or internal shocks. These factors related to political parties and party systems do not operate in a vacuum, however. Any comprehensive evaluation of the impact of these party system institutions on the policymaking process also must consider the joint influence exercised by other prominent institutions such as the presidency, cabinet, judiciary, bureaucracy, and subnational leaders (such as governors and mayors). Fortunately, the policy consequences of these and other institutions are expertly analyzed by the other chapters in this volume.

CHAPTER 3

Active Players or Rubber Stamps? An Evaluation of the Policymaking Role of Latin American Legislatures

Sebastian M. Saiegh

Legislatures are critical institutions in the effective functioning of a democratic system and in the policymaking process. Legislatures are expected to represent the needs and wishes of citizens in policymaking; identify problems and formulate and approve laws to address them; and oversee the implementation of policies by monitoring, reviewing, and investigating government activities to ensure that they are transparent, efficient, and consistent with existing laws and regulations.

The extent and nature of the role played by legislatures in the policymaking process vary greatly from country to country. At the more proactive and constructive end of the spectrum, legislatures such as the U.S. Congress are able to develop their own legislative proposals and thus participate along with the executive in directing the policy agenda. Given their policy capabilities, such legislatures are also likely to be active and effective in overseeing policy implementation. At the other end, legislatures may be fairly marginal players, serving as a rubber stamp for the executive's legislative proposals and having little capacity or willingness to scrutinize the conduct of government (Morgenstern, 2002). Between these two extremes, there is a wide area in the middle where legislatures can exhibit different degrees of activity either in simply blocking much of what the executive proposes or in reformulating and/or amending executive initiatives. Among such legislatures, there can also be considerable variation in the intensity and effectiveness with which the legislators perform the oversight role.

How the legislature plays its policymaking roles can have an important effect on the nature of policy outcomes. If the legislature is a marginal actor, this will give the executive free rein to enact policy changes that it perceives to be necessary. But the lack of legislative deliberation as policies are formulated and the weakness of oversight may mean that the policies adopted are poorly conceived in technical terms, poorly adjusted to the real needs or demands of organized interests and citizens, lacking consensus and therefore politically unsustainable, and/or ineffectively or unfairly implemented. On the other hand, legislatures that are involved more heavily in policymaking in a constructive sense can contribute to the adoption of policies that are more sustainable because they are based on a broader social and political consensus and are more carefully scrutinized in technical terms. In addition, in a constructive legislature, the effective oversight of policy implementation should increase the likelihood that policies fulfill their intended objectives rather than being carried out for the benefit of particular individuals, groups, or sectors.

Legislatures with limited capacity to play a constructive role in policymaking may nonetheless be important players because they can obstruct or veto much of what the executive proposes. Such legislatures have many of the potentially negative traits of more marginal legislatures in regard to policymaking, and they may also prevent the executive from advancing a positive agenda of policy reform. Given their limited capacity, such legislatures are also unlikely to play an effective role in overseeing the implementation of policies.

This chapter evaluates the main factors that affect the role of Latin American legislatures in the policymaking process. It compares and contrasts 18 Latin American legislatures to identify the main differences in their organizational structures, institutional features, and membership characteristics. Following IDB (2005), it presents a tentative categorization of Latin American legislatures. However, unlike this previous study, it does not rely on subjective/qualitative indicators to conduct such assessment. Instead, it uses a multidimensional scaling (MDS) technique to test if and how the dimensions used in IDB (2005) to classify these legislatures correspond to observed similarities among them.

The results show that these legislatures are primarily distributed in a two-dimensional space. The horizontal dimension can be interpreted as a representation of their relative capabilities. The vertical dimension captures how proactive or reactive these legislative bodies are. Therefore, in line with IDB (2005), the analysis reveals that four types of legislatures can indeed be identified. These findings also confirm that those legislatures with greater capabilities are the ones that play more constructive roles in the policymaking process.

Active Players or Rubber Stamps?

Against the backdrop of the region's history of dictatorial rule and *presidencialismo*, scholars had tended to consider legislatures in Latin American countries to be largely irrelevant throughout much of the twentieth century and not worthy of study in and of themselves. Some prominent experiences in the past two decades, such as the closing of the legislature by President Fujimori in Peru and the frequent use of decree powers by many Latin American presidents, continued to reinforce the commonly held view that Latin American legislatures often abdicate (or are forced to abdicate) their constitutional prerogatives to the executive.

However, recent studies suggest that while legislatures in the region in general may not be heavily involved in formulating and advocating policy change, they are nonetheless relevant to policy outcomes. Legislatures in some countries are active in policymaking in the sense of mainly being blunt veto players, blocking legislation proposed by the executive. Others, however, are involved in negotiating policy issues behind the scenes with the executive, or in amending or reformulating executive, legislative initiatives (Cox and Morgenstern, 2002; Amorim Neto, Cox, and McCubbins, 2003).

That legislatures in the region do not exist solely to rubber-stamp executive decisions is evident from data on the passage rates of executive legislative initiatives. As Figure 3.1 shows, the rate of approval of executive initiatives varies from a low of 41 percent in Costa Rica from 1986 to 1998 to a high of 96 percent in Mexico from 1982 to 1999.

On the other hand, these findings should not be interpreted as evidence indicating that in these countries legislative bodies play a central role in the policymaking process. For example, between 1982 and 1988, about six out of ten of all legislative proposals in Mexico originated from legislative initiative, but of those only one out of twenty became law (Casar, 2002). This seems to be the pattern in most Latin American countries: while individual legislators have the right to introduce bills everywhere, the legislation most likely to be enacted is initiated by the executive branch (Taylor-Robinson, 1999).

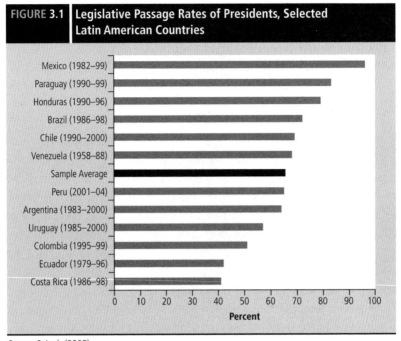

FIGURE 3.1 | **Legislative Passage Rates of Presidents, Selected Latin American Countries**

Source: Saiegh (2005).

The broader point is that these measures reveal something meaningful about executive–legislative relations, but they are of limited value in assessing a legislature's full influence on policymaking. Aside from proposing or killing legislation, legislatures can approve bills with extensive amendments. They can also exert influence outside the formal legislative arena, through bilateral negotiations between legislative leaders and executive officials as to which bills get introduced and what form such legislation takes. In addition, the executive, not wanting to face the humiliation of a legislative defeat, can anticipate the legislature's reaction in the way that it designs policy proposals (Morgenstern, 2002). Therefore, as noted in IDB (2005), the task of appraising the legislature's policymaking role in any given country is quite difficult and requires a more detailed study of each individual case.

Cross-National Evaluation

The discussion turns now to some of the cross-legislature factors that contribute to differences among legislatures with respect to their ability to play an active role in the policymaking process. Several factors drive a legislature's role in the policymaking process. These include the extent of its formal powers; the amount of political space/discretion afforded by other power holders (executives, parties); the capacity afforded by its procedures/structures/support; and the goals of the members and leaders of the legislative bodies themselves.

Fundamental Structures

Number of Houses. A first characteristic that may affect the role played by the legislature in policymaking is its unicameral or bicameral structure. Nine countries in the region (Costa Rica, Ecuador, El Salvador, Guatemala, Honduras, Nicaragua, Panama, Peru, and Venezuela) have unicameral legislatures. In principle, one would expect this organizational difference to be correlated with some political or geographical characteristics of the countries. However, bicameral cases include large countries (such as Brazil and Mexico) and small ones (such as the Dominican Republic and Uruguay). It seems that the existence of a second chamber has more to do with historical legacies than a conscious decision on the part of political leadership to adopt a particular institutional design.

Depending on the balance of legislative powers between the two chambers, a bicameral legislature can provide a separate veto point in the policymaking process. For instance, a senate elected from a single national district concurrently with the president and on a single ballot (as in Uruguay) is less likely to act as an additional veto point and does not dramatically change how territorial interests are represented. But when senators are elected separately from the president on the basis of provincial districts (as in Argentina), and representation is not tied to population, then there is a greater possibility that the upper house can become a separate veto point and accentuate the extent to which regional interests are represented in policymaking.[1]

However, as Llanos and Nolte (2003) point out, bicameral systems in Latin American are very symmetrical in terms of their institutional prerogatives. These authors develop a system of scores to measure the strength of these bicameral legislatures. Table 3.1 shows the scores for nine Latin American countries. A score of 4 means that there is extreme

---

[1] This point is elaborated on in Chapter 7 on subnational authorities.

symmetry in that particular dimension, while a score of 0 means that there is complete asymmetry. For example, a score of 4 in bill initiation means that the legislative discussion of bills can be initiated in any of the chambers; a score of 2 indicates that the lower house has the exclusive right to initiate most legislative processes; and a score of 0 is given to those instances where all legislative processes are initiated in the lower house.

As the table shows, in these nine countries there are no significant differences among the chambers with respect to their relative lawmaking powers. Therefore, given the symmetrical nature of bicameral legislatures, the analysis that follows focuses mainly on the lower house, or national assembly in the case of unicameral congresses.

Constitutional Powers. The basic forms and rules of legislatures in Latin American countries are established in their constitutions. All these legislative bodies are constitutionally created and grounded institutions. Nonetheless, there are important differences among them in their constitutional mandates.

In Mexico, the standing constitution dates from 1917, and the Costa Rican legislature has operated under the same constitution since 1949, with only the 1993 amendment regarding the role of legislative committees changing the initial set of rules governing it. Similarly, the constitution currently in place in Uruguay dates from 1967, and none of the constitutional amendments adopted from 1989 to 2004 changed the basic rules governing the structure and prerogatives of parliament. In contrast, except for Mexico, Chile, Colombia, and Costa Rica, every other country has operated under more than two different constitutions in the last six decades—five countries (Brazil, the Dominican Republic, Ecuador, Nicaragua, and Venezuela) are on their fifth—and most of them have amended their constitutions quite often. Mexico has amended its 1917 constitution more than 40 times.

These differences in the amount of constitutional "experimentation" notwithstanding, all the countries considered in this chapter have a presidential form of government. This constitutional structure seeks to divide access to policy control among different elected officials. In particular, the two fundamental characteristics of presidential systems are that the head of state is elected separately from the congress, and that the terms of the president and congress are fixed. In relation to these core features, the only notable deviation among this set of countries is

TABLE 3.1   Bicameral Symmetry in Latin America, Selected Countries

	Argentina	Bolivia	Brazil	Chile	Colombia	Dom. Rep.	Mexico	Paraguay	Uruguay
Legislative Powers	4	4	4	4	4	4	4	4	4
Bill initiation	2	2	2	2	4	4	2	4	4
Decision system	4	0	4	4	4	4	4	4	0
Oversight	4	4	4	0	4	4	4	4	2
Shared oversight	4	4	4	4	2	2	4	4	4
Impeachment	4	4	4	4	4	4	4	4	4
Total	22	18	22	18	22	22	22	24	18

Source: Llanos and Nolte (2003).

Bolivia, where congress has the responsibility of choosing among the leading two vote-winners in the presidential race if no candidate obtains an absolute majority in the first round.

Once one looks beyond these two defining characteristics, there are some other important differences among countries. Presidents have the power to appoint and remove cabinet ministers in all these countries.[2] In some cases, though, such as Colombia, Peru, Uruguay, and Venezuela, legislatures also have the power to remove ministers through censure procedures. Given the difficulty of obtaining the majorities required for censure and the president's full discretion in naming a successor, this power has not been used to a significant extent in most countries. However, the power of censure may still act as a constraint on the president's discretion in controlling the composition of his cabinet.

Aside from appointment powers, constitutions grant presidents other tools with which to insert themselves into policymaking. Generally speaking, the stronger and more diverse these powers, the more constrained the legislature is likely to be in undertaking an active and effective role in policymaking and developing its capabilities. The presidential powers that contribute to the president's ability to unilaterally change the status quo can be referred to as proactive powers (Mainwaring and Shugart, 1997; García Montero, 2008). These powers include decree powers, agenda-setting powers, and budgetary powers. Reactive powers, by contrast, allow the president to preserve the status quo against efforts by the legislature to change it. These powers include package veto and partial veto powers, and exclusive powers to initiate legislation in given policy areas.

In several countries, the constitution grants presidents the power to enact new legislation by decree, even without the legislature first delegating this authority. This authority is applicable across most policy areas in Argentina, Brazil, and Colombia, but limited to economic matters in Ecuador and fiscal matters in Peru. Although in most cases congress has the authority to rescind the decree, this power nonetheless helps the president control the legislative agenda and obtain outcomes that would otherwise not be possible. For instance, in Brazil, the president can legislate through provisional decrees (*Medidas Provisorias*), which

---

[2] A partial exception is Uruguay, where the president must seek legislative approval for cabinet appointments.

need to be ratified by congress within 60 days to remain in effect. If a provisional decree is not acted on within the first 45 days, it is automatically sent to the top of the legislative agenda. If congress does not approve the provisional decree in this first 60-day period, the president can reissue the provisional decree, but only once. Constitutions also grant many presidents in the region important agenda-setting powers (García Montero, 2008).

For instance, presidents in Brazil, Colombia, and Uruguay can declare a legislative proposal "urgent," thereby requiring congress to act within a set time frame. In Uruguay, a bill becomes law if the congress does not act within the allowed time frame. Another form of agenda-setting power, found in Brazil and Chile, is the president's ability to convene a special legislative session in which only those initiatives set forth by the executive can be debated.

The constitutions of many of the region's countries also provide presidents with mechanisms to prevent attempts by the legislature to change the status quo policies without the president's assent. The package veto, in which presidents can refrain from signing an entire bill approved by the legislature into law, is common in many presidential systems, including the United States. But many Latin American presidents are also given the power to reject individual items of bills approved by the legislature (Alemán and Schwartz, 2006).

Another form of reactive power is when the president is given the exclusive authority to initiate legislation in some policy areas. For example, in Colombia, this restriction on the legislature applies to the structure of ministries, salaries of public employees, foreign exchange, external trade and tariffs, and the national debt, among other areas. Presidential legislative monopolies (that is, areas of exclusive initiative) are also fairly extensive in Brazil and Chile.

As Table 3.2 shows, the overall legislative powers of presidents are greatest in Chile, Brazil, Ecuador, and Colombia. Proactive powers are also sizeable in Peru. Legislative powers of presidents are weakest in Bolivia, Costa Rica, Paraguay, and Nicaragua. In Paraguay, the executive branch was considerably weakened by the 1992 constitution. It deprived the president of the power to dissolve congress, and endowed the executive with relatively weak "proactive" and "reactive" powers. In the case of Costa Rica, articles 126–27 of the constitution allow the president to "amend" bills passed by congress and return them to the assembly for

TABLE 3.2 | Legislative Powers of Presidents in Latin America

Country	Proactive powers			Reactive powers					
	Decree powers[a]	Budget powers	Proactive powers subtotal[b]	Package veto	Partial veto	Exclusive initiative	Reactive powers subtotal	Plebiscite powers	Overall legislative powers[b]
Chile	0.33	0.73	0.50	0.85	0.85	0.67	0.77	1.0	0.66
Brazil	1.00	0.91	0.96	0.15	0.15	0.67	0.38	0.0	0.62
Ecuador	0.33	0.73	0.50	1.00	0.69	0.33	0.62	1.0	0.59
Colombia	0.67	0.64	0.66	0.31	0.31	0.67	0.46	1.0	0.59
Peru	0.67	0.73	0.70	0.15	0.15	0.33	0.23	1.0	0.50
Argentina	0.33	0.45	0.38	0.85	0.85	0.00	0.48	0.5	0.44
Panama	0.17	0.55	0.33	0.77	0.77	0.33	0.58	0.0	0.43
Uruguay	0.17	0.64	0.37	0.54	0.54	0.33	0.45	0.0	0.38
El Salvador	0.00	0.82	0.35	0.77	0.00	0.00	0.22	1.0	0.33
Venezuela	0.33	0.64	0.46	0.08	0.08	0.00	0.04	1.0	0.30
Guatemala	0.33	0.18	0.27	0.77	0.00	0.00	0.22	1.0	0.29
Dom. Rep.	0.00	0.64	0.27	0.92	0.15	0.00	0.31	0.0	0.27
Honduras	0.33	0.36	0.34	0.77	0.00	0.00	0.22	0.0	0.26
Mexico	0.17	0.36	0.25	0.92	0.00	0.00	0.26	0.0	0.24
Bolivia	0.00	0.27	0.12	0.85	0.00	0.33	0.38	0.0	0.23
Costa Rica	0.00	0.64	0.27	0.77	0.00	0.00	0.22	0.0	0.23
Paraguay	0.00	0.64	0.27	0.23	0.23	0.00	0.13	0.0	0.19
Nicaragua	0.00	0.73	0.31	0.15	0.15	0.00	0.09	0.0	0.19

Source: UNDP (2005).
Note: Legislative power variables are normalized on a scale of 0 to 1 based on the range of possible scores of each variable.
[a] This measure includes both the power of presidents to unilaterally make law (decree powers), and the power to shape the legislative agenda (agenda-setting powers), such as by declaring legislation "urgent," implying a reduced time frame for congress to take action.
[b] Weighted averages.

reconsideration, and article 220 of the Honduran constitution is ambiguous about the possibility of a partial veto.

While significant legislative powers give the president important levers for bargaining and shaping the legislative agenda, they usually do not substitute for the need for adequate partisan support. Decrees can be overturned, urgent legislative initiatives can be defeated, and vetoes can be overridden. Thus factors related to the party and electoral system are also key in shaping the legislature's role and the nature of executive–legislative relations.

Table 3.2 also illustrates the effect of different veto procedures on the balance of power between the executive and legislative branches of government. In particular, it shows how amendatory veto power gives the executive branch substantial leverage in the legislative decision-making process. Agenda-setting rules that give too much power to the executive may end up undermining legislators' interest in developing the capacities of the legislatures.

Partisan Dynamics and Electoral Incentives

The availability of significant legislative powers gives presidents an important lever for bargaining and shaping the legislative agenda. In fact, the use of his/her unilateral powers may in principle allow a president to implement as many of his/her desired policies as possible (Mustapic, 2002).

However, the use of executive prerogatives as a source of law has important limitations. Decrees, for example, are usually seen as an exceptional policymaking instrument or as one with specific purposes, and thus are particularly sensitive to judicial review. In contrast, the legislative approval of statutes is often more difficult to obtain, but once enacted they are sticky policy decisions. Hence, legislative passage allows chief executives to better insulate their policy choices from legal review (Remington, Smith, and Haspel, 1998; Amorim Neto, 2006). However, unlike ruling by decree, the patterns of statutory legislation are truly a product of the interactions among political parties, the legislature, and the executive. Therefore, policymaking powers granted to the president by the constitution can be as important as those powers derived from partisan support in the legislature. Table 3.3 provides information on various indicators of the degree of partisan control of the legislature by the chief executive.

TABLE 3.3	Chief Executive's Partisan Control of the Legislature					
Country	Period	Percent of seats of president's party	Percent of seats of government's party/parties	Minority governments	Portfolio coalitions	Effective number of parties
Argentina	1946–99	56.35	56.35	38.89	0.00	2.58
Bolivia	1982–99	33.08	47.92	61.11	61.11	4.15
Brazil	1946–99	34.76	66.62	15.38	82.05	4.65
Chile	1946–99	23.97	41.03	67.74	61.29	4.22
Colombia	1946–99	50.05	87.01	6.67	84.44	2.17
Costa Rica	1946–99	51.85	51.85	50.98	0.00	2.27
Dom. Rep.	1966–99	51.3	51.49	41.18	11.76	2.24
Ecuador	1979–99	20.79	26.58	100.0	61.90	5.85
El Salvador	1984–99	46.02	46.44	62.50	25.00	2.89
Guatemala	1948–99	41.95	56.39	18.42	42.11	3.01
Honduras	1957–99	55.33	59.22	8.00	24.00	2.07
Nicaragua	1984–99	56.03	56.03	25.00	0.00	2.31
Panama	1949–99	31.4	55.82	44.83	68.97	4.13
Peru	1963–99	47.44	50.86	41.18	52.94	3.13
Uruguay	1946–99	45.86	53.24	33.33	23.81	2.75
Venezuela	1946–99	42.4	46.68	48.84	25.58	3.33

Source: Cheibub, Przeworski, and Saiegh (2004).

In some countries the president's party always governs by itself (Costa Rica, Nicaragua), while in others government coalitions seem to be the norm (Brazil, Colombia). While the party of the president may not be the largest party in the legislature, by crafting government coalitions, these presidents may be able to put together a legislative contingent with a majority of the votes (Kellam, 2007).

Still, it is striking to see the pervasiveness of minority governments in Latin America. When a single party controls both the executive and legislature, then the chances for independent legislative decision making diminish. For example, a governing party (or parties) may circumscribe its role in the legislature to merely transforming government policy into law. This task, of course, will be subject to a number of constraints: proportion of seats, intraparty cohesion, the committee system, and the strength of the opposition. For example, despite having relatively weak constitutional powers, Mexican presidents before 1997 dominated policymaking, since they could count on solid majorities for the governing Partido Revolucionario Institucional (PRI) in both houses of congress. But when control over the government was divided between the PRI and their opponents in the House of Deputies, the legislature became more assertive.

While a highly fragmented party system is likely to result in a more active legislature, it may tend to limit the legislature's role to being mainly a veto player or a site of bargaining over particularistic expenditures rather than an arena for proactive policymaking or effective oversight of the executive. Having a large number of parties, especially when they are internally factionalized, is likely to limit the possibilities for coordination over policy both within the legislature and between the executive and the legislative branches (de Riz and Smulovitz, 1990).

Differences in the extent to which parties are centralized and disciplined also entail trade-offs with respect to the legislature's policymaking role. On the one hand, party centralization may help presidents secure support in the legislature and facilitate interparty negotiations in the formation of governing coalitions, thus contributing to policy adaptability. Centralized parties that are also programmatic in orientation may encourage legislators to adopt a policy focus oriented toward national public goods, rather than a focus on the delivery of more targeted and narrow benefits.

On the other hand, high levels of party centralization are likely to limit legislators' incentives to respond directly to their constituents—and the possibilities of such a direct response—as well as their incentives to participate independently in the policymaking process and in oversight responsibilities. Subservience to party leaders, especially when parties tend to be clientelistic, can contribute to a weak policy role for the legislature and weak incentives for legislators to invest in developing the capacities of congress. But while decentralized parties may encourage greater policy independence among legislators and more accountability of individual legislators to voters if parties are less cohesive, this can limit the ability of voters to hold representatives accountable on the basis of national policy positions and accomplishments, and can encourage an orientation among legislators toward satisfying narrow geographic interests (Carey and Shugart, 1995; Seddon Wallack et al., 2003; Hallerberg and Marier, 2004).

Legislators are most likely to represent constituent interests when they know precisely who their constituents are; when they interact with them frequently; and when their political futures depend on gaining and keeping constituent support. Table 3.4 presents summary information on the main features of the rules governing legislative elections (including candidate selection mechanisms) for the countries covered in this chapter. Higher values for the first three variables—*ballot, pool, and votes*—indicate that legislators have incentives to develop a personal vote. The next column provides the average district magnitude.[3] The variable *personal* combines this information into a single indicator. The last two columns provide a rank ordering of the countries.

The representation deficit in Latin America is increased by the inappropriate proportional distribution of representatives to the legislative bodies (malapportionment). This inappropriate distribution is significantly higher in the region than in the rest of the world. For example, in Argentina, smaller provinces have a minimum of five deputies and this creates a big distortion, as they should only have one or two deputies based on their population. The same is true in Brazil. While thousands of votes are needed to get elected in São Paulo, a small fraction of votes are needed to be elected in, say, Fortaleza.

Legislative Careers. Election rules and the degree of centralization of candidate nomination processes can also affect legislators' career ambitions

---

[3] District magnitude is defined as the average number of legislators elected per electoral district.

TABLE 3.4 | **Incentives for the Personal Vote and District Magnitude**

Country	Ballot	Pool	Votes	District magnitude	Personal	Personal rank	District magnitude rank
Paraguay	0	0	0	19.2	0.08	2	19
Bolivia	0	0	0	12.5	0.09	3	17
Argentina	0	0	0	8.7	0.11	5	15
El Salvador	0	0	0	8.2	0.11	6	14
Costa Rica	0	0	0	8.1	0.11	7	13
Nicaragua	0	0	0	8.1	0.11	7	13
Honduras	0	0	0	7.1	0.12	9	11
Mexico	0	0	0	4.0	0.17	11	8
Dom. Rep.	0	0	0	3.4	0.19	12	7
Venezuela	0	0	1	7.6	0.23	13	12
Guatemala	0	0	1	6.9	0.24	14	10
Uruguay	1	0	2	11.4	0.38	16	16
Panama	0	0	0	1.8	0.39	17	4
Ecuador	0	0	1	3.2	0.40	18	6
Chile	1	0	2	2.0	0.43	19	5
Peru	1	0	1	4.0	0.50	20	8
Brazil	2	0	2	16.8	0.62	21	18
Colombia	2	1	2	42.0	0.76	22	20

Source: Hallerberg and Marier (2004).

and incentives, as well as their experience. Given the very high rates of reelection (around 90 percent) and fairly decentralized party structures of the U.S. Congress, analysts assume that legislators' main motivating goals are to obtain reelection and to advance their careers in the legislature. By contrast, in Latin America, where the rate of reelection tends to be much lower, legislators typically have an incentive to work toward advancing a career outside the legislature (such as in national, state, or local government) and are also less experienced. Their career objectives are often furthered by satisfying party leaders rather than by centering their attention on satisfying constituents' interests and demands.

As shown in Figure 3.2, the rates of immediate reelection to congress in Latin America are quite low. On average, less than 40 percent of legislators return to their seats. This figure stands in sharp contrast with the reelection rates for legislators in OECD countries. In Chile and Uruguay, around 60 percent of legislators are immediately reelected, but in Argentina less than 20 percent return for a second consecutive term. In Mexico immediate reelection is not permitted, and only about 11 percent of legislators, respectively, are eventually reelected.

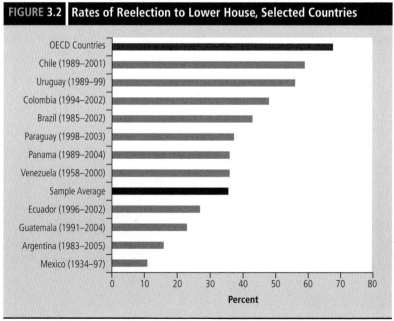

FIGURE 3.2 | Rates of Reelection to Lower House, Selected Countries

Source: Saiegh (2005).

The high levels of turnover may be seen as a sign of a "healthy" political system: the voters are voting the rascals out of office. However, this is seldom the case. In general, the biggest hurdle in the career path of Latin American legislators is posed by their own parties. Most party- or executive-dominated systems often have features that limit the development of constituency ties. The complex interactions among various electoral rules and party system characteristics are illustrated by the following examples.

In Argentina, local party leaders control the construction of the local party list. Thus legislators' ability to pursue a legislative career independently is significantly restricted. Instead, they typically seek to continue their political career in other elective or appointive offices. As a consequence, Argentine legislators have a strong incentive to maintain a good relationship with their local party leaders. These leaders have a complex political objective: they want to maximize their party's performance in their province, but at the same time they want to safeguard their position within the provincial party structure. The threat of challenge by popular legislators provides local party leaders with a strong incentive to reduce the national and provincial visibility of their local subordinates by rotating them among the various jobs the provincial party can offer. The electoral risks associated with nominating lesser-known candidates are mitigated by Argentina's electoral rules, especially the use of party-supplied ballots and closed list proportional representation. Voters tend to vote for the party list, not for the individuals on the list. A president's ability to influence legislators of his own party thus depends in part on whether the provincial party leader supports the administration (Jones et al., 2002).

In Chile, the binominal electoral system, with two members elected per district, creates strong incentives for the formation of two electoral coalitions. Parties or electoral alliances can win the two available seats only if the winning list receives at least twice the total vote of the list that obtains the second-most votes. Given electoral incentives, legislators concerned with keeping their seats in congress know that dropping out of one of the main coalitions entails significant electoral risks. The imposition of this voting system in a country characterized by around five effective political parties has resulted in majority control of the Chamber of Deputies by the governing Concertación coalition since the return to democracy in 1989. Thus electoral system-based incentives have contributed to strong legislative support for bills initiated by the executive.

Legislative Organization

The legislature's policymaking role is also affected by its organizational characteristics, which in turn are influenced by environmental factors, such as constitutional stipulations, party system dynamics, and electoral incentives. Given the unwieldy size and lack of specialization of the full congress, if legislatures are to play an active role in shaping the content of policy and overseeing the executive, they must do so through capable committees. Most legislatures in Latin America have permanent committees with specific policy jurisdictions. Legislation is routinely referred to them before being taken up by the larger chamber.

A well-designed system is one in which this definition tends to parallel the structure of the administrative or cabinet agencies. However, as Figure 3.3 shows, this is the exception rather than the rule in Latin America.

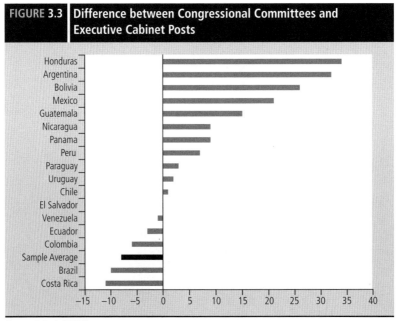

FIGURE 3.3 | Difference between Congressional Committees and Executive Cabinet Posts

Source: Saiegh (2005).

Except for El Salvador, where legislative committees "mirror" the structure of the cabinet, in most Latin American countries there are either too many (Honduras, Argentina) or too few (Brazil, Costa Rica) legislative committees relative to the size of the cabinet. The variation in the number of committees does not necessarily correspond to the size of the legislature. One would expect legislatures with many members to have relatively more committees than legislatures with few members. However, some small legislatures have relatively too many committees. Figure 3.4 shows the relative size of committees in 16 Latin American lower houses of their respective national legislatures.

The size of these bodies ranges from 513 members (Brazil) to 57 members (Costa Rica) and the number of committees from 7 (Colombia) to 48 (Honduras). The figure also includes, as a benchmark, the average ratio of the number of committees to the size of the legislature for a cross-section of non-Latin American countries. Compared to this benchmark, except for Brazil and Colombia, all the countries in this sample have too many committees relative to their size. The worst cases are Honduras, with 48 standing committees in a legislature with 128 members, and Paraguay, with 25 standing committees in an 80-legislator body.

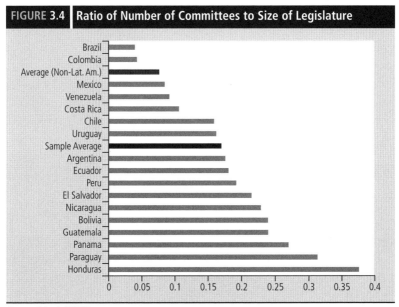

FIGURE 3.4 | Ratio of Number of Committees to Size of Legislature

Source: Saiegh (2005).

If there are a large number of committees relative to the size of the chamber, legislators may be required to serve on several committees simultaneously, which may limit their ability to concentrate their efforts and develop specialized knowledge. For example, in Argentina, committees must normally have a minimum of 15 and a maximum of 25 members, and the rules do not restrict multiple assignments. As a result, the average Argentine deputy serves on 4.5 committees. In addition, the effectiveness of the legislature can be impaired if legislation is commonly sent to multiple committees because of overlap among committees' policy jurisdictions.

Legislative rules also shape how members and committee leaders are selected. If committee memberships and leadership rotate frequently, this is likely to limit the degree of expertise that members develop and thus their policymaking effectiveness. To the extent that party leaders can exercise control over committee assignments and appointments to leadership positions, this can give them leverage in maintaining party discipline. In Brazil and Colombia, such prerogatives of party leaders to manage the committees, organize the legislative agenda, and direct public resources help impose some party discipline, despite electoral rules that allow or encourage legislator independence.

In most Latin American countries, committee and leadership assignments are made on a partisan basis. The composition of the committees is expected to reflect the partisan composition of the legislature as a whole. Instead of allocating important committee assignments and leadership positions on the basis of seniority, as has been the practice in the U.S. Congress until recently, in most Latin American legislatures party leaders or party caucuses allocate these slots on the basis of other criteria, such as party loyalty (Heath, Schwindt-Bayer, and Taylor-Robinson, 2005).

The existence of an ample and competent staff to assist legislators with the tasks of administration, research and analysis, and document preparation is vital to enable committees to evaluate bills initiated by the executive and supervise policy implementation effectively. While the scope of committee staffing varies widely from one country to another, in most countries it is deficient relative to the roles assigned to the committees. For example, in Argentina each committee has access to a secretary, an administrative secretary, and two clerical assistants. However, these personnel only perform administrative functions. In contrast, in El Salvador, each committee has only one technical assistant and one secretary, but they perform all three secretarial functions. In a few countries, professional staff are available to assist legislative committees (and parties) with research and analysis. For example, in Brazil, a research office that has about 35 professionals assists the budget committee of the lower house. Chile has a (relatively small) legislative budget research office; several professional staff persons also advise the budget committee. In Colombia, a relatively large number of professional staff members assist the budget committee. Conversely, a study of the legislatures of Argentina, Bolivia, and Honduras conducted by Rundquist and Wellborn in 1993 concluded that the committees of these countries lacked skilled staff. The authors found that most committees had a single nonpartisan staff professional employed by the secretariat, supplemented by party employed staff controlled by the chamber or committee party leadership (Rundquist and Wellborn, 1994). Hallerberg, Scartascini, and Stein (2009) show that the lack of support for budgetary analysis has not improved in most of these countries.

A Characterization of Latin American Legislatures

IDB (2005) presents a tentative categorization of Latin American legislatures. The authors group these legislatures according to the nature of their policymaking role and the intensity with which they carry out that role. In part, the nature of the role is shaped by the capabilities of the legislatures. Therefore, in their categorization, a major focus is on legislative capabilities, including the experience and qualifications of legislators, and the strength and degree of specialization of committees.

The general idea is that legislatures that have more legitimacy, more experienced legislators, and well-developed committee systems will tend to be more constructive and/or proactive. Legislatures with weaker capabilities will tend either to play a limited policymaking role or to be active, but only in a fairly obstructionist way rather than a constructive one.

Table 3.5 compares Latin American legislatures according to several indicators that attempt to measure the main dimensions of these legislative capabilities. The first two assess the confidence of citizens and businesspeople in the performance of congress. The third and fourth indicators (average years of legislator experience and percentage of

TABLE 3.5 | Measures of Legislatures' Capabilities

Country	Confidence in congress, average	Effectiveness of lawmaking bodies, average	Average experience of legislators (years)	Percentage of legislators with university education	Average number of committees per legislator
Argentina	20.5	1.6	2.9	69.6	4.50
Bolivia	19.9	1.8	3.3	78.4	1.66
Brazil	24.9	3.1	5.5	54.0	0.92
Chile	36.0	3.7	8.0	79.4	1.95
Colombia	20.3	2.7	4.0	91.6	0.86
Costa Rica	29.9	2.2	2.6	80.4	2.09
Dom. Rep.	—	2.0	3.1	49.6	3.54
Ecuador	13.3	1.7	3.5	83.1	1.26
El Salvador	27.7	2.1	3.9	64.0	2.44
Guatemala	19.9	1.8	3.2	68.4	3.24
Honduras	30.8	2.6	3.0	73.1	2.34
Mexico	27.4	2.0	1.9	89.5	2.43
Nicaragua	23.1	1.6	3.5	85.6	1.96
Panama	22.5	1.8	5.8	81.3	1.86
Paraguay	25.0	2.2	5.5	75.4	3.15
Peru	22.1	1.7	5.2	92.9	2.44
Uruguay	38.2	2.7	8.8	68.4	0.98
Venezuela	27.8	1.4	4.9	74.6	0.97

Source: IDB (2005).
— not available.

legislators with university education) attempt to gauge the qualifications and experience of legislators. The average number of committee memberships per legislator attempts to measure the degree of specialization of legislative committees, and thus their effectiveness.

Main Indicators

Confidence in Congress. The nature of the role that legislatures play is likely to influence the way that citizens view them. At the same time, the level of citizen trust in congress affects the likelihood that investments can be made in building its capacity. As seen in Table 3.5, the general public does not have a high degree of confidence in the congress in most countries of the region. On average over the past decade, according to the Latinobarometer, the general public has the most favorable view of congress in Uruguay, Chile, Honduras, and Costa Rica and the least favorable view in Ecuador, Bolivia, and Guatemala. A deficit of representation and accountability may be one the reasons behind the low esteem that legislatures have among Latin American citizens.[4]

Effectiveness of Lawmaking Bodies. In cases in which congress has little credibility, it is likely to be less effective in representing societal interests, and the executive will have a greater incentive to seek to bypass or minimize the legislature in the policymaking process. As Table 3.5 shows, the average ratings given by business executives, as reported by the World Economic Forum, are highest in Chile and Brazil and lowest in Venezuela, Nicaragua, and Argentina. The most important differences in the views of the general public and business executives are for Venezuela, where in each case the general public has a comparatively more favorable view than business executives do.[5]

Experience of Legislators. Term length is thought to influence legislative behavior, with longer terms insulating legislators more effectively

---

[4] The indicator was constructed as the average percent of respondents from 1996 to 2004 and the percentage of respondents in 2004 in the Latinobarometer survey who stated that they had a lot or some confidence in congress.

[5] This indicator is the mean score given by business executives in the 2002–05 World Economic Forum survey to the question: How effective is your national parliament/congress as a lawmaking and oversight institution?

from electoral pressures than shorter ones. The modal term in office for lower house members in the countries examined in this study is four years. The other countries have five-year terms (except for El Salvador and Mexico, where terms last for only three years). One fundamental difference across some of these legislatures is the existence in some of them of limitations on the number of terms a member may serve. In Venezuela legislators can be immediately reelected, but up to only two legislative terms, and both Mexico and Costa Rica prohibit immediate reelection of lower house members. As noted, aside from term length restrictions, rates of immediate reelection to the congress are quite low in the countries under consideration. All these factors thus have an effect on the average experience of Latin American legislators. As Table 3.5 shows, Uruguay and Chile have the most experienced of legislators, while in Mexico, Costa Rica, and Argentina, the average experience of legislators is quite low.

Legislators' Education. Legislators' behavior is shaped by a variety of factors, including personal motivations, how they view their jobs, and the variety of ways that they can respond to constituents. One plausible observable indicator of this source of heterogeneity across legislators is their educational level. Table 3.4 shows the percentage of legislators with a college degree, based on the data collected by the PELA project (García and Mateos, 2000). Peru and Colombia have the highest percentage of legislators with higher education. By contrast, less than half the legislators in the Dominican Republic have a university education.

Legislative Specialization. As noted, legislative rules shape the size of committees, how members and committee leaders are selected, and the number of committees on which each legislator can serve. As such, another indicator of a legislature's ability to enact policy changes through statutes is given by the degree of specialization of its members. The average number of committee memberships per legislator attempts to measure the degree of specialization of legislative committees, and thus their effectiveness. Table 3.5 shows that Colombia and Brazil have the most specialized committees, while Argentina, the Dominican Republic, Guatemala, and Paraguay have too many members serving on their committees.

Multidimensional Scaling

The comparison of the Latin American legislatures presented in IDB (2005) makes use of the aforementioned indicators. However, the authors rely on a set of ancillary subjective indicators and a qualitative evaluation to make their final assessment of legislatures' policymaking roles. The analysis that follows examines the robustness of such characterizations when only quantitative indicators are used, and the data are allowed to "speak for themselves," in effect.

The appropriate way to conduct such analysis is multidimensional scaling (MDS), a statistical technique for analyzing the structure of data. This method represents measurements of similarity (or dissimilarity) among pairs of objects as distances between points of a low-dimensional multidimensional space. The data, in this case, are correlations among the Latin American legislatures based on the indicators presented in Table 3.5, and the MDS representation shows them as points on a plane. The graphical display of the correlations provided by MDS enables us to literally "look" at the data and to explore their structure visually (Borg and Groenen, 2005). Besides using MDS as a method to represent the data as distances in a low-dimensional space in order to make them accessible to visual inspection, this technique also allows us to test if the dimensions by which IDB (2005) conceptually distinguishes Latin American legislatures corresponds to observed similarities among them.

Figure 3.5 presents a two-dimensional MDS representation where each national legislature is shown as a point.[6] The points are arranged in such a way that their distances correspond to their correlations. Namely, two points are close together (such as the Peruvian and Paraguayan legislatures) if their characteristics (as measured by the indicators presented in Table 3.5) are highly correlated. Conversely, two points are far apart if their characteristics are not highly correlated (such as Argentina and Brazil).

More generally, Figure 3.5 shows that these legislatures are primarily distributed along a horizontal dimension which, in accordance with IDB (2005), can be interpreted as "low capacity versus high capacity" legisla-

---

[6] The MDS representation was produced using KYST, a computer program that provides a best-possible solution in a space with a dimensionality selected in advance by the user. In this case, the best-possible solution was sought for a two-dimensional space.

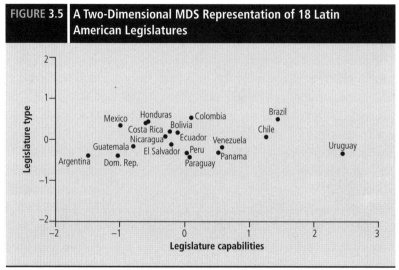

FIGURE 3.5 **A Two-Dimensional MDS Representation of 18 Latin American Legislatures**

Source: Saiegh (2005).

tures. The vertical axis, in turn, can be interpreted as a "reactive–proactive" dimension. It seems to be reflecting the fact that some legislatures play a relatively limited policymaking role (such as those in Argentina and the Dominican Republic), while others, despite being quite reactive in nature, can occasionally take the initiative in shaping the policy agenda and developing policy proposals (such as those in Colombia and Brazil).

Discussion of the Evidence

The cross-national evidence presented earlier, along with the MDS findings, provide a very good picture of the different types of legislatures in Latin America. Armed with this information, it is time to address the main questions that motivate this study: Can a characterization of Latin American legislatures be devised according to their role in the policymaking process? How do the assessments of the legislatures' capabilities that arise from the previous analysis compare to the qualitative evaluation of their roles discussed in IDB (2005)? Is it true that legislatures with greater capabilities tend to play a more constructive role in the policymaking process?

Returning to Figure 3.5, all the points in the southwest quadrant correspond to legislatures that are classified as being reactive limited/obstructionist and having low capabilities by the IDB (2005) report. In terms of the cross-national evidence presented earlier, these legislatures can be characterized as being (quasi-) marginal, somewhat obstructionist, but mostly passive. The quasi-marginal role of these legislatures is due to the excessive powers of the executive and/or the lack of professionalization of their members. These are legislatures where being a member is not worth much. Legislators cannot undertake spending initiatives and thus cannot deliver pork or public works. Most legislators in these countries often seek to continue their political careers somewhere else. Therefore, they may or may not be obstructionist, depending on how they are compensated. In the case of Argentina, control over political careers is enough to keep them in line. When the electoral mechanism is not enough, "compensations" may even be paid using monetary resources. Argentina, Peru, and Panama are good cases in point. Unless policy would directly affect legislators' interests, the president may have easy sailing. But policy reversal is also possible. Accordingly, legislation is of low quality, poorly drafted, and easily reversed.

The legislatures represented by the points in the northwest quadrant have low capabilities, but are somewhat proactive. All these legislatures were characterized by the IDB (2005) report as having medium capabilities, while also being reactive/obstructionist. They are the prototypical rubber-stamp legislatures. In these cases, most policies are decided outside of the legislature, mainly in the governing party (or parties). Executives tend to get much of what they want and the currency is mainly partisan endorsement or other government posts. Some of these legislatures were able to adopt a more active role when presidential powers were reduced (such as in Mexico in the post-PRI period). However, these legislatures do not have very good capabilities, and thus their scope of action is greatly reduced when their partisan composition is at odds with the preferences of the executive.

The points in the northeast quadrant correspond to those legislatures deemed to be reactive/constructive and endowed by high capabilities by the IDB (2005) report, with one exception (Uruguay; see below). Even though these legislatures possess greater capabilities, they still play a reactive role in the policymaking process. This limited role can be due to the excessive powers of the executive (Brazil) and/or the alignment of legislative majorities with the executive (Chile). For example, in Brazil, presidents can get their legislation passed using their extensive legislative and nonlegislative powers. In the case of Chile, individual legislators can submit initiatives under very restricted conditions. Everything indicates that these legislatures can "step up to the plate" and become more active players in the policymaking process under different institutional and/ or political conditions. (In fact, the Brazilian legislature did so when Collor was impeached.) The Colombian congress became more powerful after the 1991 reforms, but it can still be characterized more as reactive rather than proactive.

Finally, the Uruguayan legislature is located in the southeast quadrant of the MDS representation. Unlike the IDB (2005) report, which characterizes this legislature as being reactive/constructive, the analysis reveals it as reactive/obstructionist. In accordance with the IDB (2005) report, the results also indicate that Uruguayan legislators tend to be of high quality. However, these legislators tend to be quite ideological, making them hard to be "bought." Instead of compensations paid in cash or transfers, legislators are more likely to demand cabinet posts or policy compromises. Therefore, whenever the executive faces a lot of legislative opposition, the most probable consequence is political stalemate between the branches of government.

Conclusion

The main goal of this study was to fill the gap in knowledge about how Latin American legislatures operate and their role in the overall policymaking process. This study did not seek to cover every detail related to the organization and operation of legislatures in Latin America. Instead, the primary focus was to get a broad sense of the current circumstances of Latin American legislatures, and their potential to become an important actor in the policymaking process as defined by the laws, politics, and incentives faced by their members.

The evidence presented in the study indicates that the extent and nature of the role played by Latin American legislatures in the policymaking process vary greatly from country to country. At the more constructive end of the spectrum, legislatures such as those in Brazil and Chile have the potential to become active and effective players capable of participating in setting the policy agenda and overseeing policy implementation. On the other hand, other legislatures in the region lack the organization, financial resources, experienced members, and staff to serve as a mature and autonomous point of deliberation in the policy process.

Therefore, these legislatures—very much like the U.S. Congress at the end of the nineteenth century—operate more as a blunt veto player (exercising gatekeeping and some other types of delaying strategies) than as effective policymaking bodies. These results have important implications for those interested in strengthening the role of legislative institutions in the policymaking process throughout the region. The main lesson that reformers should keep in mind is that they will not be able to empower legislatures if the right incentives for individual legislators are not established first. The institutionalization of any legislature starts with the recognition on the part of its members that they need to spend part of their time and effort on building a stronger collective body. Therefore, the focus should be on the incentives that legislators must have in order to "invest" in the legislature.

CHAPTER 4

How Courts Engage in the Policymaking Process in Latin America: The Different Functions of the Judiciary

Mariana Magaldi de Sousa

Judicial reforms, embedded within the broader context of political reforms undertaken by many Latin American countries in the past 25 years, have changed the nature and the extent of courts' involvement in the policy-making process. Judges and courts—as a collective entity—have assumed a more active role in the elaboration and implementation of public policy, reflecting a process of gradual delegation of lawmaking powers from the legislature and the executive to the judiciary (Tate and Vallinder, 1995). As a result, the importance of the courts in national politics has grown (Waltman and Holland, 1988; Alivizatos, 1995; Shapiro and Stone Sweet, 2002) and recourse to the courts for the resolution of political and social conflicts has increased (Domingo, 2004; Sieder, Schjolden, and Angell, 2005). Yet a systematic understanding of how courts may engage in the policymaking process and how such an engagement actually varies across Latin American countries is still lacking.

This chapter attempts to fill this void by providing a typological framework for categorizing and comparatively assessing the scope of judicial activism (defined as the extent of courts' involvement in the policymaking process) in Latin America.[1] Another goal of the chapter is to draw attention to the possible impact of Latin American courts' activism on public policy outcomes, suggesting interesting hypotheses for future empirical research. In particular, this chapter argues that

---

[1] In this study, the definition of judicial activism is different from what is conventionally used. The term is used simply to mean courts' involvement in the policymaking process.

the varying results of judicial reforms in establishing institutions that facilitate stronger judicial independence, wider judicial review powers, improved access to justice, and enhanced communications among the three branches of government have determined the extent to which the judiciary can veto new legislation, shape legislative content, enforce the implementation of existing rules, and act as an alternative representative of society in the policymaking process.

Judicial activism, in turn, has impacted the characteristics of public policies as defined in previous volumes of this series (IDB, 2005, 2008). The public policies in countries where reforms have yielded broad judicial activism tend to be rather stable and adaptable, while the policies in countries whose reforms have limited the extent of judicial activism exhibit more volatility and rigidity.[2] Ultimately, a better conceptualization of the role of the judiciary in the policymaking process and its consequences can stimulate discussions about the appropriate interplay between law and politics in the region.

In 1970, Francisco José Moreno asserted that "[u]nfortunately there is very little written material dealing with the political role of the judiciary in Latin America" (p. 378).[3] His evaluation largely holds to this day. Despite the fact that laudable efforts have been employed in the examination and measurement of judicial independence in Latin America, systematic assessments of judicial activism in the region are scant. There are few comparable sources of statistical data on judicial decisions, and there is a paucity of conceptual schemes guiding empirical research on the role of the judiciary in the policymaking process in the region. At most, recent authors have highlighted an ongoing process of "judicialization" of politics and "politicization" of the judiciary (Tate and Vallinder, 1995; Domingo, 2004; Sieder, Schjolden, and Angell, 2005; Oliveira, 2005) and

---

[2] While a brief definition of the characteristics of public policies (stability, adaptability, credibility, and public regardedness) appears in Chapter 1, a more detailed description can be found in IDB (2005), Stein et al. (2008), and Scartascini, Stein, and Tommasi (2008).

[3] Other authors have corroborated. For instance, Gibson, Caldeira, and Baird (1998, p. 343) assert: "Despite impressive progress in understanding many aspects of cross-national politics, comparativists know precious little about the judicial and legal systems in countries outside the United States. We understand little or nothing about the degree to which various judiciaries are politicized; how judges make decisions; how, whether, and to what extent those decisions are implemented; how ordinary citizens influence courts, if at all; or what effect courts have on institutions and cultures." Similarly, Gloppen, Gargarella, and Skaar (2004, p. 2) highlight: "Studies of the political role of courts outside of the United States are scarce."

a rising impact of courts on public policy and governance (Ballard, 1999; Méndez, O'Donnell, and Pinheiro, 1999; Gargarella, 2003).

Such a relative scarcity of studies on judicial activism in Latin America is not surprising. The decades immediately preceding the 1980s were characterized by military dictatorships, recurring economic crises, and intense social instability, which did not create a propitious environment for judicial independence, "checks and balances," and the protection of civil rights and liberties. Judges often suffered from undue influence on their rulings coming from powerful private actors, other branches of government, or even higher court judges. Supreme (or constitutional) courts did not have enough powers to strike down legislation that was inconsistent with constitutional principles. Within the parameters of the civil (or Roman) law tradition followed by many Latin American countries, judges were not supposed to "create law," but rather limit their responsibilities to discovering the meaning of the text given an existing body of rules, norms, and codes. Naturally, academics, policymakers, and the general public considered the role of Latin American courts irrelevant for the politics and policies in the region (Duncan, 1976).

It was not until Latin American countries started undertaking judicial (and political) reforms in the 1980s and the 1990s and pursuing major efforts to revamp various law-related institutions that it became possible to see an increased impact of courts in the policymaking process.[4] Indeed, there are reasons to believe that the policymaking role of the judiciary is not as irrelevant and narrowly defined as traditionally supposed. First, although the speed, content, and degree of success of reforms varies across countries, experts agree that Latin American judiciaries have generally become more independent, professional, and accountable (Hammergren, 2002; Popkin, 2002). As the judiciary becomes more efficient and repositions itself vis-à-vis the other branches, the opportunities for courts to decide against the preferences of the executive or the legislatures increase, thereby activating the mechanisms of "horizontal accountability" (O'Donnell, 1999) and "checks and bal-

---

[4] In the words of Sieder, Schjolden, and Angell (2005, p. 1): "It would be wrong to exaggerate the contrast between a currently activist judiciary and a previously passive one. Courts have been significant political actors in some countries during specific periods in the twentieth century, playing both progressive and conservative roles…However, there has undoubtedly been a marked change in the nature and character of judicial involvement in political matters since the 1980s and ever greater recourse to the courts is now a marked feature of the region's contemporary democracies."

ances" (Przeworski and Maravall, 2003). Moreover, the broadening of judicial review powers has forced legislators to think about constitutional adequacy when elaborating legislation (Stone Sweet, 2000). The policy debate now includes efforts to anticipate the reaction of judicial institutions (Ferejohn, 2002) at the same time that an increasing number of citizens are choosing to protect their rights by appealing to the courts (Zemans, 1983; McCann, 1994; Sieder, 2007). Finally, the appointment of higher court judges constitutes a largely political issue. If courts were irrelevant for the policymaking process, the strategic interest in the control of appointments to the courts would not be so prevalent.

The point of departure of this chapter thus is the observation that reforms have created institutions that allow judiciaries across the region to play a number of different roles in the policymaking process. Three relevant questions emerge from this observation, which are addressed in the rest of the chapter. First, how can judiciaries engage in the policymaking process? In other words, what are the main roles that judiciaries can play in the policymaking process? Second, how do these roles vary across Latin American countries? Third, what is the impact of the extent of judicial activism on policy outcomes?

Four Potential Roles for the Judiciary in the Policymaking Process

Beyond the adjudicatory tasks of resolving civil and criminal disputes, the judiciary may engage in policymaking either directly or indirectly (Vallinder, 1994). Directly, judges are called upon to give their consent regarding specific policies and their approval is a requirement for the implementation of such policies. Indirectly, even if judges do not directly participate in the policymaking process, the mere threat of recourse to courts can prompt changes in the behavior/preferences of other political actors as well as alterations in the proposed legislation in order to avoid future judicial disapproval. In both accounts, the legislative process is said to be "juridicized" (Stone Sweet, 1992).[5] Given the difficulties of

---

[5] Another possible form of judicial involvement in the policymaking process relates to the judiciary's refusal to participate in political discussions and decisions. In this case, the judiciary would be endorsing the commonly known policy of "no policy," which could also be considered another type of engagement, albeit an absence of engagement. This study adopts a more "positive" understanding of judicial activism, however.

identifying and systematically assessing indirect judicial participation in the policymaking process, this chapter focuses only on the direct forms of judicial involvement.

Such direct involvement occurs in four major ways, depending on the nature of the effects of judicial decisions: courts can veto laws, shape their content, ensure the effective application of other policies, or act as alternative societal representative to bring law and justice to the poor and representation to the disenfranchised. While engaging in these activities, courts' decisions can have two main types of effects. First, decisions may be confined to a case or group of cases: that is, decisions may be either *inter partes* (the judicial ruling is applied to the specific case under review) or *erga omnes* (the judicial ruling is applied not solely to the specific case but also to all similar cases that might be considered in the future). Second and more broadly, judicial rulings may uphold or alter laws and policies: that is, courts' decisions may maintain or change the status quo.

At the intersection of these effects can be found four potential roles for the judiciary in the policymaking process (see Table 4.1). When a court's decision invalidates a policy or a policy proposal, and such a decision is supposed to be applied in similar cases, the judiciary is effectively vetoing a law or proposal for a law, forcing a default return to the status quo. This is when the judiciary undertakes its "veto player" role in the policymaking process.

Similarly, when the judiciary either rejects a change to existing policy but its decision is applied only to the specific case under review, it is exercising its "referee" role. In this case, courts supervise the effective implementation of public policies, acting as an external enforcer (or a referee) of agreements involving the government. Alternatively, courts can accept (the proposal for) a new law or give a new interpretation for an existing rule. In both cases, the judiciary is changing the status quo.

If its decision to change the status quo is good only for the specific case, then the judiciary is an "alternative societal representative." If the judicial decision to change the status quo is applied to other similar cases, courts are engaging in the creation of policies, exercising their "policy player" role.

These roles are neither mutually exclusive nor static. They may be used more frequently in some countries at some time than in others, varying across political systems and over time. Sometimes these judicial

TABLE 4.1	The Four Potential Roles of the Judiciary in the Policymaking Process		
		Effects on policy	
		Inter partes effects	*Erga omnes* effects
Effects on policymaking process	Maintain policy status quo	Referee role	Veto player role
	Change policy status quo	Alternative societal representative role	Policy player role

Source: Author.

roles are well accepted (and even applauded) by the government elites and the general public; at other times and in other circumstances, greater judicial involvement in the policymaking process elicits political controversies and power struggles with the executive and the legislature. The discussion that follows briefly describes each of these roles.

Veto Player Role

The first role that courts can assume is the veto player role. Following Tsebelis' (1995, 2002) work—which argues that policy change becomes more difficult as the number of veto players increases—courts assume this type of role when they do *not* grant their agreement to enact a policy change and such a decision is effective *erga omnes*. This rejection might become known either before the policy comes into effect or only after days, months, and even years of its enactment. The main requisite for this type of role is the existence of a higher court (either a constitutional court or a supreme court) responsible for constitutional adjudication (or judicial review process). If courts have the authority to declare the unconstitutionality of other legislation with *erga omnes* effects, their decisions cannot be overruled by other political actors (Tsebelis, 2002, p. 226).[6] In this case, the judiciary becomes involved in the policymaking process to the extent that courts serve as a tool to activate the horizontal mechanisms of institutional limits on political power and block certain governmental policy proposals.

---

[6] The exception is when political actors change the constitution itself, but this is more difficult to achieve, in practice.

Since the U.S. Supreme Court's decision in *Marbury v. Madison* (1803), the United States and other English-speaking countries have used judicial review as the main source of judicial involvement in policymaking (Jackson and Tate, 1992).[7] By determining whether a piece of legislation is consistent with the constitution and by requiring the barring of unconstitutional practices, judicial review grants judges the power to legitimize the application of a law. When the rulings on constitutional questions have binding *erga omnes* effects and the supreme court (or other constitutional court) sets precedents, judges effectively create or reject laws that cannot be easily bypassed by the executive or the legislature.[8] As a result, judges in common law countries have historically been largely active in the policymaking process.

The same cannot be said of courts in Latin America. Following the civil law tradition,[9] the doctrine of precedential authority is not prevalent, and judges are supposed to simply apply the pertinent parts of the legislative code to the conflict at hand. The judicial branch does not have the power to formulate new legislation, and whenever codes need to be modified, it is up to the legislature to perform the necessary changes. At most, judges interpret statutes and reject new policies given their views of the legal system as a whole. When interpreting statutes, however, judges are not engaging in their veto player role because these interpretations are applied to the concrete case and they can be overruled by new legislation (Tsebelis, 2002, p. 228).

Notwithstanding these pronounced differences between common law and civil law traditions, some studies have highlighted a process of convergence between the two legal systems in the last three decades.[10] Many Latin American countries have created constitutional courts and expanded their judicial review powers (Brewer-Carías, 1997; Navia and Ríos-Figueroa, 2005). There is a consensus that courts in the region are becoming stronger and more independent from the other branches of

---

[7] Jackson and Tate (1992, p. 4) offer a definition of judicial review: "[It] refers to the ability of a court to determine the acceptability of a given law or other official action on grounds of compatibility with *constitutional* forms."

[8] This process is commonly known as "judge-made" laws or "government by judges" (Stone Sweet, 2000).

[9] For a discussion of the characteristics of the civil (or Roman) law tradition, see Merryman (1985).

[10] See Waltman and Holland (1988, p. 85), for example.

government (Hammergren, 2002), and not surprisingly, there is some preliminary evidence of more dynamic judiciaries in the region (especially related to their veto player role).[11] In Colombia, for instance, the constitutional court, created in 1991, made use of its judicial review powers to declare unconstitutional the law proposal that criminalized the possession and consumption of personal doses of narcotic drugs (*tutela* C-221/94). Considering that Colombia suffers from a serious problem of drug consumption and trafficking, it is difficult not to see the important role played by the country's constitutional court in the policymaking process.

Overall, it is important to note that the pure existence of judicial review is not enough to characterize courts as veto players. Judges themselves must be willing to exercise constitutional control, and their propensity to use review powers is affected by various factors such as their legal educational background, the degree of their independence from other branches of government, and their personal beliefs as to what the function of the judiciary should be. Thus, when assessing the veto player role of the judiciary in the policymaking process, one needs to look beyond the formal rules of judicial review powers to analyze the other determinants of the actual propensity of courts to employ these powers.

Policy Player Role

When courts interpret laws and shape the content of policies, they are assuming their policy player role in the policymaking process. Rather than providing a simple seal of approval of policies, judiciaries are engaging in the process of crafting law when they interpret laws and statutes to determine their original meaning or when they give new interpretations to pieces of legislation. By establishing what a statute is and how it applies to specific cases, judicial rulings can change the status quo and impose *erga omnes* effects.

This type of role is especially vibrant in countries where courts maintain close interactions with the other lawmaking branches of government, and the legislature (as well as the executive) often asks the judiciary for some kind of clarification or opinion before a policy goes into effect. Institutional features favoring these kinds of activities include

---

[11] For examples, see Sieder, Schjolden, and Angell (2005).

the presence of an abstract centralized a priori model of constitutional adjudication.[12] An interesting example of the exercise of the policy player role is the Chilean constitutional tribunal. Between 1990 and 2001, various members of congress asked the tribunal for its opinion on several legislative proposals. As a result, the legislature had to rewrite more than 225 proposals before they were actually enacted (Navia and Ríos-Figueroa, 2005, p. 208).

Beyond the consultations before a law is enacted, statutory interpretation often occurs after a policy goes into effect. Indeed, courts may need to interpret laws and statutes for a variety of reasons. The technical complexity of the subject matter, various societal and technological advances, or the enactment of inconsistent statutory amendments can often raise questions about what the statute means and whether it is applicable to a certain situation. In all cases, the crux of the problem is the ambiguity of the statutory language, which makes judicial intervention necessary. Such ambiguity allows judges to be "creative" in their conceptions of the meaning of the law. Thus judges find opportunities repeatedly to impress their own preferences and value judgments onto statutory interpretation and policy content.

Some observers question why the simple interpretation of statutes can engage judges in the policymaking process. Their argument is usually two-pronged. On the one hand, supporters of "textualist" theory claim that judges do not have much room for influencing policymaking because their job is confined to deciding cases according to what the law says and not what judges may think the legislators intended.[13] On the other hand, some critics emphasize that statutory interpretation generally has *inter partes* effects without any apparent wider impact on society (Tarr, 2002).

Without denying the value of these arguments, such an understanding of statutory interpretation underestimates its importance in policymaking for two main reasons. The textualist approach is based on the assumption that the meaning of a text is *rarely* dubious. How-

---

[12] For a description of various types of constitutional adjudication models in Latin America, see Navia and Ríos-Figueroa (2005).

[13] Textualism is a philosophy of statutory interpretation that holds that the original text should guide judges in their interpretation. One of the major proponents of this notion of interpretation is U.S. Supreme Court Justice Antonin Scalia. Textualism opposes other theories of interpretation that allow judges to examine other secondary sources in order to understand the context in which the law was written and the intent of legislators.

ever, one can easily imagine various circumstances in which such an assumption would not hold, making the textualists' assumption debatable. Even if judicial rulings are supposed to have an impact solely on the parties involved, they can have broader effects on society under two main conditions.

First, through statutory interpretation, courts can make certain issues more salient, placing them at the core of political debates. If courts can draw the attention of not only academics but also the general public and the media to contested topics such as ethnic discrimination, then judicial decisions can expand their effects and have a direct influence in the policymaking process.

Second, when courts highlight serious drafting problems through statutory interpretation, they may induce the legislature to take corrective actions. In the process, an increased interaction between the judiciary and the legislature may follow in order to (re-)formulate statutes that are more clearly defined (Katzmann, 1997). In both cases, critics of statutory interpretation fail to recognize its implications for the content of policies as well as for the relationship between the judiciary and the legislature. As Katzmann (1997, pp. 48–49) notes: "When courts interpret legislation, they become an integral component of the legislative process…[statutory interpretation] has real consequences for the meaning of legislation, the shape of policy, and the allocation of power in the government system."

That is not to say that the broader effects of statutory interpretation always have positive consequences, whether intended or unintended. Rather than cooperation, statutory interpretation may elicit tensions and power struggles between the legislative and judiciary branches. The legislature, for instance, can react to courts' unfavorable statutory interpretations by attacking judicial decisions publicly and undermining the judiciary's public image. As a result, consideration of the political environment in which courts operate is of crucial importance for an understanding of the potentialities and limitations of their policy player role.

Referee Role

If the veto player role focus on the power of the courts to *nullify* policies, and the policy player role underscores the capacity of the judiciary to *elaborate* policies, the referee role emphasizes the judiciary's power to *enforce* policies through the judicial oversight function. Courts can be called upon to ensure that existing public policies are being applied effectively; in these cases, they act as an external enforcer of agreements and a mediator among contracting parties. In their referee role, courts are not primarily concerned with the interpretation of legislation or their constitutional adequacy; rather, the courts focus on the supervision of administrative activities and the resolution of day-to-day disputes involving the government that cannot be solved by the litigants alone or the regulatory agency.[14] Some examples of this role include impeding the government from levying illegitimate taxes, protecting the autonomy of an independent central bank, and oversight of federal administrative agencies (Humphries and Songer, 1999). In all circumstances, the results of judicial decisions include the maintenance of the status quo and *inter partes* effects.

After many sectors of the economy were privatized, the policymaking power of administrative (or regulatory) agencies increased in many Latin American countries. Administrative agencies in sectors ranging from telecommunications to aviation were granted the authority to issue regulations (secondary legislation) that complemented and further specified legislative mandates (primary legislation). Although explicit procedural and substantive standards were established, these agencies have largely retained a degree of discretion when designing secondary legislation (Humphries and Songer, 1999). Sometimes, this discretion is overextended, either by not following the preferences of political superiors such as the president and congress or by breaching the demands of legal requirements.[15] In these cases, important opportunities for judicial involvement arise, entangling courts in the control of bureaucratic compliance (McCubbins and Schwartz, 1984) and the review of the constitutional/statutory adequacy of regulations (Horowitz, 1994). Such involvement has allowed courts to solve common matters of time inconsistency within government as well as principal-agent problems, with significant implications for policymaking.[16]

---

[14] In the course of their oversight function, courts do interpret statutes and sometimes assess the constitutional adequacy of laws, thereby performing both their policy player and veto player roles..

[15] Administrative agencies can also fail to act. In this case, inaction can also constitute a violation of an agency's mandate.

[16] Time inconsistency is the incentive of the government to deviate in period $t+1$ from the optimal policy rule it chose in period t. The reason why time inconsistency can arise is that it might be optimal for the government to use its announced government policy rule in period t to

Indeed, many authors have underscored the existence of an independent judiciary as a precondition for central bank independence and stable monetary policy (Feld and Voigt, 2003). Others have pointed out that the judiciary, in its capacity as a referee, can help decrease governments' spending and fiscal deficits through the enforcement of fiscal responsibility laws (Alston et al., 2009). Still others have emphasized the importance of a strong judiciary in restricting regulatory capture and/ or outright corruption in the executive branch, the legislature, or in the judiciary itself (Buscaglia and Dakolias, 1999; Alt and Lassen, 2005). In Latin America, a judiciary capable of performing its referee role is particularly relevant for the region's prospects for economic growth. By limiting the incentives and ability of various Latin American governments to behave opportunistically, and by protecting the rights of domestic and foreign investors against administrative expropriation and potential abuses of the state's coercive power, courts create an environment of "legal security" in which investments in physical, financial, and human capital can thrive.

Alternative Societal Representative Role

Judges are not subject to mechanisms of electoral accountability. Unlike members of the other branches of government that participate in the policymaking process, judges are not popularly elected; thus they are not conventionally understood as legitimate representatives of society. Yet judiciaries can provide a forum for the defense of civil and social rights, uphold the enforcement of the principle of "equality before the law," and make certain issues/conflicts more salient than others; in these capacities, they can serve as a "voice" for the poor and other marginalized groups of society, who often find it difficult to influence the elaboration of public policies. When courts see themselves as the advocates of minorities or the "weak" and try to expose and rectify social injustices, they are engaging in their fourth possible role in the policymaking process: an alternative societal representative. Even though the effects of courts' decisions affect only the involved parties, they are actually helping to change the policy status quo.

---

encourage people to commit to certain actions over the near term. Once people have committed to these actions, however, government might then find it optimal to shift to a new policy rule.

During most of the twentieth century, corporatism and political parties were the main vehicles of political access and representation for marginalized groups in Latin America. Within the context of an import-substitution model of development, the state itself decided how to distribute resources and resolve social conflicts. With globalization, privatization, and the neoliberal economic reforms that followed in the 1980s and 1990s, however, markets gained in importance, becoming the main arena for societal groups to advance their interests (Correa Sutil, 1999, p. 269). Governments rapidly lost their ability to allocate social benefits. As a result, the "losers" of increased market competition have had to find new ways to fight for better and more equal opportunities. Among these, legal mobilization has allowed individuals and minority groups to press their demands and participate in the policymaking process. With the help of various social movements and nongovernmental organizations, marginalized groups in Latin America are increasingly resorting to courts as a means to secure their rights and address pressing social problems (Sieder, Schjolden, and Angell, 2005).[17]

At least in theory, the legal system has the capacity to bring law and justice to the poor and representation to the disenfranchised. It entails a set of procedures that forces the elites/majorities to listen to the claims of the poor/minorities,[18] while giving the latter the opportunity to have their rights protected[19] (Correa Sutil, 1999). Under the rubric of "public interest litigation" (or "social action litigation"), courts are capable of "[rebalancing] the distribution of legal resources, [increasing] access to justice for the disadvantaged, and [imbuing] formal legal guarantees with substantive and positive content" (Cassels, 1989, p. 497). To the extent that the judiciary capitalizes on its capabilities and leads the protection of minorities' rights,[20] courts become an alternative societal representative in the process of policy and social transformation. Even in the case of judicial decisions that are not favorable to minorities, the symbolic effects of public interest litigation and expanded public visibility may be enough to spur discussions about new social policy formulation or reform.

---

[17] For a description of this process outside Latin America, see Epp (1998).

[18] That is, courts cannot simply refuse to listen to the initiated disputes.

[19] That is because law is guided by the principle of equality and impartiality.

[20] Usually this protection takes the form of either constitutionally based efforts to strike down democratically enacted policies to the benefit of minorities, or initiation of claims for the protection of generalized interests such as the environment and other regulatory matters.

To be sure, many authors have underscored the idea of judges being active in the defense of disadvantaged groups and courts providing alternative access to political participation to those who otherwise would influence the policymaking process only in their capacity as voters. For example, in an essay about judicial policy regarding the poor, Bennett (1983, p. 61) writes: "Courts are designedly insulated from the usual levers of political influence and thus are particularly charged with ensuring that the benefits of the rule of law reach the nation's poor." Similarly, in talking about the "*amparo*" suit[21] in Mexico, Taylor (1997, p. 152) asserts: "The federal judiciary developed historically with the main purpose of bringing justice to the people and protecting human rights before that of interpreting the laws or maintaining particular principles of legal techniques."

Despite its potential for positive impacts, the use of the courts as an alternative channel for representing minorities in the policymaking process is problematic on occasion, and is not always equality-enhancing. First, there is an inherent difficulty in defining who a "minority" is. As Ely (1980) emphasizes, one of the most influential theories of when the U.S. Supreme Court should strike down democratically enacted policies is based on the existence of a "discrete and insular minority," which can be a racial or religious one. In the case of Latin America, however, courts have tried to identify such a minority in economic terms, which is a greater challenge.[22] In a region characterized by enormous social inequalities and concentration of wealth, the minority is often the rich and well-endowed rather than the poor and disadvantaged. In addition, in the process of defending the rights of the minority, the judiciary may end up being "captured" by interest groups—an outcome that calls into question the very legitimacy of the courts' role of societal representative.

Variations in Judicial Activism across Latin America: The Importance of Institutions

Many explanations have been offered to account for the recent changes in both the levels and the nature of judicial involvement in the policy-

---

[21] The *amparo* suit is often used in Spanish-speaking countries as an instrument to protect individuals' constitutional rights.

[22] Thanks to Richard Messick for this point.

making process. Some authors have argued that judges nowadays are more predisposed (and even willing) to engage in policymaking than in previous periods.[23] Others claim that public trust in the judiciary has increased, making societal groups more likely to use the courts to protect their rights and advance their policy objectives.[24] Still others believe that the recent increase in judicial activism is a product of more legislation and societal conflicts. Although the importance of these explanations should not be denied, they cannot fully account for the increased level and scope of judicial policymaking in Latin America. Changes in the institutional features of the judicial branch in particular and the political system in general also constitute a crucial determinant of the variation in judicial activism across Latin American countries.

The reforms of the 1980s and the 1990s included major efforts to change law-related institutions, with the objectives of creating more independent, efficient, professional, and accountable judiciaries. Within the context of democratization and economic liberalization, international financial institutions (such as the World Bank, the International Monetary Fund, and the Inter-American Development Bank), nongovernmental organizations, and various domestic political actors (including political parties and judges) promoted and pressured Latin American governments for renewed judicial structures and a more active role for the courts. The initiation and implementation of these reforms varied across countries, and their results were not uniform.[25] There is a consensus, however, that the institutional arrangements generated by the various judicial and political reforms have increased the levels of judicial independence, broadened courts' judicial review powers, promoted wider participation of quasi-judicial institutions, enhanced the professionalization of judges, improved access to justice, instigated society's legal mobilization, and facilitated more interaction between the judiciary and other government branches. These reform achievements can be summarized along three main dimensions of judicial activism:

---

[23] See, for example, Wolfe (1997).

[24] See, for example, Smithey and Ishiyama (2002).

[25] See Sousa (2007) for an overview of the results of judicial reforms in Latin America. Additionally, the country chapters in Hallerberg, Scartascini, and Stein (2009) show the differential impact of judiciary activism on fiscal outcomes. For example, while the improved fiscal results in Brazil may depend on the new activism of the courts (Chapter 3), they have contributed to the fiscal burden in Colombia (Chapter 4).

judicial independence, judicial powers, and quasi-judicial institutions; legal mobilization and access to justice; and interaction between the judiciary and other branches of government (see Table 4.2). Together, they constitute a good indication of both the potential for individual judges to act according to their own policy preferences, and the potential for courts—taken collectively—to be involved in the policymaking process.

For the judiciary to fill any of its four potential roles in the policy-making process, high levels of judicial independence are a prerequisite. A de facto independent judiciary is one that issues rulings that are respected and enforced by the legislative and executive branch; that receives an adequate appropriation of resources; and that is not compromised by political attempts to undermine its impartiality.[26] Certain institutions help ensure judicial independence: those that guarantee budgetary autonomy; a uniform, transparent, and merit-based appointment system; stable tenure for judges; and promotion procedures based on evaluation of performance. Without these institutions, Latin American courts simply would not be able to veto policies, shape their content, or act as a referee and a societal representative. To put it differently, judicial independence is a necessary (although not sufficient) condition for judicial activism.

Table 4.3 shows the relative rankings of judicial independence for selected Latin American countries in 1975 and 2005. Although nearly all countries moved a couple of positions either up or down, it is interesting to note how Chile, Brazil, and Uruguay achieved considerably higher levels of judicial independence, and Venezuela and Argentina seem to have encountered larger barriers to do so during this thirty-year period. While the first group of countries undertook important reforms to retain judicial budget autonomy, establish professional procedures of appointment, and maintain stable tenure for judges, the latter set of countries have often struggled with attempts by the executive branch to control judges' appointments, especially at the supreme court level. Judiciaries

---

[26] According to Shetreet (1985), judicial independence has four interrelated dimensions: substantive independence (power to make judicial decisions and exercise official duties subject to no other authority but the law); personal independence (adequately secured judicial terms of office and tenure for judges); collective independence (judicial participation in the central administration of courts); and internal independence (independence from judicial superiors and colleagues).

TABLE 4.2	The Three Dimensions of Judicial Activism
Dimension 1: Judicial independence, judicial powers, and quasi-judicial institutions	a. Judicial independence Judicial and/or political reforms have: • allowed the judiciary to achieve high levels of de facto independence from the executive and legislative branches b. Judicial review (or constitutional adjudication) powers Judicial and/or political reforms have: • allowed the constitutional courts' decisions to have *erga omnes* effects • separated the workings of the supreme court from the constitutional court • centralized judicial review powers in the hands of a constitutional court (or the supreme court)[a] • allowed members of the constitutional court to come primarily from the judicial branch (rather than through political appointments) c. Quasi-judicial institutions Judicial and/or political reforms have: • allowed quasi-judicial institutions (such as the public ministry in Brazil) to become more active in the defense of individual and collective rights • changed the nature of the constitution to widen the range of individual and collective rights
Dimension 2: Legal mobilization and access to justice	Judicial and/or political reforms have: • created effective alternative dispute resolution mechanisms • enhanced information systems • improved organization and case management • decreased the average costs of the litigation process • improved the efficiency of the litigation process • allowed social minorities (defined in terms of race, religion, purchasing power, and the like) to initiate the litigation process more frequently
Dimension 3: Interaction between the judiciary and other branches of government	Judicial and/or political reforms have: • promoted a high degree of both administrative and fiscal decentralization • stimulated fierce party competition • encouraged weak party discipline • improved the means of communication between the legislature (and the executive) and the judiciary

Source: Author.

[a] That is to say, ordinary courts cannot engage in judicial review.

TABLE 4.3	Relative Judicial Independence, Selected Latin American Countries, 1975 and 2005	
Ranking	**1975**	**2005[a]**
1 More judicial independence	Costa Rica	Uruguay (15)
2	Venezuela	Costa Rica (1)
3	Colombia	Chile (16)
4	Argentina	Brazil (12)
5	Mexico	Dom. Rep. (7)
6	El Salvador	Mexico (5)
7	Dom. Rep.	El Salvador (6)
8	Peru	Colombia (3)
9	Panama	Guatemala (11)
10	Ecuador	Bolivia (14)
11	Guatemala	Honduras (13)
12	Brazil	Peru (8)
13	Honduras	Argentina (4)
14	Bolivia	Panama (9)
15	Uruguay	Paraguay (18)
16	Chile	Ecuador (10)
17	Nicaragua	Venezuela (2)
18 Less judicial independence	Paraguay	Nicaragua (17)

Source: For 1975, Verner (1984, p. 479). For 2005, World Economic Forum (2005).
[a] 1975 rankings are in parentheses.

characterized by institutional safeguards against executive (or legislative) branch encroachment are generally more likely to engage in policymaking than their counterparts in countries where such institutional protections either do not exist or are poorly enforced.

Other sources of judicial involvement in the policymaking process are judicial review powers (or constitutional adjudication). Judicial review is the power of a court (generally the supreme court, or in some cases, the constitutional court and ordinary courts) to declare laws and other administrative acts unconstitutional. Such a power can be implicitly or explicitly guaranteed by the constitution, and it varies according to type (concrete or abstract), timing (a priori or a posteriori), jurisdiction (centralized or diffuse), standing (broad or not), and effects (*erga omnes* or *inter partes*).[27] While the United States presents a decentralized, concrete, and a posteriori model, European countries, for the most part, have centralized systems that include a mixture of a posteriori/a priori and abstract/concrete systems. In Latin America, systems tend to be more hybrid, and elements of the U.S. and European models coexist.

The existence of judicial review powers is necessary for the development of the branch's roles as veto player, policy player, and alternative societal representative. Without these powers, courts lack the tools to veto or shape policy outcomes or protect minorities from the oppression of the majorities. If verdicts are binding and effectively *erga omnes*, judicial powers are stronger. The enactment of a bill of rights and a comprehensive constitution also enhances the scope and efficiency of courts' constitutional control. While a centralized system of judicial review is often more conducive to the exercise of the veto player role, decentralized systems favor courts' role as alternative societal representative, as they prompt constitutional awareness in a larger number of judges, as well as in civil society in general. When standing is broad, more political actors can activate courts to perform either as a veto player or an alternative society representative. Abstract a priori models of constitutional adjudication help judiciaries exercise their policy player role. In general, the more opportunities judges have to examine the constitutional adequacy of legislation, the more engaged they will be in the policymaking process.

In addition, the creation of constitutional courts and their membership can further strengthen judicial review powers. If reforms have separated the workings of the constitutional court from those of the supreme court, the prospects for better efficiency in constitutionality control increase, as the case loads are distributed between two high-level courts. Also, if the members of the constitutional court come mainly from the judicial branch (rather than from the ranks of political appointees), the chances of political interference in judicial decisions decrease.

Beyond judicial independence and judicial review powers, judicial activism is reinforced by the existence of quasi-judicial institutions that are rather active in the defense of individual and collective rights, such as the Public Ministry (in Brazil) and the figure of the ombudsman. Traditionally, the ombudsman (Procurador de Derechos Humanos,

---

[27] For a thorough discussion of constitutional adjudication in Latin America, see Navia and Ríos-Figueroa (2005).

Defensor del Pueblo, or Comisionado Nacional de Derechos Humanos) was supposed to provide citizens with a way to voice their grievances against public administration, especially in cases regarded as bureaucratic arbitrariness. However, the evolution of the institution in Latin American countries, combined with the enactment of comprehensive constitutions that included a series of rights, extended the scope of the ombudsman's attention to include individual, social, and especially human rights (Uggla, 2004). Not surprisingly, ombudsmen in several Latin American countries consider themselves legitimate defenders of the public interest, further stimulating the judiciary's role of alternative representative of society.

Recent judicial reforms have also helped marginalized groups of society gain greater access to courts and legal mobilization through the creation of alternative dispute resolution entities, improvement of information systems, and changes in organizational and case management. Because courts are reactive by nature (in general they do not initiate cases against social injustices), societal demand is a second important prerequisite of judicial activism. Higher levels of access and legal mobilization thus galvanize courts, particularly in their roles of referee and alternative societal representative.

Finally, reforms in the institutional features of the political system in general have affected the nature of the relationship between the judiciary and other branches of government and/or levels of government. Certain patterns of judicial–legislative interaction and central–local relations may facilitate recourse and engagement of the courts, while others may hamper it. For instance, in countries with a high degree of both administrative and fiscal decentralization, such as Brazil, the judiciary's involvement in the policymaking process is more likely, especially in its role as a veto player. When there is a greater division of power between central and local governments, the opportunities for jurisdictional conflict and questions regarding constitutional adequacy increase. Similarly, fierce party competition and weak party discipline may allow an active judiciary to emerge, as a larger number of legislators may choose to pursue their political agendas through the courts. Effective means of communication between the legislature or the executive branch and the judiciary may also lead the latter to become more engaged in the policymaking process.

The four possible judicial roles amount to a typology that provides insights as to what judiciaries in Latin America are *capable* of doing in the policymaking process; it cannot reveal which of these roles are actually carried out in a given country. For that, one would need to analyze the achievements of the reforms undertaken in the past two decades, focusing on the elements of the three dimensions of judicial activism. To provide some sense of the scope of judicial activism in Latin America, ten selected LACs have been classified into three groups, depending on the extent of courts' participation in the policymaking process. If there is evidence (either qualitative or quantitative) that the judicial branch is involved in *three* or *all four* of the potential roles that it can undertake, then judicial activism is classified as "broad." If the judicial branch is involved in only *two* of the potential roles, then judicial activism is classified as "medium." If it is involved in only *one* or *none* of the potential roles, then judicial activism is classified as "narrow."

Table 4.4 summarizes the findings. Brazil and Chile are included in the group of "broad" judicial activism. Over the past two decades, the judiciary in these countries has tended to be actively engaged in the policymaking process, playing three or all four potential roles assigned to the branch. Conversely, Argentina, Ecuador, Paraguay, Peru, and Venezuela fall within the "narrow" category of judicial activism. In these countries, judicial review powers are limited and the judiciary is still largely dependent on the executive, which makes the branch play a rather limited role in the policymaking process. Between these two extremes, Colombia, Mexico, and Uruguay are classified as countries with "medium" levels of judicial activism. Although the scope of courts' involvement in the policymaking process is not extensive, the impact of the judiciary can be significant in the various stages of the policymaking process.

The information presented in Table 4.4 should be interpreted cautiously. Given the difficulty of gathering systematic and comparable measures of judicial activism across all Latin American countries, the classification presented is largely based on the author's subjective judgment. In the absence of direct measures of judicial activism, one plausible way to assess the level of judicial involvement in the policymaking process across Latin American countries would be to count and review supreme court (or constitutional court) decisions during the period under analysis. However, such a strategy could be misleading, since a higher number of supreme court rulings does not necessarily mean a broader engagement of the court in politics. Instead, information regarding the

TABLE 4.4 | Typology of Judicial Roles and Judicial Activism, Ten Latin American Countries

Country	Extent of judicial activism	Roles that the judiciary has undertaken the most	Areas in which the judiciary has been the most active	Features of policies
Argentina	Narrow	Veto player. Limited judicial review powers. Judicial independence is tempered by strategic behavior of judges.	Human rights and economic	Generally volatile and rigid.
Brazil	Broad	Some evidence of veto player, policy player, and impartial referee. To a lesser extent, society representative (via *Ministério Público* and also the fact that judicial review powers are somewhat decentralized), which promotes the adaptability of policies in Brazil.	Tax, pension, and land reform issues (often rules against the executive and congress). Evidence that the judicial system has a negative impact on the economy.	In terms of macro policies, stable but adaptable. Other policy issues are residual, which can be rigid (education and health) or volatile (all others).
Chile	Broad	Impartial referee (ensuring the implementation of other policy reforms), veto player (especially in human rights issues), and policy player (given the conservative nature of the supreme court, it could shape the content of policies in that direction).	Economic	Mostly stable. Both kind of policies (flexible or rigid), depending on consensus among veto players.

(continued)

TABLE 4.4 | **Typology of Judicial Roles and Judicial Activism, Ten Latin American Countries** *(continued)*

Country	Extent of judicial activism	Roles that the judiciary has undertaken the most	Areas in which the judiciary has been the most active	Features of policies
Colombia	Medium	Veto player (Constitution of 1991 empowered constitutional court to block legislation) and policy player (increased separation of purpose and judicial independence after 1991 Constitution).	Fiscal	Deterioration and greater volatility of macro policies and fiscal policies (especially after 1991 Constitution), as well as in national security. Greater rigidity in macro policies as the central bank gained greater independence; and with new constitution, local governments and the constitutional court gained power (more difficult to reach intertemporal agreements due to greater number of veto players).
Ecuador	Narrow	Veto player	Fiscal and exchange rate policy	Policies are highly volatile in areas characterized by the presence of a strong "decisive" player. Policies are rigid in areas characterized by the presence of multiple veto players. Two determinants: delegation of power by the legislators to bureaucracy; presidential control of the agenda-setting process.

(continued)

TABLE 4.4 | Typology of Judicial Roles and Judicial Activism, Ten Latin American Countries (*continued*)

Country	Extent of judicial activism	Roles that the judiciary has undertaken the most	Areas in which the judiciary has been the most active	Features of policies
Mexico	Medium	Veto player and policy player (executive has delegated some functions to the judiciary especially since the mid-1990s) at the supreme court level only. During the PRI era, Supreme Court was necessary to legitimate *pax prista*.	Mostly electoral disputes and issues regarding the redefinition of federalism. Also, tax, trade union membership, and bank interest rates	1989–97: Adaptable, coordinated, and public regarded. 1997–2004: Rigid or less adaptable, less coordinated, more transparent.
Paraguay	Narrow	Until 1993, the judiciary was dependent on the executive. Since 1993, judiciary has been somewhat autonomous but not very competent: somewhat of a veto player.	Policies of regulatory or redistributive intent	Rigid, volatile (1989–93), stable, or rather stalled policy reform (1993–present) and low public regardedness.
Peru	Narrow	The judiciary has not played effective roles in defining the national policy agenda, promoting intertemporal cooperation, and providing checks and balances on executive power.		Volatile, arbitrary, easily reversed, poor quality, and not enforced.
Uruguay	Medium	The supreme court has limited capacity to declare unconstitutionality of laws. However, the supreme court can be an effective veto player when the bill has been approved by congress and an individual citizen has been affected by it. Also evidence of policy player.	Social and financial policies	Stable (financial and commercial policies); rigid and low quality (social policies, state reform, and bankruptcy regime); volatile (discretionary public spending).
Venezuela	Narrow	With the Chávez revolution, the judiciary has become very dependent on the executive.		Volatility, incoherence, and disinvestment in policy capabilities.

Source: Author's compilations.

level of judicial independence, the scope of judicial review powers, the activism of quasi-judicial institutions, the nature of the political system, and secondary sources' accounts of judicial access and legal mobilization in each country has been used as the basis for the author's subjective judgment.

Judicial Activism and Public Policy in Latin America: Four Hypotheses

How can judicial engagement in the policymaking process affect public policy characteristics? More specifically, what is the relationship between judicial activism and the outer features of public policy: namely, stability, adaptability, credibility, and public regardedness?[28] The discussion that follows sets out four main hypotheses regarding such a relationship. Preliminary evidence supporting these hypotheses is provided in Table 4.4.

Stability

With respect to stability (ranging from stable to volatile policies):

> Hypothesis 1: As courts increase their involvement in the policymaking process, policy outcomes are more likely to be stable, holding everything else constant. Conversely, policy outcomes are likely to be more volatile, ceteris paribus, if the institutional structure encourages a narrow to medium degree of judicial activism.

Policies are stable if they persist beyond the tenure of particular officeholders or coalitions. When judicial/political reforms produce an institutional environment in which the judiciary can play only a restricted number of roles in the policymaking process, it becomes easier for political actors to bypass or discount the influence of the judiciary. Not only do the preferences of the judiciary (as a collective entity) become irrelevant, but a narrow type of judicial activism limits the number of entrance points for various political actors to have a direct impact on public policy. According to the policy literature, the fewer the actors

---

[28] See IDB (2005) for a discussion of the various possible outer features of public policy.

that can have a direct impact on policy, the easier it becomes to reach a collective consensus to implement or change policies (Tsebelis, 2002). If the number of actors influencing policymaking is restricted, the government's ability to change policies in accordance with the preferences of the governing administration increases. Thus the theoretical expectation is that policies become more volatile as judicial activism narrows, holding everything else constant. Conversely, as judicial activism broadens, the durability (stability) of policies increases.

Adaptability

With respect to adaptability (ranging from flexible to rigid policies):

> Hypothesis 2: As courts increase their involvement in the policy-making process, policies are likely to be more adaptable, holding everything else constant. Conversely, policy outcomes are likely to be less adaptable, ceteris paribus, if the institutional structure encourages a narrow to medium degree of judicial activism.

Policy rigidity and policy flexibility are two extremes of a range of possible levels of adaptability of a given policy. Adaptability means that policy can be changed promptly to respond to exogenous shocks and to allow for adjustment when mistakes occur. The inability to adapt to new circumstances reflects an intrinsic difficulty to achieve cooperation and consensus for the implementation of welfare-improving policies (Spiller and Tommasi, 2003). Such difficulty in reaching cooperation is largely due to the lack of mechanisms to resolve time-inconsistency problems. As courts assume other tasks beyond acting as a veto player (especially that of a referee), then an active judiciary can act as an enforcer of inter-temporal political transactions, solving many of the time-inconsistency problems that had impeded cooperation. As a result, it seems reasonable to expect that broader judicial activism would be associated with higher levels of policy adaptability.

Credibility

With respect to credibility of policies (ranging from credible to not-so-credible policies):

Hypothesis 3: As courts increase their involvement in the policy-making process, policy outcomes are more likely to be credible, holding everything else constant. Conversely, policy outcomes are likely to be less credible, ceteris paribus, if the institutional structure encourages a narrow to medium degree of judicial activism.

The credibility of policies—the ability to commit to a given policy once it is enacted—is intrinsically related to its stability. Stable policies suggest not only that the ability to change policies is low, but also that its "resoluteness"—the government's ability to commit to policies—is high.[29] As judicial activism broadens, policies are less subject to the whims of the different governing administrations. As a result, the commitment to enacted policies becomes more credible.

Public Regardedness

With respect to public regardedness:

Hypothesis 4: As courts increase their involvement in the poli-cymaking process, policies are more likely to be public regarded, holding everything else constant. Conversely, policy outcomes are likely to be more private regarded, ceteris paribus, if the institu-tional structure encourages a narrow to medium degree of judicial activism.

To evaluate whether policies are public or private regarded is to ask, basically, to what extent policy outcomes are geared toward spe-cial interests (Helpman and Grossman, 1996). An important body of literature has shown that incomplete information and the existence of competitive elections are important determinants of whether policies favor special interests (Baron, 1994; Lupia and McCubbins, 1994; Mehrez and Kaufmann, 1999). Beyond these determinants, Keefer (2001) has demonstrated that the number of veto players is also an important factor in explaining to what extent policies are public regarded. In analyzing the effects of "checks and balances" on banking crises, Keefer finds that

---

[29] The term "resoluteness" is from Cox and McCubbins (2001).

as the number of veto players increases, their incentives to favor special interests diminishes, independent of their preferences. According to the author, the introduction of new veto players allows for greater representation of society as well as greater influence of different society groups in the policymaking process and policy outcomes. As the influence of previously disenfranchised citizens grows, the incentives for policymakers to cater to special interests decrease. The result is that a larger number of veto players would be associated with more public-regarded policies.

As judicial activism increases, courts are more likely to be used by specific actors within the policymaking process (Ferejohn 2002). In doing so, rather than acting as a veto player in their own right, courts become a vehicle of contestation: "a veto point from which other policy actors—driven by their own interests and ideas—can contest policy, and in the process, at times exercise veto power" (Taylor, 2004, p. 332). The number of veto players then increases. Applying Keefer's (2001) reasoning: if there are more veto players in a polity, policies can be expected to be more public regarded.

Judicial Roles in Action:
The Cases of Brazil, Argentina, and Mexico

Until this point, the chapter has tried to identify the political roles of the judiciary in Latin America and how they vary across countries, making a case that the extent of judicial activism may affect the features of public policy. This section reviews three case studies, focusing on the link from reforms to institutional arrangements and the extent of courts' involvement in politics. Brazil, Argentina, and Mexico present an interesting comparison of the different roles the judiciary can play in the policymaking process. Although they are all large economies in Latin America, they have gone through somewhat different processes of judicial and political reforms, which have caused judicial activism to vary across the three cases. Brazil is an instance of broad activism, where the judiciary plays three main roles: veto player, policy player, and alternative societal representative. Argentina is characterized by a narrow type of court involvement in the policymaking process: the judiciary primarily plays a veto player role. Mexico stands between the two extremes. The judiciary is more active in vetoing policies and shaping their content. The expectations of different patterns of public policy vary according to the extent of judicial involvement. For the sake of clarity, the Brazilian case is presented first and then compared to the Mexican and Argentine cases.

Brazil

Three events stand out as crucial for understanding the process of reforms and the subsequent redefinition of the role of the judiciary in Brazil. First, the Constitution of 1988 secured judicial independence and a rather de-centralized but privileged type of constitutional adjudication. While this independence was instrumental in allowing the judiciary to take on new policymaking roles, it also created unintended negative consequences for the efficiency and the transparency of the judicial system, which has hampered the capacity of the judiciary to act as a referee. Moreover, the privatization of many public companies, coupled with the creation of many regulatory agencies, has led the judiciary to play the role of a policy player in the policymaking process. The last crucial event for understanding judicial activism in Brazil is the creation, in 1985, of a new legal instrument—the public civil suit (ação civil pública)—allowing the Public Ministry (Ministério Público) to take any person or entity to court for any violation of environmental concerns, consumer rights, the nation's artistic and cultural patrimony, the rights of senior citizens and the handicapped, and public property rights. As pointed out by Alston et al. (2008), this legal instrument expanded the role of the Public Ministry in the policymaking process beyond prosecuting criminals in the name of the state by allowing it to monitor and act in the defense of the "diffuse and collective interests" of society. All other reforms enacted since 1988, such as the restriction of judicial salaries (Constitutional Amendment 19) and the Reform of 2004 (Constitutional Amendment 45), have had fewer effects on the prospects for judicial activism.

The 1988 Constitution guaranteed an independent and well-funded branch by granting budgetary and administrative autonomy, lifetime tenure for judges, high and irreducible salaries, merit-based selection criteria, and the insurance that removal can take place only by a vote of peers following a well-defined process. In the 2005 World Economic Forum's *Global Competitiveness Report,* Brazil scores higher than most Latin American countries in quantitative measures of judicial inde-pendence, lagging behind only Uruguay, Costa Rica, and Chile. The Constitution also established decentralized judicial review powers, in which both the supreme and lower courts have the authority to rule on questions of constitutional adequacy. The combination of high levels of judicial independence and the existence of various instruments that allow individuals and other political actors to question the constitutionality of policies in different court venues was supposed to grant many opportunities for the average citizen to veto policies through the use of the courts.

In reality, however, that has not occurred. The process of contesting the constitutionality of policies at the level of the lower courts is extremely slow. Because of case backlogs and the overall low efficiency performance of the judicial sector, a claim on the constitutionality of a law can take months and even years to be heard. Even then, because lower courts' decisions are not final, cases are appealed repeatedly until they finally reach the supreme court (*Supremo Tribunal Federal*, STF). The accumulation of appeals in turn overburdens the higher level courts. The result is extremely high costs and delays in judicial rulings. These costs and delays deter the majority of the population from using the constitutionality review instruments available at the lower court level. The political actors who do use the lower courts for constitutional complaints do so in a strategic manner, to benefit from the delay of decisions.[30] In practice then, most of the constitutional challenges come from a select group of political actors, which does not include the average citizen.

Indeed, selected political actors have frequently called upon the judiciary to decide on the constitutionality of policies, especially through the use of the Direct Action of Unconstitutionality (ADIN).[31] Data provided by Rodrigues de Carvalho (2004, p. 119) for the 1988–2003 period shows that most of the ADINs were initiated by state governors (27 percent), followed by special interest groups (26 percent), and political parties (21 percent). In aggregate terms, the total number of ADINs increased sharply after 1988 and peaked in 2000. If the boost in the number of ADINs and the constant recourse to the courts to adjudicate political

---

[30] It is common in Brazil for lawyers representing individuals, firms, interest groups, or even the public sector to file claims to purposefully avoid or delay the execution of obligations (especially concerning tax payments).

[31] The ADIN is a legal instrument that allows the plaintiff to question the constitutionality of a policy directly at the *Supremo Tribunal Federal* without going through the lower courts. It can be proposed by the president, the senate leadership, the chamber of deputies leadership, state governors, the head of the Public Ministry, the Brazilian Bar Association (OAB), a political party with congressional representation, or a union or special interest group with national representation.

matters is viewed as a sign of "judicialization" of politics, then it follows that the judiciary has accepted playing new roles in the policymaking process, particularly in providing veto points for determined groups of political actors to have a direct say in the policymaking process.

Notwithstanding the barriers to widespread access to constitutional control mechanisms, the Brazilian judiciary has taken upon itself the responsibility of representing certain marginalized groups within the policymaking process, at least to a certain extent. The creation of the public civil suit and the subsequent expansion of the activities of the Public Ministry (MP) largely account for this transformation of judicial roles. According to what the Constitution stipulates, the MP is an independent entity linked to the executive and the judiciary, whose main attribute is to protect the interests of society generally conceived. Because most policy issues affect the diffuse and collective interests of society, the MP today has a large jurisdiction, as it can bring any political matter into the judicial sphere, especially through the public civil suit.[32] The MP can thus provide different sectors of society a voice and representation in the policymaking process.

To be sure, institutional characteristics have created a strong type of "political voluntarism"[33] on the part of the members of the MP. Because prosecutors enjoy high salaries and lifetime tenure, and the position is highly competitive,[34] a group of mostly young and highly qualified individuals has viewed themselves as the main protectors of society's interests and diffuse/collective rights (Arantes, 2003; Alston et al., 2008). Figure 4.1 corroborates this outlook: in a survey of prosecutors in seven Brazilian states, the large majority of the respondents believed that the MP was the institution that most contributed to the broadening and consolidation of diffuse and collective rights. As Arantes (2003, p. 9) describes it, Brazilian prosecutors' political voluntarism includes: "1) a pessimistic assessment of the capacity of civil society to defend itself by itself ('under sufficient,' in the legal jargon); 2) a pessimistic assessment of political representatives and institutions that are seen as corrupt and/or unable to fulfill their duties; and 3) an idealized conception of the MP

---

[32] See Alston et al. (2008) for a more detailed discussion of how the MP can protect the interests of society.

[33] "Political voluntarism" is a term coined by Arantes (2003).

[34] The selection process of prosecutors is done through competitive public examinations.

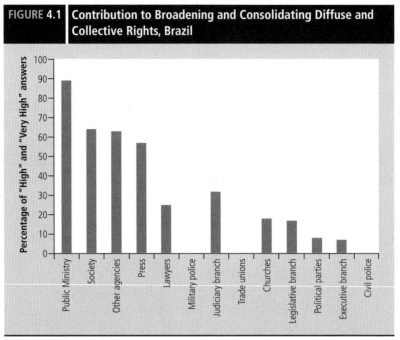

FIGURE 4.1 | Contribution to Broadening and Consolidating Diffuse and Collective Rights, Brazil

Percentage of "High" and "Very High" answers

Source: Arantes (2003, p.11).

as the preferred representative of an incapable society (albeit without an explicit grant of political power and lacking accountability mechanisms) and inept administrations that fail to enforce laws." Coupled with a number of judges who are following the so-called "alternative law movement,"[35] the MP has been instrumental for the judiciary in protecting the "weak" and the disadvantaged.

Some critics have argued that such an expansive role assigned to the MP has often interfered in the policy process in a not so constructive manner (see Arantes, 1999). Their argument is usually twofold. On the one hand, they claim that prosecutors are prone to act in a biased manner: given their own personal and partisan preferences, they are more likely to act against certain administrations than others. On the other hand, critics claim that prosecutors tend to use the media to gather public

---

[35] The "alternative law movement" started in the mid-1980s in the south of Brazil. Judges began to use their powers and the law to promote justice for those whom they considered the "oppressed" sector of the Brazilian population (mainly the poor). See Alves Maciel and Koerner (2002) for a broader discussion.

support for their case: a move that often poses barriers to the investigative process. The supporters of an active and expansive MP respond by claiming that, in most cases, the courts have ruled in favor of the rich and the powerful. Regardless of the merit of both accounts, what is clear is that the MP does exert significant influence in Brazil's policymaking process and public policy.

The third element crucial to understanding the new roles assumed by the Brazilian judiciary in the last two decades has to do with the process of politico-economic reforms more broadly understood. To the extent that Brazil has privatized a number of public companies, created regulatory agencies in various sectors, and revamped many of the state's management practices, the judiciary has been called upon to perform statutory interpretation. Because the recent economic reforms have often encompassed modifications to ordinary legislation or the constitution, greater interaction between the judiciary and the legislature as well as the executive have become inevitable. The Administrative Reform is a case in point. Before the enactment of the constitutional amendment embodying the Public Administration Reform, there were many debates concerning the legal definition of a "social organization." Although previous laws had addressed the issue, a synthetic definition of what the concept meant was still lacking (Modesto, 1997). Such a lack of textual precision led the main authors of the reform (the Ministry of Federal Administration and State Reform of Brazil, MARE) to consult the judiciary frequently. In the process, the judiciary became engaged in the policymaking process as it exercised its policy player role.

It is difficult to find evidence that courts actively play a referee role in Brazil. With some exceptions (such as cases regarding the Fiscal Responsibility Law), the judiciary has largely remained outside the debates on how to best guarantee the effective implementation of public policies. The problem of judicial overburden and large case backlogs does not allow for prompt resolutions, making it more difficult for courts to supervise government actions. In this context, judicial predictability— which is valued by international investors—is impaired, and such a lack of confidence in the institutional foundations of the country has often been translated into high levels of country risk.[36]

---

[36] For instance, there are no signs of expropriatory actions in Brazil, according to the U.S. State Department's Bureau of Public Affairs (see the Bureau's Country Background Notes at

Based on these observations, one could classify the courts' involvement (that is, judicial activism) in the Brazilian policymaking process as "broad." An evaluation of the achievements of reforms suggests that the judiciary actually plays three of the four possible roles in the policymaking process (namely, veto player, policy player, and society representative). The implication is that one would expect to see a certain pattern of policy outcomes. Given the theoretical reasoning presented in previous sections of this chapter, if everything else was held constant, one would expect to see mostly stable, adaptable, credible and public-regarded policy outcomes in Brazil. Systematically testing these hypotheses would require further research.

Argentina and Mexico

Compared to Brazil, the Argentine and the Mexican policymaking processes are less judicialized. Although both countries have undertaken important reforms in the direction of the modernization of the sector, these reforms have led to judiciaries that are markedly less independent than Brazil's. Specifically, the judicial institutional structures that arose in Argentina and Mexico are less conducive to the involvement of courts in the elaboration, implementation, and enforcement of policies. Argentina is characterized by a narrow type of judicial activism; Mexico stands between Brazil and Argentina. It should not be surprising that one would expect to find different patterns of policy outcomes.

The process of judicial reforms in Argentina gained force in the early 1990s when President Carlos Menem took over the presidency of the nation. In a context of various market-oriented economic reforms, the senate approved a law proposed by Menem to augment the number of supreme court justices from five to nine; this was the first major judicial reform in two decades. The new appointed justices were all politically biased toward Menem's Peronist government. The main result of the reform was a decrease in the level of judicial independence

---

http://www.state.gov/r/pa/ei/bgn/35640.htm). However, the Bureau highlights that, in 2003, the newly inaugurated government in one of the states refused to honor a series of contracts the previous state government had signed with a number of national and foreign investors. Although the parties involved have appealed to the local courts, the majority of the cases have not yet been resolved.

and horizontal accountability. The court effectively did not object to the constitutional legality of many presidential decrees, and judicial independence was further diminished by executive orders to pardon the military officers involved in human rights abuses during the dictatorship. The Constitutional Reform of 1994 introduced a number of other changes, which were primarily aimed at strengthening judicial institutions and increasing efficiency. The judicial council was created, the rules of appointment were modified, a new Procedural Criminal Code was promulgated, and changes to the organization of the tribunals were introduced. Overall, the reforms did not succeed in strengthening the judiciary vis-à-vis the executive branch, and the gains in efficiency were small (Dakolias et al., 2001; Santiso, 2003). Unlike the result of the reforms in Brazil, the judiciary has remained relatively weak and submissive to the other branches of government (mainly the executive branch).

Such a claim is corroborated by other measures of the success of reforms. The level of case backlogs is still significant, reflecting a judicial system that is rather slow. The sector's levels of transparency and accountability remain low and the weak rule of law (unequal protection of the law and lack of law enforcement) creates legal uncertainty (Dakolias et al., 2001). Public perception of corruption within the judiciary is high; as Dakolias et al. (2001) point out, only 13 percent of the public have confidence in the administration of justice.

In Mexico, the path of reforms has not yielded significantly different results. The efforts toward a more efficient and independent judiciary were initiated by President Ernesto Zedillo, who asserted: "I have decided that the power of the presidency cannot and should not be an omnipotent power, an omniscient power, nor an omnipresent power."[37] In the package of constitutional reforms approved by the Mexican congress in 1994, a number of changes were included that were supposed to increase the quality of supreme court justices and their judicial review powers. A new instrument of constitutional review—the "action of unconstitutionality" (AU)—was created, the number of supreme court justices was reduced from 26 to 11, the requirements for appointment became stricter, and the Federal Judicial Council was established. The senate approved the

---

[37] Mark Fineman, "Mexico's Zedillo Offers to Share Power," *Los Angeles Times*, Dec. 7, 1994, p. A9.

constitutional reforms in a 108–0 vote[38] and the reforms were well-received both in legal circles and by Mexican citizens.[39]

Notwithstanding the fact that reforms were generally desired and popular, the changes were not comprehensive and their implementation was blocked by many barriers (Human Rights Watch, 1999). Critics have pointed out that the reforms were overly concentrated at the level of the supreme court, and have failed to address a number of pressing problems in the lower courts.[40] Among these problems, critics claim that the rules of court procedure still need to be reformed to avoid the use of delaying tactics to affect the outcome of a case, and that the police force is in dire need of resources and organizational changes to mitigate the problems of corruption.[41] It is generally argued that the average Mexican cannot see the practical effects of the reforms (Suchyta, 1997).

In Argentina and Mexico, some significant reforms have occurred, although they have not been completely successful. In Argentina, the changes were geared more toward modernization at the expense of independence. In Mexico, the reverse occurred. In both cases, the strength of the judiciary vis-à-vis the other branches of government is lower than in Brazil.

Besides the different levels of judicial independence, an important institutional feature that helps explain the variation in judicial activism among the three countries is related to the nature of the constitutional court. Although none of the three countries has a separate constitutional court responsible for constitutional matters (unlike Chile), the supreme courts in Brazil, Argentina, and Mexico function differently, particularly with respect to the scope of their judicial review powers. The Argentine *Corte Suprema* (composed of nine justices) can rule on constitutional cases coming from either the appeal from lower courts or original jurisdiction. Because the cases in which it has original jurisdiction are relatively limited,[42] most of its activities consist of reviewing the decisions of lower

---

[38] "Mexico Senate OK's Judiciary Reforms," *San Antonio Express-News*, Dec. 19, 1994.

[39] According to Mark Fineman, "Mexico Moves to Counter Rebels" (*Los Angeles Times*, Dec. 21, 1994, p. A1), the reforms were supported by 84 percent of Mexicans.

[40] For a discussion, see Domingo (2000).

[41] Human Rights Watch (1999).

[42] The only cases in which the *Corte Suprema* exercises original jurisdiction are those relating to foreign powers and cases in which a province is a part (Taylor, 2004, p. 345).

courts. In Mexico, the supreme court (composed of eleven justices) has original jurisdiction only when dealing with *controversias constitucionales* and *acciones de inconstitucionalidad*.[43] The bulk of its cases come from appeals by the district and circuit courts.[44] The Argentine and Mexican supreme courts rule on a considerably lower number of cases per year than Brazil's *Supremo Tribunal Federal*.

The difference in the number of cases decided by each supreme court is also a reflection of the existence or absence of binding mechanisms. For instance, despite the lack of formal *stare decisis* mechanisms and weak *writ of certiorari* rules,[45] Argentina's rather decentralized type of constitutional adjudication is counterbalanced by supreme court jurisprudence, which customarily sets a precedent for lower court judges.[46] Similarly, in Mexico, the supreme court and circuit courts may establish jurisprudence if these courts rule five consecutive and consistent decisions on a particular case. In both cases, the existence of formal and informal binding mechanisms imposes greater uniformity in judicial decisions and serves as a filter of the appeal cases reaching the supreme court. Given that Brazil lacks these binding mechanisms, the number of appeal cases overburdens the *Supremo Tribunal Federal*.[47]

In terms of the timing of judicial review, all three countries present a posteriori constitutional review. Only Brazil allows for a priori discussions of the constitutionality of the law. In reality, given the slowness of the judicial process, it could take years before a law is reverted in Brazil or Argentina. In Mexico, the timing for review is constrained by a limit for filing unconstitutionality suits (*acciones de inconstitucionalidad*) of no more than 30 days after a law goes into effect (Taylor, 2004, p. 347).

---

[43] In *controversias constitucionales*, the supreme court settles disputes among political powers (judiciary, executive, legislature, states, and the federal government). In *acciones de inconstitucionalidad*, the supreme court decides on the constitutional adequacy of laws.

[44] Unlike in Argentina, the appellate jurisdiction of Mexican supreme court is considerably limited by law to specific situations.

[45] *Stare decisis* is the legal principle by which judges are obliged to obey the precedents established by prior decisions. A *writ of certiorari* currently means an order by a higher court directing a lower court, tribunal, or public authority to send the record in a given case for review. Rules of *writ of certiorari* were created in 1990 but it has not been widely used.

[46] The power of supreme court jurisprudence in Argentina can be considered an informal binding mechanism. In some circumstances, lower court judges do not feel obliged to follow it..

[47] An instrument to remedy the lack of binding mechanisms in Brazil was recently introduced with the Reform of 2004 and the institution of the *Súmula Vinculante* (a supreme court decision that must be followed by lower courts).

Finally, neither in Argentina nor in Mexico did the reforms ensure a broader former standing than in Brazil.[48] As mentioned, in Argentina, only when foreign nations or provincial governments are involved in a case can they have privileged access to bring a constitutional review case directly to the supreme court. Unlike the other two countries, political parties are not allowed to have special standing. Formal standing is broader in Mexico than in Argentina, but narrower than in Brazil. The Brazilian constitution allows the largest number of groups to have direct access to the highest court of the country. In all three countries, individuals' access to the highest courts is limited to the parts in appeal or in case of *amparo* suits. However, given the *inter partes* nature of the *amparo* suit, the impact of individuals on policy outcomes is rather constrained.

The importance of these institutional arrangements for the types of roles the judiciary can play in Argentina and Mexico is clear. First, in neither of these countries does the judiciary act as an alternative representative of society. Not only is formal standing narrow (especially in Argentina), but the levels of access to the judicial system are still rather low. Moreover, the Argentine and the Mexican constitutions have not assigned the resources or the role of the guarantor of collective and social interests to the *Ministério Público*, as the Brazilian constitution has. Regardless of the historical and political explanations, the fact is that comparatively speaking, Argentine and Mexican citizens have not gained much of a voice within the judicial branch.

Furthermore, as in Brazil, it is difficult to find evidence that the judiciary in Mexico and in Argentina plays the role of a referee. Judicial unpredictability continues to be an important characteristic of those judicial systems, especially because of the diffuse nature of judicial review. With few binding mechanisms, appeals and repeat cases have clogged the work of the supreme court as well as lower courts. The inevitable delay in the enforcement of contracts and the mediation of conflicts undermines both the credibility and effectiveness of public policies.

In terms of shaping policy, the judiciary in Mexico has played a more active role than the judiciary in Argentina. The Argentine supreme court does not have a priori judicial review power, meaning that there is no opportunity for the judiciary to get involved in policy debates

---

[48] Here, standing means the possibility of political actors initiating a constitutional review process. Standing can predetermine the influence of political actors in the policymaking process.

before the law is enacted; this somewhat constrains its ability to tilt the content of the policy toward its preferences. In addition, binding mechanisms are more operational in Mexico than in Argentina, which allows supreme court justices to construct jurisprudence over a policy with universal effects.

Finally, both qualitative and quantitative evidence suggests that courts do play a veto player role in Argentina and Mexico (as well as in Brazil). As courts become increasingly independent and judicial mechanisms of checks and balances are increasingly activated (through more extensive judicial powers), it becomes more difficult to bypass the courts' preferences in all stages of the policymaking process. As shown by various studies,[49] after the judicial reforms of 1994, the Mexican supreme court has shown a willingness to act independently from the judiciary in many policy areas, even though the same cannot be said about the lower courts. In Argentina, lower court judges have been found to act strategically against the government.[50] In both cases, policy change becomes more difficult if it does not receive the courts' approval.

Argentina's narrow judicial activism would be expected to give rise to policies that are mostly unstable, rigid, not credible, and private regarded, In Mexico, where judicial activism can be classified as medium, policies would be expected to be more stable, adaptable, credible, and public regarded.

Conclusion

Over the past two decades, Latin American countries have gone through an important process of judicial reform, albeit at a different pace. Within the context of political and economic liberalization, these reforms aimed at increasing levels of judicial independence, efficiency, and access to justice, and eliminating corrupt practices. Although the simultaneous achievement of all these goals has proved difficult (if not impossible!), reforms have generated distinct institutional structures. This analysis shows that different institutional arrangements allow for a range of judicial involvement in the policymaking process: the judiciary can act as a veto player, policy player, referee, and alternative representative of

---

[49] See, for example, Domingo (2000).
[50] See Helmke (2002); Iaryczower, Spiller, and Tommasi (2002).

society. Judicial activism in turn is an important factor in determining public policy outcomes. The overall message is clear: the judiciary is increasing its impact on the policymaking process in Latin America.

Such a message should resonate with the public law literature, which draws attention to the capacity of the judiciary to influence policymaking—but does not systematically identify the various possible roles courts can play in the policymaking process. It should also enrich the literature on reforms in Latin America, which highlight the need for judicial reforms—but does not make the connection between reforms, judicial policymaking, and policy outcomes. Finally, the message of an increased importance of judiciaries in the policymaking process in Latin America can prove most of the public policy literature wrong, since that literature does not consider courts as relevant policymakers.

Most importantly, the greater impact of judiciaries in the policy-making process in various Latin American countries can spur important debates in Latin America (as has occurred in France and the United States) about the legitimacy of judicial engagement in the policymaking process. Proponents of judicial policymaking claim that the engagement of the judiciary in the policymaking process is necessary to maintain "checks and balances" and to protect the interests of minorities. Critics respond by arguing that "judge-made law" goes against the principles of popular sovereignty and liberal democracy because judges are not accountable to the electorate. At the heart of the discussions is a normative question of what should be the ideal relationship between law and politics.

This study has attempted to make the concept of judicial activism more explicit. It has also made the case that institutional structure is a necessary determinant of the extent of courts' involvement in the policymaking process, although not a sufficient one. Even though other factors—such as the attitudes of judges or strategic interactions with various political actors—might account for the increasing judicialization of politics in Latin America, these explanations are only partial. The structure of judicial institutions is what ultimately paves the way for courts to veto laws, shape their content, enforce other public policies, or act as an alternative representative of society. While making the argument that institutions matter is not so difficult, measuring and systematically comparing the reformed judiciaries across countries remains a challenge. Further refinements in the definitions, classifications, and measurements of the possible judicial roles are still necessary.

As a suggestion for further research, a comprehensive study evalu-ating the hypotheses offered in the fourth section of this study would be of great value. Scholarly writings on the judiciary in Latin America have not focused enough attention on the impact of courts' involvement in the policymaking process on the characteristics of public policies. A comprehensive study of this issue would fill a void.

CHAPTER 5

Inside the Cabinet:
The Influence of Ministers
in the Policymaking Process

Cecilia Martínez-Gallardo

The vast authority that is delegated to cabinet ministers in Latin American presidential countries stands in sharp contrast with the lack of academic work on cabinet politics and its influence on policymaking.[1] Very little is known about the composition of cabinets,[2] how often cabinets meet, how decisions are made in them, and how consequential they are for policymaking. Only recently have scholars begun to investigate cabinet formation and cabinet change, including the conditions under which presidents will choose to integrate coalition cabinets and the effects of different cabinet formation strategies on the stability of the government (Cheibub, Przeworski, and Saiegh, 2004; Amorim Neto, 2006; Martínez-Gallardo, 2008).

This gap in the literature is especially surprising given evidence that cabinet formation and change matter for policymaking. The institutions and procedures that organize the formation and operation of the cabinet determine the ease with which coordination can occur, as well as the quality and efficiency of the government's work. First, cabinet formation determines the number of political parties in government, the relationship between them (and between them and other political institutions), and the ease with which policy can be changed. Indeed, government formation is central to arguments about the capacity of

---

[1] This chapter focuses mainly on the presidential systems of continental Latin America.

[2] An important exception is the work by Escobar-Lemmon and Taylor-Robinson (2005) on women's participation in Latin American cabinets.

presidential institutions to sustain democratic government (see Martínez-Gallardo, 2005). Second, the structure of the cabinet itself is crucial in making possible the kinds of relationships—between cabinet members and between them and the bureaucracy—that allow coordination and flexibility in policymaking.

Third, stable tenures allow ministers to build relationships of co-operation and accountability, to gain essential expertise, and to reach intertemporal agreements, all central to making better policy. Conversely, rapid cabinet turnover—through its effect on the accumulation of expertise and information and its role in shaping relationships of accountability between politicians and bureaucrats—has been linked to economic outcomes such as higher spending (Amorim Neto and Borsani, 2004) and volatile inflation rates (Aisen and Veiga, 2008).

These institutions vary widely across presidential countries. This chapter describes this variation across Latin America and explores the mechanisms that relate these institutions to the policymaking process.

The Role of Latin American Cabinets in Policymaking

The lack of attention to cabinet politics is due at least partly to the ambiguous role that cabinet ministers play in presidential political arrangements. In pure presidential systems, executive power falls solely on the president, who is both head of state and head of the government. In this sense, cabinet ministers have a narrow *formal* role as aides to the president.[3] In contrast to parliamentary cabinets, cabinets in presidential systems are not collectively responsible to the legislature and individual ministers are accountable only to the president. This position has placed them largely outside the framework of formal institutions and thus largely beyond the type of scrutiny, public and academic, that other institutional actors face.

Despite their limited formal role, in practice individual ministers or groups of ministers do play important roles in the policymaking process. Together with the bureaucracies they head, ministers have

---

[3] Some presidential constitutions provide for some limited control of ministerial appointments by the legislature, but in general presidents tend to dominate the appointment and dismissal of ministers (Shugart and Carey, 1992). By contrast, in parliamentary systems, ministers are typically members of parliament and are directly responsible to it, both collectively and individually (see Laver and Shepsle, 1994).

a near-monopoly in the design of policy, with occasional input from political parties and/or interest groups. They are also important in the legislative phase of policymaking, where they typically have the task of pushing the executive's proposals through congress. And they are in charge of turning approved laws into concrete policy outcomes, both through rulemaking and through implementation by the executive agencies that they head.

First, cabinet ministers (and the bureaucracies they head) are the dominant players in the design of policy in every Latin American country. Practically everywhere, presidents count on "key institutional sources of expertise located at the bureaucratic apparatus" (Bergara et al., 2006, p. 34) to aid them in the design of policy. By contrast, legislatures and political parties rarely have comparable resources at their disposal that allow them to compete in the formulation of public policy. Exceptions to this trend exist, however, in countries where the legislature is increasingly professionalized (in Mexico, for example, the share of legislative proposals introduced by the president dropped from 76.9 percent in 1994–97 to 18.2 percent in 2000–03; see Lehoucq et al., 2008), or where other specific institutional actors have developed the resources to design policies (the National Security Council in Chile, for example; see Aninat et al., 2008). But, by and large, cabinet ministers remain the main source for policy expertise and policy proposals.

Second, although only presidents can formally initiate legislation,[4] cabinet ministers play an important role in guiding the president's agenda through congress. Much of their work in support of the president's legislative agenda is done behind closed doors, in consultations with members of congress and their staff, but some formal institutions reinforce this role. In some places, ministers participate actively in debates over the executive's proposals. Almost everywhere, legislatures have the right to summon ministers to appear before them, and in most countries ministers are often called upon to explain, defend, or clarify law initiatives that fall within their area of competence. These initiatives (called *comparecencias* or *citatorios*) give ministers a forum in which they can justify and push the government's agenda. Additionally, ministers are

---

[4] Some presidents cannot initiate legislation. As Shugart and Carey (1992) note, however, the absence of this power is not a significant obstacle since any president can find a legislator to introduce a desired bill.

usually required to present reports on their activities to congress (called *informes* or *memorias*) and these instances are often also used to make arguments in favor of the president's program.

Third, ministers are central in the implementation stage of the policymaking process. Most obviously, they head the agencies in charge of executing the laws approved in congress. But they also aid presidents in one of their most consequential tasks: rulemaking (*función/potestad reglamentaria*).[5] Through rulemaking, presidents turn broad principles approved in the legislature into workable policies with the sole restriction of not altering the "spirit" of approved laws or "transgressing" their original meaning. Although the effects of rulemaking on outcomes in Latin America have not been widely studied, it seems certain that they allow executives wide flexibility in shaping the specific content of policies.[6] Two features common to most countries in the region further increase the importance of rulemaking as a source of ministerial influence on the policymaking process. First, the extent to which executive bureaucracies can deviate in the application of constitutional principles (the extent of *bureaucratic drift*) will tend to be higher where judicial review of executive acts is weaker, as it tends to be across the region. Second, the lack of legislative influence over agency design and decision making (as well as its lack of input into the appointment process) means that once the law is passed, congress effectively relinquishes any control in the implementation of the law.

In sum, the formal role of ministers as aides to the president translates in practice into a central position in the policymaking process. Cabinet ministers are the principal source of policy expertise, they are central in pushing the president's agenda through the legislature, and they are the leading force behind policy implementation—especially in a context where judicial and legislative oversight of executive bureaucracies is weak.

---

[5] Formally, this is an attribute of the president, not of ministers. This distinction was explicitly held up by the Ecuadorian Supreme Court in April 1994 in a case regarding a ministerial decree (*acuerdo ministerial*) by the minister of foreign affairs. An exception is the case of Brazil, where both the president and ministers have rulemaking powers (see Arts. 87-2 and 84-4).

[6] In contrast, there is a wide body of work on delegation by congress to agencies in the executive branch in the United States. See Chapter 1 of Epstein and O'Halloran (1999) for a review of this literature.

Features of Cabinets and Policymaking

Despite their privileged position in the political system, the extent to which cabinet ministers shape policies varies widely across countries. This variation depends to a large extent on the ability of ministers to coordinate and to cooperate with other political institutions in ways that make *better* policies more likely. Although cabinet ministers are obviously crucial in shaping the *content* of policies, the rest of this chapter follows Spiller, Stein, and Tommasi (2008) in focusing on the features of cabinet politics that allow them to improve the *quality* of policies: that is, to reach and enforce intertemporal agreements that foster policies that are stable, of higher quality, and adaptable to changing circumstances.[7]

Three aspects of cabinets are central to policymaking. First, *cabinet formation* determines the number of actors involved in cabinet decision making and their skills, the nature of the relationship among them, and between them and their political principals. Cooperation should be enhanced where authority is divided among fewer actors with the requisite policy skills, and where relationships of delegation and accountability are clear. Second, the *structure of the cabinet*, as well as the nature of decision-making rules and practices, are crucial in determining whether interministerial coordination is possible. Third, *cabinet stability* is central to the possibility of long-term transactions that are requisite for stable and coherent policies. A certain degree of stability allows policy continuity, makes the accumulation of experience possible, and allows the establishment of relationships of trust between politicians and bureaucrats.

Cabinet Formation

Cabinet formation has long been a central area of research in the literature on parliamentary politics. The emphasis has been on the aspects of the political and institutional environment that determine the type of cabinet that is formed—the number of parties involved and whether or not they have a parliamentary majority—as well as the links between

---

[7] That is, to foster policies with certain favorable outer features, in the parlance of Spiller, Stein, and Tommasi (2008).

the process of cabinet formation and the government's performance.[8] In contrast, a comparable literature on government formation in presidential systems had not evolved until recently.[9] Through this work, scholars have begun to gain a better understanding of how institutions affect patterns of government formation, including coalition formation, the partisanship of cabinets, and their stability. But there is still much to learn about how the process of government formation impacts policymaking in these systems.

This section describes differences across presidential regimes in patterns of government formation and suggests ways in which these differences might affect policymaking. It focuses specifically on how the independence of origin and survival of the executive and the dominant role of the president in cabinet politics shape patterns of government formation. These defining institutional features of presidentialism interact with the electoral and party systems to shape the incentives that presidents have to include—or not—other parties in the government coalition and to change the composition of the cabinet throughout their term in response to changing conditions.

The main defining feature of government formation in presidential systems is the absence of a relationship of dependence between the executive and the legislature. In pure parliamentary systems the executive depends on the approval of a parliamentary majority for its survival; this implies both parliamentary approval of cabinet positions and parliamentary oversight of cabinet actions. In presidential systems, by contrast, the executive and the legislature are separately elected; they do not depend on each other for survival. In practice this means that the president does not need the approval of a majority in the legislature to name the cabinet, and that the government can stay in office even when a legislative majority exists that would support the formation of an alternative government.

A consequence of independence of survival is that the relationship of accountability between the president, the cabinet, and the legislature is different from what is observed in parliamentary systems. While in

---

[8] This literature is extremely large and it is impossible to cite it all here. For some examples, see Dodd (1976); Warwick (1979, 1992, 1994); Powell (1982); King et al. (1990); Diermeier and Merlo (2000); Diermeier and Stevenson (2000); and Strøm and Swindle (2002).

[9] For some examples, see Kellam (2007); Martínez-Gallardo (2005, 2008); Amorim Neto (2006); Negretto (2006); and Araujo, Pereira, and Raile (2008).

parliamentary systems the executive derives from, and is responsible to, parliament (see Laver and Shepsle, 1996), in presidential systems the president can largely name and dismiss the members of the government without legislative interference and the cabinet is responsible only to the president. Over time, however, some Latin American constitutions have been modified to include some legislative control over the appointment process. Typically, this has been done by giving the president and the legislature shared responsibility over the dismissal of ministers— through a vote of censure, for example—as a way to keep the executive in check.[10] In a handful of cases, the separation of origin and survival has been modified by giving the executive the authority to dissolve the legislature. In both Uruguay and Peru, dissolution can be invoked only as a response to interbranch conflict over a vote of censure from the legislature (Shugart and Carey, 1992), but the conditions under which this can happen are so restrictive that they have not worked in favor of the president (Pérez-Liñán, 2005).

In terms of policymaking, the possibility of censure might give the legislature a tool to delay the implementation of the president's agenda—especially if the president does not have a legislative majority. However, even where the censure procedure is binding (as in Colombia, Guatemala, Peru, Uruguay, Venezuela, and for the chief of the cabinet in Argentina), the president is in charge of appointing the replacement for the dismissed minister. Hence the role of the legislature is merely a negative one and the president remains the central figure in government formation in Latin American countries. Shugart and Carey (1992, p. 118) argue that where the legislature can censure ministers but cannot participate in restructuring the government, the potential exists for conflict and instability.

A second consequence of independent survival is that presidents are not required to include other parties in the cabinet in order to assemble a government supported by a parliamentary majority. Instead, presidents are largely free to decide whether to seek the participation of other parties or to govern alone. Because they can continue in office

---

[10] Censure exists in Argentina, Bolivia, Colombia, Ecuador, El Salvador, Guatemala, Paraguay, Peru, Uruguay, and Venezuela, although there is variation in the circumstances under which the legislature can censure a minister and the majority needed to overrule the legislature's decision. See Shugart and Carey (1992); Mainwaring and Shugart (1997); Casar (1998).

even if they do not have the support of a majority of the legislature, the incentives to build governing coalitions are weaker than in parliamentary systems. However, despite the traditional notion that presidential systems lack incentives for coalition building, presidents still need a supportive legislative majority in order to pass their political agenda and they will use government formation to get this support.

Table 5.1 shows that it is actually common for Latin American presidents to form governing coalitions. In a study of patterns of government formation across 12 Latin American countries, Martínez-Gallardo (2008) finds that coalition governments were formed 52 percent of the time (see also Deheza, 1998; Cheibub, Przeworski, and Saiegh, 2004).[11] The table also shows, however, that the frequency with which governing coalitions are formed varies widely from country to country—from Brazil and Chile, where coalition governments dominated during the entire period of study, to Mexico and Costa Rica, where single-party governments were the norm.

The most evident source of variation in coalition formation is variation in the incentives presidents face in seeking legislative support for their legislative agenda. The incentives to build coalitions will be greater where the electoral system tends to produce minority presidents more frequently: that is, presidents who are not supported by a party with majority representation in the legislature. Indeed, of all presidents elected without majority support in the legislature, 65 percent formed coalitions. In contrast, of all presidents elected with majority support, only 28 percent formed a coalition. Minority presidents, in turn, are more likely as the fragmentation of the party system increases (and the probability of the president's party having a majority of seats decreases). In Table 5.1, the four countries with the highest legislative fragmentation (as measured by the mean Herfindahl index)—Brazil, Ecuador, Bolivia, and Chile—never had a majority president in the period of study and had coalition governments well over 60 percent of the time. In contrast, Costa Rica and Mexico had low relative fragmentation, produced presidents with majority status more than half the time, and never experienced a coalition government.

---

[11] Martínez-Gallardo's data include South American countries, Mexico, and Costa Rica between 1982 and 2003 (start and end dates vary by country). Observations are country-months. Deheza (1998) studies 123 cabinets and finds that 56 percent were coalitions.

TABLE 5.1	Prevalence of Coalitions in Latin America, 1982–2003			
Country	Proportion coalition[a]	Prop. majority president[b]	Herfindahl index (mean)	No. of parties in government
Brazil	1.00	0.00	0.14	4.74
Chile	1.00	0.00	0.24	4.90
Uruguay	0.91	0.00	0.32	2.31
Peru	0.89	0.68	0.34	2.44
Colombia	0.81	0.36	0.41	2.14
Bolivia	0.80	0.00	0.24	2.75
Ecuador	0.60	0.00	0.17	2.34
Paraguay	0.30	0.65	0.46	1.37
Venezuela	0.22	0.42	0.33	1.32
Argentina	0.18	0.31	0.38	1.24
Costa Rica	0.00	0.55	0.42	1.00
Mexico	0.00	0.84	0.43	1.00
Total	0.52	0.34	0.33	2.13

Source: Martínez-Gallardo (2005).
[a] Proportion of country-months where ministers of more than one party were represented in the cabinet.
[b] Proportion of country-months where the president's party had a majority of seats in the legislature.

An additional source of variation in the incentives to form coalition governments is the legislative authority vested in the president. If coalitions are formed to overcome the obstacles faced by presidents in getting their agenda through congress, one should expect presidents with strong unilateral legislative authority to be less likely to use ministerial positions to build a majority government. In fact, Amorim Neto (2006) finds that across Latin America presidents with decree authority and extensive veto powers typically staff their cabinets with technocrats and cronies (rather than partisan ministers) and that they fail to distribute portfolios proportionally across all parties in the governing coalition. Martínez-Gallardo (2008) finds that once formed, coalitions tend to be more stable (last longer unchanged) when the president has stronger agenda-setting authority.

The formation of governing coalitions might impact policymaking in several ways. In the parliamentary literature, where coalition politics have been widely studied, a common theme is that coordination will be enhanced where policymaking authority is divided among few actors. The expectation is that a lower number of political players—and a higher degree of ideological convergence among them—will be more conducive to political cooperation (Huber, 1998; Treisman, 2000; Spiller and Tommasi, 2003). The most obvious empirical implication of this literature is that reaching agreements and making decisions should be less costly in single-party governments and that coalition cabinets should find it more difficult to coordinate over policy. Empirically, Martínez-Gallardo (2008) finds that more parties in the government translate into more unstable coalitions, even after controlling for coalition status.

Policymaking in Argentina during the *Alianza* coalition government (1999–2001) illustrates the potential coordination challenges involved in making policy when more parties are involved. During the *Alianza* between the Radicals and FREPASO, although most ministries were headed by Radicals, FREPASO was given the labor and social affairs ministries. Power was further divided within ministries, through the appointment of under-ministers from a party different from the minister's. In social affairs, for example, the minister was from FREPASO, the under-minister was a Radical; the ministry was further divided into five areas or *Secretarias*, three occupied by FREPASO officials and two by Radicals. Interviews confirmed that this arrangement made coordination difficult because lines of command were cut off as officials responded to their party leader, instead of the minister.[12]

A further challenge for the *Alianza* was that the government could typically not count on supportive legislative majorities. In general, the ability of cabinets to coordinate will also be contingent on whether or not the coalition has a majority. The need to negotiate working majorities on every issue is bound to make coordination more costly and policymaking less efficient. Martínez-Gallardo (2005) finds that in Latin America, turnover of individual ministers tends to be consistently higher when the government does not have a stable legislative majority. This finding points to the fact that during minority governments, cabinet positions will be used as side-payments to construct majorities and this will result in higher cabinet instability. High turnover, as discussed below, will make coordination over policy harder to achieve.

---

[12] Interview with Maria Matilde Ollier, July 2001. Ollier is Associate Professor of Political Science at the Universidad Nacional de San Martín, Buenos Aires, and was chief of staff in the Labor and Social Affairs Ministry during the *Alianza* government.

Another important factor that affects the ease with which agreements will be reached in the cabinet during coalition governments is the extent to which coalition partners are ideologically connected: when the parties in government are ideologically close, agreement should be easier to achieve as the transaction costs of coalition bargaining are minimized (Axelrod, 1970; de Swann, 1973). In the parliamentary literature, ideologically connected cabinets have been found to survive longer than ideologically divided cabinets where greater compromises are necessary (Warwick, 1994). The same logic also applies to a certain degree in single-party governments: big-tent parties should have more difficulty getting all their members in the government aligned, while more hierarchical or ideological parties should find it easier to coordinate over policy. Martínez-Gallardo (2008) tests the proposition that coalitions with less ideological fragmentation are more stable for Latin American presidential systems and finds that although the empirical relationship seems to go in the expected direction, the relationship is not robust.[13]

A related distinction is between cabinets composed mostly of partisan and nonpartisan ministers. The most common argument about partisanship and policymaking is that cabinets composed of nonpartisan ministers ought to find it easier to agree on a diagnosis of the problem at hand and to coordinate over a policy prescription.[14] On the other hand, while it might be true that depoliticization of policy issues might help coordination within the cabinet, party loyalty and incentives might also work as a cohesive force and aid coordination. Again, there is practically no work that tests these arguments empirically. The type of policy agreement assumed in these arguments is very hard to measure directly. However, Figure 5.1 shows how the partisanship of ministers affects the stability of their tenures.[15] If indeed nonpartisan ministers are less susceptible to political cycles, we would expect them to have longer tenures. As the figure suggests, however, it seems that cabinets with *more* partisan

---

[13] Stability is measured in terms of changes in the partisan composition of the cabinet. Ideological fragmentation is measured both as the standard deviation for the ideology of all parties in the coalition and as the distance between the right-most and left-most parties in the coalition.

[14] See, for example, Haggard and Kaufman (1992).

[15] Data on cabinet partisanship come from Amorim Neto (2006) and were reproduced with permission of the author.

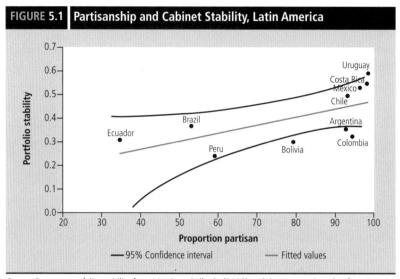

FIGURE 5.1 | Partisanship and Cabinet Stability, Latin America

Source: Data on portfolio stability from Martínez-Gallardo (2005) and data on partisanship from Amorim Neto (2006).

ministers are actually more stable than ones with more nonpartisan or independent ministers. Perhaps not surprisingly bonds of politics seem to be strong.[16] Further evidence is given by Martínez-Gallardo (2008): the duration of coalition governments in Latin America is also higher when the share of independents in the cabinet is lower. It is hard to know at this stage whether the relationship goes only from the selection of nonpartisan ministers to higher stability or whether presidents who find themselves in a situation of crisis name nonpartisan ministers as a way to broaden their base of support and shore up the stability of their government. In either case, it seems clear that on average presidential cabinets tend to be more stable where less nonpartisan ministers are appointed. This is true both at the level of individual turnover of ministers and of partisan membership in the coalition.

In sum, cabinet formation is crucial to explaining patterns of policymaking across Latin American political regimes. Electoral insti-

---

[16] The level of partisanship of cabinets could be expected to affect the *public regardedness* of policies. Mostly partisan cabinets will have more incentives to deliver "pork" to their constituencies than cabinets composed primarily of nonpartisan ministers. In more partisan cabinets, policies would tend to be more narrowly construed: designed to benefit a particular constituency and not necessarily the public good.

tutions play an important role in shaping the incentives of presidents about whether to incorporate other parties into the cabinet or whether to rule alone. Despite traditional notions, coalitions are common in the region; thus the institutions that shape coalition politics (the number of parties in government, their ideological proximity, the incorporation of independent ministers) are also central in shaping the capacity for coordination within the cabinet, as well as the ease with which the cabinet can cooperate with other political actors by shaping relationships of delegation and accountability.

Structure of the Cabinet

The structure of an organization (the number of decision-making units and the relationship between them) is important in defining specific arenas where decisions are made and the degree to which these encourage cooperation and facilitate the exchange of ideas among members. In the case of presidential cabinets, the number of ministries shapes patterns of coordination and the efficiency of policymaking efforts. How these units organize for work also affects the flexibility of policy outcomes and their quality. This section analyzes four specific aspects of cabinet organization—the number of portfolios, the coordination of the cabinet, the creation of thematic cabinets, and the existence of dominant portfolios—and their impact on policymaking.

First, the number of policymaking units with jurisdiction over policy is related to the ability to develop policy that is consistent over time and that is implemented coherently. When authority over policy is divided among a larger number of players, cooperative outcomes are harder to achieve and policy outcomes will tend to reflect this. Figure 5.2 shows the number of ministries for Latin American countries in 2005 and 2008. The size of the cabinet varies widely, from more than 27 ministries in Venezuela to nine in Paraguay, and it varies over time and within countries but across different administrations. In Costa Rica, for example, President Figueres named almost 10 ministers more than President Calderón had before him; in Brazil cabinets had as few as 17 ministers under President Collor and as many as 30 under President Cardoso.

These figures, however, mask an additional source of inefficiency in policymaking: independently of the number of ministries, bureaucratic agencies are often created that have functions that overlap with those of

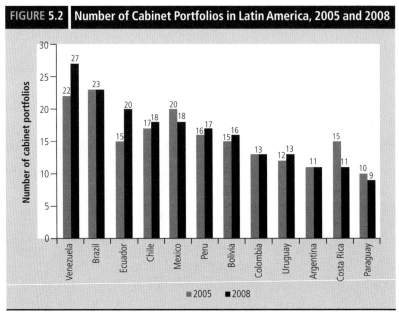

FIGURE 5.2 | Number of Cabinet Portfolios in Latin America, 2005 and 2008

Source: Information gathered from the government Web pages.

the ministry. One example is social policymaking in Argentina, where the existence of multiple agencies with overlapping jurisdiction, and the existence of a parallel bureaucracy composed mainly of temporary officials (*contratos especiales*), have typically made coordination among ministers and between them and the bureaucrats in their agencies difficult and has made it hard to attain coherent policy (interview with M. Ollier, 2001; Oszlak, 2002; Spiller and Tommasi, 2003).[17]

Another important feature of cabinet structure is how ministers organize for work. As argued, little is known about cabinet decision making in presidential systems, and less still about how different patterns of cabinet organization impact policymaking.[18] The discussion that follows describes the three distinct types of organization that characterize most

---

[17] A good example is provided by Oszlak (2002). The ministry of labor during the Alfonsín administration had a secretary of labor and a secretary of social security, under which were undersecretaries for labor, for social security, for labor and social security, and a coordinating undersecretary.

[18] In contrast, there is a substantial body of work on cabinet decision making in parliamentary regimes. See, for example, Blondel and Müller-Rommel (1993); Laver and Shepsle (1994); Andeweg (2000).

Latin American cabinets and speculate about how they might affect policymaking. The first relates to patterns of delegation from the president to a cabinet "coordinator," the second is the formation of subgroups of ministers organized around specific policy issues, and the third is the dominance of certain portfolios within the cabinet.

Formally, the president is the head of the administration in all presidential systems. Typically, he or she delegates authority directly to cabinet ministers, who then have wide authority to make policy in their jurisdiction. However, it is not unusual for the president to delegate the task of coordinating the work of the cabinet to a member of the cabinet. Indeed, there has been a growing trend in some presidential systems to separate the role of the president as head of state from tasks related to the administration of the government and to delegate these to a cabinet member (Valadés, 2005). Three models of cabinet coordination dominate among the presidential systems of Latin America.

In the first model, the constitution defines a position that is explicitly given the task of administering the government and, more specifically, of interministerial coordination. The two clearest examples of this sort of arrangement are Argentina and Peru. In other countries, the position is defined in a secondary law or in practice. This is the case in Venezuela (Ministerio de la Secretaría de la Presidencia), Chile (Ministerio Secretaría General de la Presidencia), Bolivia (Ministro de la Presidencia), and Honduras (Ministro de la Presidencia). The second mode of cabinet coordination is modeled after the Office of the Presidency in the United States, where the task of coordinating the cabinet's work is moved from the context of the government itself to the inner circle of the presidential staff. An example of this model is the Office of the Presidency in Mexico. Other examples include the Ministério da Casa Civil in Brazil, the Secretaría General de la Presidencia in Colombia, and the Secretaría General de la Presidencia in Ecuador.[19] A third model relies on the vice president to carry out the tasks of coordinating the cabinet.[20]

Where a coordinating institution exists, one of its main tasks is to aid the president in fulfilling his or her legislative powers and to serve as

---

[19] The occupant of this position typically has the same rank as other ministers.

[20] In Nicaragua and Guatemala, the vice president takes over the presidency of the Consejo de Ministros in the president's absence. In other cases, as in Colombia, Peru, and Venezuela, there is both a vice president and a "coordinator" of the cabinet.

an intermediary between the presidency and the legislature. In part, the idea is to relieve the president of some of the political tension and potential conflict that can come from negotiations with congress. In practice, the relationship between the cabinet "coordinator" and other ministers is different in every country and the degree to which the coordinator actually exercises influence over cabinet decision making varies widely, too. In Mexico, for example, the Office of the Presidency was created in 1989 and its head exercised substantial influence, organizing cabinet meetings, setting the president's agenda, suggesting priorities, and managing relationships among ministers.[21] This influence, however, declined under President Fox (2000–06). According to government officials, although the office (now divided into two areas) had some influence on the president, its heads did not hold much clout with particular ministers and thus were not able to perform coordination duties effectively.[22]

The most usual model of cabinet work across these countries, however, tends to be through thematic cabinets or committees. This arrangement exists in the law in Peru, Venezuela, and more recently, Ecuador, and is common almost everywhere—although it is difficult to know how frequently these cabinets meet and how successful they are in aiding coordination.[23] In Mexico, for example, cabinets have usually been divided for work into thematic cabinets; these, in turn, have changed according to the priorities of the government.[24] In Argentina, the success of thematic cabinets as coordination devices has also been varied. For example, the social cabinet (Gabinete Social Federal) was formally created

---

[21] Other important tasks of the Jefe de la Oficina de la Presidencia (JOP) were setting the president's agenda, suggesting topics that the president should prioritize, and managing relationships among cabinet members. Interview with Luis Téllez, JOP for President Ernesto Zedillo, Mexico City, June 2001.

[22] Interview with a former official in President Fox's staff, Mexico City, March 2005.

[23] In Ecuador a law was passed in 2002 that created six Coordinating Portfolios, or Ministerios Coordinadores. Their function is to coordinate the policies and actions of the ministries under their jurisdiction (production, social development, political economy, security, politics, and national and cultural heritage).

[24] During President Ernesto Zedillo's administration, there was a security cabinet (Gabinete de Seguridad), an economic cabinet (Gabinete Económico), and an agrarian affairs cabinet (Gabinete Agropecuario). According to the Chief of the Office of the Presidency, the first two met more frequently. President Fox organized his government around three thematic cabinets: growth with quality, order and respect, and human and social development. However, again, the perception is that coordination among ministers was not very successful. Interview with a former minister of the Salinas administration, Mexico City, June 2001.

in 1993, but did not operate. A second attempt was made at the end of President Menem's term; this social cabinet operated between 1997 and 2001. In 2002 it was replaced by the National Council for Coordination of Social Policies. However, conflicts between the agencies involved and a lack of resources have prevented these instances from functioning as effective policy coordination devices and have reduced them to a venue for information exchange and minimal operative coordination (Repetto and Potenza, 2005).

The importance of cabinet meetings also depends on the type of government. In coalition governments, decisions are typically made within political parties and coordination takes place in other settings: bilateral meetings between cabinet ministers or coalition committees composed of a small number of high-ranking politicians from the parties in government.[25] During the coalition *Alianza* government in Argentina, for example, government officials interviewed complained that "nothing happened" at cabinet meetings and that this dynamic was repeated within ministries. People reported to their party, not to the government, and this translated into severed chains of communication.[26]

The third important feature of cabinet organization in Latin America is the role that individual ministers play in the policymaking process. In most countries, a reduced number of ministers tend to play a predominant role in policymaking. This is particularly true of finance ministers. The centrality of the finance minister across the region can hardly be exaggerated. They dominate the budget process and this position has made them essential to the president's political strategy. Control over money has also placed them in a privileged position with respect to other ministers and, in some cases, with respect to regional governors too (see, for example, Hallerberg and Marier, 2004; Cárdenas et al., 2008). During the 1980s and 1990s, this influence was typically magnified by their role in designing and pushing through structural reforms (Centeno and Silva, 1998; Teichman, 2001; Camp, 2002).

Finance ministers typically go through more competitive recruitment, which often combines personal loyalty and technical expertise

---

[25] On decision making in coalition cabinets in parliamentary democracies, see Huber and McCarty (2001); Martin (2004); and Timmermans (2006).

[26] Interview with political appointees in the ministry of social affairs during De la Rúa's administration, Buenos Aires, June 2001.

(see Aninat et al., 2008; Cárdenas, Junguito, and Pachón, 2008), as well as intense scrutiny both from groups within the country and abroad. At least in part, recruiting finance ministers with a high level of skill or expertise is meant to shield them from political cycles and thus enable them to make better policy. Whether or not this goal is achieved depends greatly on the country. One measure of the extent to which finance ministers are actually shielded from political shocks is their stability. Figure 5.3 shows the tenures of finance ministers across Latin America, measured as a proportion of a presidential term. The longest-lasting finance ministers during the 1990s are found in Uruguay, where they lasted 76 percent of the presidential term. Next are finance ministers in Mexico and Chile, who lasted around 60 percent of a term on average, followed by ministers in Costa Rica and Colombia, who were in their positions around 40 percent of a term. Other ministers, however, are very unstable; in Ecuador and Peru, ministers held office for 16 percent and 23 percent of a presidential term, on average.[27]

Overall, finance ministers were in office an average of 18.52 months. This compares negatively with the duration of foreign, defense, and labor ministers (24.41 months, 21.20 months, and 20.10 months, respectively), but favorably with ministers of the interior (17.10 months), justice (16.74 months), and agriculture (18.14 months). Indeed, in a multivariate analysis, Martínez-Gallardo (2005) finds that, on average, finance ministers in Latin America tend to have shorter tenures than other ministers. This stands in sharp contrast with findings in the literature on parliamentary governments, where finance ministers tend to have more stable tenures (see Huber and Martínez-Gallardo, 2003).

In sum, coordination within the cabinet is less costly when the number of ministries is not too large and they are organized around topics that overlap as little as possible. The way in which these ministries are organized for work is also central to efforts for coordination and efficiency in the policymaking process. Although differences exist, most cabinets work through smaller groups organized around relevant topics. There is also a trend toward delegating some administrative tasks to a cabinet coordinator, although the specific roles this figure plays and its

---

[27] Using the same data shown here, Martínez-Gallardo (2005, chapter 4) shows that finance ministers are more unstable than other ministers at the beginning of their term, but that if they survive this "trial" period, they then become relatively more stable.

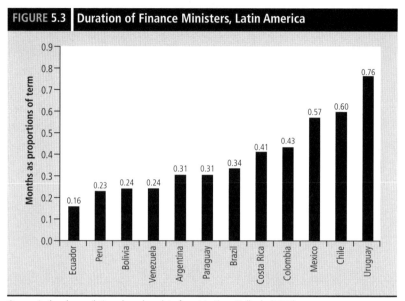

FIGURE 5.3 | Duration of Finance Ministers, Latin America

Source: Authors' compilations, based on data from Martínez-Gallardo (2005).

relative influence vary throughout the region. Finally, one of the most prominent features of cabinets in Latin America, particularly since the economic reforms of the 1990s, is the centrality of finance ministers and their influence on economic policymaking and, through their role in the budget process, on other policy areas as well.[28]

Stability of Cabinets

The ability of ministers to coordinate is not only related to the identity and the number of political players but also to how often they change. Patterns of stability like those shown above for finance ministers are closely related to the ability of political actors to reach cooperative outcomes. In general, when there is uncertainty about whether a politician will be in office in the next period, politicians do not fully internalize the costs associated with their policy choices (Persson and Tabellini, 2000) and they are unable to commit credibly to intertemporal arrangements. In terms of cabinet politics in particular, a certain degree of stability is

---

[28] For several examples, see Teichman (2001). The degree to which the finance minister dominates the budget process varies across countries; see Hallerberg and Marier (2004).

also necessary to promote long-term policies and, importantly, to see the implementation of programs and policy through to completion. Frequent turnover promotes short-sightedness in policymaking and favors outcomes that have short-term benefits, regardless of how costly they might be in the longer run, since their costs will not be borne by current decision makers. In the academic literature, cabinet instability has also been associated with severed relationships of accountability between politicians and bureaucrats, with weak accumulation of experience, and with policy instability and inconsistency.

First, stable tenures help ministers establish credibility within the bureaucracy and ascertain their authority, as well as establish relationships of control and accountability. Managing large agencies demands that different actors with often divergent interests work together; turnover makes coordination among different levels of the agency difficult. In a context of high instability, officials, "subject to suspicion from newcomers and asked to follow widely divergent policy directions, will expectedly tend to adopt a cautious and defensive attitude towards new incumbents" (Oszlak, 2002, p. 222; see also Huber, 1998; Blondel, 1985). Further, leadership vacuums produced by rapid turnover will tend to leave room for inefficiency and even corruption in executive agencies (Chang, Lewis, and McCarty, 2000).

Second, more stable tenures contribute to the accumulation of policy expertise and experience. Even if cabinet ministers do not have a professional background or previous experience in the policy area they head, they can acquire this experience while in their post. Continuity allows them to develop expertise specific to the policy area in which they work and to develop skills (political, managerial) that are likely to improve the quality of their performance. The accumulation of knowledge and the creation of institutional memory are impeded when there is high turnover, as priorities tend to shift and learning has to start anew. The lack of incentives to gain information tends to make informational asymmetry between politicians and permanent bureaucrats worse, and this asymmetry is likely to lead to bureaucratic drift (Huber and Shipan, 2002).

Last, more stable and coherent policy outcomes should be expected where ministers have longer tenures, especially when they remain in a specific portfolio, thus allowing them to follow the policies they put in place to completion. In contrast, policy switches or bureaucratic inaction should be expected where ministers are changed frequently.[29] The relationship between instability and policy outcomes has been studied most widely in the political economy literature (Persson and Tabellini, 2000). Economic policy is one of the best examples of an arena where political instability is likely to induce myopic behavior, as actors who expect to leave their positions soon do not internalize the future cost of their decisions. Empirically, this myopic behavior has been shown to increase public debt and reduce public investment and growth (Ozler and Tabellini, 1991; Alesina et al., 1992; Cukierman, Edwards, and Tabellini, 1992; Amorim Neto and Borsani, 2004). To differing degrees, the same is true in many other areas where intertemporal bargains are crucial to cooperative outcomes.[30]

In general, cabinet stability is low in Latin America, compared to other regions.[31] According to data from Martínez-Gallardo (2005), between 1985 and 2003, 19 percent of all ministers in South America, Mexico, and Costa Rica remained six months or less in the same portfolio and less than a third (30 percent) had tenures of more than two years (with presidential terms that vary between four and six years). Tenure length varies widely across countries, however. Table 5.2 presents summary data on the duration, in months, of cabinet ministers in these countries. Given that most ministers leave their position when the president who appointed them does, the last column of the table shows average tenure lengths as proportions of the length of the term. The most stable country

---

[29] One manifestation of this type of inaction is the under-execution of the budget in the Argentinean bureaucracy. Interestingly, Abuelafia et al. (2009) find that the longer the period a minister has been in office, the less the under-execution of the budget. That is, it seems that ministers—and the people who work with them—learn the workings of the bureaucracy while in office. The relationship between ministerial turnover and under-execution of the budget was confirmed in interviews with an official in the ministry of social affairs during the government of President De la Rúa (Rosalia Cortés, Buenos Aires, June 2001).

[30] There is very little empirical work connecting turnover in the cabinet to policy performance outside the economic arena. For examples in other policy arenas, see Huber (1998) on health care cost containment, Corrales (2004) on education, and Abuelafia et al. (2009) on the effect of turnover on the ability of bureaucrats to execute the budget.

[31] For reference, Chang, Lewis, and McCarty (2000) find that the average tenure of political appointees in the United States is 33 months for all positions (down to assistant secretaries), and 34.7 months (almost three years) for secretaries only (with a presidential term of four years). Their data cover the period 1789–2000. Not much work has been done on the stability of individual ministers in parliamentary systems, but there is some evidence that they are more stable than ministers in presidential countries, in particular in Latin America (see Blondel, 1985; Przeworski et al., 2000; Martínez-Gallardo, 2005).

TABLE 5.2	Duration of Ministers, by Country, 1990–2003 (months)						
Country	N	Mean	SD	Min	Max	Term[a]	Mean/Term
Peru	188	13.29	11.18	1	64	5	0.22
Venezuela	165	18.98	15.57	1	59	6	0.28
Bolivia	213	13.77	10.69	1	47	4	0.29
Ecuador	160	18.02	13.80	2	47	5	0.30
Colombia	211	14.87	9.09	1	47	4	0.31
Argentina	125	20.17	18.51	1	106	5	0.34
Brazil	106	16.76	18.04	1	95	4	0.35
Paraguay	77	21.57	16.94	3	73	5	0.36
Chile	56	31.07	18.79	5	71	5	0.52
Mexico	92	39.59	26.87	1	135	6	0.55
Costa Rica	113	27.86	14.34	3	47	4	0.58
Uruguay	85	29.30	22.10	1	105	4	0.61
All countries	1,591	19.84	17.08	1	135	4.75	0.39

Source: Martínez-Gallardo (2005).
Note: Excludes presidents and administrations who were still in office by the end of 2003. Includes a subset of the ten most important portfolios.
[a] Chile and Argentina changed the length of the presidential term during the time of the study: Argentina from four to six years and back to four years; and Chile from four to six years. Numbers in the table for these countries are averages.

by this measure is Uruguay, where ministers are in office an average of 61 percent of the four-year term, followed by Costa Rica and Mexico. On the other side of the scale, ministers in Peru, Venezuela, Bolivia, Ecuador, and Colombia are in office less than a third of the length of the presidential term.

A related measure of the difficulty of coordinating policy is the number of ministers that occupy a portfolio throughout an administration. As before, cooperative outcomes will be harder to achieve where the number of players within a portfolio is large and where their identity (and priorities) tend to change often. Figure 5.4 shows the number of ministers per ministry in the most important portfolios in the same 12 Latin American countries.[32] The variation between countries is striking. During this period, the average number of ministers per portfolio in

---

[32] See Martínez-Gallardo (2005) for data sources and for a complete list of the top portfolios for each country.

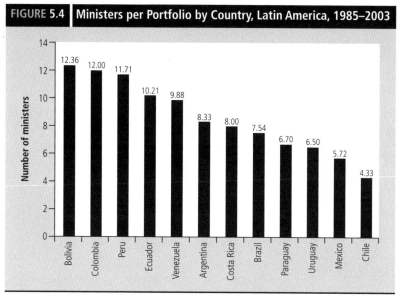

FIGURE 5.4 | **Ministers per Portfolio by Country, Latin America, 1985–2003**

Source: Constructed by the author with data from Martínez-Gallardo (2005).

Chile was slightly over four; in Peru, Colombia, and Bolivia, the average was nearly three times greater (between 11 and 12 ministers, on average).

To summarize, rapid turnover shortens the time horizon of policy-makers, who tend to favor policies that have benefits they can capitalize on in the short run, regardless of their potential future costs. A certain degree of cabinet stability is necessary to promote the accumulation of knowledge and expertise that fosters better policies. Stability helps build relationships of authority and control within the agencies of the executive, which are central to policy implementation.

The flip side of cabinet stability is the ability of presidents to change their cabinet in response to changing circumstances during their term.[33] Cabinet changes sometimes respond to the need for innovation in policy—the need to bring new people to the decision-making process and, with them, new skills and ideas. Overly long tenures can lead to stasis, complacency, and even corruption. In the context of presidential

---

[33] There is little work on the use of appointments by presidents in Latin America to deal with changes in the policy environment (see Martínez-Gallardo 2005), but there is some evidence that in parliamentary systems presidents use this mechanism to react to crises (see Dewan and Dowding, 2005).

systems, a certain amount of turnover might act as a "safety valve" that protects the president from ongoing crises (Mainwaring and Shugart, 1997). Unfortunately, from an empirical perspective, the point at which healthy stability turns into unhealthy stasis is hard to pin down systematically.[34]

A Characterization of Latin American Cabinets

In the study of presidential political systems, the president's role in policymaking has been widely studied and documented. The role of the president's closest advisors—his or her cabinet ministers—has been largely ignored, however. This chapter has taken a step toward redressing this oversight by surveying some of the most prominent features of cabinets in Latin America and the main mechanisms through which they affect policymaking.

The chapter highlights both similarities in cabinet politics across Latin America and the enormous variation in how cabinets work. There are many differences in how cabinet members are appointed, especially in the number of parties involved in cabinet formation, in how they organize for work (although there is a growing trend for presidents to delegate coordination tasks to someone else), and in the degree to which cabinet instability is problematic for policymaking. But there are also some common trends. One of these is the key role that individual ministers play in every stage of the political process. The predominant role of finance ministers in policymaking is another constant throughout the region. A third common trend is the relatively low level of cabinet stability that prevails in most Latin American countries.

The big question is, what is the significance of these features of cabinet politics? Does it matter how large the cabinet is? Does rapid turnover of ministers really affect policy outputs? Given the limited evidence available on the subject of cabinet politics, it is hard to give unambiguous answers to these questions. In concluding, however, this study looks briefly at some preliminary evidence.[35]

---

[34] For a discussion in the context of parliamentary systems, see Huber and Martínez-Gallardo (2004).

[35] Recently, some authors have started to analyze the effect of cabinet characteristics on policy in a wider cross-section of countries but without looking specifically at presidential countries.

Table 5.3 uses the data set out in the chapter and classifies countries according to the extent to which each feature of cabinet politics is present. In spite of the limitations of the data, some clear patterns emerge. Several cases stand out. Venezuela, Peru, and Ecuador have unusually large and unstable cabinets, even in the economic policy arena, where ministers tend to have short terms. In Peru, the existence of strong censure authority in the legislature is an additional source of tension and instability. On the other end of the scale, Uruguay has a small number of portfolios, as well as a small number of ministers per portfolio, low levels of cabinet instability, and long-lasting finance ministers. In Costa Rica, cabinets have been remarkably stable, organized around cohesive and disciplined political parties. In Mexico, cabinets have been rather large but levels of stability have been high compared to other places, including stable finance ministers, who have a strong influence over the design of economic policy.

Connecting the trends shown in Table 5.3 with policy outcomes, as measured by the index of the quality of policy constructed for the IDB report *The Politics of Policies* (IDB, 2005), yields evidence that these factors matter—although some important exceptions exist (Stein and Tommasi, 2007).[36] Among the 12 countries in Table 5.3, Venezuela, Peru, and Ecuador are all below the mean level of policy performance. Uruguay, Costa Rica, and Mexico all score as high on the policy index. The most notable exception is Brazil, which scores low on measures of cabinet stability but is ranked among the top policy performers, and Bolivia, which scores higher in the quality of its policies than one would expect given its relatively high cabinet instability.

The policy index includes several dimensions of policy outcomes (stability, adaptability, enforcement, coordination and coherence, public regardedness, and efficiency). Cabinet politics should be expected to affect each dimension differently. In particular, the most direct relationship should be expected between the stability of cabinets and the stability of policy outcomes. This study has argued that cabinet instability is bound

---

For example, Scartascini, Stein, and Tommasi (2008) present preliminary evidence showing that cabinet stability matters for explaining the characteristics of policies, particularly the degree of coordination of public policies, and Wehner (2009) studies the impact of the number of ministries on fiscal results.

[36] The authors have recently expanded the database to cover a wider cross-section of countries (Scartascini, Stein, and Tommasi, 2008; Berkman et al., 2009).

TABLE 5.3 | Some Basic Features of Latin American Cabinets

Variable	Argentina	Bolivia	Brazil	Chile	Colombia	Costa Rica	Ecuador	Mexico	Paraguay	Peru	Uruguay	Venezuela
Censure	L	VL	—	—	M	—	VL	—	VL	VH	VH	M
Duration of finance minister	M	L	M	VH	H	H	VL	VH	M	VL	VH	L
Number of portfolios	VL	M	VH	H	L	VL	VH	H	VL	M	L	VH
Ministerial duration	M	H	M	L	H	VL	H	VL	M	VH	VL	VH
Ministers per portfolio	M	VH	M	VL	VH	M	H	VL	L	VH	L	H

Source: Author's compilation from various sources.

— not available.

VH: very high. H: high. M: medium. VL: very low. L: low.

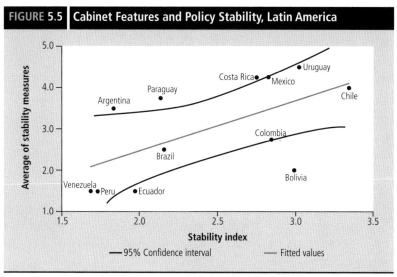

FIGURE 5.5 | **Cabinet Features and Policy Stability, Latin America**

Source: Data on cabinet stability from Martínez-Gallardo (2005) and data on policy stability from IDB (2005).

to have a negative effect on the ability of ministers to credibly commit to long-term policy outcomes and that shifts in policy are bound to result when constant turnover prevails. This claim appears to be supported by the available evidence. Figure 5.5 plots an average of the measures of cabinet stability presented in the chapter and in Stein and Tommasi's index of policy stability. The figure shows a significant upward slope, connecting grater cabinet stability to policy stability.[37]

Both Table 5.3 and Figure 5.5 provide preliminary support for the idea that cabinet politics indeed matter for policy performance in the presidential countries of Latin America. Where cabinet decision making is more fragmented and cabinets are more unstable, policymaking tends to suffer. Whether these variables are related systematically across a wide cross-section of presidential systems remains to be tested in future research.

---

[37] The correlation between the two variables is .6 and is significant at the p<.05 level.

CHAPTER 6

The Weakest Link: The Bureaucracy and Civil Service Systems in Latin America

Laura Zuvanic and Mercedes Iacoviello, with Ana Laura Rodríguez Gusta

The bureaucracy is commonly understood as a body of officials, an organizational apparatus, or even an employment system. As an institution, the bureaucracy can be seen as a coordinated set of operating rules and guidelines whose purpose is to guarantee the continuity, coherence, and relevance of public policies on the one hand, and prevent the discretionary exercise of public power, on the other. Overall, the bureaucracy is a crucial player in the design and execution of public policy. From the point of view of the policymaking process, the bureaucracy is particularly important because it is the body in charge of preparing, executing, controlling, and evaluating public policies. Accordingly, the bureaucracy is a central institution in the effective functioning of the democratic system and oversight of the rule of law. This is especially true given the growing challenges facing public policies in Latin America.

The bureaucracy can act as a brake on arbitrary actions, be a safeguard of legal certainty, and be crucial for effective and efficient government action. However, these roles can be fulfilled only if the bureaucracy fulfills certain characteristics. Only an impartial and transparent bureaucracy can generate legal certainty. A professional bureaucracy helps limit the adoption of opportunist policies and strengthens the confidence of actors to comply fully with the commitments they contract as part of the agreements into which they enter. Moreover, a correctly functioning bureaucracy prevents capture of public policies by corporate interests (Evans, 1992). In the more specific sphere of the decision-making process, a professional bureaucracy can be an additional channel to reinforce intertemporal political agreements. As explained in Chapter 1 and further developed in Spiller, Stein, and Tommasi (2008), intertemporal cooperation increases the effectiveness of policies by limiting the possibility of reversing decisions on the basis of short-term considerations.

Unfortunately, the bureaucracy seldom plays this role in Latin America. The reality of the region is one of states with a weak capacity to execute public policies. To a large extent, this weakness has been associated with the low level of professionalization and stability of the bureaucracies of Latin American countries. Some studies have suggested that bureaucracy has functioned as an employment system in the hands of politicians and corporate interests. As a result, bureaucracies in the region are seldom characterized by regularized and impersonal procedures and employment decisions based on technical qualifications and merit (Klingner and Pallavicini Campos, 2001; Prats i Catalá, 2003).

There is no formal definition of the role of the bureaucracy in the national policymaking processes in the region: from design to execution, including evaluation, control, and follow-up, and provision of inputs for discussion of policy alternatives. Constitutions only vaguely mention the role of "service" to the nation by public employees. Civil service statutes define the obligations with respect to compliance with laws and regulations, tasks and functions, the orders of superiors, and responsibility for public property, leaving vague how public officials should contribute to and be involved with public policy, even in its most mechanical and operational aspects.

One might expect that the regulations covering the career ladders of officials would provide more information about the expected performance of bureaucratic bodies. For each occupational group, the regulations define levels of responsibility and the type of function to be performed. However, the low level of development of systems of work organization in the region leads to an ad hoc definition of jobs and job profiles, which are not part of more global criteria related to the functions and roles assigned to specific sectors of the bureaucracy.

This chapter shows that the region's bureaucracies take on diverse roles that are very often contradictory. This diversity varies according to their degree of professionalism and neutrality with respect to the execution of public policies. Bureaucracies also vary according to their degree of stability and capacity to adapt, and their orientation to the public interest—or, to the contrary, their use as a private resource by the political parties or even by the public employees themselves, who are able to defend their interests because they are protected by job security.

Characterization of Latin American Bureaucracies: Strategic Human Resource Management

To what extent are bureaucracies equipped with the institutional attributes needed to manage increasingly complex public policies in changing conditions? To guarantee some stability in the results of public policies, an independent and stable bureaucracy must be assured. This type of bureaucracy depends on the effectiveness of rules and practices that adhere to criteria of merit, accountability, transparency, and flexibility (Grindle, 1997).

In other words, the procedures, rules, and practices of public employment to a large extent influence the institutional capacity and effectiveness of the bureaucracy in designing and executing public policy. The rules of public employment are (or are not) a source of motivation for officials, as well as monitoring their activities and the quality of their work and results.

What is the current situation in the region? The discussion that follows takes a detailed look at the situation of Latin American civil services in order to identify some common trends and highlight the differences between national cases. This empirical exercise takes as a reference point for evaluation the integrated model of strategic human resources management proposed by Francisco Longo (2002, 2004).

This study takes into account the development of the civil service based on adjustments between organizational strategy and the behavior of officials. It proposes a system-based approach to human resources management. It takes a broad view of the functioning of human resource management that integrates internal context, environment, strategy, and results in an analysis of the coherence of the organizational strategy.

In line with this broad view, this study examines a series of human resource management subsystems, covering human resource planning, organization of work, employment, performance, pay, development, and human and social relations (see Table 6.1).

This study uses findings from an evaluation of civil services in 18 countries of the region according to the reference model (Echebarría,

TABLE 6.1 | **Integrated Human Resources Management Model**

Human resources planning

Availability of information for management. Provision for personnel based on strategic priorities. Flexible planning that adapts to changes. High degree of technological improvement and reasonable payroll costs.

Work organization	Employment management	Performance management	Compensation management	Development management
Jobs designed based on criteria of management, job enrichment. Profiles expressed in terms of competences and based on technical studies.	Open recruitment based on suitability, with guarantees to prevent arbitrary actions and discrimination. Selection based on profiles of competence, validated instruments, technical criteria. Disciplinary mechanisms, mobility, control of absenteeism. Separation, dismissal for noncompliance not arbitrary.	Performance objectives related to strategic objectives, communicated to employees. Support for employees' work and performance, evaluated in relation to fixed standards in an efficient and fair system.	Pay policy linked to organizational strategy. Internal and external equity. Reasonable salary costs. Efficient nonwage incentives and benefit schemes. Strategies for nonmonetary recognition.	Flexible career plans, including horizontal promotion. Promotion based on performance and development of competences. Training oriented to collective learning, with design and evaluation based on the organizational strategy.

Human and social relations management

Developed, balanced, and efficient labor relations system to prevent and resolve conflicts, with union influence on HR policies. Health practices and social benefits adapted to the context and appreciated by employees. Strategies to improve labor climate and communication.

Source: Authors' compilations based on Longo (2002).

2006). This same conceptual model was taken as the basis for preparation of the Ibero-American Civil Service Charter (CLAD, 2003), which was approved by the countries of the region as the standard at which their public personnel management should aim.

Taking this integrated strategic model of human resources management as point of reference, what can be said about the region? First, the region's civil services are very far from the proposed model. Instead of the integrated strategic management that the model suggests, the region seems to be characterized by a segmented human resources management, with decisions and procedures that are more random than planned (Iacoviello, 2006). These characteristics can be more or less dysfunctional in relation to the design and execution of public policies depending on the national environment in question. Despite the deficiencies, some of the human resource management subsystems of the model are closer to the proposed standard.

Consider first qualitative and quantitative human resources planning, which suffer from important deficiencies in the region. The planning of government policies and budget projections concerning personnel are rarely coordinated with the public sector's institutional indicators and organizational strategies. On the contrary, the planning of policy guidelines is often separated from their human resources needs, producing serious mismatches between the personnel needed for implementation of successful public policies and the personnel available. This gap results in ineffective instruments of government coordination.

These shortcomings are compounded by the great difficulty of establishing systems of updated, relevant, and reliable information suitable for use by senior public service heads and supervisors in personnel management. The construction of these information systems also must contend with considerable vagueness in the definition of jobs and profiles in public organizations, which is intensified by the difficulties of carrying out an effective evaluation of the performance of organizations and their members. With respect to pay, efforts are centered only on guaranteeing the formal administration of wages, without any effective coordination with the organizational strategy and with the development of incentive systems for individuals. These shortcomings in the pay system affect effort. It is common to find situations where public policies are implemented with difficulty because inequalities in the pay of officials or even low wages among certain specialized occupation groups do not foster the necessary levels of commitment to the work. Some researchers have called this gap "substantive absenteeism."[1] There are only a few cases in the region of pay structures that act as positive incentives.

Latin American countries have different methods of hiring and promoting officials. In some, admission into public employment occurs only through political connections. In others, some admission schemes are based on merit criteria used in the selection and promotion of employees—although with clear difficulties of implementation. Other countries have solid merit systems in recruitment and promotion of employees, with Brazil a leading case. Because of the importance of merit in the construction of an efficient bureaucratic body to implement public policies, and because the caliber of the bureaucracy based on merit varies considerably in the region, the discussion that follows focuses on analyzing how merit criteria influence decisions in entry, promotion, and dismissal of personnel.

Merit Criteria in the Region

How are the most capable candidates selected from a set of aspirants? What mechanisms are used to attract aspirants in the first place? Are the mechanisms particularistic or do they offer comparable opportunities to similarly qualified personnel? Are the officials selected those who are most capable or those with personal or political connections to the bosses in power? To tackle these questions, this study works with a *merit index* prepared for the reference management model.

This index measures to what extent objective, technical, and professional procedures exist and are followed to recruit, select, promote, compensate, and dismiss employees from an organization. By evaluating ten critical points,[2] this index offers a summary measure of the effective guarantees of professionalism in the civil service and the effective protection of officials from arbitrariness, politicization, and private benefit-seeking. Merit is displayed in the practices of selection, promotion, and dismissal of officials from the state apparatus. Following this

---

[1] We thank Humberto Martins for suggesting the use of this term.

[2] The methodology evaluates 93 critical points that reflect best practices in relation to the various aspects of human resource management. Each index is constructed as a weighted average of a selection of critical points. Evaluation is based on analysis by a team of experts of quantitative and qualitative information.

index, merit not only includes professional or occupational qualifications, but also the expertise acquired in practice and the capacities needed to work in more specific areas.

The merits of a candidate can be evaluated through objective procedures (knowledge tests) or subjective ones (interviews). They also involve open competition mechanisms and universal procedures for aspiring to a position in the public sector. Ideally, only the suitability of the candidate should be taken into account in human resources management, leaving aside considerations that have nothing to do with job performance, such as attributed characteristics or political loyalties.

Low values on the scale from 0 to 100 imply absence of objective, universal, and technical considerations, while high values reflect established merit criteria in personnel management practices.

In general in the region, the merit index suggests that the systematic and institutionalized use of merit criteria for selection, promotion, and dismissal of employees is infrequent. This situation is reflected in an average of only 33 points (out of 100) for Latin American countries, although, as discussed later, there is an enormous spread—between 87 points for Brazil and 2 points for Panama.

Paradoxically, one of the most developed normative aspects of civil services in the region is the selection of employees based on meritocratic principles, which has even achieved constitutional status in some nations. There has been no lack of attempts to introduce merit-based competition for recruitment of new employees, but with very uneven success. Moreover, it is not common to promote personnel to other, more responsible posts based on their merits and work qualities. When there are objective promotion practices, they are based more on length of service than merit, understood as performance. Finally, dismissal of career officials is very difficult; when it occurs, it does not necessarily reflect bad performance but political "purges" (which can involve tortuous legal questions for many years).

Based on these trends, use of merit in bureaucratic bodies varies from country to country, as can be seen in Figure 6.1. Brazil, Chile, and Costa Rica head the list, with indexes between 55 and 90 (out of 100), which reflects widespread acceptance of the principles of merit in decisions on selection, promotion, and dismissal of public servants. Brazil, Chile, and Costa Rica are the three cases where merit criteria are most embedded in personnel management, putting them—in principle—in

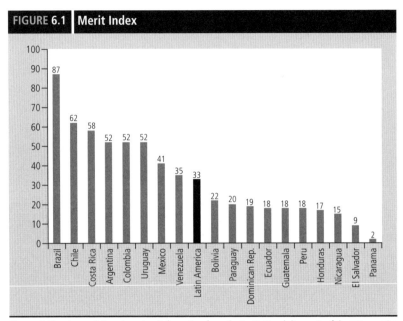

FIGURE 6.1 | Merit Index

Source: Authors' compilations based on information from the institutional diagnosis of the 18 countries analyzed (Iacoviello and Zuvanic, 2005).
Scale 0 to 100.

the best situation for the tasks of preparation, implementation, and control of public policies.

Brazil has a considerably institutionalized universal system for covering positions through public competitions for both functional careers and temporary posts under the Labor Contract Law. In Costa Rica, merit is the prevailing principle (based on the Civil Service Statute of 1953) and recruitment is open to all candidates, with the possibility of dismissal for reasons of poor performance. In Chile, the Administrative Statute (1989) establishes competitions for entry into different areas; the New Deal on Employment Law (2004) introduces merit criteria for selection to posts of free appointment through the Senior Public Management System.

The next group of countries, with indexes between 30 and 55, includes Argentina, Colombia, Uruguay, Mexico, and Venezuela. Here, merit-based practices coexist with traditions of political patronage. A third group of countries—Bolivia, Paraguay, the Dominican Republic, Ecuador, Peru, and the Central American countries (except Costa Rica)—have indexes below 30 points. This indicates strong politicization of decisions on selection, promotion, and dismissal; in addition to the

absence of institutionalized merit-based criteria for selecting personnel, there are no protection mechanisms against arbitrary practices in
personnel management.

Mexico, Venezuela, and Colombia have very politicized situations,
but with a strong movement to include merit in personnel management
based on new legal frameworks. In contrast, Uruguay and Argentina
illustrate how attempts to develop an administrative career and reform
the civil service have stagnated because of prohibition on entry of new
employees into the workforce. This is made worse by the use of parallel
recruiting mechanisms, particularly in programs with international
funds for implementing sectoral public policies. Under the same nu-
merical result, countries display two very disparate tendencies: those
that are trying to put situations of strong politicization behind them
and introduce rules based on professionalization criteria still in their
infancy; and countries with a longer tradition of administrative careers
that have stagnated, with length of service predominant in considering
criteria of personnel management.[3]

Finally, there are the countries with the lowest levels of merit, with
strong politicization of personnel decisions. In some cases, political
interference violates the principles of merit established by law. In other
cases, legal ambiguity permits political favoritism. Politicization of entry
and dismissal leads to the general absence of career systems. In several
of these countries, the party membership of employees can be predicted
by their year of entry (Geddes, 1994).

In Panama, Honduras, Nicaragua, Guatemala, Peru, and Ecuador,
a mass replacement of officials occurs every time the administration
changes. This type of "revolving door" is a problem because public
policies need continuity of resources for follow-up and control. If the
most capable employees with specific knowledge are dismissed, then
policies will be affected. Ironically in these countries, the laws establish
merit-based entry—in some cases for decades. In Paraguay and in the
civil service segment in the Dominican Republic, legal ambiguity encourages a high level of politicization of recruitment decisions because
only minimum standards are required for entry. In El Salvador, there
is a curious "institutionalization" of a special selection procedure for

---

[3] The change of administration in Uruguay has put professionalization of the civil service back
on the reform agenda as one of the priority reforms.

candidates suggested by politicians. In Bolivia, political criteria continue to predominate in personnel decisions, although the institutions that have reformed under the umbrella of institutional reform projects—usually financed by external donors—have hired personnel through open public competition.

Variations in Functional Capacity

Apart from merit, the integrated model of strategic personnel management calls for bureaucracies to have certain capacities to attract, retain, and manage qualified personnel. What influence do civil service practices and procedures have on the work motivation and commitment of employees? Can these structures promote a real vocation of public service, with officials committed to the quality of their work and service to citizens?

The functional capacity index[4] evaluates how and how much existing procedures and practices in the civil service can influence employee behavior, and if they serve the purpose of strengthening the commitment of officials to the institution and to their jobs. Functional capacity does not operate in a vacuum, but is influenced by the quality of the systems of pay and performance evaluation. The perception of an equitable compensation in relation to the private sector (external equity) and to the rest of the public sector (internal equity) is a requirement for attracting, motivating, and committing trained personnel. The motivation and retention of officials are also affected by the nature and extent of follow up of individual, group, and institutional performance, and the degree to which performance effectively influences decisions affecting careers (assignment of tasks, promotion, monetary or nonmonetary recognition).

So what is the state of functional capacity in the region? What are the values for the reference index? The average for this index in the countries of the region is 30 (out of 100), with a maximum of 61 for Brazil and a minimum of 11 for Honduras. As can be seen in Figure 6.2, the spread of the results is high, but less than for the merit index.

---

[4] This index is constructed on the basis of a weighted average of the valuation of 41 critical points that reflect a series of best practices associated with the capacity of the system to guarantee key competences for public management (competence); its effectiveness for creating incentives for productivity, learning and quality of service (incentive effectiveness); and its flexibility for promoting adaptation to change (flexibility).

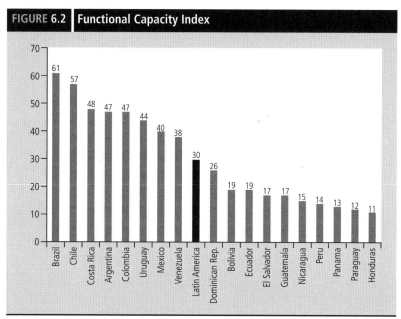

FIGURE 6.2 | Functional Capacity Index

Source: Authors' compilations based on information from the institutional diagnosis of the 18 countries analyzed (Iacoviello and Zuvanic, 2005).
Scale 0 to 100.

In general, the civil services of the region have fairly undeveloped management systems. Likewise, there is no real wage policy. In practice, wage policy is determined by budgetary restrictions, which generate decisions that undermine the objective of guaranteeing the internal and external equity of remuneration. There are few experiences of variable remuneration systems that effectively relate individual performance to compliance with targets. Those that do exist are arbitrary. In most cases, attempts to associate incentives with individual performance tend to generate conduct outside the norms, such as rotation of officials with maximum qualifications during the evaluation period, to give all officials the opportunity to access an additional bonus, which undermines the system.

Despite these tendencies in management of pay and performance, the functional capacity of the region's bureaucracies is not homogeneous. As seen in Figure 6.2, Brazil and Chile have indexes of close to 60 points out of 100. Their indexes reflect ordered systems of wage management with relative internal equity, and the existence of processes aimed at improving wage competitiveness, along with evaluation processes that take into account group and institutional management.

These countries have more developed and coordinated systems of performance management, wage structure, and incentive systems. For example, in Chile, pay management is centralized, which promotes a high degree of fiscal discipline. With pay associated with aspects of management (such as the Management Improvement Programs) based on institutional and collective incentives, the Chilean civil service has achieved some flexibility in its functional capacity. Brazil has reformed its wage structure, with important efforts to make it competitive based on benchmarking studies. Individual and institutional performance evaluation schemes have also been developed.

The next group of countries, which have indexes between 35 and 50 points, consists of Costa Rica, Argentina, Colombia, Uruguay, Mexico, and Venezuela. This group, despite having made some pay reforms, is characterized by the persistence of strong internal inequities and very low competitiveness of the managerial salaries when compared with similar occupations in the private sector. Performance evaluation is practiced only for show. It is not transformed into a reliable management tool capable of distinguishing between good and average performance. In Venezuela and Colombia, the system is distorted by the excessive benevolence of supervisors, while in Argentina and Uruguay the problem is a forced rotation of scores for the high performers. That is, despite actual performance, the best scores are assigned to different officials each year as a reaction to the forced distribution of evaluations that establishes a maximum percentage of employees that can be assigned to each evaluation category. Consequently, some high performers may not be rewarded as such because of the preestablished fixed proportions across the staff distribution. An exception is Costa Rica, which has a slightly broader development of evaluation practices. At the other extreme, in Mexico, evaluation practices are pending implementation. With respect to pay management, progress in terms of definition of wage scales based on tasks and levels of responsibility is held back by situations of internal inequity and problems of wage competitiveness in the managerial sectors. The inequity is based on the multiple sources of additional compensation which continue to represent an important part of remuneration (despite attempts at unification). For example, in Colombia, additional pay represents 50 percent of the basic wage, on average.

The countries with the lowest functional capacity (between 10 and 25 points) are the Dominican Republic, Bolivia, Ecuador, El Salvador,

Guatemala, Nicaragua, Peru, Panama, Paraguay, and Honduras. These countries have multiple pay criteria with no relation or coordination, coupled with the absence of systematic and transparent information on remuneration, together with high levels of inequality and almost total absence of any kind of performance evaluation criteria.

Pay criteria vary greatly for different groups of officials, so it is not possible to guarantee a minimum of internal equity to which levels of responsibility or complexity of tasks and pay levels can be associated. Consequently, lack of motivation or the sense of inequality in the civil service is not surprising. The cases of Peru and Ecuador are paradigmatic in this respect. In Peru, only 40 percent of wages are paid by the unified payroll, which makes it practically impossible to obtain information for wage management. In Ecuador, the enormous diversity of regimes creates deep internal inequities, which create "classes of bureaucrats." The term "golden bureaucracy" is usually used to refer to sectors with privileged pay—which creates envy and resistance in other bureaucratic groups. Moreover, several of these countries have not even established individual performance evaluations (Panama, Nicaragua, Paraguay, and Guatemala), or such evaluations are undertaken only in pilot bodies (Bolivia), in some restricted sectors (the Dominican Republic), or for personnel under special statutes (Honduras).

So far, the discussion has considered the aspects of merit and functional capacity separately. It is possible to examine them together; in this way, a "summary" of the characteristics of the national civil services can be obtained, based on simultaneous consideration of these aspects.

Bureaucratic Configurations

Are some bureaucracies more professional and others less professional? Are some more flexible, with the capacity to adapt to the environment? Are others more focused on procedures?

Looking at bureaucracies broadly this way means approaching them as organizational configurations. By configuration is meant the global form and logic of the functioning of a civil service; this covers the set of practices and structures that produce its peculiar attributes. Two different ways of working with the organizational configuration approach follow. Both are empirical but each takes a different level of analysis as reference.

In the first way, bureaucratic configurations are distinguished by the level of development of their management systems. This approach aims to demonstrate the state of the civil service in any given country. The unit of analysis continues to be the national case. The objective of the exercise is to classify the countries of the region by the degree of development of their civil service taken as a whole. This degree is established in relation to the human resources management model used as reference (Longo, 2002). The advantage of this approach is to provide a "summary" view of the bureaucracy of a particular country.

The second way changes the level of analysis and the aspects of interest in question. The level of analysis becomes the organization, whether taken individually or as a set of organizations with common attributes, rather than the national case. From this point of view, it would be incorrect to say that a national case has a single bureaucracy; rather it has multiple types of bureaucracies or organizational configurations. The advantage of this approach is that it offers a view of the variations existing inside a single national bureaucracy.

Bureaucratic Configurations by Level of Development of the Civil Service

Considering the merit and functional capacity indexes simultaneously, the countries analyzed can be grouped according to three levels of bureaucratic development (see Figure 6.3). Brazil and Chile stand out: their civil services are more developed. In relative terms, these two countries have institutionalized civil services with practices that take into account the abilities and credentials of officials, and structures that tend to maintain and develop a higher quality of work in the service.

These countries construct their professional civil service in different ways. While Brazil is a more classic bureaucracy in its procedures and structure, Chile has elements close to the New Public Management in its personnel management.[5] Aside from these important differences, both cases converge in the use of criteria where performance-related achievements and work incentives play a central role for public officials.

---

[5] New Public Management is a broad term used to describe the new management philosophy that has accompanied the institutional reforms since the 1980s, which tried to bring about both greater cost-efficiency and organizational flexibility.

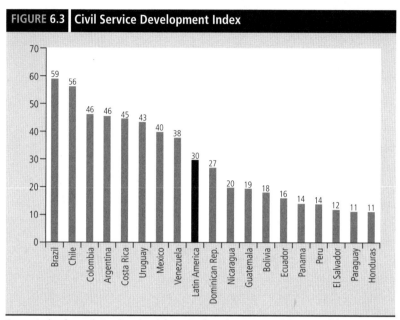

FIGURE 6.3 | Civil Service Development Index

Source: Authors' compilations based on information from the institutional diagnosis of the 18 countries analyzed (Iacoviello and Zuvanic, 2005).
Scale 0 to 100.

A second group of countries has civil service systems that can be classified as intermediate: Colombia, Argentina, Costa Rica, Uruguay, Mexico, and Venezuela. Their bureaucracies are relatively well structured. In some posts a high percentage of officials have achieved job security, so there is a certain permanence to the bureaucracy. However, some of the guarantees of merit or management tools that permit effective utilization of the competences of employees, groups, and institutions have not been consolidated.

A third group of countries has bureaucracies with minimal development: the civil service system either cannot guarantee the selection and retention of competent personnel or does not possess management mechanisms that effectively influence the behavior of officials. This group includes the Dominican Republic, Nicaragua, Guatemala, Bolivia, Ecuador, Panama, Peru, El Salvador, Paraguay, and Honduras. Here, politicization is so strong that it hinders the development of a professional civil service.

Aside from these general comments on the comparison between different countries, civil service systems do not exist as homogeneous and uniform structures. For this reason this study proposes a typology that reflects the bureaucratic configurations that coexist in the systems of public employment in the region.

Bureaucratic Configurations Combining Autonomy and Technical Capacity

Bureaucracies even in the same country are far from being homogeneous actors. A civil service is a set of complex and interdependent organizations with differences with respect to the use of merit and functional capacity. Admitting the possibility of this heterogeneity can provide some clues to understanding the internal dynamic of the state apparatus and the degree to which different parts of the bureaucracy can play different (and even contradictory) roles in the public policy cycle, even in the same country.

Such heterogeneity is better observed from a public policy approach rather than a self-contained bureaucratic analysis approach. The emphasis on trying to understand bureaucracies from the point of view of the design and execution of public policies means that merit becomes relevant insofar as it strengthens the autonomy of bureaucracies and helps them develop their own prestige and institutional culture. Functional capacity also takes on renewed importance from the point of view of public policies because such policies require increasing technical skills for execution.

Taking the existence of this heterogeneity as starting point, and using individual public organizations (or sets of them) as unit of analysis, a typology is created that is appropriate for the different types of bureaucracies found in the countries of the region. Bureaucracies are mapped onto two axes: *autonomy* and *technical capacity*. Four distinctive categories result from the intersection of two axes: variables that relate to merit and functional capacity.[6]

What does autonomy mean? Autonomy means the degree of isolation from political manipulation and from rent-seeking interests outside the state.[7] This variable is one of the central aspects considered in the merit index presented in the previous section.

---

[6] This typology is based on the one in Zuvanic and Iacoviello (2005).

[7] This definition of autonomy is similar to that presented by Peter Evans and called embedded autonomy (1992). The difference is that this study puts more emphasis on autonomy in relation to the use of public posts as resources for exchange by the political parties.

Bureaucracies protected from political interference can act more professionally without being captured by external special interests. Autonomy means that a bureaucratic body is governed by its own regulations and rules. Nevertheless, extreme degrees of autonomy—or its exercise not subject to norms—can lead to bureaucrats becoming corporative actors that favor their own interests over the public interest.

What does technical capacity mean? The bureaucracy is partly a system for doing a job: delivering goods and services to citizens. The production processes of these goods and services, together with the use of technology, require that the competences of officials be developed so that they have the skills needed to solve efficiently the problems that arise during their work.

Technical capacity thus does not only depend on whether the officials have the credentials to support a position, but also on the work skills they need to perform their tasks, whether acquired through formal education or on the job. The bureaucracy must also offer the incentives to put these competences to work. At this point, aspects of the "merit" variable come into play that go beyond a simple guarantee of political noninterference, in combination with aspects of the "functional capacity" variable, which has an impact on the motivation and commitment of officials.

By crossing these two variables, a typology emerges that results in four categories of bureaucracy: administrative, parallel, patronage, and meritocratic. Figure 6.4 summarizes these four categories. How are these categories related to national civil services? First, different types of bureaucracy can coexist in one country. For example, some organizations in the civil service in Argentina are patronage bureaucracies (some of the provincial or even municipal bureaucracies). Others are administrative bureaucracies (the segment of administrative posts in national government ministries). There are also parallel bureaucracies (those of international programs), and meritocratic bureaucracies (the central bank).

Second, a national civil service can be characterized as administrative, parallel, patronage, or meritocratic if one of these four categories is the dominant type among its public organizations. If a broad majority of the organizations of a given civil service fall into one specific type of bureaucracy, then by aggregation, it can be said that a national civil

FIGURE 6.4 | Bureaucratic Configurations and Prevailing Roles

High	Administrative bureaucracy	Meritocratic bureaucracy
Autonomy	• Formal merit criteria, not always utilized • Recruitment on political grounds, but job security • Partial reflection of frustrated attempts to develop a Weberian bureaucracy Limited ability for policymaking and implementing.	• Permanent public officials, recruited on basis of merit and incorporated into professional careers; incentives favor professional performance • Specific tasks Expresses opinions and acts, contributes to stability of policies.
	Patronage bureaucracy	**Parallel bureaucracy**
	• Temporary public officials • Entry based on party loyalty/membership • Political resource Absent from the policymaking and implementation process, except in basic functions.	• Senior personnel with flexible contracts, not integrated into the permanent body • Occasionally important in design and execution of policies and projects Participate in the process, but with a low contribution to the stability of policies and to strengthening of the capacities of the state.
Low		
	Low Capacity High	

Source: Zuvanic and Iacoviello (2005).

service is a specific bureaucratic type. But it is highly plausible that a national civil service will be *hybrid*, combining two or more of the four categories of bureaucracies.

The typology presented has heuristic purposes, which are intended to introduce a more complex level of analysis into the evaluation protocols of civil services. This approach is also useful because each type of bureaucracy is related to a different performance of public policies, which will theoretically permit bureaucratic forms to be associated with the performance of public policies in future work.

Administrative Bureaucracy

This type of bureaucracy is characterized by a high level of autonomy backed by strong protection against "capricious" political interference and special interests—mainly because of the job security that officials enjoy. However, it has a low level of technical capacity since its tasks are related to standardized procedures. This is the bureaucracy that typically executes the classic administrative functions, especially in the ministries.

This type of bureaucracy is observed in central government bodies subject to a general statute that regulates public employment and establishes a formal administrative career; however, these statutes acquire a uniquely ceremonial value without any great consequence for day-to-day activity. This category includes the cases of Ecuador, Peru, and Venezuela, along with the unionized segment in Mexico, as well as the central administrations of Argentina, Costa Rica, and Uruguay—although with a somewhat higher degree of technical capacity.

In these countries, the administrative bureaucracy displays some singular characteristics. Traditionally, officials have been appointed on the basis of more political or particularistic criteria than exclusively meritocratic ones, but in general tend to have stability. It is precisely the job security clause (very often with constitutional status) that gives this bureaucracy its autonomy, even against the vicissitudes of political change.

The history of these organizations suggests that administrative bureaucracies, at least in the form in which they exist in the countries of the region, represent truncated or halfway attempts to develop rational, hierarchical, merit-based bureaucracies that could strengthen their technical capacity. Recently, these have been the bureaucracies most affected by budgetary cuts and vacancy freezes (in Argentina, Peru, and Uruguay), including retirement incentive packages, in the attempts at state reform during the 1990s.

Their low levels of technical competence and of orientation toward adding value have been difficult to transform. By way of illustration, the training programs implemented do not necessarily lead to an increase in technical competence. An important structural limit that these bureaucracies face is the fact that their tasks are generally routine and standardized in public policy environments of low uncertainty.

What is the role of this type of bureaucracy in relation to public policy? In general, administrative bureaucracy has little capacity to play an active role in the different stages of the public policy cycle. With respect to policy design and crafting, its scant technical capacity prevents it from having any real influence in the decision-making phase. Moreover, policy design, crafting, and decision making take place in the ministries, reinforcing the isolation of the administrative bureaucracy, which is perceived by the political leadership as a mere operational body or even as an obstacle to implementation.

The flip side is that these bureaucracies have little potential for transforming themselves into a resource for political exchange because of the stability of officials and their lack of importance for public policy, especially in strategic cases. Paradoxically, this lack of political attractiveness has made them irrelevant for several of the region's governments: they have nothing to gain and nothing to lose from them.

Despite this situation, administrative bureaucracies occasionally assume an important role in implementation, although with a bias toward formalism and control of bureaucratic procedures rather than effective and substantive management of services.

Patronage Bureaucracy

This type of bureaucracy is formed by public officials who enter the administration—usually temporarily—because of certain criteria of political loyalty or party membership, with no consideration of their technical capacity. These bureaucracies are fragile because a change in the government party or even simple shuffling of authorities in a ministry can result in mass changes of officials.

This type of bureaucracy has no autonomy in the political system—which manages it arbitrarily, even in relation to dismissals. It does not develop technical capacity because what is at stake is political favor rather than interest in recruiting officials with the competences needed to implement complex public policies.

The most severe cases are in the Central American countries (except Costa Rica), and in the Dominican Republic, Paraguay, and Bolivia (except in some meritocratic enclaves). Some of these characteristics also exist in specific bureaucracies in certain countries, such as Argentina, Colombia, and Peru, under transitory or special employment regimes that give the government increased flexibility in appointments and dismissals.

The role that patronage bureaucracy can come to exercise in public policy is linked to its primary character as a political resource of the governing party. This type of bureaucracy is an extension of the partisan political actor, and it can exercise a certain veto power over professional or meritocratic bureaucratic segments with which it comes into conflict. Its role in policymaking or implementation is almost irrelevant, except on the operative plane of the most simple and routine tasks. It has a strong presence in delivery of social services.

Parallel Bureaucracy

This type—also known as "technical team" or "project team" bureaucracy—is formed by technocrats or professionals whose special mode of entry into the state is through flexible and fixed-term contractual forms, a practice especially prevalent in the region during the 1990s under the "management by project" system (Martínez Nogueira, 2002). Their salaries are usually higher than those of the rest of the personnel in the public administration.

Although these bureaucracies have developed in practically all countries in the region, they are much more frequent in those with less developed civil services. The intention is to cover the lack of qualified human resources in the permanent workforce with external experts, as happens in the Central American countries.

Because of their system of recruitment and the temporary nature of their positions, this bureaucracy is characterized by a very low level of autonomy with respect to the executive branch: the employment relationship clearly depends on the political will of the executive to hire personnel and renew their contracts. This employment regime is usually governed by regulations on service contracts or other extraordinary legal forms. The personnel hired are not part of the permanent structures of the public administration, although renewal of these contracts has become routine in various countries.

These groups of officials do not necessarily respond to a political party, even though their entry is through these mechanisms. Bambaci, Spiller, and Tommasi (2007) argue that, in the case of Argentina, these "temporary bureaucrats" tend to respond to the individual political patron who brings them to the post.

Their technical capacity is high, precisely because their recruitment is based on the expert knowledge needed to implement sectoral public policies and specific programs. They have specialized knowledge in some specific policy area. In most cases they have been hired to cover specific technical needs, and in some cases have developed technical–political aptitudes. They usually form parallel institutions—or what have been called "parallel ministries"—inside and outside the ordinary departments, as in Argentina and Mexico. These structures can be more or less successful, and more or less resisted by the other internal bureaucratic actors, because they form areas that are differentiated and not complementary to the regular administrative apparatus (Martínez Nogueira, 2002).

Technocratic bureaucracies can take different forms. Some versions have teams of technical advisers who perform key roles in designing policy alternatives. These technocrats are close to the head of the executive branch or have important contacts with international cooperation organizations, which means that their voice is heard at the time of policy design.

At other times, this bureaucracy focuses on guaranteeing execution of policies or projects, or effective delivery of certain public services. The category includes the organizations that negotiate projects with international financing or social funds.

What is the relation between this type of bureaucracy and public policies? These technical teams take on extraordinary challenges in the design and execution of public policy. They are hired for new work schemes that require increased coordination between the state and civil society, closer relations with international credit organizations, and technical abilities not usually associated with the permanent administrative workforce. These parallel bureaucracies have promoted new public policy schemes, such as those that involve implementation in public–private institutional networks.

However, when it comes to long-term execution of public policies, these parallel bureaucracies are of little use for building lasting institutions because of their temporary nature and special relationship with the executive branch. In general, at the end of the project little is left of the institutions set up for its execution and the learning process ends with the departure of the technical personnel. Martínez Nogueira (2002) cautions that a close association between the public policies implemented in the framework of these parallel bureaucracies and the ministerial action of a specific government can create important political vulnerabilities and uncertainties with respect to continuity of the efforts.

Meritocratic Bureaucracy

This category represents the Weberian classical ideal: this body of officials is recruited by open mechanisms in which their credentials and merits have priority. After selection, they execute the tasks in the framework of structured professional careers with good opportunities for mobility and learning, and with a series of incentives for the professional performance of the work.

This type of bureaucracy is characterized by a combination of high level of autonomy and technical capacity. First, the autonomy is based on the stability of the officials and on development of a career where political interests respect organizational hierarchies. Second, technical capacity is based on the relevance of the credentials and competencies, and the training and learning on the job that takes place in the framework of structured professional careers where promotion and advance are tied to a higher degree of complexity of tasks and exercise of responsibility.

Meritocratic bureaucracies form a specific culture, although sometimes an isolated one, with strong group cohesion, which can produce institutional bias. They also claim autonomous decision-making spaces, which in many cases create conflicts for them with other government departments. They can form alliances with other departments and even with external social interests, which grants them capacity to mediate between these different interests but also opens them to capture.

Meritocratic bureaucracies predominate in the civil services of Brazil and Chile. They are also observed in various countries among the special bodies linked to the fiscal or economic bureaucracy. Central banks, regulatory agencies, and tax administrations tend to be meritocratic bureaucracies. Examples include the National Tax Administration Superintendency (SUNAT) in Peru, and the Internal Tax Service in Chile. These meritocratic bureaucracies also exist in the professional career segment in Mexico, and among diplomatic corps in various countries of the region (the most outstanding case being Itamaratí in Brazil). In Argentina, a paradigmatic case of this type of bureaucracy is the so-called Government Administrators, a cross-cutting body of officials recruited on the basis of merit, who have highly technical careers.

In general, these bureaucracies are very active in the execution of public policy, and influence their design, if not directly at least indirectly. They are bureaucracies with specific obligations related to sectoral policies. They respond to thematic areas of public policy that require a degree of training or specialized knowledge. This gives them the opinions and capacity to influence the area in which they act, and makes them important actors for sustaining the stability and public interest orientation of policies.

Hybrid Forms

The empirical reality of the region goes beyond the categories that can be theoretically derived. Some hybrids or bureaucratic configurations are halfway between the categories mentioned and cannot be clearly classified in one or other type. One of the most readily identified hybrids is the social sector bureaucracies such as education and health personnel. These are situated halfway between administrative and meritocratic bureaucracies, with important national variations.

Health and education personnel are recruited on the basis of merit criteria, to some extent. Doctors and teachers must have credentials for accessing a public post where these specific profiles are required, which is an attribute of meritocratic bureaucracies. This minimal criterion—possession of the relevant credentials—is accompanied in some countries by public competition; in these cases, these bureaucracies show more mixed characteristics.

The degree of professional structuring of careers varies considerably. Thus there are important shortcomings in the use of criteria based on performance and on-the-job learning as mechanisms for selecting and rewarding personnel. Very often length of service has replaced other factors in promotion—especially in careers in education—which moves this bureaucracy away from meritocratic characteristics and brings it closer to the processes of more classic administrations.

The relation between these hybrid bureaucracies and public policies is complex and goes beyond the theoretical associations that this chapter aims to establish. However, their high capacity for lobbying or at least blocking initiatives to reform public policies, and their unionization, should be mentioned. In recent experiences in the region—such as in the administrations of Lula da Silva in Brazil and Tabaré Vázquez in Uruguay—these bodies and their professional associations have been invited to take part in dialogues on the design and formulation of the sectoral public policies that concern them.

The strategies that have been developed in relation to reforming bureaucracy in Latin America have included attempts to generate merit-based career systems for the administration as a whole, as well as efforts

FIGURE 6.5 | Examples of Bureaucratic Configurations

High	Administrative bureaucracy	Meritocratic bureaucracy
	National administration (Ecuador, Peru, Venezuela) National administration (Argentina, Costa Rica, Ecuador) Operating levels (unionized in Mexico)	Central banks Tax administration (Argentina, Chile, Mexico, Peru) External service National administration (Brazil, Chile) Senior Level [Government administrators (AG) body in Argentina, civil service in Chile, Professional Service in Mexico]
(Autonomy)	Patronage bureaucracy National administration (Bolivia except for meritocratic enclaves, Central American countries, Paraguay) Transitory appointments (Argentina, Colombia, Peru)	Parallel bureaucracy Groups of technical advisors Execution units of international cooperation projects (especially in Central America)
Low	Low Capacity High	

Source: Zuvanic and Iacoviello (2005).

to professionalize some specific areas, such as health and education services or tax administration. In other cases, efforts have concentrated on upgrading the professionalism of the managerial segment, as recently occurred in Chile and Mexico. This range of processes has coexisted with patronage practices and with the increasingly pronounced trend, since the 1990s, toward adopting flexible mechanisms to incorporate technical staff. In short, bureaucracy in Latin America presents a mosaic of options, which this study has attempted to systematize in the proposed typology (see Figure 6.5).

Conclusion

This chapter began by proposing that the bureaucracy has a potential role as guarantor of the democratic system and the rule of law. As an independent and professional body, the bureaucracy can guarantee the continuity and coherence of policies and prevent discretionary actions in the exercise of political power. However, in Latin America, bureaucracies usually do not play this role because they lack professionalization and stability.

The region's civil services are characterized by a low level of development, which suggests negligible capacity in most of the region's bureaucracies for taking an active role in the policymaking process. In addition, in the constitutions and statutes of the countries of the region, the expected role of the bureaucracy is defined in excessively generic terms, emphasizing compliance with norms, established procedures, and respect for hierarchical authority as central tenets.

This chapter has shown that the performance levels of the region's bureaucracies vary according to the degree in which regulations and work practices promote merit and the effective capacity of officials, along with the level of professionalism and neutrality of the various groups of officials. To come closer to a characterization of the bureaucracies in the region, the study began by analyzing the bureaucracies of each country in broad terms by comparing 18 national civil services in the region with a strategic integrated human resources management model. This exercise confirmed the general weakness of the civil service systems in the region in terms of the level of merit put into practice and the capacity of the system to manage personnel performance. Both the merit and functional capacity indexes show regional averages of around 30 percent of the scale.

Since both indexes yield a broad dispersion of results, it is possible to analyze these two indexes together, and thereby distinguish different degrees of development and integration of the human resources management systems among the states in the region.

Brazil and Chile are the two cases that stand out because of the higher level of development of their civil services. Costa Rica is a special case among the Central American countries. At the other extreme, the most critical situation occurs in the other Central American countries, and in the cases of Bolivia, Ecuador, Paraguay, and Peru. In these countries, politicization is so strong that it is impossible to create a professional civil service, or guarantee recruitment and retention of competent personnel, or implement management mechanisms to influence the working conduct of officials. The other countries (Argentina, Colombia, Mexico, Uruguay, and Venezuela) have partially formed civil service systems that have not achieved consolidation in terms of guarantees of merit or efficient tools to manage the human resources of the state.

Apart from these general trends in national civil services, it is clear that the "bureaucracy" is not homogeneous, but that different types of bureaucracies coexist in each country, each with its own logic, criteria, and roles. These varieties coexist because it has not been possible to fully develop the traditional Weberian model in the region. In many countries, to supplement their own bureaucracies, a strategy of hiring technical teams under more flexible employment schemes has been pursued.

The typology described captures this diversity by crossing two variables: the *autonomy* of each bureaucratic group with respect to political power, particularly in terms of guarantees against possible arbitrariness; and the *technical capacity* to solve problems related to management efficiently. Four bureaucratic types emerge from this interaction: administrative, patronage, parallel, and meritocratic bureaucracies. Each has different characteristics in relation to its possible role in the policymaking process. According to the predominance of the types in each country, the role of the bureaucracy can vary considerably. At one end of the spectrum is the informal veto, either through specific actions to block the design or implementation of a policy or passive resistance by way of organizational culture. At the other end is an active role that can result not only in stimulus for a specific policy, but also in collaboration and cooperation to sustain or improve that policy.

Although the main objective of this typology is descriptive, it implies a preference for the meritocratic model, since that model maximizes the capacity of the bureaucracy and provides the necessary autonomy that protects it from arbitrariness. But this implicit preference does not mean that one can simply extrapolate a lesson about how to develop a reasonably strong, capable, and neutral bureaucracy in Latin America. The typology opens the discussion to explore the complex institutional framework and the deep social, political, and economic patterns that have generated these diverse "configurations";[8] it does not intend to establish what *should be done*.

With this consideration in mind, and given the differing levels of development of civil services and the complex variations in each

---

[8] Interest in the institutional determinants of public policies is increasing, and the perspective of the political economy is particularly interesting in analyzing civil service reforms in Latin America. Some efforts along these lines can be found in Geddes (1994); Heredia (2002); Scartascini (2008); Heredia and Schneider (2003); Spiller and Tommasi (2003); IDB (2005); Iacoviello and Zuvanic (2006); and Bambaci, Spiller, and Tommasi (2007).

national case, what are the prospects for strengthening Latin American civil service systems?

The cases of Brazil and Chile are exceptional in terms of the consistency of the state human resources policy and the level of institutionalization of personnel management. Both these aspects result in a positive evaluation of their possibilities of consolidation as meritocratic bureaucracies. In Central America, Costa Rica is an exception; even without reform initiatives it has had a consistent record of progressive advances in introducing merit criteria into the system, and strong institutionalization of human resources management. Thus the system now characterized as administrative bureaucracy has possibilities of moving toward a meritocratic bureaucracy.

In the group with intermediate development of civil services, Argentina, Uruguay, and Venezuela do not have initiatives to stimulate consolidation of their systems, so the possibility of consolidation is low despite the existence of meritocratic enclaves. These three countries have introduced some level of professionalization into personnel management, and have begun to institutionalize some areas of human resources. Thus there is a base on which to anchor a reform project.

Colombia and Mexico have also achieved some development of their civil services and have meritocratic structures in certain areas, and have better prospects for their consolidation based on reform initiatives in progress. The reasons are different in each case: the strong institutionalization of the human resources function in Colombia, and the political stimulus given to the reform in Mexico, which reverses the weakness of the previous norms and institutions in relation to the civil service.

The countries with the weakest bureaucracies, which feature elements of patronage and strong dependence on parallel structures, include Bolivia, the Dominican Republic, El Salvador, Honduras, Panama, and Paraguay. These countries have no reform initiatives under way, while there are reform movements in Guatemala and Nicaragua. Reform initiatives are also taking place in Ecuador and Peru, which this study identifies as administrative bureaucracies, although they are also affected by elements of patronage. However, the reforms in the countries of this group are considered to have little prospect for success because they are not backed by a certain preexisting normative consistency or by the institutionalization of areas that could lead the way.

The countries of the region have stated their intention to develop meritocratic systems for their personnel management, as established by the Ibero-American Civil Service Charter. There are many starting points for each country, and the priority areas differ according to the level of development of the norms and practices of the civil service.

However, a key aspect to be considered for all the countries of the region is that institutions do not operate in a vacuum. The transformation of civil service systems requires consensus building, above all. The multiplicity of actors involved must be willing and interested in laying the base for a real civil service system in these countries. The only way to guarantee a certain level of legitimacy for civil service systems is to generate a consensus-based strategy that establishes clear rules and is accepted by all actors.

There is a wide gap between the normative view of the expected role of bureaucracies and the existing situation in Latin American countries. However, the stakes for closing that gap, and for improving bureaucracies, are high. As argued, the bureaucracy is a central institution for the democratic system and for governance. Efforts aimed at promoting highly capable and neutral bureaucracies oriented to serving the public interest are critically important to improving the quality of governance and the quality of life of Latin American citizens.

CHAPTER 7

Decentralizing Power in Latin America: The Role of Governors in National Policymaking

Francisco Monaldi

This chapter evaluates the role played by regional players, governors, and regional party leaders in the national policymaking process of Latin America's democracies. It focuses on the institutional determinants of the governors' influence at the national stage, and on the effect that their influence has over the type of policymaking process that develops.[1]

There is an extensive literature studying the recent wave of decentralization in the region (Gibson, 2004; Montero and Samuels, 2004; O'Neill, 2003, 2005). Most of this literature has focused either on the determinants of decentralization or on its effects on the policies that have been decentralized (such as education and health care). There has also been a significant theoretical and comparative literature on the relationship between federalism and the political system, and between federalism and fiscal and economic performance (Rodden, 2004, 2006; Weingast, 2005). There has been relatively less attention paid to the comparative determinants and effects of the role played by regional players in the national policymaking process. The recent literature on Argentina's political system and its fiscal federal arrangement has been a notable exception (Jones et al., 2001, 2002; Spiller and Tommasi, 2003, 2007).[2] Similarly, the literature on Brazilian politics has generated an

---

[1] In this chapter, the expression "regional" is used interchangeably with "subnational" to refer to intermediate levels of government called "states" in places like the United States and Venezuela and "provinces" in places like Argentina and Canada.

[2] This makes sense because it is the country in the region in which governors play the most significant role.

interesting debate on how influential the country's governors are and on how they exert their influence (Samuels and Mainwaring, 2004; Alston et al., 2008). This chapter aims to provide a comparative study of the governors' role in the region, taking advantage of the rich theoretical and empirical literature that exists on the related subjects mentioned above.

Across the region, the role and influence of regional authorities differ dramatically. In Argentina, governors are very significant players, influencing their province's legislative delegation and bargaining with the president to barter congressional votes in exchange for resources. As a result, the country has had a volatile and fragmented policymaking process, with especially negative effects on fiscal performance. Similarly, in Brazil, Mexico, and Venezuela, governors have played a prominent role in some circumstances, sometimes with negative consequences for the fiscal stability of the country. In contrast, during other periods governors have had a very minor role in the design and approval of national policies. In countries like Chile and Uruguay, regional authorities have not played a relevant role in the national policy stage. What explains this variation over time and space? What are the incentives of governors in the national policy game? How do governors play in it? These are the questions this chapter aims to answer in the context of the Latin American region.

The chapter shows how, under certain circumstances, governors have perverse incentives that introduce problematic features into the policymaking process. In particular, it shows that if the institutional framework does not properly solve the *commons problem*—the incentive to over-extract resources from the center to favor regional constituencies—a significant influence of the governors in nationwide policymaking could engender a political system with little intertemporal cooperation and a tendency to generate volatile policies. Moreover, powerful governors could contribute to weakening the degree of nationalization of the party system, inducing a fragmented and unstable party system (Leiras, 2006).

The study proposes that to a large extent the role that governors play in the national policymaking process is determined by the particular configuration of institutions in each country. The key institutional determinants are: the method of selecting regional authorities; the federal or unitary constitutional structure; the federal fiscal arrangement; and the electoral system and party structure. Governors will have relatively little influence on the national political stage if they are: appointed by the president; operating in a unitary political structure, with no territorial legislative chamber; in a country with a low level of expenditure decentralization and a low vertical imbalance; and in an electoral system that promotes presidential coattails and nationalized parties. In order to understand the specific role that governors play, however, it is necessary to analyze the full institutional context. Some individual factors could have a different effect (even the opposite) if combined with other factors.

Regional Authorities and the National Policymaking Process

This section explores the role that subnational authorities, particularly governors, play on the national policy stage, and how their participation transforms the policymaking game. It analyzes the incentive structure and capabilities of subnational actors. In particular, it concentrates on the interaction between governors and presidents in the legislative and fiscal arenas.

In some cases governors have the incentives and the capacities to have a significant influence on the discussion and approval of legislation. In other cases, they do not have the motivation or the influence to do so. The institutional foundations that generate these different results are discussed in the next section.

Political decentralization, through the election of subnational authorities, may well induce many positive effects over democratic governance and the efficient provision of public services. Among other possible advantages, it could bring decision making closer to the citizens, improve accountability, increase innovation and competition between regions, and allow for flexible and tailored policies in heterogeneous societies. Moreover, under certain conditions, federalism has been an effective mechanism to create governmental commitment to property rights, by limiting the power of the national authorities to expropriate investors, helping the development of markets. For example, in the United States, state governments have significant policy autonomy and the existence of a "market-preserving federalism" has been proposed as one of the key institutional foundations for its exceptional record of economic growth (Weingast, 2005). However, it is important to notice that governors in the United States, despite their significant authority in regional policy, play a very limited role in national policymaking.

Notwithstanding the many potential benefits of having elected governors, their influence over national policymaking could promote noncooperative and uncoordinated national policies under certain circumstances. Governors, if elected, have incentives to obtain resources and advantages for their regions potentially at the expense of welfare-maximizing national policies. As a result, if political institutions do not provide the right incentives and effective limits to the power of subnational authorities, the governors may exert a detrimental influence on national policymaking.

The policymaking process in Latin America, particularly at the design and approval stages, is centered on two main actors: the president and the legislature. All countries in Latin America have presidential systems, and presidents are the central players in the national policymaking process. Presidents are generally elected by national popular majorities and are accountable for the effectiveness of national policies, such as macroeconomic policies. Although, the institutional setting could provide some perverse incentives for presidents (such as inducing political fiscal cycles), national leaders generally have incentives to care for polity-wide goals, in contrast to governors. Presidents generally prefer controlling more fiscal resources at the center to accomplish their objectives; they are interested in being able to pass their policy agenda in the legislature; they internalize the national fiscal constraint; they care for the coherence between national and regional policies; and they are interested in achieving effective policy implementation. Still, presidents might also face some perverse incentives with respect to regional governments. For example, they could prefer to transfer politically problematic responsibilities to the subnational authorities, without transferring sufficient resources to attend to them.

As shown in the next section, the incentives of national legislators depend crucially on the electoral and the party systems. The influence of subnational authorities over legislators is one of the most powerful tools they have in national policymaking. Under certain institutional frameworks, governors can have a significant influence over the careers of legislators. As a result, presidents and national party leaders may need to negotiate with regional authorities to obtain a legislative majority to pass a reform.

Regional authorities, like presidents and legislators, have incentives to do whatever is necessary to further their political careers. How they do it depends on the institutional details: for example, if governors are elected or if they are appointed by the president. In contrast to presidents, elected regional authorities are focused on regional issues. As a result, the direct election of governors has several potential public policy advantages. For example, it makes regional governments more responsive to the local electorates and it can encourage federal competition and policy innovation.

Nonetheless, having regional elected governments may generate collective dilemmas in terms of national policymaking. If the institutional framework does not provide incentives, or imposes restrictions that make regional governments internalize the national objectives, governors may be tempted to use their bargaining power to obtain resources and secure their career advancement at the expense of desirable national policy goals, such as fiscal stability. For example, governors would like to obtain the political benefits of spending revenues collected at the center, without the political costs of collecting them. As a result of this lack of internalization of the national budget restriction, governors have incentives to overspend the *common pool* resources. Moreover, if they are facing fiscal difficulties, governors might pressure the central government to bail them out. Since a region's default could be costly for the national government, under certain institutional circumstances, the central power would not be able to credibly commit to refrain from bailing out a province. Thus, this situation creates a soft budget constraint that in turn provides incentives for regional profligacy. In addition to the *fiscal commons problem*, the negotiations between governors and the national executive generate difficulties for the coordination of a variety of policies, particularly during the implementation phase.

A crucial variable promoting the commons problem is the extent to which regional governments depend on central revenues for their expenditures. A high *vertical imbalance*—the difference between expenditures and regionally generated revenues—induces high incentives for regional players to invest time and resources in order to influence national policymaking. Argentina and the United States, both highly decentralized federal countries, differ crucially in this respect. U.S. governors face a budget financed mostly by statewide taxes and have significant limits on deficit spending. In contrast, governors in Argentina finance most of their spending with resources from the central government and face a softer budget constraint. As a result, one of the main activities of Argentinean governors is playing the fiscal federal game, while in the

United States, governors focus more on developing regional (state-level) sources of finance.

Even if governors are perfect agents of their regional electorates, the fiscal commons problem may arise from a combination of a high vertical imbalance and a perverse federal fiscal structure. Regional electorates would like their governor to extract as much as possible from the center and tax them as little as possible. Similarly, regional voters may want their governor to veto important national reforms that affect them. If the institutional framework provides governors with veto power, they may obstruct welfare-maximizing national policies. As a result, absent the right incentive structure, improving democracy at the regional level does not necessarily solve the coordination problem.

The coordination problems might be compounded if the governors face little competition in their regions and are capable of extracting high rents from holding on to power. In such a case, their perverse role in national politics would reinforce their hold on power as regional *caudillos*.[3] That seems to be the case in Argentina, where governors use their manipulation of the national fiscal game to increase their hold on regional power, and in turn use their regional dominance to control the nominations and the careers of national legislators (Ardanaz, Leiras, and Tommasi, 2009).

To further their political careers, governors desire to obtain financial resources to implement their preferred policies and increase their constituent support, but they may also need political support from the center to win regional elections. As a result, the electoral system and the party structure could affect the incentives that the governors have, making them internalize the costs of their lack of cooperation with the national leaders. In some well-functioning federal systems, such as Germany, strong and disciplined parties typically play this crucial role. For example, governors of the same party of a popular national executive would confront the electoral consequences of defecting from the national party line. In addition, if the lack of cooperation from a governor of the same party as the federal administration results in policy failure at the

---

[3] *Caudillo* is a Spanish word usually describing political–military leaders at the head of (often local) authoritarian powers. It is sometimes translated as "warlord" or "strongman". The root of *caudillismo* lies in Spanish colonial policy of supplementing small cadres of professional, full-time soldiers with large militia forces recruited from local populations to maintain public order.

national level, the negative effects on its party label might generate a negative impact over his electoral support (Wibbels, 2005).

As argued, governors may have incentives to over-extract resources from the center and block legislative reforms that they do not like, but that does not mean that they have the capacity to do so. Such capacity depends crucially on the influence that regional authorities have over congress and the president. Governors can play a significant role in the national legislative process if the institutional setting, as well as other factors, provides them with the capacity to pressure legislators, and thus influence the legislative agenda or veto the approval of federal legislation. If governors control the nomination of legislators for reelection or have some control over the legislators' future political careers, for example, they can influence legislative decision making significantly. As a result, legislative actions would favor the interests of regional authorities instead of the objectives of national party leaders or presidents.

Regional leaders trade the votes they "control" in the legislature with presidents and national party leaders in exchange for fiscal resources or other desirable goodies. When the main political transaction to obtain a legislative majority for reforming the policy status quo is based on the exchange of fiscal resources for legislative votes, the national policymaking process becomes a vast commons problem.

If the national legislative process can be influenced by governors via the control of their regions' legislative delegation, the transaction costs of legislating may also increase significantly. Compare such a scenario with the one arising from repeated bargaining between a few national party leaders who control their parties' congressional delegation, as has been the case in Chile, Costa Rica, and Uruguay (or Venezuela before 1989). In the latter scenario, the probability of reaching a cooperative federal policymaking process is much higher due to the lower number of actors and the polity-wide incentives of the main actors.

On the other extreme, compare the governors' control over congressional delegations with the more decentralized negotiation with individual legislators, as is the case in the U.S. Congress. In contrast to individual legislators, governors may constitute veto players if they control a significant block of legislators (as in Argentina, and during specific periods in Brazil). In the United States, weak parties do not translate into influential governors because neither the national party leaders nor the governors control the nominations.

To understand the nature of the votes for resources transaction, take the example of Venezuela before 1989. Governors were appointed by the president, while congressional delegations were tightly controlled by national leaders. As a result, governors did not have any influence on the legislature and the fiscal negotiations faced no regional commons problem. In contrast, during the 1990s, with the direct election of governors and the decline in control over the legislators by the national party leaders (due also to changes in the electoral system), fiscal reforms increasingly had to be negotiated with the governors. As a result, in order to pass fiscal reforms to reduce the large fiscal deficits at the center, new fiscal transfers to the regions also had to be passed, partially offsetting the reforms' purpose.

Similarly, in Brazil in the 1980s, governors exerted significant influence over the legislative process, blocking fiscal reforms and borrowing on the expectation of federal bailouts, which induced macroeconomic instability. In the 1990s, institutional reforms that significantly limited the influence of governors reduced the tendency toward fiscal profligacy. In contrast, in Argentina, during the 1990s, the control of governors over the legislative process made it particularly difficult to reach a fiscal bargain to control of the large fiscal deficits, contributing to the macroeconomic debacle that ensued.

Governors may have another bargaining chip when negotiating directly with the president, if they have autonomous agenda control over certain policy domains that are important to the national executive. This is particularly relevant in federal countries. In addition, governors may obstruct the implementation of some national policies, such as social policies that are executed by the central government in cooperation with the regional governments. Finally, governors may use their capacity to affect national policy goals, such as macroeconomic stability, as a bargaining tool with presidents. For example, they can affect the national economy by abusing their fiscal or quasi-monetary policy authority.

In essence, presidents want to get support for the approval of laws, policy coherence, effectiveness, and fiscal responsibility from the regional leaders. To the extent that regional leaders can provide or withhold votes in the legislature, cooperate (or not) on the implementation of national policies, and cooperate (or not) with macroeconomic stability, they will be able to extract resources and career opportunities from the president and the national party leaders.

Institutional Foundations of the Role of Regional Authorities in the National Policymaking Process

The literature showing how political institutions shape the policymaking process and its policy outcomes is growing (see, for example, Haggard and McCubbins, 2001; Stepan, 2004b; Spiller and Tommasi, 2007; Stein et al., 2008). This section explores how the institutional framework of a country interacts with other factors to shape the different roles of subnational authorities in the national policymaking process.[4]

Political institutions and the structure of the party system are fundamental determinants of the role that subnational authorities play at the national stage. They shape the incentives, capabilities, and opportunities of subnational actors, determining the relative bargaining power that these actors have. Institutions and party structures also determine the number of effective veto points in the policymaking structure that arise from the existence of subnational levels of government (Stepan, 2004a, 2004b), and the degree of cooperation between national and subnational authorities in the national policymaking process (Spiller, Stein, and Tommasi, 2008).

The most salient institutional and party variables determining the willingness and ability of subnational political actors to influence national policymaking are: the method of selecting subnational authorities; the existence of a federal constitutional structure, including territorial bicameralism; the existence of malapportionment; the federal fiscal arrangement; and the electoral and party system. Other factors such as the presidential powers and the internal structure of the legislature may also have some impact.

All these institutional and structural variables do not operate in isolation. A given feature may have different effects—and sometimes even opposite ones—depending on the full institutional context. For example, having a single closed and blocked list proportional system for electing the national legislators will have radically different effects if governors are elected than if they are not. If governors are appointed

---

[4] Inevitably, the problem of endogeneity arises in this type of analysis. For example, in the short term it might be reasonable to take the borrowing authority of subnational authorities as given, and analyze how it affects their bargaining power with the national executive. However, using a longer-term perspective, it becomes evident that the borrowing autonomy is itself, to a large extent, a result of the role that regional actors play in the political system. As will be shown, in the last decade there have been significant changes in the borrowing autonomy of subnational governments in the region.

(as in Venezuela before 1989), this electoral system strengthens national party leaders. On the contrary, if they are elected (as in Argentina), this will tend to strengthen the governors' role as party leaders. Similarly, the effects of having elected governors could differ depending on whether the electoral system is majoritarian with single-member districts (as in the United States) or proportional with closed lists (as in Argentina).

Although this chapter focuses on democratic political regimes, it is important to acknowledge the influence of regime type over the role played by regional leaders. Authoritarian and semi-authoritarian regimes have been generally characterized by the centralization of power and the suppression of autonomous subnational power. The various military regimes in Argentina and Brazil, as well as the elected hegemonic regimes of Perón in Argentina, Fujimori in Peru, Chávez in Venezuela, and the PRI in Mexico, all have recentralized political power to some extent. There have been some exceptional cases, like Brazil and Mexico, where the transition toward open democracy was initiated with competitive elections at the subnational level, resulting in a significant transformation of the policymaking game (Ochoa-Reza, 2004; Samuels, 2004).

Method of Selecting Subnational Authorities

Two methods are generally used for selecting governors: popular election and appointment by the president. The popular election of governors provides them with incentives and tools to have a more relevant role in the national policymaking process. Competitively elected governors have incentives to cater to their constituency and pursue regional goals at the expense of national objectives.[5] In contrast, when subnational authorities are appointed and removed by the president, they have strong incentives to behave as agents of the national executive.

In general, the evidence shows that once elected, subnational authorities gain a powerful regional constituency, which makes political recentralization relatively costly under democracy. However, as the regional examples mentioned above and the case of Putin in Russia illustrate, semi-democratic regimes have been able to significantly diminish the role of governors on the national democratic stage.

---

[5] Even if they cannot be reelected, they still have similar regional incentives in order to advance their political careers in other national or regional positions.

Federal Constitutional Structure (and Territorial Bicameralism)

In general, governors play a more significant role in formally federal countries. However, having a formally federal constitution is not a necessary or sufficient condition for subnational political influence. The effects of the federal label become relevant only when fundamental elements of a federal structure are in place, such as elected subnational authorities and territorial bicameralism.

Governors can be powerful, regardless of the constitutional label, if the specific institutions and the party structure establish the incentives and opportunities for the regional leaders to exercise influence.[6] There are examples of countries that are not formally federal or even democratic, but which have provided significant power and authority to the subnational levels of government (such as China in the last two decades). Moreover, there are examples of formally federal countries, such as Mexico and Venezuela, in which governors became significant players only after they began being competitively elected. In addition, the robustly federal structure of the U.S. Constitution, which provides very significant regional (in that case, state) autonomy, induces a moderate role of governors in national policymaking. However, as discussed below, some specific institutional features that are typical of federalism seem to have an important impact on the influence of governors. As the Latin American evidence shows, once the subnational authorities become elected, the federal features typically become "activated."

Of particular relevance is the fact that federal countries usually have two chambers in the legislature and one of them, generally called the senate, is based on territorial representation of subnational units rather than on population.[7] The composition of the federal territorial chamber is defined by a different electorate from the one electing the president or the population-based chamber, creating a potential

---

[6] The classic work on federalism by William Riker (1964) claimed that the existence of a federal structure is not relevant for the national policymaking process. According to this view, which is supported by recent research, it is the party structure that defines the influence of regional authorities over national policy (Díaz-Cayeros, 2004; Stepan, 2004a).

[7] There are few exceptions to the rule. One is Venezuela after the 1999 Constitution promoted by President Chávez, which made the legislature unicameral. Another is Colombia where the 1991 Constitution made the senate elected in a nationwide district. In spite of that change in formal institutions, former practices have carried through and many senators are still elected from narrow geographical constituencies (Crisp and Ingall, 2002).

"separation of purpose" between them. As a result, the senate can become a separate institutional veto point (Stepan, 2004b).[8] This veto point can be particularly relevant if the senate has symmetric responsibilities with the lower chamber (Stepan, 2004b).[9] In addition, the electoral district of senators typically coincides with that of the governors, increasing the electoral connection between them.[10]

Malapportionment

Malapportionment refers to the overrepresentation of underpopulated provinces in the legislature; that is, the extent to which the political representation in the legislature violates the "one person–one vote" maxim. Malapportionment strengthens the power of subnational legislators from the less populated areas (which constitute the majority of the regions). As a consequence, overrepresented states typically receive a disproportionately high share of per capita resources, controlling for other factors (Kraemer, 1997; Gibson, Calvo, and Falleti, 2004; Snyder and Samuels, 2004). There are at least two channels by which this disproportionality may result from the national policymaking game. First, if presidents have discretion over the resource allocation and governors control their region's legislative delegation, it would be cheaper for the president to "buy" the support of governors from the small over-represented regions. Similarly, if the legislature controls the expenditure allocation, legislators from over-represented regions in malapportioned legislatures can obtain more per capita resources.

The existence of malapportionment, combined with the presence of powerful governors and regionally motivated legislators, could have a significant effect on the policymaking process, introducing a rural bias and representing a significant constraint on reforms supported by large national majorities.[11]

---

[8] In the United States, the president is elected by an electoral college, which reduces the differential in the electors of congress and the president.

[9] For example, in Brazil the senate typically constitutes a relevant additional veto player.

[10] In Argentina, until the mid-1990s, national senators were elected by the regional legislative assemblies, where governors had a significant influence. As a result, governors and regional bosses controlled the senate delegation (Jones et al., 2002). This pattern has largely continued even after the change to direct election (Ardanaz, Leiras, and Tommasi,, 2009).

[11] Stepan (2004b) argues that in the case of Argentina and Brazil, this allows small regional minorities to have a potential veto over national policymaking.

The Federal Fiscal Arrangement

The incentives of subnational actors are significantly shaped by the ways in which they can fund their spending. The fiscal federal rules are a crucial determinant of the role played by subnational actors in the national policymaking process. Even though, these rules are themselves a result of the higher-level policymaking game between national and subnational officials, analytically they can be considered fixed in the short run.[12]

Five basic elements of the federal fiscal rules determine the incentives and opportunities of regional actors: the taxing authority of subnational governments; the degree of expenditure decentralization; the relationship between regional expenditures and regionally collected revenues (or vertical imbalance); the borrowing autonomy of subnational governments; and the discretion over the central government transfers to the regions (Stein, 1999; Haggard and Webb, 2004).

In particular, the federal fiscal rules determine how "hard" the regional budget constraint is; that is, if governors face a real budget restriction, or if in case of fiscal difficulties they can readily reach to the federal government for a bailout. If governors face a "soft" budget constraint, they have the incentives and opportunity to be fiscally irresponsible. The existence of a soft budget constraint provides bargaining power to the governors because they can credibly affect the fiscal performance of the country.

In addition, a significant taxing authority and a high degree of expenditure decentralization provide regional governments with autonomy and resources that can be used to influence other actors in the policymaking game. Thus governors can become relevant political players, offering career opportunities and campaign resources to legislators, and even campaign funding for the presidential reelection campaign.

The existence of a high vertical imbalance—the degree in which the regions are financed with central revenues—makes the regional governments highly dependent on the national government. This dependency might be used as a powerful bargaining tool by the national authorities.

---

[12] See Tommasi (2006) for an account of the coevolution of and interaction among federal fiscal arrangements and national policymaking in Argentina.

However, it could be a double-edged sword for presidents because the imbalance also creates incentives for subnational authorities to spend without the political costs of raising revenues. As a result, a high vertical imbalance combined with a soft budget constraint provides subnational governments with a tool to make the national executive hostage to their fiscal profligacy. Moreover, if governors control the legislative delegation, they can extract more national fiscal resources in exchange for legislative votes.

The discretionary nature of central government transfers, although generally favorable to the president, also constitutes a mixed blessing for him or her. On the one hand, the discretionary use of funds allows the president to use them to negotiate effectively with the governors. On the other hand, the more discretionary the system of transfers is, the less capable the president is to credibly commit not to bail out the regions, and the more politicized the fiscal game becomes. In countries like Argentina and Venezuela, most transfers are automatic; that is, nondiscretionary. In such cases, the problem for the national authorities is the lack of flexibility that automatic transfers bring to fiscal policy.[13]

The Electoral and Party System

The electoral rules and the party structure are also very important because they provide the incentive framework for national legislators. The electoral system and the party structure may provide governors with powerful tools to influence national legislators. The influence of governors in the nomination process and the careers of national legislators, the concurrency between the subnational and national legislative elections, and other factors that favor denationalized and decentralized party structures, potentially increase the power of governors.

The degree of nationalization of the party system—the extent to which parties' support is relatively constant across the different provinces—affects the prospects of influence by regional party leaders. If

---

[13] In Argentina, although the largest portion of transfers are automatic, there is still substantial room for discretion at the margin. That is the source of substantial gaming and has important effects on political behavior. Among other things, it influences the selection of governors toward types able to play this game, not necessarily the most competent or most honest characters (Jones, Meloni, and Tommasi, 2009).

the party system is concentrated in a few nationalized and centrally disciplined parties, the role of regional leaders generally will be limited (Leiras, 2006).

Alternatively, if the party system is regionalized or fragmented and national authorities cannot control the party's delegation to congress, the potential for regional leaders to exert influence on the national policy stage increases. The above characteristics are significantly determined by the electoral system and the intraparty electoral rules (see discussion that follows). In addition, the party structure is determined by other exogenous factors such as the social, economic, and geographical cleavages present in the country.

Control of Nominations and Careers. Among the most powerful tools to affect policy design and approval that regional authorities have at their disposal are control of the nominations for national legislative elections and the influence they have over the political careers of national legislators. If the candidates' nomination and order in the ballot are decided at the subnational level, governors can use their political and financial resources to influence the election of legislators. In that case, the regional congressional delegation to the national legislature has incentives to vote more according to the governor's interests than to the national party leaders' or president's directives.

Connection between the National and Subnational Elections. The timing between national and subnational elections is another institutional element that has significant effects on the role of governors in national policymaking, largely through its influence on the party structure. If elections for the legislature occur concurrently with the subnational elections and separately from presidential elections, the legislators' vote will be influenced by the coattails from the governors' votes.[14] In contrast, if the national legislative elections are always held concurrently with the presidential elections and separate from the regional

---

[14] In the case of Argentina, until 2004 subnational governments set the dates of gubernatorial elections. This allowed each governor to pick and choose whether to coattail with national elections or not depending on their political convenience (Calvo and Micozzi, 2005; Ardanaz, Leiras, and Tommasi, 2009). A similar practice was used once in Venezuela by the national legislature to maximize gubernatorial coattails (see discussion below).

elections, the presidential coattails will affect the legislative election results.[15]

In addition to the timing connection, the coattails will also be influenced by the structure of the ballot. If the ballot is structured to maximize the connection between the presidential and the legislative vote, presidential coattails could be stronger.[16] The key issue is which coattails are more relevant for the legislators to get elected: the presidential or the gubernatorial coattails. Other things equal, governors will have a stronger bargaining position in the national policymaking process if their coattails are the most relevant.

Additional Elements of the Electoral and Party System. The electoral rules affect the degree of nationalization, fragmentation, and discipline of the party system (Geddes and Benton, 1997; Cox, 1999; see also Chapter 2, this volume). Fragmentation and lack of discipline in the party system might reinforce the power of regional authorities. High district magnitude proportional systems, not concurrent with the presidential elections, with low electoral thresholds, would tend to produce more fragmented party systems. An open list or single-member district system would tend to induce a lower degree of party discipline. Party fragmentation and lack of discipline could make it difficult for the president to obtain a legislative majority. In such cases, if governors can control legislators, their influence over national policy will be magnified, particularly in cases where a few regional delegations are pivotal in the legislature (Geddes and Benton, 1997).

If the electoral system—or other factors—encourages the existence and survival of regional parties, and if those regional parties are pivotal, the power of some governors and regional bosses who lead this type of party could be quite significant. In some countries, registration

---

[15] "Coattails" refers to the positive effect over a candidate's vote exerted by a copartisan elected concurrently. For example, if a governor is very popular, the high turnout of voters in favor of his reelection would benefit his copartisans.

[16] For example, in Venezuela before 1989, the presidential vote and all the legislative seats were elected through the use of cards that were placed next to each other in the ballot—and both had the photo of the presidential candidate (without the names of the legislative candidates). However, Leiras (2006) finds that in the case of Argentina when elections for governors are held concurrently with presidential elections, the gubernatorial coattails are more powerful than the presidential coattails. Samuels (2004) has a similar finding for Brazil. This occurs despite a ballot structure that should favor presidential coattails. These studies suggest that in countries where the governors are powerful, the gubernatorial coattails are significant.

requirements make it very difficult for regional parties to survive. In other countries (like Argentina), the electoral system makes it easy for regional (provincial) parties to survive. As a result, some provincial parties have survived for decades controlling certain regions and sometimes extracting significant resources from the center when they have had a pivotal role in the national legislature. Similarly, in Venezuela after the direct election of regional authorities was introduced in 1989, the party system became more fragmented, and regional parties began to play a significant role in the national policymaking process.

Other Variables

From the discussion of the institutional elements relevant to this study, one conclusion can be made: any factor that significantly modifies the bargaining power of either the national actors (president, national party leaders) or subnational actors (governors, regional party leaders) can have an impact on the policymaking role that subnational players have in a specific country. As a result, idiosyncratic factors that significantly strengthen the negotiation power of one side may have a large impact on the national policymaking. For example, presidents with high popular support due to their ability to stop hyperinflation (such as Menem in Argentina, and Cardoso in Brazil) may be in a better negotiating position with legislators, limiting the potential influence of governors. In contrast, weak and unpopular presidents could face a harder time limiting the governors' influence.

Some presidential powers can be particularly useful to negotiate with legislators or regional governors. For example, if the president has a line-item veto over the budget approval, he or she can selectively use it to obtain the support of legislators looking to obtain pork for their regions (as in Brazil). Similarly if the president has wide discretion over some regionally allocated expenditure, he or she can use it to negotiate the vote of a regionally based politician (legislator or governor).

The rules for designing and approving legislation can also be a factor strengthening the national party leaders and limiting the power of regional leaders. For example, the internal rules of the legislature could provide party leaders with tools for disciplining their party's congressional delegation, curtailing the centrifugal influence of regional leaders, as seems to be the case in Brazil and Colombia.

Comparing the Role of Regional Authorities in Latin America

Despite a general trend toward political and fiscal decentralization during the last two decades, there are still substantial differences in the role and influence of subnational authorities across Latin America. In almost all countries mayors are now elected, and regional authorities (governors) are elected in a majority of the countries. However, in some countries governors play a more important role in national policymaking than in others, and the influence of governors in each country has changed over time.

Table 7.1 compares six countries. It shows whether the role played by governors in selected countries has been high, moderate, or low over time and summarizes the institutional determinants of that role. Argentina's democracy has been an outlier, where governors have played a very significant and systematic role in national policymaking, particularly through their influence over national legislators. Subnational influence has generally translated into negative effects on fiscal performance and macroeconomic stability, as well as on the quality of policies (Spiller and Tommasi, 2007) and of democracy (Ardanaz, Leiras, and Tommasi, 2009; Jones, Meloni, and Tommasi, 2009). Similarly, in Brazil in the 1980s and early 1990s, governors played a perverse role by obstructing macroeconomic reform. However, in the Brazilian case the institutional reforms introduced by President Cardoso significantly diminished the perverse influence of governors over the national policymaking.

In Venezuela and Mexico, governors increased their influence in the 1990s; nonetheless, their role in national policymaking is much more limited than in Argentina or Brazil. Moreover, in Venezuela, the recentralization of power by President Chávez has dramatically reduced the influence that governors had in the 1990s. In Colombia, the influence of governors increased once they were elected rather than appointed, but is still low compared to the federal countries—even though regional politicians have traditionally played a prominent role in Colombia's congress.

In the rest of Latin America, the influence of governors is very low or nonexistent, although it can be expected to increase in countries where election of governors has recently replaced appointment, such as Bolivia, Paraguay, and Peru. In Table 7.1, Chile is presented as a representative of the countries in the region in which regional authorities do not play a role in the national policymaking process.

TABLE 7.1   The Influence of Governors and Determinants of That Influence, Selected Latin American Countries

	Argentina	Brazil	Chile	Colombia	Mexico	Venezuela
Influence of governors	High	High before mid-1990s; Moderate thereafter	No influence	Low	Moderate	No influence before 1989 Moderate in 1990s Low after 2000
Governors elected	Yes, since 1983	Yes, since 1982	No	Yes, since 1991	Yes, competitively since 1990s	Yes, since 1989
Formally federal	Yes	Yes	No	No	Yes	Yes
Territorial bicameralism	Yes	Yes	Yes	No	Yes	No
Malapportionment	High	High	High	Very low	Low	Moderate
Degree of expenditure decentralization	High	High	Low	High	Moderate	Moderate
Vertical imbalance	High	Moderate	High	Moderate	High	High
Borrowing autonomy	High	High	No	Low	Low	No
Governors or president coattails are/were significant (concurrency)	Both governors and presidents, depending on circumstances	Governors, in 1986 and 1990; After 1994, presidents	Presidents have big coattails	No	Presidents and partially governors	Governors only in 1998; Presidents until 2000

(continued on next page)

TABLE 7.1   The Influence of Governors and Determinants of That Influence, Selected Latin American Countries (continued)

	Argentina	Brazil	Chile	Colombia	Mexico	Venezuela
Influence of governors over nomination/election of legislators	High	Moderate; Declined after 1994	Low	Moderate	Moderate	Low before 1993; High in 1990s; Moderate after 2000
Influence of governors over future careers of legislators	High	High	Low	Moderate, increasing	High, increasing after 1990	Low before 1989; High in 1990s; Moderate after 2000
Governors are major contenders for presidency	Yes	Yes	No	Yes, after 1991	Yes, especially since 1990s	Yes, after 1989
Degree of nationalization of party system	Low	Low	Moderate	Moderate	Moderate	High before 1990; Low in 1990s; High since 2005
Importance of regional (provincial) parties	Moderate	Low	No	No	No	No before 1989; Moderate thereafter

Source: Author's compilations.

Selecting Subnational Authorities in the Region

In Latin America, governors are elected in Argentina, Bolivia, Brazil, Colombia, Mexico, Paraguay, and Peru. Argentina and Brazil have a history of electing governors for close to a century, with repeated interruptions under the military regimes. In Colombia, Paraguay, and Venezuela, governors have been elected for a little more than a decade. In Mexico, despite a long history of regional elections, such elections became competitive only starting in 1989. In Peru, governors were elected for the first time in 1990, but two years later, during President Fujimori's administration, provincial governments were abolished. In 2002, regional elections were reinstated. Bolivia began electing governors only in 2006. Until recently in Ecuador, provincial *prefectos* were elected, but governors were appointed.[17] In Uruguay *intendentes* are elected, but there are no governors.[18] In other countries, including Chile and Costa Rica, the president continues to appoint the governors. In some of the smaller countries, there are no regional executives.

The empirical evidence in Latin America supports the notion that only when governors are elected do they have the incentives and capabilities to affect national policy. In all the countries in which governors play a significant role, they are popularly elected. In fact, the countries where governors have been elected for the longest period of time, such as Argentina and Brazil, are the ones where they have played the most significant role. In countries where they have always been appointed, such as Chile and Ecuador, governors have generally had a minor role in the national policymaking process (Eaton, 2004a, 2004b; Mejía Acosta et al., 2008).

Likewise, in countries in which governors were previously appointed and became elected, the power and significance of governors have by and large increased appreciably. For example, in Venezuela, governors had been freely appointed and removed by the president throughout its democratic history (1958–88). In that period they had a minimal role in the national policymaking process and were agents of the central executive.

---

[17] Until the 2008 Constitution was enacted, there was some confusing overlap between the authority of *prefectos* (elected provincial authorities) and governors (appointed provincial authorities). The 2008 Constitutions unified the authority on elected governors.

[18] *Intendentes* are the municipal (*departamentos*) executives. However, given the small size of Uruguay, some municipalities represent a relatively large portion of territory or population.

In contrast, since 1989 when they became popularly elected, governors have increasingly played a more important role in the legislative process. They have also become leading contenders for the presidential elections (Monaldi et al., 2008). In Colombia, a less dramatic transformation in the role of governors also started with their popular election in 1992 (Cárdenas, Junguito, and Pachón, 2008). In Mexico, governors have been formally elected for decades, having some influence in the ruling PRI internal politics, but they became much more influential in the 1990s when regional elections became free and competitive (Díaz-Cayeros, 2004; Ochoa-Reza, 2004; Santín Del Río, 2004).

Still, as argued, the degree to which having elected subnational authorities matters depends on the interaction with other institutional features of the country and the party structure. For example, in Chile and Uruguay, where in the last decade subnational authorities have become directly elected (at the municipal and departmental levels, respectively), the existence of centralized party structures that control all nominations has limited the political effect of subnational elections, according to Eaton (2004b). However, even in these countries, elections have to some extent weakened the "traditional sources of national control over sub-national officials" (Eaton, 2004b, p. 19).

Federal versus Unitary Countries

Only four countries in the region have a constitutional federal structure: Argentina, Brazil, Mexico, and Venezuela. The rest are formally unitary, even though some are relatively decentralized in practice, like Bolivia and Colombia.

During the last decade, in the four federal countries, governors have played a more significant role in the national policymaking process relative to the other countries in the region. However, this fact should not be interpreted to mean that having a de jure federal structure is a necessary or sufficient condition for subnational political power. In Mexico and Venezuela until the 1980s, power was extremely centralized at the national level. Then, in both countries in the 1990s, without a formal change in the constitutional structure, there was a significant change in the role of subnational authorities in the policymaking process.

In the case of Venezuela, the change after 1989 can be largely attributed to the election of governors and mayors. In the case of Mexico, it can be mostly attributed to the opening of the formerly hegemonic party regime. In fact, some authors have argued that these two countries should not have been considered federal before the recent institutional changes that allowed popular election of governors (Stepan, 2004a).

The key point that these examples show is that the decisive factor is not whether the constitution defines the country as federal or unitary, but whether the specific institutions (federal or not) and the party structure establish incentives and opportunities for the regional leaders to exercise influence in the national policymaking process.[19]

Territorial Bicameralism and High Malapportionment

In Latin America, nine countries have bicameral legislatures—Argentina, Bolivia, Brazil, Chile, Colombia, the Dominican Republic, Mexico, Paraguay, and Uruguay—including three of the four federal countries. Territorial bicameralism has been the norm in federal countries. Since 1999, Venezuela has been the only federal country in the region, and one of the few in the world, that is not bicameral.[20] In some unitary countries like Colombia, Paraguay, and Uruguay, the second chamber is not structured based on territorial representation.

Territorial bicameralism has had different effects depending on other elements of the electoral and party systems. When the party system has been relatively concentrated, centralized, nationalized, and disciplined, as in Chile, Uruguay, and Venezuela before 1989, and Mexico before 1997, the effect of the separation of powers between chambers and the president has been minimized by the unity of purpose. In those cases, the senate generally has not represented an additional veto point.

In contrast, in Argentina and Brazil, the territorial chamber has been a significant veto player in which the regional leaders have had a significant influence. In Argentina, until the mid-1990s, the national senators were elected by the regional legislative assemblies, where governors had a significant influence. As a result, governors and regional bosses controlled the province's senate delegation. Even today with the

---

[19] As argued, in other regions of the world, there are examples of countries that are not formally federal or even democratic, but that have provided significant power and authority to the subnational levels of government (for example, China in the last two decades).

[20] Before 1999, Venezuela had a territorially based senate.

direct election of the senators, regional authorities exert a large influence (Ardanaz, Leiras, and Tommasi, 2009). In Brazil, the powerful senate has also served as a vehicle for the governors' influence.

As explained, the territorial chambers typically have high malapportionment. For example, in the upper chambers of Argentina, Brazil, and Mexico (as in the United States), the least populated states have the same representation as the highly populated states. As a result, in Argentina, one vote in the province of Tierra del Fuego is equivalent to 180 votes in the province of Buenos Aires, in terms of its representation in the senate. Similarly, one vote in the state of Roraima in Brazil is equivalent to 144 votes in the state of São Paulo (Gibson, Calvo, and Falleti, 2004).

The *malapportionment index* reflects the percentage of seats that are not allocated equally among the voters (see Figure 7.1, for the senate, and Figure 7.2, for the lower chamber). An index of zero means that all seats are allocated with equal representation. An index of 0.5 means that 50 percent of the seats are given to regions that would have not received them if equally allocated according to the population (Snyder and Samuels, 2004). As can be seen in Figure 7.1, Argentina with an index of 0.49, and Brazil with an index of 0.40, had the highest malapportionment in the senate. In contrast, Mexico had the least malapportioned territorial chamber, with an index of 0.23. Notice that the nonterritorially based senates, such as those of Colombia, Paraguay, and Uruguay, have a malapportionment index of zero. This is a result of the fact that these chambers are elected using only one national electoral district.

A more surprising fact, shown in Figure 7.2, is the significance of malapportionment in the population-based lower chambers. In Argentina, Bolivia, Brazil, Chile, Colombia, and Ecuador, more than 10 percent or more of the lower chamber is malapportioned. This is a result, in part, of the existence of lower and upper limits to the number of deputies that a certain region may have.[21]

Federal Fiscal Arrangements

Of the six countries with higher expenditure decentralization in Latin America as of 1995, four were the federal countries in which governors

---

[21] In addition, it may be the result of not adjusting for the population migration between regions, typically from rural to urban areas (Snyder and Samuels, 2004).

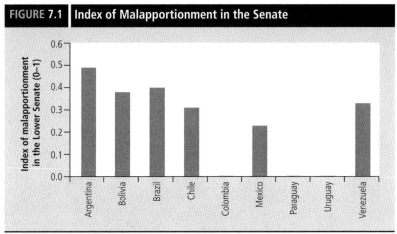

FIGURE 7.1 | Index of Malapportionment in the Senate

Source: Snyder and Samuels (2004).
Index = 0 to 1

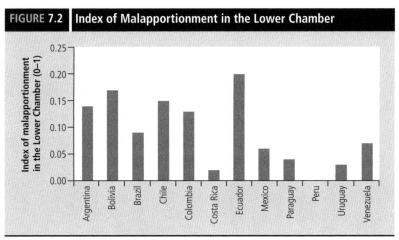

FIGURE 7.2 | Index of Malapportionment in the Lower Chamber

Source: Snyder and Samuels (2004).
Index = 0 to 1

played a significant role at the national stage: Argentina, Brazil, Mexico, and Venezuela. The other two were unitary: Bolivia and Colombia (see Figure 7.3). Four of the top five were federal as of 2004, this time with the exception of Colombia (see Figure 7.4). However, in Colombia regional politicians play a relatively influential role.

The vertical imbalance, the portion of regional expenditures financed by the center, is highest in Venezuela, Chile, and Mexico, followed

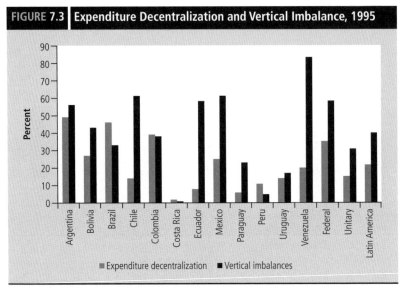

FIGURE 7.3 | Expenditure Decentralization and Vertical Imbalance, 1995

Source: Stein (1999).
Expenditure decentralization (%) = Subnational/total government spending
Vertical imbalance (%) = Intergovernmental transfers/subnational total revenues

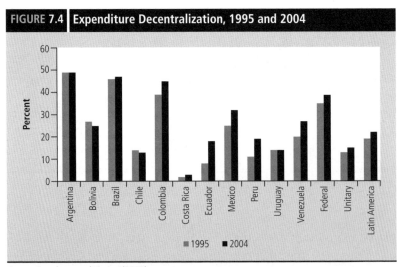

FIGURE 7.4 | Expenditure Decentralization, 1995 and 2004

Source: Daughters and Harper (2007).
Expenditure decentralization (%) = Subnational/total government spending

by Ecuador and Argentina (see Figure 7.3). In Chile and Ecuador, the low levels of expenditure decentralization and the existence of appointed governors greatly limit the relevance of the fiscal commons. In Mexico and Venezuela, the still moderate levels of expenditure decentralization also reduce the magnitude of the commons problem. In Brazil, although expenditure decentralization is quite high, the vertical imbalance is moderate, making the states less dependent on the center, and thus limiting the perverse incentives of the common pool. In contrast, Argentina has both high expenditure decentralization and a high vertical imbalance, maximizing the perverse incentives for powerful governors.

Moreover, the combination of a high vertical imbalance and high expenditure decentralization with significant influence of the governors over congressional delegations creates the conditions for making the fiscal federal game a transaction of trading resources for votes, as has been the case in Argentina (and to a lesser extent in Brazil during the 1980s and Venezuela during the 1990s). In Colombia the vertical imbalance is lower, as is the influence of governors over legislators; as a result, there are fewer incentives for this type of transaction.

Electoral System and Party Structure

As explained, the electoral system and party structure are key determinants of the role of governors in national politics. The discussion that follows describes specific elements in selected countries of the region: the governors' influence over the legislators' nominations and careers; the importance of gubernatorial coattails (concurrency and ballot structure); the degree of nationalization of the party system; and the prominence of regional parties. Across the region, these dimensions vary significantly.

In Argentina, regional party leaders have a significant influence in the nomination process of national legislators. Nominations are decided at the provincial level by primaries, assembly elections, or elite agreement. Regional party bosses are the key players in the nomination process; in particular, ruling governors are usually able to impose their candidates (De Luca, Jones, and Tula, 2002). The combination of control over nominations with a closed list proportional electoral system gives governors a powerful tool to discipline their legislative delegation to the national congress. Moreover, since governors control a large part of the budget, they can provide future career opportunities to legislators.

In Brazil, congressional candidates are typically nominated by regional conventions in which governors have had a moderate influence, but such influence has been declining since the 1990s. In contrast to those in Argentina, Brazil's legislators have some autonomy from party leaders to obtain reelection, due to the open list electoral system.[22]

In Mexico, governors have had a small but increasing influence over the nomination process and some degree of control over the future career of legislators. According to the Mexican constitution, legislators cannot be reelected, and therefore cannot become professional legislators.

In Venezuela during the 1990s, regional authorities increased their influence over the nomination process, especially in regionally based parties. Finally, in Colombia, the multiple list system has allowed individual legislators some autonomy to get reelected. Regional party machines had some influence even before the election of governors. In contrast, in Chile, Costa Rica, Paraguay, Uruguay, and Venezuela (before 1989), national party leaders have been the most relevant actors in the nomination process.

Presidential coattails have been important in some countries in the region, providing presidents with a powerful negotiation tool. For example, in Venezuela in the 1960s and 1970s, national and regional legislative elections were always held concurrently with presidential elections, and voters could not split their vote between the national and the regional legislative levels. The ballot was structured so as to maximize the connection between the presidential vote and the other votes. As a result, presidential coattails were amplified and influenced every other political office; only a small proportion of the votes were split (Monaldi et al., 2008). Similarly, until 2000 in Uruguay, all elections were held concurrently with the presidential one, and votes could not be split between the national vote and regional vote (including the regional executive). As a result, the presidential vote pulled even the gubernatorial vote. Since 2000, when for the first time the national and gubernatorial vote could be split, the results have been significantly different.

In contrast in Brazil, the influence of gubernatorial coattails over the national legislature was very significant during the first few elections during the transition toward democracy. Before there were free presiden-

---

[22] There is a significant dispute in the literature on Brazilian politics over the extent of the influence of governors over legislators (see discussion below).

tial elections, the military organized a legislative election concurrent with subnational elections in 1982. Similarly in 1986 and 1990, legislative and regional elections were held concurrently and separately from presidential elections. As a result, legislators had a significant electoral connection with governors, and the national party system was highly influenced by regional politics. To some extent, the highly fragmented nature of the Brazilian party system has been attributed to the electoral system and the role of regional politics in national elections (Willis, Garman, and Haggard, 1999; Samuels, 2004). However, after 1994, the elections to the legislature have been fully concurrent with the presidential elections. This has weakened the power of governors over national legislators and strengthened the president's power.

Another example of the power of gubernatorial coattails is provided by the Venezuelan elections of 1998. The traditional parties, which controlled all the regional governments, separated the legislative elections from the presidential elections. This was an attempt to avoid the presidential coattails of a Chávez presidential victory. Instead they held the legislative elections earlier, concurrently with the regional elections. The electoral trick worked, and the gubernatorial coattails allowed the traditional parties to obtain a significant majority in congress, despite the landslide presidential victory of Chávez later the same year.[23]

Across the region, the timing between national and subnational elections varies widely. In Argentina, half the lower chamber and a third of the upper chamber are elected concurrently with the president and some governors. The rest are elected in midterm elections concurrent with some gubernatorial elections. As a result, the effect of timing is mixed (Jones et al., 2001). As mentioned, currently in Brazil, legislators' elections are held fully concurrent with presidential elections (Alston et al., 2008). In Mexico, the system is also mixed, with midterm elections coinciding with some gubernatorial elections. In Colombia, there is full concurrency with the presidential elections. In Venezuela, the 1999 Constitution created a system with little concurrency since the president has a six-year term; congress, a five-year term; and governors, a four-year term.

---

[23] To get rid of the congress in which his party faced strong opposition, Chávez convoked a Constitutional Assembly and later elections for a new legislature were held. In those new elections, Chávez's supporters obtained a comfortable majority.

To analyze the *nationalization* of the party systems in Latin America, Jones constructed an index of the national policy incentives provided by the electoral and political institutions (see Chapter 2, this volume). The lowest national incentive scores were obtained by Brazil, Colombia, Argentina, Chile, Venezuela, and Mexico, in that order. With the exception of Chile, these are the countries with a more significant role for regional authorities.

The Chilean exception may be explained by the peculiar binomial electoral system and the fact that regional authorities are not elected. However, one logical prediction would be that if Chile introduces regional elections and transitions to a more proportional electoral system, the role of regional politicians would increase dramatically and the party system would become more fragmented and less nationalized than it is today.

The index of vote nationalization calculated by Jones, which measures the extent to which the voting results are homogenous across regions, gives the lowest scores to Peru, Ecuador, Argentina, Venezuela, and Brazil, in that order.[24] Again, with the exception of Mexico, the countries with a more relevant role of regional actors are among the bottom five. In Argentina, Brazil, and Venezuela, the low nationalization of the vote feeds and is reinforced by the influence of governors in national policymaking.

In contrast, the low levels of vote nationalization in the cases of Ecuador and Peru may be explainable by their traditionally strong geographical cleavages. However, this geographical fragmentation, if combined with regional elections—as have been recently implemented in Peru—may produce a centrifugal effect in the national policymaking.

In some countries such as Argentina, the electoral system makes it easy for regional parties to survive. As a result, some regional parties have survived for decades controlling certain regions and sometimes extracting significant resources from the center when they have had a pivotal role in the national legislature. Similarly, in Venezuela after the direct election of regional authorities was introduced in 1989, the party system fragmented significantly, and regional parties have started to play a significant role in the national policymaking process.

---

[24] These results imply that in these countries, the vote of each party varies considerably across regions.

The Role of Governors in Argentina, Brazil, Venezuela, Mexico, and Colombia

The last part of this section briefly describes the role of governors in the five countries where they have played a more significant role. These brief case studies are presented to show how the full configuration of institutions determines the role of governors. Each institutional feature considered in isolation is typically not sufficient—or often even necessary—to explain the influence of regional authorities in national politics.

Argentina

Governors play a central role in Argentina's national policymaking process. Governors have been elected for most of Argentina's democratic history—most recently since democracy was reestablished in 1983. The country is formally federal. Compared to other formally federal countries in the region, like Mexico and Venezuela, regional governments have authority over significant policy areas (Faletti, 2004; Gibson and Faletti, 2004). Argentina has a bicameral congress with a territorially based senate. Until the mid-1990s, the provincial legislatures elected the members of the national senate. As shown in Figures 7.1 and 7.2, it has the region's highest malapportionment in the upper chamber and the third highest malapportionment in the lower chamber.[25] In particular, sparsely populated provinces are highly overrepresented. This federal, bicameral–territorial system generates multiple veto points. A small group of governors may, under certain circumstances, constitute a veto player. This is particularly relevant when the president is in legislative minority as was the case with President Raúl Alfonsín.

As can be seen in Figures 7.3 and 7.4, expenditure decentralization is the highest in Latin America. Moreover, it has a large vertical fiscal imbalance, though not the highest in the region (see Figure 7.3); thus the regional governments are highly dependent on the national government. The revenue transfers have been made increasingly rigid, yet discretion at the margin is still the source of significant gaming and accountability and policy distortions (Tommasi, 2006; Jones, Meloni, and Tommasi, 2009). Borrowing by regional governments has

---

[25] Provinces have a minimum of five deputies, regardless of their population.

created a soft budget constraint, and regions have been repeatedly bailed out.

In Argentina, the electoral system is proportional representation with closed lists. Provincial party leaders and governors play a very influential role in the nomination process for legislative elections. This combination provides governors with significant control over the provincial delegation to the national legislature.[26] In practice the party system is more fragmented than it appears from simply counting party labels. Political careers are largely made at the regional level, providing additional leverage to regional leaders. There is partial concurrency between regional and midterm legislative elections and between presidential and legislative elections. More importantly, it is relatively easy to survive as a regional (provincial) party. Provincial parties are relevant players and sometimes have been pivotal in the legislature. As a result they have been able to extract significant resources from the center (Acuña, Galiani, and Tommasi, 2007).

The Argentine institutional framework and party structure provide the basis for the very significant role governors and regional party bosses play in the national policymaking process. According to Spiller and Tommasi (2003, 2007), this institutional setting has created a policymaking game with an excessive number of players and high transaction costs. The common pool problem and vertical fiscal imbalance induce the governors and presidents to behave in an uncooperative way, making it difficult to obtain long-term policy commitments. The control that regional party bosses have over legislators produces a high turnover in congress because bosses do not want legislators to get reelected and become autonomous. This mechanism generates amateur and shortsighted legislators.

As a result of the way the policymaking process works, the federal fiscal mechanisms have often been the subject of opportunistic manipulation by both the governors and the center. For example, in 1988, Peronist governors forced President Alfonsín to accept a new transfers law that gave them a higher share of fiscal revenues and solidified the malapportionment of revenues to less-populated provinces (Garman, Haggard, and Willis, 2001). On occasion, the solution to permanent renegotiation has been to create highly inflexible and inefficient transfer

---

[26] By contrast, in the United States, the single-member district system with open primaries does not allow the governor control over the state's delegation to Congress.

mechanisms, generating difficulties for fiscal adjustment. The macroeco-nomic implosion of 2001 has been partly attributed to these rigidities, as exemplified by the transfer law of 1999, which guaranteed the provinces a fixed nominal transfer, forcing the central government to raise debt to finance the provinces. The Argentine case shows how powerful governors with perverse incentives may have catastrophic consequences.

Brazil

In Brazil, governors have been elected for more than a century, with some authoritarian interruptions. Since 1982, with the transition to democratic rule, regional elections have been reestablished. The first three legislative and regional elections (1982, 1986, and 1990) were held concurrently, separated from presidential elections (maximizing guber-natorial coattails). However, since 1994, there has been full concurrency between legislative and presidential elections, increasing the influence of presidents.

The constitutional structure is formally federal, and significant authority is given to subnational officials. It has a bicameral–territo-rial congress with high senate malapportionment and moderate lower chamber malapportionment. Expenditure decentralization is high by regional standards, but the vertical fiscal imbalance is moderate. As a result, governors have less common pool incentive than in the cases of Argentina, Mexico, or Venezuela.

Governors have some influence in the nomination of legislators, but it seems to have declined in the last decade. There is some debate in the literature about how significant the influence of governors is over the legislative delegation of their region. The party system is highly fragmented by regional standards, but parties are relatively disciplined (Samuels, 2003; Alston et al., 2008; Cheibub, Figueiredo, and Limongi, 2009).

The institutional framework provided governors with incentives and some powerful tools to influence legislators between 1982 and 1994. First, the full concurrency of regional and congressional elections, completely separated from presidential elections, maximized governors' coattails. Second, the capacity to borrow, and the soft budget constraint, made the governors powerful players in the fiscal game with national authorities. Third, the federal structure, the direct election of governors, and the regional control over resources still provide some incentives and tools to influence legislators. However, in the 1990s, the first two factors described above changed radically. Congressional elections are now held fully concurrent with presidential elections, maximizing presidential coattails. More importantly, the reforms of the fiscal federal rules by President Cardoso hardened the budget constraint and radically diminished the bargaining tools of governors.

In addition to his presidential coattails, Cardoso had the advantage of the high popularity derived from his successful halt of hyperinflation, and the perception that the regional governments' profligacy was one of the roots of macroeconomic instability. This situation provided him with a unique opportunity to renegotiate the fiscal rules in a way that limited the power of regional governments.

According to Alston et al. (2008), the explanation for the presidential reign over governors, which has characterized the administrations of both Cardoso and Lula, has some additional institutional roots, arising from the powers of the president and the internal structure of congress. In particular, the presidential partial veto over amendments (equivalent to a line item veto) provides a powerful negotiating tool with legislators looking to provide pork to their regions to secure reelection. Also, the internal rules of the Brazilian congress provide tools for national party leaders to discipline their party delegations.

Venezuela

In Venezuela, the election of governors in 1989 produced a significant transformation in the policymaking process. The decline of the long-established party system can be partially attributed to the influence of political decentralization. In contrast to the previous democratic history, characterized by few and stable actors and resulting in cooperative agreements, the period after political decentralization was characterized by multiple actors, high electoral volatility, and institutional instability. As a consequence, it was more difficult to generate cooperative agreements among politicians or to create an adequate environment for sustainable reforms and long-term policy commitments.

The two most significant institutional changes that occurred were: the introduction of direct elections for governors and mayors in 1989;[27]

---

[27] These regional authorities were elected for three-year terms, with one immediate reelection.

and the modification of the legislature's electoral system, from pure proportional representation to a mixed-member system of personalized proportional representation in 1993. These changes helped significantly weaken the power of traditional parties and national party leaders. Also, in the context of a change in electoral preferences, these institutional transformations contributed to an increase in party fragmentation, volatility, and legislative turnover (Monaldi et al., 2008). The transformation of the policymaking process, along with the multiplication of relevant policy actors, substantially increased transaction costs. Unlike the previous period, in which political exchanges were conducted at low transaction cost in small groups, in this period transactions were negotiated among a larger number of players in more open and conflictive arenas.

Key legislation approved at the national level (either by congress or by executive decree) had to be negotiated with regional actors. Proponents had to introduce regional considerations to gain the support of governors. For example, in the 1990s, legislators were able to push reforms to deepen fiscal transfers to the regions despite the opposition from national party leaders and the national executive. Regional leaders have powerful incentives to extract more resources from the center, given that Venezuela has the largest vertical fiscal imbalance in Latin America, and the rules of distribution of fiscal resources have become slightly more discretionary.

The lack of discipline of legislators was expressed not only in the increasing independence in policy issues vis-à-vis the party leader, but also by desertions from the parties that had nominated them. Factions within consolidated political parties have split off during the 1989–2004 period, creating their own independent legislative groups. The institutional reforms contributed to the erosion of the strict control that party leaders exercised over nomination procedures. This, in turn, weakened party discipline in the legislature.

In 1998, congress approved the separation for the first time of the legislative and presidential elections due on that year. Congressional elections were set to coincide instead with regional elections, before the presidential elections.[28] As a result, these legislative elections generated

---

[28] This modification was designed by the traditional parties to reduce the coattail effects that a potential landslide victory by Chávez might produce on the legislature. Instead, the parties planned to build their support in congress based on the strength of their governors (and their coattails).

the largest political fragmentation in Venezuela's history (more than six effective parties).

Although Venezuela was formally federal for more than a century, it was only in 1989, after the initiation of the direct elections of governors and mayors, that the dormant federal system was activated. There are two key institutional elements of Venezuela's federalism that transformed its party politics: the increasing competition and higher number of electoral arenas (at the subnational level); and the possibility of reelection for governors and mayors, as well as the nonconcurrency between regional and presidential elections. These institutional features provided new regional political actors with an opportunity to gain independence vis-à-vis the national authorities. As a result, a coalition of governors was able to promote and pass legislation increasing the transfer of oil royalties from the central government. Similarly, in order to approve the value-added tax law, the government had to increase transfers to the regions (González and Mascareño, 2004; Penfold-Becerra, 2004a, 2004b; Villasmil et al., 2007; Monaldi et al., 2008). Fiscal decentralization significantly increased, as can be seen in Figure 7.4

After the election of President Chávez in 1998, a progressive recentralization of powers has occurred. The Constitution of 1999, although formally federal, centralized power at the national level and eliminated the territorial legislative chamber. A failed attempt at constitutional reform in 2007 would have dramatically weakened the authority of governors. Even though the president's reform proposal lost a referendum (by a slim margin), the government continued the recentralization of power using its large majority in the legislature. In particular, the government has systematically used its authority to weaken the opposition governors. As in Putin's Russia and Fujimori's Peru, political decentralization has been largely reversed (Manzano et al., 2009).

Mexico

In Mexico, regional elections were not competitive until 1989, when the PRI lost its first governorship. Before the 1980s, Mexico's single-party hegemonic regime had been extremely centralized. For decades the national government had recentralized tax revenues that were in the hands of the states. Governors had some influence in the PRI, but they were mainly agents of the president. In practice, most governors were selected by the president and the national leadership, which could remove them if need be.

Starting in the 1990s, and particularly with the separation of powers generated by divided government in 1998, governors have increasingly played a relevant role in national policymaking (Beer, 2004; Mizrahi, 2004). The position of governor is now a key stepping-stone for the presidency. By contrast, in the PRI-dominated era, the national cabinet positions were the key launch pads. Still, the patronage networks that governors control have allowed them some influence over legislators.

The competitive election of governors in a system that is constitutionally federal has activated Mexican federalism, resulting in a much more decentralized national policymaking process. This already has had significant implications. For example, Lehoucq et al. (2008) attribute the increasing decentralization of fiscal expenditures (as can be seen in Figure 7.4) to the combination of divided government and political decentralization. At the end of 1999, the opposition governors, which had become a majority, demanded a change in the fiscal pact. As a result, congress approved a program of grants to the states and institutionalized transfer programs that used to be controlled by the president.

Colombia

The Colombian case is peculiar because the country is formally unitary, but significantly decentralized. It ranks third after Argentina and Brazil in terms of expenditure decentralization (see Figure 7.4). However, it does not have a high vertical imbalance by regional standards (see Figure 7.3). Political decentralization started in 1988 with the election of mayors and continued in 1991 with the election of governors. The 1991 Constitution advanced significantly toward fiscal decentralization (Falleti, 1999; Cárdenas, Junguito, and Pachón, 2008).

Governors are much less influential in the national policymaking in Colombia than in the federal countries of the region. However, Colombia has had a long history of regional party bosses playing a relevant political role. The explanation might be rooted in the geographical fragmentation of the country, but institutionally it has been the consequence of an electoral system that allows for multiple party lists. As a result, political parties are conglomerates of party factions (similar to Japan) that maintain some autonomy. This feature has provided regional party bosses with some leverage in national policymaking. Compared to regional standards, Colombia is characterized by higher intraparty competition. This feature can be largely attributed to the electoral system.

Moreover, factionalism and regionalization are on the rise. The combination of this electoral system with the recent elections of regional authorities might have been instrumental in the decline of the traditional two-party system and the proliferation of regional and local parties. The creation of a national district for the senate, contrary to expectations, has fueled the regionalization of the party system. Each national list for the senate typically elects only the first member of the list. As a result, instead of creating a national constituency, the system allowed regional factions to obtain representation (Crisp and Ingall, 2002).

Paradoxically, even though the system strengthens regional party factions, it does not provide governors with the same influence over legislators that they have in Argentina. The reason is that individual politicians have easier access to the nomination (in this respect similar to the United States) since they can make their own list. Moreover, the 1991 constitutional rules on campaign finance provide individual candidates with public resources, weakening the power of national party leaders that used to distribute the resources. Despite the increasing factionalism of the Colombian party system, Cárdenas, Junguito, and Pachón (2008) show that the internal rules of the congress provide national party leaders with significant leverage to maintain a relatively high degree of discipline.

Conclusion

This chapter has shown that the significant influence of governors in the national policymaking process can potentially generate uncoordinated and contradictory policies. Elected governors have a regional constituency, different from the national constituency of the president and national party leaders. Thus, unless political institutions and the party structure make the governors internalize the welfare of the national constituency, governors may have incentives to obtain advantages and resources from the center at the expense of nationwide goals such as macroeconomic stability.

The institutional conditions that maximize the influence of governors in national politics are: the direct elections of governors; the existence of a federal structure, including a territorial chamber and a malapportioned legislature; a federal fiscal arrangement that has high expenditure decentralization and a high vertical imbalance, combined with regional borrowing capacity, creating the conditions for a soft budget constraint; an electoral system in which governors control the nominations for the national congress and that maximizes gubernatorial coattails; and a party structure that is not nationalized or fragmented, and that encourages pivotal regional parties (partly a result of the electoral system).

Having elected governors has many advantages, including improving electoral accountability and the regional delivery of public goods. As a result, it does not seem reasonable to solve the commons problem by giving the president the authority to appoint all governors. Moreover, even if it were normatively reasonable, once governors are elected, the policy would be very difficult to reverse in a democracy. The cases of Fujimori and Putin, however, suggest that it is possible in a semi-authoritarian regime.

Similarly, political decentralization and a functioning federal system may prove effective mechanisms to govern large or heterogeneous countries and can generate credible commitment over the protection of property rights. As a result, it seems that a more productive avenue for research and action would be to design the electoral and party structure to provide incentives to allow the president and national party leaders to make the governors internalize the national interest.

The systemic nature of the electoral and party structure makes it particularly difficult to reform. A change in one feature might produce unintended consequences in other areas. However, mechanisms that provide the president with bargaining tools in the legislature and improve the nationalization and national discipline of parties would be among the political reforms that should be evaluated in case the governors have become a centrifugal force to the political system.

It is also important to have a well-designed federal fiscal arrangement that reduces the commons problem, either by creating a stronger link between regional taxation and spending or by designing a credible and fiscally sound transfer system. However, the federal fiscal bargain is usually endogenous to the political system—and it is itself a subject of bargaining between the central government and the subnational governments. As a result, when the federal fiscal structure generates perverse incentives, as in Argentina, it is difficult to renegotiate the terms given that it would affect the interests of the governors, who are highly influential in the legislature and within parties. Presidents should use the windows of opportunity provided by specific political shocks to create a hard budget constraint for the regions, as was skillfully done by President Cardoso in Brazil.

Even though governors have represented a real menace to macro-economic and political stability only in Argentina and in some periods in Brazil, the analysis of this chapter shows that in other countries, such as Bolivia, Chile, Ecuador, and Peru, political decentralization, if not well designed and implemented, could increase the lack of coordination in policymaking and could worsen macroeconomic performance. The case of political decentralization in Venezuela shows how it could lead to party system fragmentation and volatility. In the end, the decline of the party system, partly induced by decentralization, led at the other extreme to the excessive centralization of power and to the weakening of democratic institutions.

CHAPTER 8

Business Politics and Policymaking in Contemporary Latin America

Ben Ross Schneider

Business, especially domestic business, is usually a key participant in policymaking. As most policies, especially market and state reforms, redistribute resources, businesspeople are likely to be among those with the most intense preferences regarding policy outcomes, in terms of both policy content (how specific policies affect them) and the longer-term "outer features" of the policymaking process (such as the stability and credibility of policies). Moreover, among social groups, business is the one with the most resources to invest in politics. However, despite the common prominence of business in policymaking, patterns of business participation vary widely across Latin America and are not easily captured in simple models of politics.

Business participation in policymaking varies over time, across policy areas, and across countries along three interrelated dimensions. First, business participation can be collective and organized or dispersed and individual. Among industrialized countries, for example, business tends to be more organized in northern Europe and Japan, much less organized in the United States, and ranging in between in other English-speaking and southern European countries (see Lehne, 2006). Second, business input can be formal and open or informal and largely opaque. This dimension tends to covary with the organizational dimension, but does not overlap completely. Participation through business associations is typically formal, structured, known to many, and covered by the press. Personal networks, in contrast, involve very small numbers and are often largely invisible, even to other participants in policymaking.

Third, business input varies by the channels of influence that predominate in mediating business participation: deliberative or consultative councils, corporatist tripartite bargaining, lobbying, campaign and party finance, networks and appointments to government positions, and of course, outright corruption. Businesspeople will often avail themselves of a number of these channels simultaneously, but comparative analysis helps single out which are primary in particular countries. For example, Japan and other Asian countries have relied heavily on deliberative councils that bring together representatives of government and business to discuss a wide range of policy issues. Campaign contributions and legislative lobbying are more central to business politics in the United States and Japan than in most European countries, and obviously are more important in democratic regimes than dictatorships. Lastly, the appointment of businesspeople to top policymaking positions in government varies greatly across nations, from thousands of appointments in the United States and many countries of Latin America to virtually none in most other industrialized countries.[1]

Conceptual Frameworks

Scholars often mean very different things when they say "business." Distinguishing among five conceptual approaches to the analysis of business contrasts these meanings and illuminates the various ways that business can participate in policymaking: as capital, as sector, as firm, as association, and as individuals and participants in policy networks (Haggard, Maxfield, and Schneider, 1997). Through capital mobility and flight, business as capital can have an indirect, uncoordinated, impersonal effect on policies as policymakers try to anticipate policies that are likely to keep and attract capital (Mahon, 1996; Maxfield, 1997).[2]

Business as Capital. While capital mobility imposes significant constraints on policymakers, it is not a deliberate form of business participation

---

[1] To capture the variations and nuances of business relations and power in Latin America, this study drew on a series of interviews with business leaders. See list of business leaders interviewed in Schneider (2005).

[2] Capital flows could also be further disaggregated to consider foreign direct investment (FDI), portfolio investment, and loans (commercial and public), and are sensitive to different kinds of policies (Maxfield, 1998; Mosley, 2003).

in policymaking; nor is it a major dimension of variation, since capital movements are relatively unrestricted throughout Latin America. However, it is important to note this background constraint because it tends to narrow the range of policy options that government officials consider, and contributes to making business politics less contentious and politically destabilizing in the twenty-first century than it was in the twentieth when business mobilized to fight major battles over property rights, labor mobilization, socialism, and the basic parameters of capitalist development.

Business as Sector. This conceptual approach is one of the most popular in the literature on international political economy and in many analyses of recent market-oriented reform in developing countries.[3] This approach follows from the conventional Olsonian wisdom that businesses will be better able to overcome obstacles to collective action if they are small in number and homogeneous, as they usually are in capital-intensive sectors (Olson, 1965). Later approaches deepened the theoretical underpinnings with careful conceptualizations of asset specificity: the more specific a firm's assets, the more likely it is to engage in collective action and politics. Conceptualizing business as sector is often a useful "first cut" because sectoral cleavages in Latin America are accentuated, and because many policies have very uneven distributions of costs and benefits across sectors. However, taken too far, sectoral analysis can obscure other bases of business politics such as corporate structure, business associations, and business networks that regularly swamp sectoral considerations (Schneider, 2004a, Chapter 2; Schneider, 2004b, pp. 458–64).

Business as Firm. In this concept, firms are the primary units of analysis, and business politics vary largely according to corporate structure. Two core features of corporate ownership—multisectoral conglomeration and dominance of multinational corporations (MNCs) in key manufacturing sectors—distinguish Latin America from other regions and affect business–government relations (Guillén, 2000, 2001).[4] Diversified

---

[3] Major works include Frieden (1991) and Shafer (1994). For recent reviews, see Alt et al. (1996) and Frieden and Martin (2002).

[4] Firm size also differentiates business preferences in politics (Thacker, 2000; Shadlen, 2004). Another striking characteristic of firms of all sizes in Latin America is the persistence of family

conglomerates have more encompassing interests, which, combined with their huge size and small number, should facilitate collective action and coordination, in principle. According to this logic, conglomerates should support more public-regarding policies designed to improve the functioning of the economy as a whole. MNCs, because they can shift investment to other countries (exit), tend to be less committed interlocutors in longer-term policy implementation and institution building. To the extent that MNCs influence policy more through anticipated reactions than deliberate political activity, MNCs resemble the effects of the first concept of business as capital. At a minimum, ownership variables like multisectoral conglomeration and MNCs complicate simple deductions about business preferences on policy and straightforward predictions about their political behavior. Conglomeration and foreign ownership both open up exit options for firms in particular sectors. If, for example, policies threaten a stand-alone, single-sector firm, that firm is more likely to use voice and politics to change the policy. In contrast, MNCs and conglomerates are more likely to weigh the costs and benefits of voice versus exit.

Business as Association. In this concept, taken up at greater length in the next section, the way business organizes and the longer institutionalization of business associations are primary factors in explaining patterns of business participation in policymaking. The major variations along this organizational dimension include whether associations are voluntary or state-chartered (corporatist), whether they are encompassing or sectoral, whether they are based on production or employment relations, and whether they represent primarily large or small firms.

Business as Network. In this concept, the analysis turns to examining how individual businesspeople can participate directly through appointment to government positions or close personal connections to top policymakers in personal or policy networks (Teichman, 2001). Personalized business–government networks can sometimes evolve out of long-standing social and kinship relations, as well as common

---

ownership and management. This variable has not been extensively researched or theorized, but there are good reasons to expect that the political behavior of firms will differ according to whether or not they are managed by family owners or professional managers.

schooling and university training. More short-term network connections can also emerge out of career movement back and forth between the public and private sectors. As in the United States, most presidents in Latin America appoint thousands of people, including many from business, to top policymaking positions. There are some exceptions, notably Chile after 1990 and Mexico for most of the twentieth century, where presidents invited very few businesspeople into government, but in most other countries businesspeople circulate regularly in and out of government. The movement between the public and private sectors is probably greatest in Colombia, but businesspeople are also common in government in Argentina, Brazil, and Peru. Such movement creates ready-made networks for sharing information and debating policy options.

Portfolios of Business Investment in Politics ·

Another, partially overlapping framework for analyzing variations in business participation is in terms of the *portfolio* of political investments made by business. Businesspeople can invest in a range of political activities from business associations, to financing parties and candidates, to networking with government officials, to outright bribery. In principle, rational businesspeople should balance their *portfolio* of political investments to take advantage of evolving opportunities by shifting political investments to activities that generate the greatest return. Where business concentrates its political investments is largely a function of the perceived opportunities for influence offered by the political system (see Tarrow, 1998). Some features of the opportunity structure are relatively fixed by long-standing institutional features of the political system; others, though, can be created or closed by individual policymakers. So, while variations in patterns of business politics are relatively stable, they are not immutable, and policymakers can have decisive and relatively short-term impacts on those patterns. Explaining the origins of these patterns is beyond the scope of this study, but the conclusion briefly returns to this issue of business politics as an *object* of policymaking.

Associations

Table 8.1 presents some basic information on the strength and age of encompassing associations in some of the largest countries in Latin

America. On this dimension, countries like Chile, Colombia, and Mexico follow a more European or Japanese model of business organization compared to a more "American" style of fragmentation in Brazil and Argentina. Among the remaining larger countries, Peru and Venezuela both have fairly well-organized economy-wide encompassing associations in CONIFIEP and Fedecamaras, respectively. Almost all the smaller countries, with the significant exception of Uruguay, have economy-wide encompassing associations (see Durand and Silva, 1998).

The mere existence of voluntary encompassing associations is one good indicator of the amounts prominent capitalists invest in collective action. The rough estimates of staff give a further proxy useful for cross-country comparisons of the material investments members make in their associations. Other indicators of organizational strength would include the time businesspeople invest in associations and the quality of internal representation. Although they cannot be summarized in a table, historical instances of organizational capacity to aggregate or reconcile member interests were more common in the histories of encompassing associations in Chile, Colombia, and Mexico than in Argentina and Brazil.[5]

Beyond economy-wide associations, wide variation also exists among encompassing associations for industry and for agriculture.[6] Agricultural associations were some of the first to form in the region, although most had faded as organizations by the late twentieth century, except for some in narrower sectors like coffee (Federacafe). Agricultural associations tended to be stronger in countries with less diversified agriculture and larger landholdings, as in Argentina, Chile, and Colombia (Smith, 1969; Wright, 1982; Schneider, 2004a, pp. 39–40). In industry, Chile and Colombia have the strongest voluntary associations in the region. The industry association in Argentina, UIA (Unión Industrial Argentina), enjoyed some periods of strength but after the 1940s suffered from internal division and competition from rival associations. Non-

---

[5] Institutional or organizational strength refers to these internal characteristics—material resources and internal intermediation—not to the amount of power or influence of the association in the political system.

[6] Commerce and finance are other major sectors with significant associational activity. However, there is less variation across the region. Commerce associations tend to be weak, largely because they organize so many thousands of small retailers, except at the municipal level. In contrast, financial and banking associations tend everywhere to be strong and well organized, largely because they organize a small number of very large firms, except where they are divided between foreign and domestic firms.

TABLE 8.1	Voluntary Encompassing Business Associations, Latin America		
	Association	**Scope**	**Staff**
Strong encompassing associations			
Mexico	Coparmex (1929)	economy-wide	30
	CMHN (1962)	economy-wide	0
	CCE (1975)	economy-wide	80
Chile	CPC (1935)	economy-wide	8
	Sofofa (1883)	industry	50
Colombia	Federacafe (1927)	coffee	3,500
	ANDI (1944)	industry	150
	CG (1991)	economy-wide	3
Weak encompassing associations			
Argentina	UIA (1886)	industry	50
	AEA (2002)	economy-wide	8
Brazil	IEDI (1989)	industry	8
	Ação Empresarial (1993)	economy-wide	0

Source: Schneider (2004a). The year the association was established is in parentheses.
Figures for staff are rough estimates for average total employment in the late twentieth century.

Ação Empresarial–Business Action, Brazil
AEA–Asociación Empresaria Argentina
ANDI–Asociación Nacional de Industriales
CCE–Consejo Coordinador Empresarial
CG–Consejo Gremial
CMHN–Consejo Mexicano de Hombres de Negocios
Coparmex–Confederación Patronal de la República
  Mexicana

CPC–Confederación de la Producción y del
  Comercio
Federacafe–Federación Nacional de Cafeteros
  de Colombia
IEDI–Instituto de Estudos de Desenvolvimento
  Industrial
Sofofa–Sociedad de Fomento Fabril
UIA–Unión Industrial Argentina

voluntary, corporatist associations in Brazil and Mexico gave industry federations the appearance of institutional strength, but behind the façade they were much weaker, in large part due to state controls on internal organization. These controls were especially debilitating in Brazil, where the regional structure of representation gives marginal industry federations from states in the rural northeast control of the national industry confederation, Confederação Nacional de Indústria (CNI).

Business associations participate in policymaking in a number of ways. First, leaders of associations appear regularly in the press. Newspapers often assign reporters to cover business associations, and they contact associations almost daily for reactions to government announcements and breaking economic news. In addition, associations invest in their own press and dissemination departments and call press conferences to announce policy positions. Some associations also have sophisticated research departments that collect data relevant to sectoral performance. Associations use the opportunity of announcing, say, monthly employment statistics to comment on policy issues of the day. Some leaders contend that this press presence may be the most important lever, albeit indirect, that business has to influence policy.[7]

Leaders of associations also talk directly to policymakers. Associations may invite officials to events or to make presentations, or they may ask for appointments. For instance, an annual report to the members on the activities of the president of the economy-wide Consejo Coordinador Empresarial (CCE) noted dozens of meetings with various cabinet ministers (CCE, 1987). These meetings are often ad hoc and called to address short-term issues, but in some countries meetings are more routine. Again in Mexico, the Consejo Mexicano de Hombres de Negocios (CMHN) hosted monthly luncheons and the CCE hosts monthly dinners, mostly with ministers from the economic area. It is often unclear exactly what influence these meals have on policy, but they certainly expand access and dialogue.

In other cases, governments can institutionalize business input into policymaking or oversight councils (considered further later). These forums, sometimes called consultative or deliberative councils, are typically granted functional authority over certain policy areas that can range from broad macro issues such as monetary policy and stabilization plans to labor issues like minimum wages and training, to narrow technical issues like animal husbandry. These councils have fixed membership that usually includes representatives from relevant ministries and business associations. A small number of councils also include representatives from labor or other organized social groups. If the council decides on policy with formal votes, then business rarely has a majority of votes or even veto power. However, representatives from business associations usually have a good deal of informal influence because they can use common committee tactics to slow unfavorable policies and can bring considerable technical expertise to bear on discussions.[8] Lastly,

---

[7] Interview with Jorge Blanco Villegas, President of Unión Industrial Argentina (UIA), 1993–97, May 3, 2000. Analyses of Colombian associations emphasize their strong presence in the media (Urrutia, 1983, pp. 45, 82).

[8] Once invited to join councils, associations usually create or expand professional research departments. See Urrutia (1983) for a discussion of informal influence on councils.

governments may grant complete policy authority, along with public resources, to associations. For example, the Colombian coffee confederation, Federacafe, has control over an export tax and other resources and is responsible for financing, promoting, and marketing Colombian coffee. Brazilian industry federations receive a 1 percent payroll tax to promote worker training; the government collects the tax but turns it over to federations that in turn decide how to spend it.

Although it is beyond the scope of this chapter to attempt an explanation for the wide variation across Latin America in the strength of business associations, it is worth noting some of the main causes [Schneider (2004a) provides a full discussion]. As Olson would expect, most strong associations provide some selective benefit to members only, ranging from control over an export tax in the case of Federacafe, to a genealogical registry for cattle in the case of Sociedad Rural Argentina, to monthly luncheons with ministers for CMHN. Furthermore, in most cases, the most significant benefits are granted by the state. In cases where the state has granted control over public funds to associations, firms have had incentives to join the association and contribute to its institutional strength. Less tangible benefits, such as regular access to top policymakers (as in the CMHN luncheons mentioned earlier) or to policymaking councils, also encouraged businesspeople to join associations, as well as contribute to and participate in them.

Legislative Lobbying

In the wake of democratization, more avenues for business participation in policymaking have opened up, particularly in political parties and congress. Unfortunately, there are few empirical studies of lobbying by business (see Diniz and Boschi, 2004, focusing on Brazil, for a major exception). However, sporadic evidence suggests that business is increasing its contacts with elected politicians. As business moves to invest more in lobbying the legislature, its influence tends to become more fragmented and particularistic, and therefore ineffectual on general issues, what Diniz and Boschi (2004) call an "Americanization" of business politics. There are a number of reasons for this fragmentation. For one, individual contributors are likely to seek legislators' assistance on issues relating specifically to their firms, such as resolving particular administrative problems in the bureaucracy.

Moreover, business associations, by custom or legal restriction, do not contribute to political campaigns in Latin America, and their influence with legislators is likely to be less than that of major contributors, who tend to come from individual firms. An interesting exception, which tends to prove the general rule, is the sophisticated lobbying operation of the CNI, Brazil's national industry confederation. Its lobbying wing COAL (Coordenação de Assuntos Legislativos) grew from a small operation in Brasília in the late 1980s to a large and sophisticated lobby in the 1990s.[9] By the mid-1990s, COAL had 21 employees and accounted for close to half of CNI staff in Brasília. In contrast, legislative lobbying in the economy-wide CCE in Mexico was still incipient by 2003, in part because the legislature began exercising a more active policy role only after 1997, when the president's party lost its majority in Congress for the first time in many decades.[10]

In most countries, individual companies also frequently lobby the executive branch. Systematic, cross-national data are lacking, but some general patterns emerge in policy studies. For one, pressuring officials in the executive is usually ad hoc and informal (without a more organized lobbying office that is more commonly associated with new legislative lobbying). Moreover, contact is often sporadic, reactive, and/ or crisis-driven, as businesspeople seek out officials for help with, or relief from, particular policy decisions. Lastly, as in legislative lobbying, contact with the executive usually involves small numbers of firms with narrow interests.

Electoral Politics, Parties, and Campaign Contributions

According to press reports, in February 1995, at a private dinner with several dozen wealthy businessmen, Mexican President Carlos Salinas de Gortari announced to them that they had all made a lot of money during his government and that he expected them each to donate $25 million to the Partido Revolucionario Institucional (PRI) to help finance the election of his successor (Oppenheimer, 1998). These reports generated heated debate and portended important changes in politics in Latin America (the possible privatization of the PRI, not least among them).

---

[9] Interview with Carlos Alberto Cidade, May 27, 1995.

[10] Interview with Luis Miguel Pando, February 26, 2003.

For one, redemocratization in the region would inevitably lead to ever more expensive campaigns and require governments to decide how they would be financed. And, as the Salinas dinner made clear, big money was most likely to come from big business.

Over the last decade most of the large countries of Latin America reformed the legal framework for campaign finance (Griner and Zovatto, 2004). Although complex and varied, several patterns emerge in campaign finance laws in the region (Payne et al., 2002). Most legal frameworks prohibit foreign contributions (to the probable relief of many MNCs), maintain some public funding, limit maximum contributions, and provide some free media access. There are also a wide range of other restrictions in smaller numbers of countries, including prohibitions on paid advertising or contributions from government contractors and business associations, as well as different stipulations on eligibility for public funding. Taken together, these laws represent a systematic effort to limit the private cost of elections and to reduce dependence on business contributions, both overall and by particular kinds of business. Nonetheless, a lot of money flows from business into elections, both legally and illegally. There are few studies of compliance, but sporadic evidence from Latin America, as well as experiences in other consolidated democracies, suggest that there are many ways to circumvent restrictions on business contributions.[11]

Despite the flow of millions of dollars into electoral campaigns, there are several reasons to doubt that this flow buys business a great deal of leverage in most policy processes. The first is a common collective action problem: businesses contribute to individual legislators, who do not have much impact on policy except in collective votes, while it is nearly impossible for business contributors to coordinate to exercise collective pressure. In the Brazilian state of São Paulo, for example, construction firms depend heavily on government contracts and therefore contribute a lot to congressional campaigns. Most large firms have at least one deputy in Brasília whom they can call on to help sort out problems with the federal bureaucracy. However, the industry as a whole cannot get "their deputies" to vote together on policies of common interest to

---

[11] Another way that electoral politics opens up avenues for business influence is for business-people to run for office themselves. In Brazil, for example, estimates of the percentage of deputies with business backgrounds range from one-quarter to one-half of the deputies elected between 1985 and 2002 (see Schneider, 2004a, Chapter 4). In Mexico, Fox and many Panistas had business backgrounds.

all construction firms, such as housing or highway programs.[12] Where parties are stronger in organizing policy-relevant votes and collective campaign funding, they can help solve this collective action problem; however, such parties are rare in Latin America. Another problem for contributors is that turnover is very high in most legislatures (100 percent in Mexico, by law) so that incumbents, once in office, have weak incentives to heed their contributors.

Contributions to presidents, many of whom can now stand for reelection, may suffer less from these problems of collective action and lapses in attentiveness after the election; however, the contributions must be very large. Moreover, very large contributors are likely to give to both sides (as is common in the United States) as insurance to be sure the winner does not retaliate. In the 2002 elections in Colombia, for example, the Santo Domingo group, one of the four leading business groups, gave $300,000 to Uribe and $300,000 to his closest contender (Njaim, 2004). Such electoral promiscuity is not likely to enhance contributors' policy influence, though it likely keeps channels of access open.

A study of campaign finance in Brazil lists more than a dozen scandals involving major alleged infractions of Brazil's electoral law in the 20 years since the return of freer and more competitive elections in the 1980s (Fleischer, 2002). The long list confirms several suspicions about campaign finance. First, laws are difficult to enforce and easy to circumvent. Second, irregularities and scandals involve all major parties, from left to right, and all levels, from municipal to presidential campaigns. Third, in cases where the scandal revolved around alleged favoritism for business contributors after the election, favors were mostly in the form of individualized, private-regarding benefits, as in privatization policies, rather than collective influence on broad policy issues.

Networks

In most countries, informal personal relations connect at least some economic and government elites. These connections can result from family ties, attendance at the same schools (usually private) and universities, studying abroad, or overlapping in previous career stages.

---

[12] Interview with Eduardo Capobianco, January 28, 1993.

In Latin America, high socioeconomic stratification and geographic concentration in capital cities facilitate the formation of elite networks. It is often difficult to tell what impact these networks have on policy-making, in part because the relations are informal and opaque, when not deliberately secretive. Analysts argue that intense networks can contribute to everything from shared world views to spot transactions and private-regarding policies designed to favor only the firms of particular network participants (see Teichman, 2001). Narrower networks between particular firms and policymakers that are closed to other elites seem more likely to generate private-regarding policies than do open, expansive networks. At a minimum, personal networks open up channels of access and communication. In terms of the portfolio analogy, to the extent that businesspeople feel they have sufficient access through informal networks, they will have weaker incentives to invest in other formal channels like business associations or election campaigns.

The extent of networks is difficult to measure empirically. The most in-depth analyses of networks in Latin America cover Mexico during the years of PRI dominance (Smith, 1979; Camp, 1989; Centeno, 1994).[13] This research documented the remarkable and long-standing absence of networks linking economic and political elites. On the other end of the spectrum, public and private elites in Colombia seem in most periods to be thoroughly networked and interconnected. Although not as extensively documented as in Mexico, most political elites in Colombia follow careers that weave in and out of government and private firms or business associations (Juárez, 1995; Schneider, 2004a, pp. 148–50). Table 8.2 provides further comparisons among recent governments in terms of the number of businesspeople appointed to the cabinet. This table confirms both the expected expansion of businesspeople in the Fox government in Mexico, as well as the continued patterns of business representation in governments in Colombia and business exclusion in Concertación governments in Chile.

Some public–private network relations may result from decades of social interaction. Others can be created (or destroyed) overnight by political appointments of businesspeople to government. In Mexico,

---

[13] The greater scholarly attention paid to networks in Mexico is partly the result of better data (the government published biographical information on all top policymakers) and partly due to the importance of networks in intra-elite politics generally.

TABLE 8.2	Business Appointees in Selected Government Cabinets		
Country	President	Number of business appointees	Percent of business appointees
Argentina	Kirchner (2003–05)	0	0
	Duhalde (2002–03)	1	8
	De la Rúa (1999–2002)	1	9
Chile	Lagos (2002–05)	0	0
Colombia	Uribe (2002–05)	7	54
Mexico	Fox (2000–05)	5	25
Peru	Toledo (2001–05)	7	27

Source: Author's compilations from government and periodical sources. Years covered are in parentheses.

the inauguration of Vicente Fox in 2000 transformed from one day to the next the previous pattern of relative absence of personal networks between business and government. Fox was himself a former businessman (and therefore had personal connections of his own to many businesspeople) and also appointed other ministers from the private sector.[14] Even in countries with fairly long-standing traditions of appointing businesspeople, as in Argentina, Brazil, and Colombia, practices can vary widely from one government to the next. In Brazil, for example, Presidents Fernando Collor de Mello and, curiously, Lula (Luiz Inácio Lula da Silva) appointed more prominent representatives of the private sector as ministers than did president Fernando Henrique Cardoso.[15] One hypothesis is that political leaders who already have good networks with business when they come to power, as did Cardoso and his inner circle from São Paulo, have fewer incentives to appoint businesspeople than do outsider leaders like Lula, Carlos Menem, or Augusto Pinochet, who lacked ties to big business prior to becoming president.

From a broader comparative perspective, a pan-American pattern of appointing businesspeople that is common to most of Latin America as well as the United States has emerged. This pattern contrasts sharply

---

[14] For example, the minister of labor, Carlos Abascal, came from the employers' confederation Coparmex. Francisco Gil Díaz, the first minister of finance, came from a telecommunications company, though he had been there only a few years and had a long public career before that.

[15] Marcílio Marques Moreira, Collor de Mello's minister of the economy in 1991–92, had a long career in banking. Lula's main business appointees were Roberto Rodrigues (agriculture), Luis Furlan (development), and Henrique Meirelle (president of the central bank).

with patterns in most of the rest of the world. For the most part, these networks seem to bias policies generally in favor of business, although not necessarily in particularistic ways. Some exceptions that prove this rule include Chile in the 1970s and Argentina under Menem. In these instances of crony capitalism (a term best reserved for these kinds of exclusive networks and particularistic policy benefits), political leaders appointed businesspeople from a few of the largest conglomerates and thereby established very narrow and closed networks. Many of the early policies enacted by these governments in turn favored the few firms represented in these networks (Silva, 1996; Schamis, 2002; Teichman, 2001).

Corruption

Beyond legal forms of participation in policymaking, business sometimes buys influence directly. The term corruption covers a wide range of behaviors, from petty *mordidas* paid to traffic cops to large-scale embezzlement of public funds. The form of corruption relevant to this analysis is private-sector bribes to public officials in exchange for favorable changes to economic policies. As such, this is a fairly rare form of corruption, even in systems widely perceived as corrupt. Bribery also suffers from free riding, in the sense that firms are likely to consider direct corruption only if they can capture all the benefits, which means they are likely to consider it only in case of policies that are very narrow in scope (see discussion that follows). Most documented scandals of business bribery seem to be related more frequently to policy implementation (when funds, contracts, or opportunities are distributed to particular firms) than to policy formulation.

According to the indices compiled by Transparency International, levels of perceived corruption vary widely across Latin America. In the overall rankings, the countries in Table 8.3 cluster in three groups by 2004. A "cleaner" set that includes Chile, Uruguay, and Costa Rica, is grouped around the least corrupt quartile. A middle group comprised of Brazil, Colombia, Mexico, and Peru hovers just above the median. Three countries perceived as more corrupt—Argentina, Venezuela, and Bolivia—cluster around the bottom quartile. By 2008, some of the country scores had changed, but the relative ranking of the three groups was the same.

TABLE 8.3	Perceived Corruption in Latin America, 1996 and 2004					
	Score	1996 rank	Percentile	Score	2004 rank	Percentile	Change in score
Chile	6.8	21	0.38	7.4	20	0.14	+ 0.6
Uruguay	—	—	—	6.2	28	0.19	—
Costa Rica	—	—	—	4.9	41	0.28	—
Brazil	3	40	0.74	3.9	59	0.41	+ 0.9
Colombia	2.7	42	0.77	3.8	60	0.41	+ 1.1
Mexico	3.3	38	0.70	3.6	64	0.44	+ 0.3
Peru	—	—	—	3.5	67	0.46	
Argentina	3.4	35	0.64	2.5	108	0.74	−0.9
Venezuela	2.5	48	0.88	2.3	114	0.78	−0.2
Bolivia	3.4	36	0.66	2.2	122	0.84	−1.2

Source: Transparency International Corruption Perceptions Index for 1996 and 2004 (http://www.transparency.org).
The surveys included 54 countries in 1996 and 145 countries in 2004.
— not included in the 1996 survey.

Overall it is difficult to relate these corruption rankings directly to different patterns of business politics. First, it is important to remember that these rankings are based on opinion surveys (and these surveys have been sensitive to scandals that appear in the media). Second, they are aggregate measures that do not separate out specific forms of business corruption. However, these rankings at least signal the possibility that corruption is a more likely form of business influence in countries ranked toward the bottom of the list than in those at the top.

Portfolio Distribution and Opportunity Structure

Table 8.4 offers a rough comparative assessment of how business distributes its political investments across major countries of the region. As noted, businesspeople should rebalance their portfolios of political investments to take maximum advantage of the opportunities offered by the political system. In countries where policymakers pay less attention to associations, as in Argentina and Brazil, business tends not to invest much time or money in them. Where government leaders have institutionalized business input through associations, then businesspeople have strong incentives to invest in associations and build institutional

TABLE 8.4	Portfolio Distribution of Political Activity by Business since the 1990s				
	Campaigns and elections	Lobbying congress	Business associations	Personal networks	Corruption
Argentina, 1990s	Medium	Medium	Low	Medium	High
Brazil, 1990s	Medium	Medium	Low	Medium	Medium
Chile, 1990	Medium	Low	High	Low	Low
Colombia	Medium	Low	High	High	Medium
Mexico, 1990s	Low	Low	High	Low	Medium
Mexico, 2000	Medium	Medium	Medium	Medium	Medium

Source: Author's estimates based on preceding text.

capacity for long-term intermediation. This was evident historically in Chile, Colombia, and Mexico, and in the 1990s in trade negotiations, particularly in Chile and Mexico. The Chilean political system in the 1990s continued to favor investment in associations. However, as macro issues faded from the policy agenda, the economy-wide encompassing association Confederación de la Producción y del Comercio (CPC) became less valuable to business. Moreover, negotiations for Chile's entry into MERCOSUR sidelined CPC because it was unable to mediate the very divergent positions of industry and agriculture regarding the regional agreement. However, other consultative councils continued to draw on associations (see Muñoz, 2000).

More importantly for a portfolio analysis, the Chilean political system does not offer many opportunities for alternative political investments.[16] For example, the executive branch dominates in policymaking, but is relatively insulated from direct lobbying and from personal networks since no businesspeople have been appointed to Concertación cabinets. Moreover, the bureaucracy is more professionalized and Weberian than the mean for Latin America, and perceived corruption is correspondingly low (Chile is ranked the lowest in Latin America, just behind the United States).[17] The Chilean electoral system takes much of the suspense out of legislative elections and reduces incentives for business to invest in

---

[16] This analysis of the Chilean political system draws mostly on Aninat et al. (2008). See also Siavelis (2000); Baldez and Carey (2002).

[17] Transparency International Corruption Perceptions Index for 2004, pp. 4–5.

parties and elections. In the binomial electoral system, the two parties or coalitions that get the most votes in each electoral district each send a representative to the legislature. If the second-ranked coalition gets less than one-third of the vote (or less than half of the first-place party or coalition), then the first-ranked party gets both representatives. This two-thirds hurdle is so high as to make it virtually assured that each coalition, in what has become essentially a two-coalition system, will win representation in each district, and therefore the two coalitions have close to even representation in the lower house of the legislature. Through the mid-2000s, the deciding, swing votes were thus in the upper chamber held by senators that were appointed instead of popularly elected (nine seats out of 47 to 49 during the 1990–2006 period had such characteristics). The influence of these unelected senators was magnified by the artificially generated parity in the lower chamber. However, once again, incentives to invest in elections and parties were reduced because these senators (as well as past presidents who are life members) were not elected.

Business investment in politics varies by opportunities for influence, but also by the amount the government can actually accomplish. So, for example, the CMHN luncheons and CCE dinners that were so valuable to business under Salinas (1988–94) in the heyday of market reform meant much less under Fox, whose government was deadlocked and accomplished little in terms of new policy initiatives. Businesspeople felt that access to the Fox government was excellent, but they sometimes declined opportunities to discuss policy issues with the government because they doubted the government would be able to accomplish anything. In other instances, associations revised and limited their policy proposals to things they thought the executive branch could do on its own, without legislative approval.[18]

Business Politics and Types of Policies

Distinctive patterns of business politics vary across countries; they also vary by the type of policy. For the analysis of business politics, as well as more generally, policies can be usefully disaggregated in terms of varia-

---

[18] Interviews with Alejandro Martínez Gallardo (February 24, 2003) and Luis Miguel Pando (February 26, 2003).

TABLE 8.5	Scope and Implementation in Policymaking

Implementation speed	Broad scope	Narrow scope
Rapid implementation	Uniform changes in tariffs, pensions, or tax rates; fiscal decentralization	Privatization, deregulation
Lengthy implementation	Administrative reform, educational reform	Sectoral reregulation (public utilities such as energy and telecommunications)

Source: Author.

tions in economic scope, time for implementation, as well as variations in the types of costs and benefits expected. Table 8.5 classifies policies by whether their impact is broad in scope, as in across-the-board changes in tax rates or education, or narrow in scope, as in policies that directly affect only one sector, such as privatizing firms or regulating newly private firms. The vertical axis distinguishes policies according to how long they take to implement. Some policies, such as lowering tariffs or deregulating sectors, can be enacted overnight with the stroke of a pen. Other policies, especially those dependent on changing institutions and the behavior of large groups of people, including many so-called second-generation reforms, take years and often decades to implement.

For policies that are broad in scope, most business sectors have a hard time acting collectively to participate in policymaking, especially if they lack strong encompassing associations. This can be a boon for policymakers if they fear business opposition, as with trade liberalization, where collective business opposition did not materialize (see Naím, 1993). For narrower policies, the challenge is to prevent policy capture by the most intensely interested groups. To the extent that business participation is more collective or encompassing, then the implementation of narrow policies can be more public-regarding. The implication of the second distinction among policies by length of implementation directs attention to possibilities for institutionalized participation by business in policymaking. That is, business participation, especially collective participation, is unlikely to have much impact on longer-term policies unless business has strong associations and institutionalized access to the relevant policy forums.

Table 8.6 makes a related set of distinctions among costs (and benefits) of policies that are certain or uncertain, and immediate or longer

TABLE 8.6	Distribution of Costs in Policymaking	
Time period	Certain costs	Uncertain costs
Immediate	Changes in tax rates, pension reform	Privatization, deregulation
Longer term	Future scheduled changes in taxes or pension benefits	Trade liberalization, reregulation, pension privatization

Source: Author.

term. Changes in tax rates and pension benefits, for example, often have immediate and certain distributional costs. Other kinds of policies, especially many market-oriented reforms, tend to have more uncertain costs. In cases of privatization, for example, new owners normally lay off workers, but exactly when and how many is uncertain. Moreover, short-term crises and reform bundling can make most costs uncertain because multiple economic parameters are moving simultaneously, often in different directions. Lastly, social policy (education and health care) and administrative reform require large, long-term investments in institutional reform and have uncertain consequences. In general, business, as well as other affected groups, are most likely to mobilize when costs are certain and short-term. Longer-term, second-generation reforms with diffuse and uncertain costs and benefits do not seem to elicit sustained business engagement, either for or against (Kaufman and Nelson, 2004a).

Having laid out distinctions among various forms of business politics and various types of policy, the analysis can now recombine these component pieces in an effort to identify better and worse patterns of policymaking and specify what sorts of business participation resolve particular dilemmas in policymaking. From a pessimistic point of view, business tends to pursue its narrow, firm-level or sector-level interests using more opaque means of direct influence through networks, lobbying, campaign contributions, and corruption. In this view, business participation produces rents and inefficiency, and ultimately lowers social welfare. The solutions are to reduce the scope of policymaking to a minimum (night-watchman state) and hermetically seal off all remaining policymaking. Optimists (and a range of pragmatists and realists) believe that business can contribute to resolving a number of problems in policymaking, including, in abstract terms, problems of information, coordination, flexibility, credibility, and commitment.[19] In this more sanguine view, the challenge is to find the mechanisms and institutions that channel business participation away from rent seeking toward problem solving.

For example, the values of rigidity and resoluteness in policymaking are typically seen in signaling credible commitments to investors, who are then expected to invest according to new, rigid rules. However, rigid rules and policies lose credibility when conditions change to make them untenable. Negotiation between government and business is one possibility for maintaining flexibility and adaptability—and at the same time credible commitment to a new overall policy or development trajectory. Most policies have little initial credibility and then gain credibility as they are strengthened by politics and process. The best arrangements for intertemporal commitments are through building credibility in the *process* of policymaking and ongoing adjustment over time (Rodrik, 2007).

Cases of Business–Government Collaboration in Policymaking and Implementation

Starting with distinctions among policy types discussed in the previous section, this section turns to consider some empirical studies of policymaking that illustrate how business participation can solve some of the challenges of policymaking. Taking first policies that have fairly certain, short-term costs and benefits and that affect the economy as a whole, like tax reform and pensions, the main contribution business can make is providing information—ideally, aggregated information—and offering consensus or majority views. That is, information is costly for policymakers. The task of reconciling divergent interests among business is also costly. In these instances, partial information and strong, narrow preferences (of the sorts that characterize business lobbying on tax policy in the United States) are not likely to lead to fair, simple tax codes (see Martin, 1991).

A positive case from recent Latin American experience comes from Chile in the early 1990s (Weyland, 1997). The Concertación government

---

[19] See Doner and Schneider (2000) for a full consideration of contributions that business associations can make to economic governance; Hall and Soskice (2001) on coordination problems generally, and Rodrik (2007) on the importance of business participation to making industrial policy.

that took over from the authoritarian regime in 1990 had campaigned on a platform of increased social spending and taxation. Business expected tax reform to be high on the agenda of the new civilian government, and some segments of the business community admitted that increased social spending was desirable. The Concertación government negotiated closely with the economy-wide CPC to reach agreement on new tax rates and terms (some tax increases were to be temporary and lapse after a few years). Business in turn lobbied the right-wing opposition parties in congress to support the government proposal.[20]

After 1985, democratic governments in Brazil also increased taxes to the point where the tax share of GDP is now ranked among the highest in Latin America and developing countries generally. However, business has consistently opposed tax increases and argued strenuously for a simplification of taxes and a shift away from taxes on production that put Brazilian manufacturers at a disadvantage vis-à-vis foreign competitors. As noted, Brazilian business lacks an economy-wide association to coordinate sustained participation in tax policy, and existing peak organizations in industry and other sectors have not represented the private sector well.[21] In one remarkable example, the leader of the national industry confederation (CNI), Albano Franco, who was also a senator, voted in favor of a tax increase that industry strongly opposed (Schneider, 1997–98, p. 102). In addition, as noted, the lobbying power of business in congress in Brazil is dispersed and uncoordinated, and therefore can do little to help articulate coherent business positions on broad policy issues like tax reform.

Other economy-wide policies—such as regional integration agreements and macro stabilization—may have more uncertain costs over a longer period, and therefore benefit from more active commitments by business. In such cases, business can contribute not only aggregated information, but also make credible commitments and negotiate adjustments over time, if conditions change. Appropriate forums for these kinds of exchanges generally involve policy councils (or tripartite bargaining arrangements) and strong business associations, as in the cases

---

[20] By the 2000s, business mobilized to block further tax increases (Fairfield, forthcoming).

[21] Sectoral associations in Brazil did sometimes coordinate through loose entities like the UBE or Ação Empresarial, but neither of these entities had lasting organizational power (Schneider, 2004a, Chapter 4).

of stabilization pacts in Mexico and in trade negotiations in Mexico and Chile in the 1990s.

The stabilization pacts in Mexico in the late 1980s were among the most successful ever attempted in Latin America.[22] In early 1987, in the context of rising inflation (cresting over 100 percent), a presidential election campaign (and hence presumed pressures for capital flight), and other fiscal strains, top policymakers in the government of Miguel de la Madrid convened meetings with business (represented through the economy-wide CCE) and labor. These pacts, monthly at first, contained commitments from all three parties on increases in wages and prices. Exceeding most expectations, the pacts brought inflation down below 20 percent over the course of the first year, without provoking a sharp recession. The intense negotiations, sometimes lasting most of a weekend, allowed business and government representatives to achieve the elusive balance between commitment and flexibility. In contrast to the success of tripartite pacts in Mexico, business and governments in Argentina and Brazil in the 1980s and 1990s occasionally attempted to negotiate stabilization agreements, but without having any real impact on macro stabilization. These proto-pacts broke down for a number of reasons, but the fact that business in both countries lacked economy-wide associations was certainly a contributing factor.

Regional integration was another policy in the 1990s that was broad in scope and had fairly uncertain, longer-term consequences for many businesses (Schneider, 2004b). Government negotiators in Mexico and Chile devised mechanisms for incorporating business input at all stages of negotiations. For example, in preparation for NAFTA negotiations, the Mexican government asked business associations to prepare studies on the likely impact of NAFTA on their sectors. Then, as negotiations progressed—for NAFTA in Mexico and for MERCOSUR and other agreements in Chile—government officials brought business into the figurative *"cuarto al lado"* or "room next door." In some instances, the room was literally next door; in others, business representatives sat right at the bargaining table; and in others, they were in constant phone contact. In Argentina and Brazil, in contrast, business was largely excluded from negotiations for MERCOSUR, and the agreement

---

[22] The literature on the pacts in Mexico is extensive. For overviews and bibliography, see Kaufman, Bazdresch, and Heredia (1994); Ortega (2002); Schneider (2004a, Chapter 8).

suffered subsequently from a lack of engagement by, and support from, business (Schneider, 2001).[23]

Education reform is also in the category of long-term policies with uncertain costs and broad scope. One puzzle of the 1990s is why business was not active in pressing governments for improving education (Kaufman and Nelson, 2004a).[24] Most observers thought education and vocational training would be essential to upgrading and competing in international markets, yet business has not been in the vanguard of groups demanding more commitment to education. The conclusion to a broad comparative study of policymaking in health care and education was that "broader business and industrial associations outside the health and education sectors were not engaged, even though in principle they have a stake in more efficient and effective health and education systems" (Kaufman and Nelson, 2004b, p. 503).

There are several possible reasons for business indifference to education policy. First, education policy is broad in scope and takes a long time to implement, and the problem for business participation is both one of collective action and of finding institutionalized means for coordinating participation over the longer term. Second, beyond the usual obstacles to collective action, some segments of business may actually be opposed to increased investment in education. One study in northeast Brazil found that business felt that greater investment in education in skills would lead workers to leave the state and undermine the advantages the state had in attracting investors interested in low labor costs (Tendler, 2002). Lastly, in the period since the 1990s, business in most countries may have had fewer worries about scarcities of skilled labor (Agosin, Fernández-Arias, and Jaramillo, 2009).[25]

Most countries of Latin America entered the 1990s with antiquated and inadequate port facilities. In the wake of trade liberalization, port

---

[23] See also Bouzas and Avogadro (2002), Motta Veiga (2002), and the other country studies in IDB (2002). Motta Veiga notes a trend toward greater participation by organized business, especially the CNI, in Brazil's trade negotiations in the 2000s (interview with Ricardo Markwald, May 28, 2002).

[24] Business was also not engaged in pension reform, except for financial institutions in the implementation phase of some privatization programs (Madrid, 2003b, pp. 202–03).

[25] The initial business response to import competition in the 1990s was to reduce employment and upgrade capital equipment. Layoffs flooded the labor market with skilled workers, and reduced employer incentives to push for investment in education (interview with a member of the board of Pão de Açucar, September 13, 2004).

reform soon became a rallying cry for business. Port reform is somewhat less broad in scope because it affects only importers and exporters directly, but it is still subject to familiar problems of collective action. However, the expected benefits are often large and fairly well known, so affected businesses have strong incentives to invest in pushing reform. The story of port reform in Brazil in the early 1990s reveals the capacity for collective action on the issue of port reform, but also the importance of institutionalized business participation in order to accompany longer-term implementation (Doctor, 2000). Business in Brazil mobilized an impressive lobbying operation in Brasília through the informal Ação Empresarial (a loose coordinating body for major sectoral associations) that effectively targeted both executive and legislative branches. Sustained business pressure helped move port reform through congress, which passed major new legislation relatively quickly. However, after this legislative victory, business demobilized, not suspecting that reform implementation would stall without continued pressure from business.

Another set of policies are designed to promote narrower, often sectoral changes in the economy. These policies used to be lumped together under the label industrial policy, but are often now called export promotion.[26] Information costs for narrower policies are somewhat lower, but uncertainty is greater, business commitment is essential, and implementation takes longer and is subject to more potential exogenous shocks. Yet, despite the complexity of export promotion, there are few successful examples of ongoing business/government collaboration to expand and upgrade exports—examples of the sort common in Asia. Export promotion in Latin America—even in some of the showcase sectors like Brazilian aircraft, Mexican auto parts, or Chilean timber and fish—seems to be a fairly top-down, government-directed policy process with little formal or institutionalized participation by business.[27]

Policies of privatization, deregulation, and reregulation are usually among the narrowest kinds of policies in terms of scope and number of businesses directly affected. Sectoral policies in these areas also generate

---

[26] On the success of export promotion in Latin America, see Schurman (1996), Wise (1999), and Schrank and Kurtz (2005). For a general defense of industrial policy, see Rodrik (2004). Schrank and Kurtz found that, among different types of promotion policies, credit support had a greater positive impact on exports than tax incentives.

[27] One exception is Asocoflores and Colombian flower exports (Méndez, 1993; Juárez, 1995).

uncertainties and offer major opportunities for large gains and losses, both short- and long-term. Business politics are therefore understandably intense. Moreover, because the policies are so narrow, business participation tends to be individual, opaque, and open to suspicions of favoritism and corruption (Schamis, 2002; Etchemendy, 2009). The design of policymaking is therefore usually intended precisely to exclude business and protect policymakers from lobbying. Reducing the discretion of policymakers by outsourcing evaluation studies, or using public auctions and closed bids, all reduce the ability of officials to bias the outcomes in favor of particular firms.

Looking more broadly across all types of policies, longer-term, credible processes and intertemporal agreement among strategic policy actors usually requires iterated interaction under changing economic conditions, as well as some institution building.[28] For business participants in the policy process, several institutional mechanisms can facilitate credible intertemporal commitment. One institution is a policy council, usually a joint public–private consultation board that by statute includes representation from organized business. These public–private policy councils were widespread in high-growth countries of Asia, especially Japan, Korea, Singapore, and Taiwan (Schwartz, 1992; Campos and Root, 1996). Consultative councils were also common in recent periods in Colombia, Chile, Costa Rica, and Mexico (Clark, 2001). Effective representation by business (or other social groups) seems to require that most of the seats reserved for business come from business associations.

The contrast in business participation in Chile before and after 1982 is stark, and illustrates the difference consultation can make (Silva, 1996). In the first phase of radical neoliberal restructuring (1975–82), policymakers excluded business associations and closed off formal channels of business participation in policymaking, although policy networks between top economic policymakers and a handful of conglomerates were very tight (Schamis, 2002). After 1983, the Pinochet government adopted a very different approach by shifting network connections to associations (by appointing representatives of associations

---

[28] Although less widely researched, and beyond the scope of this chapter, it is also worth noting that there are several important experiences of close business–government collaboration at the subnational level. Relations between business and provincial governments have historically been especially close in Monterrey (Nuevo León) and Medellín (Antiochia). See also Snyder (2001) on coffee in Mexico, and Montero (2001) on industry in Minas Gerais.

to government positions) and by creating many new policy forums to incorporate regular business input, again especially from associations, into policymaking. The pragmatic policies in the 1980s, formulated in consultation with business, generated high growth and consolidated market reforms.[29]

Another mechanism that may, over time, contribute to longer-term agreements between government and business actors is coalition government (Hall and Soskice, 2001, p. 49). This is the case in Europe, where some parties have been long-standing members of regularly reshuffled parliamentary coalitions. Recent examples of long-standing coalition partners are not common in the presidential systems in Latin America, but would include the PMDB and PFL in Brazil and the parties in the Concertación coalition in Chile (Amorim Neto, 2002). In contrast, strongly majoritarian systems like Argentina, Mexico, and Venezuela produce large shifts in governments and preclude stronger intertemporal commitments.

Political parties in Costa Rica have, over time, worked out an innovative arrangement for minority representation and infusing greater stability in policymaking, despite a two-party system with constitutional prohibition against immediate reelection. Policymakers delegated authority over many areas of economic and social policy to scores of decentralized agencies. By 1994, the so-called autonomous sector spent 30 percent of GDP—as much as the rest of the central government (Lehoucq, 2005, p. 19). The constitutionally enforced alternation of parties in power encouraged outgoing governments to delegate policymaking authority in order to insulate it from the incoming government. By the 1970s, as the autonomous sector continued to expand rapidly, the two largest parties came to an agreement on an ingenious arrangement to allow for greater central control of the autonomous sector, as well as the direct, ongoing representation of the party out of power. Known as the "4/3 Law," this arrangement allows the president to appoint four of the board members and allows the party with the second-largest number

---

[29] Brazil has had a number of private–public councils, including many related to monetary policy; however, the representatives from the private sector were individuals selected by the government who had little impact on policy. Most recently the Lula government created the CDES (Conselho de Desenvolvimento Econômico e Social) to promote dialogue between business, labor, and other social groups. However, again, most of the business members were individuals rather than representatives of associations.

of votes to appoint the other three board members (Lehoucq, 2005, p. 20). For business and other economic agents, this arrangement creates expectations of greater policy continuity and institutional stability from one government to the next.

The goal of this section was to provide empirical examples of business participation in different kinds of policies, ranging from tripartite negotiations on macro-stabilization programs to ongoing consultative forums for narrower policies of all sorts. In most of these empirical studies of actual policymaking, business participation tends to come through direct contact between top officials in the executive branch and individual businesspeople or representatives of business associations. The fact that other branches of government and other political actors like parties are less visible in mediating business participation reflects the continued dominance of the executive branch, both in nondemocratic settings and in recent democracies, especially those trying to manage acute economic crises. However, as democracies consolidate and crisis conditions fade, legislatures and judiciaries are likely to loom larger as mediators in economic policymaking and therefore as sites for more active business participation (Corrales, 2002; Eaton, 2002).

Conclusion

In terms of general patterns of policymaking, or what Spiller, Stein, and Tommasi (2008) refer to as the outer features of policymaking, several aspects of business participation deserve highlighting. First, the more encompassing the organization representing business, the more likely business influence will push policy toward the public-regarding end of the policy continuum (Olson, 1982, p. 50). Encompassing business representation comes primarily on issues relevant to large numbers of businesspeople and through formal associations, though it may occasionally also come through parties and networks. Business influences that tend toward the private-regarding end of the continuum are likely to arise in instances of narrow policies, or in the implementation of broader policies, and when business representation occurs predominantly through channels involving small numbers of firms or individuals. This fragmented representation is more common in political systems that lack encompassing associations and that privilege business participation in policy networks and lobbying.

Transparency in the policy process also encourages business participants to push for more public-regarding positions (public-regarding in the minimum sense of promoting greater allocative efficiency and not favoring particular interests). Transparency is partly a function of the capacity of the media to follow the policymaking process, but also of the general openness of the policy process. Beyond these systemic features, formal business organization and representation tend to make its influence more transparent; that is, if business is represented through associations, and if business has positions on policy councils, then business representatives are more likely to press more public-regarding preferences.

Lastly, two features of business participation favor longer intertemporal commitments among policymakers and businesspeople. The first, and institutionally strongest, is the representation of business on policy councils. This representation turns every policy discussion into a segment of a repeated game. Both policymakers and business representatives have incentives to develop reputations and to not renege on agreements reached in the policy council. If, in contrast, either side knows there is no provision for future meetings and negotiations, then temptations to renege are greater and intertemporal commitments consequently less credible and likely. The other feature of business politics that contributes to intertemporal commitment is informal. Long-standing policy networks can lower information costs across the public–private divide, and contribute to perceptions on both sides that the other side is not likely to do anything rash that would significantly harm the other. In this case, the intertemporal commitment is in fact diffuse and unspecified; it is more a set of shared expectations that, when problems or external shocks arise, they will be worked out in a reasonable fashion (see Thorp, 1991).

The analysis in this chapter of contemporary variations in business organization and patterns of participation in policymaking takes these variations largely as given. Other work traces the origins of these variations back to accumulated state actions that either favored or discouraged organization and close collaboration in policymaking (Schneider, 2004a). A core finding of this research was that the more state actors drew business associations into policymaking, and the more government officials delegated responsibility for policy implementation to associations, the greater were business incentives to invest in the institutional capacity of these associations. Although policymakers rarely had strengthening associations as a policy priority, the fact that these state actions affected business organization and participation in policy makes clear that these outcomes could in fact be objects of policy. At a minimum, strengthening incentives for collective action should be one of the important externalities that policymakers consider when evaluating policy alternatives.

CHAPTER 9

Labor Organizations and Their Role in the Era of Political and Economic Reform

M. Victoria Murillo and Andrew Schrank

Latin America's free-market revolution has been diverted—if not necessarily derailed—by a combination of "reform fatigue" and electoral competition (Sandbrook et al., 2006, p. 76). Left-leaning candidates have taken power in Argentina, Brazil, Chile, Ecuador, and Uruguay. Bolivia and Venezuela are governed by self-styled opponents of "savage capitalism."[1] And even moderate leaders are calling for heterodox alternatives to the erstwhile Washington Consensus. "You have to design policies based on growth and stability that can produce social welfare," argues President Leonel Fernández of the Dominican Republic. "And you have to have mechanisms of social solidarity that are additional to the market. That means looking at the European model that is based not just on the free market but on policies that take into account these social factors."[2]

Observers part company, however, over the likely consequences of the ongoing backlash against free-market reform. While some North American pundits and policymakers predict a return to the "bad old days" of inflation, austerity, and crisis,[3] and therefore decry the growth of "radical populism" in Latin America (LeoGrande, 2005), their critics

---

[1] See David Lynch, "Anger over Free-Market Reforms Fuels Leftward Swing in Latin America," *USA Today*, February 9, 2006, p. 1B.

[2] See Leonel Fernández, "We Shouldn't Get Ideological about Latin America's Problems," *FT.com*, March 10, 2006.

[3] Brian Kelly, "The Legacy of a Liberator Named Bolivar," *U.S. News and World Report*, May 15, 2006, pp. 10–11.

draw a distinction between the admittedly populist presidents of the Andean countries and their allegedly social democratic neighbors to the south.[4]

Who is correct? Does the rise of the democratic left presage the dawn of Latin American social democracy or a return to the bygone era of stop–go macroeconomic policymaking and crisis? The answers are anything but obvious, but they will almost certainly be determined at least in part by the strategies and tactics of organized labor. After all, the labor movement continues to play a dual role in the region's policymaking process. Unions and their members defend their traditional rights and privileges through industrial action (such as collective bargaining, strikes, and slowdowns) and political activity (through lobbying, lawsuits, and mass mobilization). At the same time, they offer their public- and private-sector interlocutors a potentially powerful ally in the pursuit of more encompassing and enduring intertemporal agreements. A substantial and growing body of social scientific literature therefore portrays the potential for a "positive class compromise" (Wright, 2000) as a contingent product of the nature and degree of working class organization.[5]

The Nature and Growth of Organized Labor in Latin America: Structural Factors

Organized labor is simultaneously a producer and product of the policymaking process. Unions and their members have not only defended and taken advantage of policies like regulation, protection, and the nationalization of industry—not to mention the public provision of a

---

[4] Michael Shifter, 2005. "Don't Buy Those Latin American Labels," *Los Angeles Times*, December 24, 2005, p. A28. Indira Lakshmanan, "A Growing Fight for Power on Latin American Left," *Boston Globe*, June 4, 2006, p. A6. See also Castañeda (2006); Sandbrook et al. (2006); Valenzuela (2006).

[5] Erik Wright (2000, p. 958) defines a "positive class compromise" as "a non-zero-sum game between workers and capitalists, a game in which both parties can improve their position through various forms of active, mutual cooperation." Wright posits a reverse-J-curve relationship between working class associational power and the realization of capitalist class interests. Employer interests are maximized by an atomized and disorganized working class. They decline with the growth of working class organization and political power. And they begin to rise again—albeit to a second-best level from the employer's perspective—when working class organization begins to have a positive impact on capitalist class interest by facilitating solutions to collective action problems in the realms of demand management, macroeconomic policymaking, training and skill formation, technology policy, and the like. See Calmfors and Driffill (1988) and Scarpetta and Tressel (2002) for empirical models that are broadly consistent with Wright's claim.

variety of social services—but have also resisted and suffered under the weight of their rollback and removal. A general equilibrium approach to the policymaking process is therefore particularly well-suited to the study of Latin American labor.

This discussion begins to formulate and deploy a general equilibrium approach by distinguishing two crucial determinants of organized labor's role in the policymaking process: goals and resources.

> Determinant 1. Organized labor's principal *goals* are material. Union members delegate authority to union leaders who, at least in principle, trade credible commitments regarding the actions and behavior of their members (labor peace, productivity targets, voting behavior, and the like) for a variety of material concessions (wages, benefits, and social services).

> Determinant 2. Organized labor's principal resources are human. Union members not only exercise de facto control over key aspects of production and distribution in market economies but simultaneously constitute a well-organized voting bloc capable of rewarding and punishing politicians in electoral democracies. Labor unions therefore aggregate and defend the material and political interests of their members through industrial action and political activity.

Latin American employers have traditionally been hostile to collective action on the shop floor. The region's workers have therefore been particularly fond of electoral strategies (Hawkins, 1967; Roberts, 2002). For example, Latin American unions made explicit bargains with labor-backed parties like the Argentine Partido Justicialista (PJ), the Mexican Partido Revolucionario Institucional (PRI), Peru's Alianza Popular Revolucionaria Americana (APRA), and Venezuela's Acción Democrática (AD) in the middle of the twentieth century. Labor-backed parties have responded to electoral imperatives and the relatively small size of the salaried labor force by appealing to peasant, middle, informal, and formal working class elements in various combinations, and have therefore been labeled "catch-all" parties by their observers and critics alike (Hawkins, 1967; Dix, 1989). However, they have almost invariably relied upon *core* constituencies of unions and their members, and have therefore incorporated labor through a complicated array of "inducements," like official recognition, monopolies of representation, compulsory membership, and "constraints" on union autonomy (Collier and Collier, 1979, 1991).[6]

The postwar era of import-substituting industrialization—and *étatisme*[7] more generally—constitutes the high water mark for the alliance of party and union in Latin America. Labor-backed parties deployed tariffs, quotas, and a host of regulatory devices designed to guarantee electoral majorities in the short run and to foster industrial development in the long run. Labor unions therefore gained members and influence in a wide array of protected and state-owned (or publicly subsidized) enterprises.

Nevertheless, Latin American unions continued to bear the scars of their mid-twentieth century origins well into the subsequent era of debt, dictatorship, crisis, and adjustment. Take, for example, the geography and demography of labor organization. Unions have traditionally been more encompassing and influential in the larger political economies of Mexico and South America, where political and economic imperatives conspired to foster aggressive industrial development efforts in the era of the Great Depression, than in their smaller and less consistently democratic neighbors, where policymakers faced "neither the temptation nor the opportunity to engage in large-scale import-substitution" (Seers, 1982, p. 86; see also Bronstein, 1997, p. 7; Frundt, 2002, p. 19)—a pattern that flies in the face of the pronounced *positive* relationship between openness and union density found in the advanced industrial countries (Ingham, 1974; Cameron, 1978; Katzenstein, 1985).[8]

Figure 9.1 plots the relationship between openness (the ratio of imports to GDP) and union density in 18 Latin American countries at the dawn of the region's debt crisis. Trade exposure is relatively low and union affiliation is relatively high in traditionally labor-mobilizing

---

[6] By way of contrast, the business associations discussed by Schneider (2004) generally lacked official partisan ties and their members therefore exercised political influence through personal linkages and economic influence.

[7] "*Étatisme*" refers to an effort to give the state a more prominent role in the production and distribution of goods and services.

[8] According to Murillo (2000, p. 144), the "West European version of corporatism assumes open economies and societal corporatism. The Latin American version assumes closed economies and puts greater emphasis on the use of state institutions to control labor organization."

FIGURE 9.1 | Openness and Unionization in Latin America, 1981–85

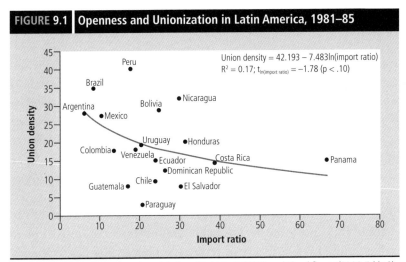

Source: Authors' calculations based on data from World Bank (2005) and Blanchflower (2006, Table 2).
Note: The import ratio is the average ratio of imports to gross domestic product between 1981 and 1985 (World Bank, 2005). Union density is the estimated percentage of union members in the workforce as a whole between 1981 and 1985 (Blanchflower, 2006).

political economies like Argentina, Brazil, Mexico, and Peru, where party–union linkages had fostered intensive industrial development efforts in potentially expansive domestic markets in the middle of the century. The relationship is reversed in traditionally elitist or exclusionary polities like the Dominican Republic, El Salvador, and Paraguay, where neither industrial development nor democratization had kept pace and labor had been drawn not toward populist parties like the PJ and AD but toward movements of the radical or revolutionary left (Frundt, 2002). The principal exceptions to the rule are Bolivia and Nicaragua—where unions gained members and influence by defending and taking advantage of more thoroughgoing social (or national) revolutions in the 1950s and 1970s, respectively (Nash, 1979; Stahler-Sholk, 1995).[9]

---

[9] The Federation of Mineworkers of Bolivia (Federación Sindical de Trabajadores Mineros de Bolivia, or FSTMB) constituted the traditional backbone of the Bolivian labor movement. "After the historical 1952 revolution," according to Harry Sanabria (2000, p. 60), "the FSTMB, whose phalanxes of armed miners were crucial for the revolution's success, came to wield enormous influence on the labor and political scene." Nicaraguan unions reaped the rewards of revolution a quarter of a century later. According to Richard Stahler-Sholk (1995, p. 79), the number of union members rose from 11 percent to 56 percent of the salaried labor force in the immediate aftermath of the Sandinista victory.

Crisis and Adjustment in the Late Twentieth Century: Organizational Variables

Labor's willingness and ability to influence the policymaking process are circumscribed by the organizational structure of the labor movement, as well as its relative size. Organizational factors include the *centralization* of unions (the number and nature of peak associations[10]), *collective bargaining* (at the local, firm, or industry level), and the nature and degree of *partisan competition* for labor's support. Table 9.1 includes the value of each variable for Latin America's traditionally inclusionary regimes in the 1980s.

The first two variables impinge on organized labor's ability to exercise influence over the policymaking process, not only through industrial and political action during the period of policy formation but also through the regulation of union or member behavior during the period of policy implementation. Only *encompassing* organizations with the authority to negotiate and enforce *nationwide* agreements can avoid free-riding by their members and challenges from rival unions (see Levitsky and Way, 1998, p. 183) and thereby make credible—and at least potentially public-regarding—intertemporal agreements with public and private-sector officials (Calmfors and Driffill, 1988; Wright, 2000; Scarpetta and Tressel, 2002). By way of contrast, the third variable influences organized labor's policy preferences and political options. Leadership competition from insurgent or opposition parties raises the cost and reduces the benefit of loyalty to traditional party allies, for insurgents not only disdain and discredit "blind" loyalty but simultaneously give union leaders an exit option (Burgess, 1998b).

Organizational variables are particularly salient at the implementation stage of the policymaking process—when key actors are tempted to defect from their formal commitments or informal bargains. Take the case of price stabilization. While workers reap the rewards of price stability, and therefore tend to embrace anti-inflationary measures in theory, they pay a high price for wage restraint, and therefore tend to undermine stabilization in practice. Thus, Ian Roxborough (1992, p. 645) portrays the

---

[10] Peak associations are organizations of organizations (or umbrella groups) that attempt to aggregate the interests of their affiliates and members. A highly centralized peak labor association would therefore count most of the country's unions and union members as affiliates or members.

TABLE 9.1	Union Organizational Structure in the 1980s		
Country	Union centralization (no. of peak associations)	Collective bargaining: Dominant level	Partisan competition: Incumbents at risk?
Argentina	Single	Industry	No
Brazil	Multiple	Local	Yes
Chile	Single	Firm	Yes
Colombia	Multiple	Firm/Craft	Yes
Mexico	Dominant	Industry/Local	No
Peru	Multiple	Firm	Yes
Uruguay	Single	Industry	No
Venezuela	Dominant	Local/Industry	Yes

Source: McGuire (1997, p. 268) and authors.

whole problem of inertial inflation as the Prisoner's Dilemma. "Unions will be 'suckers' if they agree to wage controls in a context where prices continue to rise; employers will be 'suckers' if they operate price controls in a situation where a tight labour market (or government intervention) enables unions to push up real wages so rapidly that profit margins are threatened." And the "suboptimal stable solution" of persistent inflation is therefore a common feature of Latin American history.

Policymakers can pursue price stability by either effacing or embracing organized labor. While military rulers pursued the repressive option in Brazil and the Southern Cone in the 1970s, according to the late Dudley Seers (1982, p. 83), they found that radical parties and trade unions did not "cease to be important, especially at the factory level," in their traditional industrial redoubts. In Brazil and Argentina, therefore, prices continued to double almost every year throughout the latter part of the decade.

They continued to accelerate into the 1980s, when democratically elected governments adopted, but could not enforce, anti-inflationary social pacts like the *Austral* and *Cruzado* plans (Roxborough, 1992). According to Roxborough (1992, p. 646), the plans foundered on the shoals of organizational factors like "divisions within both labour and business, the lack of trust between actors, generalised attempts to be 'free riders,' the technocratic orientations of the Argentine and Brazilian governments, and the confrontational strategies pursued by important segments of the labour movements in each country."

By way of contrast, Mexico avoided hyperinflationary episodes in the 1970s and adopted a relatively successful anti-inflationary pact when prices nonetheless began to rise in the 1980s. What differentiated Mexico's *Pacto de Estabilidad y Crecimiento Económico* (PECE) from either the *Austral* or *Cruzado* plans? According to Roxborough, Mexican trade unions and business associations "played an important role in policing the pact and in restraining their more impatient members." After all, Mexico not only featured "a relatively high level of unionization" by Latin American standards, but also played host to more powerful and encompassing labor and business associations than either Brazil or Argentina. "Mexican unions are well organized in a peak organization (the Congreso del Trabajo) with approximately 90% of all unions and union members," Roxborough concludes, and the country's employers are "well organised in a number of peak associations" as well (Roxborough 1992, p. 659; see also Schneider, 2004a, on business associations more generally).

In short, the PRI's more or less successful effort to combat inflation presupposed robust ties to encompassing associations of powerful member unions. By way of contrast, Argentina's Confederación General de Trabajo (CGT) had no authority over individual member unions, little capacity to prevent free riding, and an alliance with the opposition PJ that gave it an incentive to undercut—rather than support—anti-inflationary measures adopted by the governing Radical Party.[11] Finally, Brazil's Central Única dos Trabalhadores (CUT)—one of two rival peak associations—had long-standing ties to the principal opposition party and therefore had an incentive to defect rather than cooperate.[12]

Partisan alliances between encompassing union confederations and policymakers do not necessarily guarantee intertemporal agreement, however, for union behavior is also likely to be circumscribed by the nature and degree of competition for labor's political support. Take the case of Venezuela. While unions and labor leaders have traditionally been affiliated with the Confederación de Trabajadores de Venezuela

---

[11] The CGT called more than a dozen general strikes against the Alfonsín administration during the 1980s.

[12] Some might trace Mexico's relative anti-inflationary success to authoritarian rule. A substantial body of literature documents the persistence of genuine bargaining between the PRI and the CTM unions, however, and Roxborough discounts the idea that the unions were mere "puppets" of the state (Roxborough, 1992, p. 619). Furthermore, Mexico outperformed Argentina and Brazil on macroeconomic criteria during their respective authoritarian interludes as well (see, for example, Seers, 1982, p. 84).

(CTV), and have therefore been linked to AD, they confronted leadership competition from left-wing parties like the Causa R and the Movimiento Electoral del Pueblo in the early 1990s, and therefore demonstrated their independence and refusal to "sell out" by opposing their traditional ally's stabilization and reform measures—for better or for worse (Burgess, 1998a; Murillo, 2000).

Conflict and Compensation in the Reform Era: Policy Scope and Impact

The free-market reforms that followed hard on the heels of macroeconomic stabilization threatened organized labor in myriad ways. Economic liberalization and market opening placed the solvency of protected firms and the jobs of their unionized workers at risk. Privatization and fiscal austerity threatened public-sector employment and nonwage subsidies, as well. Efforts to deregulate labor markets promised to erode union influence throughout the economy and polity. Unemployment and the rollback of the social safety net raised the cost of job loss and lowered labor's bargaining power. And the intensification of international competition militated against improvements in wages, benefits, and working conditions more generally (Bronstein, 1997).

Unions have certainly suffered under the weight of crisis and reform. Organized labor's share of the Latin American labor force apparently declined from an average of 25 percent in the early 1980s to an average of 16.3 percent by the mid-1990s (IDB, 2003, p. 233). Wages, benefits, and working conditions have suffered as well—albeit less uniformly.

Organized labor's reactions to the reforms in question varied by issue area as well as by country, however, and they therefore deserve closer scrutiny. Economic policy reforms vary along two relevant dimensions: the *scope* and the *intensity* of their impact on unions and their members (see Table 9.2).

Labor unions have neither the will nor the ability to resist low-intensity reforms like tax reform or sectoral deregulation. They may voice their opposition, but they will save their limited resources for more important battles—especially during times of crisis.[13]

---

[13] Organized labor is by no means the sole arbiter of reform's advance, however, and low-intensity reforms may therefore face powerful sources of opposition and support outside the

TABLE 9.2	A Typology of Economic Reforms and Union Responses	
	Scope of impact	
Intensity of impact	Broad	Narrow
High	Rollback (labor law reform)	Compensation (privatization, social sector reform)
Low	Tacit acceptance (tax reform)	Tacit acceptance (telecommunications or energy deregulation)

Source: Adapted from Madrid (2003a, p. 62).

Labor Law Reform: Rollback

Labor unions respond to crisis by devoting their limited resources to campaigns that are broad in scope—that affect all or most of their members—and intense in impact. Labor law reform constitutes the archetypal example (Madrid, 2003a). Labor market flexibility is a threat not only to the wages, benefits, and working conditions of individual union members but to the very survival of the labor movement itself. And Latin American unions therefore redoubled their efforts to combat the deregulation of their markets in the late 1980s and 1990s.

The results of their efforts are by now clear. "Over the past 15 to 20 years there have been some attempts to reform labour laws," according to Simeon Djankov of the World Bank. "They have either been reversed completely or even further inflexibilities created."[14]

The labor market arguably constitutes the Achilles' heel of the liberal model—and the Waterloo of the Washington Consensus (Lora and Panizza, 2003, p. 128; Pagés, 2004, p. 67; Singh et al., 2005, pp. 17–18). While market reforms in the areas of trade, investment, and public procurement and ownership are designed and expected to engender the efficient reallocation of human as well as physical resources, and therefore all but *presuppose* the *deregulation* of the labor market, they threaten labor's traditional rights and privileges, and therefore

---

labor movement. Lora and Panizza (2003, p. 127) suggest that reform's advance has been greatest in trade and finance, moderate in taxation and privatization, and nonexistent or even negative in the labor market.

[14] Djankov, quoted in Richard Lapper, "Cutting the Ties that Bind," *Financial Times,* March 29, 2004, p. 2.

tend to *provoke* efforts to *reregulate* the labor market (Murillo, 2005; Murillo and Schrank, 2005). The point is not merely that unions aggregate their interests and resources to block the deregulation of the labor market *pace* (Madrid, 2003a), but that they push for *new* labor market regulations in order to offset or provide counter threats to their interests in *other* policy domains. Thus the "double movement" between "economic liberalism" and "social protection," christened by Karl Polanyi in the middle of the twentieth century, is alive and well in Latin America today—for better or for worse (Polanyi, 1944, p. 132; see also Piore and Schrank, 2006).

This study further examined the seemingly paradoxical growth of labor market regulation during the era of free-market reform (1985–2000) by disaggregating Latin American labor laws into their individual and collective components. The former regulate wages, benefits, and working conditions. The latter regulate organization, collective bargaining, and the right to strike. While 10 of 16 reforms to individual labor law rolled back preexisting regulations, and thereby increased labor market flexibility, 13 of 18 reforms to collective labor law added new regulations, and thereby undercut flexibility (Murillo, 2005; Murillo and Schrank, 2005). The reform pattern is consistent with this chapter's interpretation of union strategy, for collective labor law not only affects all unionized workers but provides the very foundation of their organizational existence, whereas individual labor law affects all workers regardless of their associational status and is therefore less central to union leaders.

The ability of organized labor to extract concessions in the realm of collective labor law is puzzling, however, for the free-market reforms adopted in the 1990s not only placed enormous pressure on labor costs, and thereby militated against the empowerment of organized labor in theory, but also provoked mass layoffs in the heavily unionized manufacturing and public sectors, and thereby militated against the empowerment of organized labor in practice. Why, then, did policymakers grant labor's demands? Union influence over the policymaking process in regard to collective labor law presupposed support from two different allies—labor-backed parties at home, and labor-backed policymakers overseas—in two different political and economic contexts. While labor-backed parties adopted relatively union-friendly labor reforms in traditionally *inclusionary* polities like Argentina and Venezuela, and thereby compensated their core constituents for liberal reforms in other issue areas, labor-backed policymakers in the United States conditioned preferential access to their own market on the recognition and defense of core labor standards in traditionally *exclusionary* polities like El Salvador and the Dominican Republic, and thereby appeased their own core constituencies (organized labor, human rights activists) at a time of unprecedented import penetration (Murillo and Schrank, 2005). The former trajectory is more common in the traditionally labor-mobilizing polities of South America, where import-substituting industrialization fostered the growth of labor-backed parties in the postwar era. The latter is the norm in the traditionally exclusionary environs of Central America, where more vulnerable unions decided to compensate for their impotence at home by searching for alliance partners overseas.

North American labor and human rights activists constituted all but ideal allies. After all, the U.S. Trade and Tariff Act of 1984 not only forces recipients of "better than most-favored nation" access to the U.S. market to take steps toward the defense of core labor standards, but also allows interested parties like labor and human rights activists to petition the United States Trade Representative (USTR) to review their records, evaluate their laws, and eventually even withdraw their access to the Generalized System of Preferences (GSP) for noncompliance. North American labor and human rights groups therefore petitioned the USTR on behalf of their Latin American associates throughout the late 1980s and 1990s (Frundt, 1998; Anner, 2002; Murillo and Schrank, 2005).

The petitioning process transforms the principal axis of the debate over labor law reform in the exporting country from *class* to *sector*. After all, the prospect of labor law reform typically pits workers, who are armed with their votes, the occasional lawsuit, and the threat of mass mobilization and strike (M.L. Cook, 2002, p. 16), against employers, who are armed with campaign contributions, lobbyists, and the implicit or explicit threat of an investment strike of their own (Barrett, 2001, p. 597). By tying market access to labor law reform, however, the USTR gives employers in the tradable sector an incentive to betray their class for their sector—that is, to defect from the latent capitalist coalition and to join forces with workers and activists in support of regulations that will in all likelihood burden employers in the nontradable sector as well.

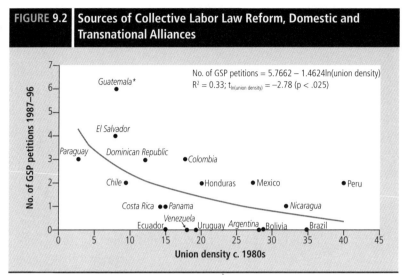

FIGURE 9.2 | Sources of Collective Labor Law Reform, Domestic and Transnational Alliances

$$\text{No. of GSP petitions} = 5.7662 - 1.4624\ln(\text{union density})$$
$$R^2 = 0.33;\ t_{\ln(\text{union density})} = -2.78\ (p < .025)$$

Source: The number of GSP petitions is from CBO (1997); union density is from Blanchflower (2006); and collective labor law reforms (italicized countries) are from Murillo and Schrank (2005, p. 975).
Note: Guatemala adopted a union-friendly labor law reform in the early 1990s but subsequently deregulated. Argentina deregulated and later reregulated. Nicaragua regulated, deregulated, and later reregulated again. The scatterplot is included for ease of presentation. A more statistically satisfying multivariate negative binomial model yields consistent results and is available from the authors upon request. Neither Chile, Mexico, nor Nicaragua is currently party to the GSP; however, all Latin American countries, including Chile, Mexico, and Nicaragua, were party to the system in the late twentieth century.

Figure 9.2 plots the number of GSP petitions filed per country between 1987 and 1996 by the level of union density in the early 1980s. The names of countries that reformed their collective labor laws in a union-friendly direction appear in italics. The data suggest that domestic and transnational alliances are for the most part substitutes rather than complements. While labor-backed parties adopted precautionary or compensatory reforms in traditional union strongholds like Argentina and Venezuela, transnational alliances achieved similar ends through trade conditionality in traditionally exclusionary environments like Paraguay, the Dominican Republic, and Central America.[15]

---

[15] The principal exceptions—Chile and Nicaragua—are rendered difficult to classify as either inclusionary or exclusionary due to their radically shifting political fortunes over the course of the past quarter of a century. Chile is a traditionally inclusionary polity with an unprecedented authoritarian interlude. Nicaragua is a traditionally exclusionary polity forever changed by a decade of socialist rule. Domestic and transnational alliances may therefore have proven complementary in one or both countries.

The results are neither trivial nor cosmetic. After all, the PJ not only centralized collective bargaining but reaffirmed union monopolies of representation and control over social services in Argentina (Etchemendy, 2001; M.L. Cook, 2002; Murillo, 2005; Murillo and Schrank, 2005; Etchemendy and Collier, 2007). AD made broadly similar concessions to the CTV in Venezuela (Burgess, 1998a; M.L. Cook, 1998; Murillo, 2005). The Concertación tempered the most liberal aspects of the military-era labor law in Chile (Pulido, 2001; Murillo, 2005). And Central American and Caribbean policymakers not only traded their traditionally repressive labor laws for preferential access to the U.S. market but redoubled their notoriously lax enforcement efforts as well. For example, the Guatemalans and Salvadorans doubled the size of their respective enforcement divisions in the 1990s and early 2000s. And the Dominicans not only tripled the size of their own enforcement division but adopted new hiring criteria—including legal credentials and competitive examinations—and employment guarantees, as well (Piore and Schrank, 2006; Schrank, 2009).

The reforms underway in Central America and the Caribbean are by no means uncontroversial. The International Labour Organization (ILO) acknowledges a number of "pending" issues, including limits to freedom of association (ILO, 2003, p. 3; see also ILO, 2004). And the ILO's approach to international standard setting is controversial, in any event (Caraway, 2006). But the laws on the books today are—by almost any metric—more favorable to organized labor than their predecessors. The average Central American country has ratified 50 percent more ILO conventions today than a quarter of a century ago (ILO, 2006).[16] The subregion actually outperforms the rest of Latin America on the ILO's newly established "intentions and commitments index" (ILO, 2002, pp. 57–58, Table 1b). And proponents of international labor standards tend not only to praise the "new and improved labor codes" (Douglas, Ferguson, and Klett, 2004, p. 298) on their merits but to acknowledge their all but revolutionary nature as well.

---

[16] Nancy Chau and Ravi Kanbur demonstrate that ILO ratifications are systematically related to a number of exogenous variables and are, among other things, "an indicator of higher domestic standards" (see Chau and Kanbur, 2002, p. 22).

Privatization and Trade Liberalization: Compensation

Massive resistance and rollback are neither likely nor necessary in the face of reforms that are narrower in scope and correspondingly asymmetrical in impact. On the one hand, unions find it hard to muster widespread support for campaigns against asymmetrical or divisive reforms like privatization and trade liberalization. Unions that are unlikely to be affected by the reforms are neither willing to devote their scarce resources to altruistic or ideologically motivated campaigns nor able to ensure that their efforts will be rewarded by reciprocal "tit for tat" behavior down the road. On the other hand, policymakers tend to purchase union support for narrow reforms with compensatory measures and side-payments. "Where reforms only affect a few unions," writes Raúl Madrid (2003a, p. 63), "it is much easier to compensate the losers, which can mitigate their opposition to reform. Compensation may involve rewarding the leaders of the unions with government posts or providing the unions with some sort of financial compensation (such as a stake in the privatized enterprise), which can typically only be doled out to a limited number of unions or union leaders."

There are many examples of such compromises/negotiations (Oxhorn, 2005). President Carlos Menem derailed opposition to the privatization of petroleum, railroads, and public utilities in Argentina by giving Peronist labor leaders lucrative positions in his government (Levitsky and Way, 1998, p. 177; Manzetti, 1999, pp. 96–97; Madrid, 2003a, pp. 72–73). The PRI pursued broadly similar tactics in Mexico (Brachet-Márquez, 1992, p. 108; Macleod, 1998, p. 33). And Brazilian policymakers continue to offer dissident union leaders jobs and contracts in their country's insatiable—but not necessarily ineffective—labor bureaucracy (Houtzager, 2001, p. 20; Damiani, 2003, pp. 102–04). "Given the precariousness of the labor market in Brazil," writes Thomas Skidmore, "these relatively well-paid positions have great appeal to all but the most dedicated political activists" (Skidmore, 2004, p. 141).

Government jobs are not simply payoffs to individual labor leaders, however, but are a form of "social linkage" (Levitsky and Way, 1998, p. 177) that *facilitates* financial compensation. For example, the PJ not only staffed the Argentine labor ministry and national health administration agency with loyal labor leaders but used their presence to negotiate important "material exchanges" (Levitsky and Way, 1998, p. 177), including a bailout of union debts, the preservation of labor's virtual monopoly over the provision of health insurance, and union participation in the newly created market for worker's compensation (Murillo, 2000; Etchemendy, 2001; M.L. Cook, 2002).[17]

Financial compensation is a particularly prominent feature of privatization, however, and tends to accrue to party-affiliated unions with de facto—if not necessarily de jure—monopolies of representation in their respective public-sector activities (Murillo, 2001). While powerful unions of public employees offer their partisan allies a potential threat (defection) as well as a political opportunity (loyalty), and are therefore able to demand compensation for their support, their decentralized or divided counterparts offer allied policymakers little more than aggravation, and are therefore unable to demand comparable concessions. Take, for example, the case of privatization in Venezuela. President Carlos Andrés Pérez offered the cohesive and combative employees of the state telecommunications monopoly an ownership stake in their prospective private employer—as well as representation on the board of directors and a variety of contract and employment guarantees—but ran roughshod over objections to the private provision of education emanating from fragmented unions of ideologically heterogeneous teachers (Murillo, 2001).[18]

Nor is Venezuela unique. Argentina and Mexico not only offered their own telecommunications workers broadly similar concessions in the run-up to privatization in the 1990s, but compensated their electrical workers and their encompassing organizations as well (Murillo, 2001). A similar dynamic emerged when labor-backed policymakers pursued trade reform and entered regional integration initiatives. For example,

---

[17] The "government jobs for political loyalty" strategy may well *depend* upon the concomitant compensation of the rank-and-file, rather than its repression or exclusion. According to Karen Remmer, the labor leaders who challenged the Pinochet regime in the late 1970s included traditional moderates who had been appointed to a variety of government posts in the immediate aftermath of the coup, only to defect from the military regime following the "application of controls to the trade union movement as a whole" in the mid-1970s. "As the implications of these controls became clearer, both in response to the elaboration of the government's political plans and the functioning of its economic policies," she concludes, "the junta's base of trade union support disintegrated" (Remmer, 1980, p. 291). See Kurtz (1999) for a broader account of the junta's rightward drift and corresponding alienation of moderate elements in the trade unions and the Christian Democratic Party.

[18] A sectoral account of the divergent outcomes is gainsaid by the fact that the PRI compensated the well-organized Mexican teachers for broadly similar reforms (Murillo, 2001).

Argentina and Venezuela offered encompassing unions of automobile workers a variety of compensatory measures, including a commitment to human resource development, input into personnel decisions, and supplementary tariffs and quotas (Murillo, 2001; Etchemendy, 2001). Labor unions have been relentless advocates of antidumping and countervailing duties throughout the region (Guasch and Rajapatriana, 1998). And Marcelo Olarreaga and his colleagues find that deviations from liberal tariff regimes are associated with a proxy for labor union influence in both Mexico and the Southern Cone (Olarreaga and Isidro Soloaga, 1998, p. 314; de Melo, Grether, and Olarreaga, 1999, p. 19).

Murillo (2001) traces concessions to two different union strategies—*restraint* and *militancy*—and offers a bivariate explanation of their occurrence and consequences. The first variable, partisan competition for labor's political support, affects the likelihood and degree of union militancy. While labor leaders are ideologically and instrumentally connected to their partisan allies, and therefore tend to exercise restraint when their partisan loyalties go unchallenged, they are ultimately committed to their own survival, and therefore tend to embrace militancy when their alliances and authority are threatened by dissident factions from rival parties. The second variable, interunion competition for members, affects the payoff to restraint and militancy. While encompassing unions have much to offer their traditional party allies, and are therefore able to extract meaningful concessions regardless of whether they pursue restraint or militancy, their fragmented counterparts have decidedly less influence, and are therefore unable to extract comparable concessions (see Table 9.3).

Murillo's framework offers a compelling explanation of the nature of economic adjustment under labor-backed parties in the 1980s and

TABLE 9.3	Union Strategies and Outcomes	
	Partisan competition for labor leadership	
	One-party monopoly	*Multiparty competition*
Interunion competition for members	*Monopoly/ Encompassing unions*	Cooperation (effective restraint)	Opposition (effective militancy)
	Competition/ Competitive unions	Subordination (ineffective restraint)	Resistance (ineffective militancy)

Source: Adapted from Murillo (2000, p. 153).

1990s. While powerful leaders of encompassing unions are paid hand-somely for their loyalty in normal times, and therefore tend to exercise restraint where possible, they are threatened by rank-and-file defection to more radical parties and tendencies in times of crisis, and therefore tend to adopt militant postures. According to Murillo, Venezuelan tele-communications workers responded to left-wing appeals by abandoning restraint for militancy in the early 1990s. Argentine militants dispelled a dissident faction of telecommunications workers in Buenos Aires and moved in the opposite direction (from militancy to restraint) over the same period. Mexican telecommunications workers practiced loyalty to the PRI in the face of market reform throughout the period. However, labor-backed policymakers offer their more encompassing union allies concessions regardless of whether they are pursuing restraint or militancy. The key to compensation is therefore the degree of union concentration or fragmentation rather than the intensity of partisan competition for labor's support (Murillo, 2001).[19]

Nevertheless, Murillo's model of compensation is designed to account for market reforms undertaken by populist or labor-backed parties—that is, a "Nixon-goes-to-China" scenario (Cukierman and Tommasi, 1998)—and therefore leaves a number of questions unanswered. Do elite-based or center-right parties compensate unions for costly free-market reforms? And, if so, how and why? While the dynamics of compensation are likely to differ in the absence of labor–party linkages, the extant literature is all but silent on the question of how. This study

---

[19] Argentina and Mexico evince a wide array of compensatory strategies. Some unions used their influence in the executive and legislative branches of the Argentine government, and the occasional show of force, to derail labor law reform, modify health care reform, and mitigate the more threatening aspects of pension reform (Etchemendy, 2001; Murillo, 2001; Madrid, 2003a). Other Argentine unions adapted to privatization and deregulation by negotiating employee stock ownership agreements, union buyouts of privatized assets, and potentially lucrative positions in the provision of private pension funds, workplace accident insurance, and health care. Finally, a third group reinvented itself by breaking with the PJ entirely, denouncing corporatism, and establishing a new Congress of Argentine Workers (Murillo, 1997a). A similar pattern can be observed in Mexico. The more traditional PRI unions used their political influence to derail labor law reform and the proposed overhaul of the public housing system. By way of contrast, the so-called "new" unions, including teachers and telephone workers, modernized and participated in privatization and provision of social services on favorable terms. Finally, the more independent unions that had emerged in the 1970s continued to denounce free-market reform *and* corporatism. In both countries, therefore, the proposed labor law reform would link anti-corporatist unions and employers to no avail (Murillo, 1997b, 2001).

therefore offers—but does not systematically test or defend—a "divide-and-conquer" hypothesis as a first step toward formulating an answer. The hypothesis departs from the distinct goals of mass- and elite-based parties vis-à-vis organized labor. While labor-backed parties need to defend their working class allies (and alliances) from the high cost of adjustment, and therefore view compensation as a form of cement, their center-right rivals need to prevent their working class enemies from impeding costly adjustment, and therefore view compensation as a potential solvent—that is, a wedge that will divide an otherwise threatening opposition. Thus, Brazilian officials defused the appeals of militant union leaders who opposed privatization by offering their rank-and-file constituents shares in firms like Usiminas and Embraer on particularly attractive terms (Montero, 1998). And the Chamorro government used a similar divide-and-conquer strategy to neutralize Sandinista opposition to privatization in Nicaragua (Prevost, 1996, pp. 312–14).

The point is most assuredly not that cooptation and fragmentation are easy or that policymakers always achieve their goals. Unions have not only extracted concessions from their political representatives, but have at times waylaid their plans entirely. For example, Uruguayan workers and their allies blocked the privatization of their state-owned telecommunications monopoly in a nationwide referendum in the early 1990s.[20] Unions in Ecuador used industrial action to achieve broadly similar ends a decade later.[21] And Mexican oil workers continue to resist "any measures perceived to be back door privatization" of PEMEX.[22]

Public service providers are particularly adept at exercising influence over the policymaking process—and their influence arguably grows *after* policy adoption. Take, for example, the case of medical professionals like doctors and nurses. The services they provide are not only essential but nontradable; that is, they are largely insulated from international competition. Their "positional power," or disruptive potential, is therefore

---

[20] Nathaniel Nash, "Uruguayans Still Resisting Call to Modernize Economy," *New York Times*, February 28, 1993, p. A21.

[21] Nicholas Moss, "Three Strikes in Ecuador's Privatisation Series," *Financial Times*, June 14, 2002, p. 3.

[22] Richard Lapper, "Change Is Needed but Far from Easy at PEMEX: Unless Reforms are Imposed on the State Oil Monopoly the Country Could Rely on Imports by 2015," *Financial Times*, December 13, 2005, p. 2.

enormous (Perrone, Wright, and Griffin, 1984, p. 414; see also Eckstein, 2004, p. 14). Nor are Latin American service providers unique. On the contrary, Geoff Garrett and Christopher Way found that public-sector workers who are insulated from international competition were less likely to exercise wage restraint in the developed market economies, as well (Garrett and Way, 1995).

Medical professionals have used their positional power to combat privatization and spending cuts throughout the region. In fact, Julio Savino of the Pan American Health Organization has identified more than 100 nationwide strikes of health service providers in more than a dozen different Latin American countries since 2003, and has traced their origins to privatization, austerity, and salary disputes (Scavino, 2005). Salvadoran doctors and nurses have been among the most vocal, as well as the most persistent, critics of privatization and austerity,[23] but they are not alone. Medical professionals have made repeated appeals for higher salaries, better resources, more stable career paths, and an end to contracting out in countries like Bolivia, Peru, the Dominican Republic, Honduras, and Nicaragua. Policymakers have responded to their appeals by raising their salaries, abandoning (or at times postponing) privatization, creating new institutions for interest intermediation, and in a number of important cases stepping down.

Striking medical professionals are by no means omnipotent; policymakers have also responded with threats, dismissals, and outright repression.[24] But Scavino (2005, esp. pp. 7–8) notes that doctors have irreplaceable skills and a high degree of legitimacy among the general public and therefore tend to achieve their goals with surprising frequency. Nor are they alone. A substantial and growing body of research suggests that skilled public sector professionals are at the forefront of Latin America's new protest movements—and generally command a good deal of public support (Eckstein, 2004). Thus, the locus of organizational and oppositional activity appears to have moved from the private sector to the public sector over time.

---

[23] Catherine Elton, "Working Class in El Salvador Fighting Medical Privatization," *Houston Chronicle*, March 9, 2003, p. A32.

[24] Lucía Navas and Haydée Brenes, "MINSA alista despidos." *El Nuevo Diario* (Managua), January 23, 2006. Available online at http://impreso.elnuevodiario.com.ni/2006/01/23/nacionales/10944.

Conclusion

Organized labor has played and will continue to play an important part in the Latin American policymaking process. While unions and their members have suffered enormously under the combined weight of austerity and adjustment, and are therefore at their low ebb in terms of membership and influence on the proverbial shop floor, they are neither dead nor particularly docile—their relatively "low level of strike activity" notwithstanding (Kurtz, 2004, p. 276). On the contrary, Susan Eckstein holds that private-sector strikes have been rendered "risky and ineffective" (Eckstein, 2004, p. 28) by globalization and that unions have therefore redoubled their efforts to pursue their goals in the political arena. Organized labor not only formed the backbones of the movements that brought presidents like Lula, Néstor (and later Cristina Fernández de) Kirchner, and Evo Morales to power but also played a key part in the impeachment or ouster of their predecessors (including Fernando Collor de Mello, Gonzalo Sánchez de Lozada, and Carlos Mesa). And Kathryn Hochstetler (2006) finds that unions have been at the forefront of successful as well as unsuccessful movements to depose democratically elected presidents throughout Latin America over the past quarter of a century.

Latin American unions have a number of valuable assets at their disposal and continue to use their assets to defend the interests of their members. They command the loyalty of millions of individual workers and their families. They take advantage of alliances with political parties, social movements, and their fellow trade unionists at home and abroad. They control strategic activities in their respective public and, to an admittedly lesser degree, private sectors. They are certainly no more likely to disappear now than 30 years ago—when they survived not only the debt crisis and austerity but the imprisonment, torture, and systematic murder of their leaders.

The question, therefore, is not whether but how workers and their representative organizations will influence the region's political process in the years to come. Will they embrace (and be embraced by) formal institutions and arrangements? Or will they be condemned to outsider status and drawn toward extra-parliamentary activity? While North American officials are at best ambivalent and at worst pessimistic about the current state of affairs, and are particularly exercised by the apparent rebirth of the Latin American left, their cynicism is not entirely warranted.

After all, European labor relations are marked by a vibrant and by no means threatening tradition of democratic corporatism. Latin American industrial relations bear the scars of corporatism—both democratic and authoritarian—as well. A number of the compromises and concessions that marked the free-market reform era arguably served to underscore, rather than undermine, the region's corporatist tendencies. Financial compensation has transformed tens of thousands of workers into stock owners and stakeholders in some of the region's largest firms (see Kikeri, 1998, p. 22). Unions have engaged in tripartite negotiations over wages, prices, reforms, and working conditions (Bronstein, 1995). Labor ministries have adopted a "tutelary" Franco-Iberian approach to labor market regulation and law enforcement (Piore and Schrank, 2006; Pires, 2008; Schrank, 2009). And vocational education and training institutions have not only grown in size and scope throughout the region but have made successful—if modest—efforts to mimic the German "dual system" of workforce development as well (Gallart, 2001; Galhardi, 2002).

The point is most assuredly not that Latin America is beginning to look like Western Europe. Nothing could be further from the truth. The aforementioned examples are limited in scope as well as significance. They are matched—and perhaps even outnumbered—by anti-corporatist or liberal counterexamples. And Latin American labor unions continue to lose members, money, and influence at an alarming rate.

The point is simply that Latin America's deepest tendencies are corporatist rather than liberal; that corporatist institutions are not obviously inferior to liberal ones from the standpoint of growth and distribution; and that policymakers who are interested in forging durable intertemporal agreements capable of generating sustainable long-run development should at the very least consider embracing and improving, rather than eliminating, Latin American corporatism. After all, European history offers at least some reason to believe that corporatist institutions can be improved over time. Latin American history offers little reason to believe that they can be eliminated over time—and no reason at all to believe that their elimination would constitute or give birth to an improvement in living standards in any event.

CHAPTER 10

The Latin American News Media and the Policymaking Process

Sallie Hughes

Latin American policy studies typically do not explore the role of the news media as participants or even influential outsiders in the policymaking process. If mentioned at all, the press usually appears as a passive intermediary in a two-step process linking elite messages and mass opinion. Media are conceptualized as conduits for elite information without direct consideration of how news media messages are constructed or what influences they might have on policymakers, the policy process, or public opinion about policy options (Moreno, 1996; Armijo and Faucher, 2002; Heredia and Schneider, 2003; Hochstetler, 2003; Wampler, 2004).[1]

Armijo and Faucher, for example, refer to news media as an "elite-controlled resource" (2002, p. 20). Heredia and Schneider speak of the need "to package" unpopular reforms within popular proposals (2003, pp. 7, 8), but do not explore under what conditions media may unwrap those packages for public display. Several authors advise reformers to control how policy is framed in political discussions and public perceptions, without analyzing how to convince the media to reflect such framing (Bresser-Pereira, 2003; Panizza, 2004).

On the other hand, regional media analysts approach the media and policy nexus by analyzing the rise (and sometimes decline) of

[1] An exception is Cortázar Velarde (2002), as well as studies of media influence in communications policymaking including Hughes (2009), Hughes and Prado (forthcoming), and Sosa Plata and Gómez García (2008). Johnson's forthcoming article, "The Media's Dual Role: 'Watchdog' and Guardian of their Own Interests," is an important addition to these studies.

media-centered political scandals or assertive journalism in the region (Waisbord, 1996, 2000; Hughes, 2006; Peruzzotti and Smulovitz, 2006; Pinto, 2009a, 2009b) as well as in the large literature examining media effects in elections (Moreno, 1996; Lawson et al., 2007; Porto, 2007; Hughes and Guerrero, 2009). However, neither of these approaches has developed into a full line of scholarly inquiry into media influences on policy or public opinion.

While researchers have failed to fully engage the issue, Latin American politicians perceive huge media influences on policymaking. These include the ability of news coverage to set the policymaking agenda, accelerate the pace of decision making, change the incentives for policy support, and increase the costs of rent seeking. As a chief executive said, "The media today have a power that can bring down a minister, that can influence a policy, and that is setting the agenda."[2]

Research based in the United States suggests that policymakers' perceptions of media effects are as important as real, measurable influences because perceptions prompt policymakers to anticipate future media behavior as they strategize and act on current policy decisions and their presentation to the public (O'Heffernan, 1991; Zaller, 1994). Accordingly, some Latin American governments have begun to implement the "strategic communication" techniques now pervasive in U.S. politics and policymaking (Kernell, 1997; T.E. Cook, 1998; Bennett, 2003). The goals of strategic communication are to develop and communicate a message that promotes a political goal. To do so, strategic communication specialists use polls, focus groups, and reaction groups of opinion leaders to shape messages that target specific audiences, typically via the mass media. In the United States, these techniques are not typically used to gather better information to guide politicians in their policy decisions, Bennett writes, but to find "the right language to sell already-made decisions to the public" (2003, p. 141).

While studies of their use in Latin American policymaking are rare,[3] Latin American political consultants have embraced U.S. tech-

---

[2] Quoted in UNDP (2004, p. 169). Translated by author from the original Spanish, "Los medios hoy tienen un poder que puede tumbar un ministro, que puede influir en una política y que está marcando la agenda."

[3] See Conaghan and de la Torre (2008) for a study on Ecuadorian President Rafael Correa's use of these techniques to secure constitutional reform.

niques (Plasser, 2000, 2001)—and, one could posit, their objectives as well. How polls and focus groups are used—to measure public opinion to guide policymaking, to persuade public opinion to support already determined policy, or some combination of both—would seem to depend on the needs and philosophies of policymakers.

The goal of strategic communication programs can be to obtain elected office, which is most typical in Latin America, or to promote a public policy, which is less common (Plasser, 2000, 2001; Bennett, 2003).[4] Latin American politicians guided by *consultores políticos* (political consultants) or *asesores de imagen* (image consultants) have used strategic communication techniques in election campaigns since the 1980s (Plasser, 2000). The use of policy-focused polls and focus groups in Latin America probably began in earnest with Mexican President Carlos Salinas de Gortari (1988–94), who established that country's first presidential polling office in 1989 (Moreno, 1996; Gamboa, 1999).

Theorists posit two reasons for the proliferation of strategic communication techniques internationally. The first is the international diffusion of ideas through education and professional networks such as the Latin American Political Consultants Association (ALACOP), established in 1995. The second is comprised of endogenous factors associated with processes of modernization and secularization. In the Latin American case, these are primarily political liberalization and the related need to address public opinion in a more efficient way, but also the uneven move toward catch-all parties and candidate-centered elections (Plasser, 2000; Carey, 2003; Coppedge, 2003; Dresser, 2003; Levitsky and Cameron, 2003; Hallin and Mancini, 2004).

Anecdotal evidence suggests that even small Latin American countries now conduct polls and focus groups when they launch large program initiatives. The Government of Nicaragua, for example, hired an international consulting firm to create the communication strategies for its National Development Plan in 2003. The company used an opinion poll, focus groups, and opinion leader discussion groups to identify key

---

[4] Personal interview with Juan Carlos Gamboa, president of Development Communication Consultants and former Senior Vice President for Public Affairs at Fleishman-Hillard, Miami, October 17, 2005. Gamboa has worked directly with the Governments of Ecuador, El Salvador, Guatemala, Honduras, Mexico, Nicaragua, and Panama. Author review of presidential Web sites, government communication policies, and national press reports in 12 countries. See also Hughes (2000) and Tilson (2004).

audiences, design tactics to reach them, and create the name, slogan, and key messages of the program (Fleishman-Hillard International Communication, 2003).

This author's review in 2005 of presidential Web sites, government communication policies, and national press reports for 12 countries found that larger countries have created full-time offices dedicated to conducting polls, focus groups, and other strategic marketing techniques to shape public opinion and test political messages for the media (Hughes, 2005). Brazil and Mexico stand out. Both countries had created cabinet-level offices dedicated to measuring, analyzing, and shaping public opinion. Chilean President Ricardo Lagos had a permanent group of advisors dedicated to measuring public opinion for strategic communication and image making, referred to in political circles by their location, "the second floor of La Moneda" (Amaro, 2001; Ruiz-Tagle, 2005). Argentina's Communication Secretariat, housed in the cabinet chief minister's office, is charged with these functions (Government of Argentina, 2003). Colombia's presidents seem to have relied upon ad hoc advisors (López, 2003),[5] as have other countries' governments.

Complementing strategic communication practices is another set of techniques known in the comparative literature as "news management." Like strategic communication, the proliferation of these practices is a response to news media in market-oriented democracies that have simultaneously become more important in governing, more conflictive and personality-centered, and less controlled by legitimizing ideologies or strong-arm tactics (Swanson, 2004). The aims of news management are to enhance the uniformity, salience, and credibility of messages about government, policy, and politicians carried in the news media. The ultimate goal of news management is not only to insert messages in news coverage, but to influence the interpretive frames that journalists emphasize when covering a news issue or event. The frame—for example, whether street protest is represented as a legitimate pressure tactic or an inconvenience to motorists—determines the sources, questions, and informational hierarchies that journalists use in their news stories (Altheide, 1996; Bennett, 2003). Setting and controlling news frames are

---

[5] See also Isolda María Vélez Holguín, "A Pastrana le cobraron en imagen sus errores," *El Colombiano*, online edition, Medellín, Colombia, 2002. Available online at http://www.elcolombiano. com/proyectos/balancepresidencial/textos/imagen/pastrana.htm.

crucial for policymakers. For example, reformers in Brazil eventually were able to frame administrative reform as a way to empower state action by creating greater efficiency rather than as part of a neoliberal plot to slash unionized government jobs (Bresser-Pereira, 2003).

Swanson (2004, p. 51) identifies the common techniques of news management internationally:

"... politicians and officials have become more sophisticated and effective at manipulating news coverage by such means as staging events that are guaranteed to satisfy journalists' commercial need for interesting video pictures, timing statements and actions to meet news deadlines, staying 'on message' to attract coverage to well-chosen campaign themes, and the omnipresent 'spin' by which political actors try to shape journalists' reports to partisan advantage."

In most government communications offices, publishing press releases and transcripts of speeches is the norm. However, like strategic communications, more sophisticated news management techniques have begun to be used to further image building and, at times, policymaking goals. In Mexico's Vicente Fox administration, former press secretary Martha Sahagún set weekly agendas of themes that would be promoted in the press and e-mailed "the line of the day" to cabinet secretaries during her brief tenure. She was unsuccessful at creating a coherent agenda or uniformity of message because cabinet ministers rebelled and either made their own statements or leaked information about internal discord to the press (Hughes, 2000). Sahagún did have some successes, especially in creating highly visual "pseudo-events." She was able to place video and photos in a number of national media of President Vicente Fox eating with street children before his inaugural address. Her masterstroke was "the kiss beamed around the world"— photos of her own wedding to the president one year after his electoral victory—which some say supplanted critical reviews of Fox's first year in office that otherwise would have received prominent play on that day. These events may have helped Fox's personal popularity, but could not overcome an opposition-controlled congress, resistance within his own political party, or no-reelection rules that distance Mexican legislators from their constituents.

Like Sahagún, former Chilean Press Secretary Patricia Politzer's policy of centralizing the press agenda and messages was undermined when presidential advisors cut off her access to the president (Amaro, 2001). Ministers were particularly upset at her rule prohibiting off-the-record interviews.

In Argentina, the Communications Media Secretariat under Néstor Kirchner published a sophisticated communications plan that closely follows the tenets of strategic communication and news management. It included systematic use of polls, media audience surveys, and content monitoring of news to determine the government's "positioning" in public opinion, as well as "inter-ministerial coordination" meetings to set a common communications agenda and message of the day (Government of Argentina, 2003). Despite the plan, some Argentine journalists said that in practice only the chief cabinet minister spoke to reporters and that old-style cronyism involving lucrative advertising contracts was used to tame the press. The tactic proved especially effective during an economic crisis that slashed readership and private-sector advertising (Committee to Protect Journalists, 2003; Inter-American Press Association, 2005).[6]

Cronyism, propagandist use of state media, and old-style repression in media–state relations are not new in democratic Latin America. Frequently in the last two decades, elected politicians across the region have turned to less-than-democratic techniques to co-opt and control critical media outlets or individual journalists. These include protecting broadcasters from competition in some countries, while distributing broadcast frequencies to friends, family, or political allies inside and outside of government in others. As in Argentina, manipulating the award of government advertising contracts remains common. In Peru, Alberto Fujimori was famous for creating tabloid newspapers that personally attacked journalists and buying off other media owners outright (Costa and Brener, 1997; Conaghan, 2002; Rockwell and Janus, 2003; Hughes and Lawson, 2004, 2005; Tilson, 2004). This author's research

---

[6] See also Dario Gallo, "Amor por encargo: el gobierno usa 80 millones en avisos para presionar a medios y conseguir oficialismo," *Noticias*, Buenos Aires, March 7, 2004. Dario Gallo, "Domesticados. Por qué los rebeldes de ayer se volvieron dóciles con el Kirchnerismo," *Noticias*, Buenos Aires, October 16, 2004. In addition, personal interview with reporter covering the president's office for a national Argentine newspaper; name withheld by request.

in Mexico suggests that state efforts to co-opt or repress are met with press collusion, acquiescence, or resistance depending on the economic circumstances of the media outlet, nature of the repression, and normative orientations of media owners and individual journalists, in the case of private-sector media. For state-owned media, norms and organizational autonomy seem most important in determining journalistic autonomy (Hughes and Lawson, 2004; Hughes, 2006).

Latin American policymakers thus perceive strong media influences and have taken concrete steps to control them. How then can the media's role in the policymaking process be delineated? The comparative literature on media and policymaking is growing in the United States and Western Europe, especially in regard to foreign policy (O'Heffernan, 1991; Entman, 2004; Paletz and Bennett, 1994), but an integrated theory has not emerged even there (Spitzer, 1993; Jacobs and Shapiro, 1996). In the United States, most research cites only a handful of empirical studies, especially Linsky (1986) and O'Heffernan (1991), who use a mixture of in-depth interviews, surveys of policymakers, and case studies. The Latin American literature, as noted above, apparently includes no in-depth empirical studies of the relationship.

A first step toward understanding the role of the press in the policymaking process in Latin America would be to map the distinctive stages of the policymaking process, and hypothesize about media influences at each step based upon the available literature. With this in mind, the remainder of this chapter does the following. First, it maps the stages and media influences on the policymaking process in democratic systems based on the comparative literature and considering the particularities of Latin American democracies, using cases from the region where known. Next, it presents the characteristics and determinants of successful policymaking based on Spiller, Stein, and Tommasi (2008), and analyzes how news media may influence these determinants. Finally, it discusses methodologies for future research.

This study takes as a point of departure the observation that policymakers' perceptions that media affect public opinion is what matters; it does not discuss the empirical disputes on media effects on public opinion, which in any case are usually located outside of the Latin American experience. As noted, several studies in the United States find that as long as policymakers *believe* the media affect public opinion, then they will modify their behavior in accordance with those beliefs.

The Policymaking Process

The policymaking process has four stages in which media can exert influence: problem formation or agenda building, policy formulation, policy adoption, and policy implementation. These are explored in turn in the discussion that follows.

Agenda Building

During the problem formation phase of the policymaking process, when issues in need of policy attention are identified and prioritized, media can bring to light issues that policymakers had not considered or did not view as urgent. This is the sometimes-powerful policy agenda-setting—or "agenda-building"—function of the news media. It has been identified in study after study of media and policymaking in the United States, as well as accounts of the media and social movements in Latin America (Knudson, 1998; Hammond, 2004). In effect, politicians scan the media as a form of "surrogate public agenda," especially when opinion polls are lacking (Pritchard, 1992).

Reporting on policy-relevant events or issues is punctuated by moments of intense scrutiny followed by periods of little interest. Media attention is driven by events (including the pseudo-events of news management), governmental process, calculated leaks, the cultures of news organizations, and the personal and professional interests of media owners and journalists. Events such as land occupations, marches, or congressional hearings timed to coincide with what Kriesi calls "the media attention cycle" can be used by both governmental and nongovernmental actors to gain press attention, especially when the events "resonate" with what the cultures of news outlets decide are legitimate and newsworthy (2004, pp. 197–98). Scandalous or "irruptive" policy issue domains are treated prominently in news coverage, while technical, incremental, or chronic problems such as poverty are ignored unless they can be personalized or dramatized (Protess et al., 1991; Waisbord, 2000). Hammond found this pattern in his review of coverage of the Landless Farmworkers Movement (MST) in Brazil (2004, pp. 72–73). The MST gained press attention during land takeovers in rural areas of the state of São Paulo in the 1990s. Farmland occupations, which are frequent in Brazil, could easily be defined as too common to be news.

What attracted the news coverage was the possibility or appearance of violence, which dominated the news coverage. The underlying causes of the occupations—farmland concentration, idle land held fallow by wealthy owners, and the issue of farm worker poverty—"are never news" (Hammond, 2004, p. 73).

MST coverage highlights another role of media in the agenda-building stage of the policymaking process. Rather than acting alone, journalists and media organizations act in tacit or open alliance with news sources, be they reformers, whistleblowers, or political cliques engaged in "politics by other means" to prod government investigations (Molotch et al., 1987; Protess et al., 1991; Ginsberg and Shefter, 2002). The MST, for example, directly courted the media. While much of the coverage they received could be described as negative, they succeeded in elevating agrarian reform among policymakers' priorities because public opinion supported their cause (Alston, Libecap, and Mueller, 2005). Similarly, the Zapatista movement in Chiapas, Mexico used the national and international media to pressure for indigenous rights legislation long after the 10 days of open fighting that initially attracted the coverage (Knudson, 1998).

The interaction between reporters and policymakers has been referred to as "mutual exploitation" in the United States (Linsky, 1986; O'Heffernan, 1991, 1994). Each set of actors uses the other to fulfill their own interests. In South America, Waisbord points out that muckrakers are "not the lone rangers" (2000, p. 116). They act in tandem with sources, based upon the demands of journalistic narrative for conflict, a culture privileging official sources, and the political and economic interests of media owners. Pérez-Liñán notes that "everyday, politicians of diverse parties in different countries criticize their opponents in press conferences, negotiate the approval of conflictive laws, and adopt 'tough' positions to obtain political benefits" (2003b, p. 151). This interaction can devolve into "politics by other means," or politicians' use of the media to harm partisan or personal rivals. This is usually achieved through anonymous tips made to trusted reporters. Depending on the resource constraints, training, professional ethics, political ideologies, or business motivations of the publication, the tip may be investigated thoroughly or published based on superficial confirmation (Waisbord, 2000, pp. 103–16).

The case of reform of foreign adoption of children in Guatemala is illustrative of the agenda-building role of the media, as well as how journalists and reformists inside and outside of government mutually exploit one another to reach objectives of problem solving, publicity, prestige, and commercial profit. The newspaper *La Prensa Libre* published an exposé on abuses of child adoption in October 2004 after a UNICEF delegate publicly criticized the country for having "the worst" foreign adoption legislation in the world. The problem of potential abuses in foreign adoptions was well known among nongovernmental organizations (NGOs) and government child welfare agencies prior to the public criticism from UNICEF, but there had been little movement to remedy the problem. Prompted by the high-profile event and new high-level interest in the issue, *La Prensa Libre* examined the law and found it riddled with loopholes, including the lack of criminal penalties for those who sell children via adoption, which can cost between $15,000 and $30,000. The newspaper's editors placed the articles and photos on the front page, and timed the coverage to coincide with an international conference of prestigious media owners in Antigua, which *La Prensa Libre*'s owners helped host. Three months later, in January, the newspaper followed up with another prominent article on the growing number of adoptions in the country, again citing reformers who urged congress to accelerate the drafting of a new law. In February 2005, First Lady Wendy de Berger's office told the foreign press she had sent a proposal to congress that would better regulate adoptions by foreign couples.[7]

La Prensa Libre's front-page coverage buttressed the efforts of NGOs such as the Social Movement for Children's Rights, as well as would-be reformers inside the Guatemalan government, including the attorney general for children and adolescent issues and the first lady, who had announced the formation of a group to propose a new law just days after the UNICEF announcement. The articles signaled to the wider bureaucracy that there was presidential-level interest in the issue and presented information that had to be addressed during negotiations over the new law. It also framed the issue as an international embarrassment and moral aberration that had to be addressed through legislative reform.

---

[7] Luisa Rodríguez, "Adopciones: falta de ley ideal, las convierte en negocio. El derecho de un niño a tener una familia se utiliza para lucrar," *La Prensa Libre*, Guatemala City, Guatemala, October 24, 2004, p. 1A. Leonardo Cereser, "3,500 trámites de adopciones en el 2004. El 90 por ciento de las solicitudes era de parejas de Estados Unidos," *La Prensa Libre*, online edition, Guatemala City, Guatemala, January 6, 2005. Herald Wire Service, "Guatemala: Foreign Adoptions May Be Regulated," *The Miami Herald*, February 9, 2005, p. 12A.

In only one paragraph deep into the January article did the leader of a pro-adoption NGO suggest the problem was being exaggerated.

While unregulated adoptions in Guatemala may indeed be a serious problem, that is not necessarily the case of all media reports. Sometimes unverified or purposely exaggerated claims are repeated in the press so often that they take on the status of taken-for-granted fact (T.E. Cook, 1998, p. 129). Under such circumstances, news coverage has the potential to miscue policymakers, diverting their attention from arguably more pressing problems. Pollster Marta Lagos, for example, has questioned whether prominent media coverage of crime news has elevated public insecurity to a place on the political agenda that it does not deserve. She bases her argument on the apparent contradiction between Latin Americans' belief that crime has "increased a lot" in the last 12 months (ranging from 85 percent to 96 percent, by country), with their feeling of safety in their neighborhoods (an average of 65 percent across the region) (Lagos, 2003). Studies in the United States suggest that television coverage of crime does increase fear of crime (Romer, Aday, and Jamieson, 2003), but a context of declining U.S. crime rates complicates the transferral of these findings to Latin America, where crime rates are indeed rising.

Policy Formulation

Since media coverage tends to portray a policy-relevant event or issue in crisis terms, media coverage prompts a sense of urgency. The pressure to act quickly and visibly is especially strong when coverage is negative, as is the bulk of policy-relevant news coverage. Sometimes, the urgency is stated directly in the form of media demands for action. In a famous U.S. case, 239 families were evacuated from the Love Canal area of New York State in 1979 after a pilot study leaked to the press suggested an "immediate health hazard" for area residents from the toxic waste dumps in the neighborhood. Those findings were later found to be faulty and the EPA administrator involved described her decision to move the families as the worst in her career (Linsky, 1986, pp. 71–81).

Similarly in Argentina, Rinne notes, economic policymakers sometimes felt intense media pressure for high-profile action during its recent economic and political crises. As inflation spiraled or protests erupted in 2001 and 2002, news accounts demanded that policymakers "do something"—but not what (Rinne, 2003). Coverage of Mexico's 300,000-person "mega-march" against kidnapping in 2004 also demanded action. The newspaper *Reforma* in Mexico City ran a daily countdown—on its front page and in a Web site animation—of the number of days President Vicente Fox had left until the end of a 90-day deadline he set for his administration to fulfill the demands of march organizers. The crime victims' march followed public outrage about the murder of a middle-class woman abducted from an upscale mall in the capital.[8]

Media and policy studies find that this kind of irruptive, negative, and commanding coverage has consequences. It changes the criteria for policy evaluation, speeds up the policymaking process, raises the level of decision making above where it would normally be, and encourages policymakers to take symbolic measures rather than to engage in long-term problem solving (Linsky, 1986; Paletz, 1998; Pritchard, 1992). In the Mexican case, state governments in central Mexico immediately launched a series of dragnets through crime-ridden neighborhoods after the "mega-march," which in turn were dubbed "mega-operations." That many of those arrested soon had to be released was lost in the barrage of television coverage portraying the government as decisive.[9] While the police were probably not reacting to media coverage alone, given the enormous size of the march, the event's magnitude and media coverage acted together to push officials toward the rapid and high-profile response.

Another way that media can influence policy formation is through the frames used to structure news stories. Journalists use latent interpretive frames to structure and organize news stories, even simple ones. The struggle to control news frames has been found to be one of the most important aspects of the media–policymaker relationship in the United States, and seems increasingly relevant in Latin America (Gamson and Modigliani, 1989; Knudson, 1998; Entman, 2000, 2004; Hammond, 2004).

Frames in the news help define the context of the policy environment for the actors involved in the policymaking process. The media's influence arises in part from their ability to frame an issue in a way that favors one policy proposal or another. This happens because frames confer legitimacy on certain actors, policy proposals, and views of the

---

[8] Yetlaneci Alcaraz and Nayeli Cortés, "Sacuden al país," *El Universal*, Mexico City, June 28, 2004, p. 1A. *Reforma*, "La cuenta regresiva," *Reforma*, Mexico City, August 16, 2004, p. 1A.

[9] Claudia Bolaños, "Reinician disputas Ebrard y Bátiz tras megaoperativo," *El Universal*, Mexico City, July 15, 2004, p. 1A.

world, but also because they can effectively block certain options from entering the public consciousness. The media frame of an issue and the public's definition of the problem are not necessarily one and the same, but media frames are strongly connected to public conceptions and, as importantly, to policymakers' perceptions of the policymaking context. Entman writes of U.S. foreign policy, "Media affect perceived public opinion—the general sense of the public's opinions that is held by most observers, including politicians and journalists. Much of politics today is the struggle among contending politicians to induce the media to construct a particular perception of what public opinion is" (2000, p. 21).

Policymakers in Uruguay and Brazil understood that it was important to frame administrative reform proposals for the public in ways that resonated with national political cultures valuing the role of the state in the economy. In Uruguay, policymakers adopted a low-key strategy to avoid extended debate. The rhetoric of the reform used a "legitimizing discourse" of strengthening state efficiency to play to Uruguayan public opinion, which approved of state-owned enterprises, as well as to neutralized union opposition. Perhaps more importantly in this case, the reform was spread throughout a large budget bill and its implementation was decentralized, in a successful attempt to avoid scrutiny by the press (Panizza, 2004).

In Brazil, a high-profile federal administration minister took his case for state reform directly to the public and the press after losing control of the initial problem definition. Minister Luiz Carlos Bresser-Pereira went public with clear language and a direct argument, redefining the reform as one that would enhance state capacity rather than curtail it. He explains how he reversed the frame of administrative reform in Brazil:

> "The media played a pivotal role in the debate. Initially, journalists were interested only in the short-term and fiscal aspects of the reform: downsizing, the breakdown of stability or the tenure rule for civil servants, and the salary cap that would eliminate some extremely high salaries. Journalists had little interest in the more positive, medium-term objectives of the reform, such as the new role for the public non-state sector, the increase in efficiency, the client-citizen focus, the new human resources policies, and the yearly recruiting for state careers. But I was able to insert the new ideas, so that, little by little, it became evident that I was not, as

my adversaries suggested, the 'henchman of civil servants,' the 'damned neo-liberal' or the 'market fundamentalist' who wanted to erase the state. On the contrary, my message involved rebuilding the state..." (Bresser-Pereira, 2003, p. 99).

Policy Adoption

The role of the news media during the policy adoption phase depends on the volume of attention. When there is little coverage, the urgency for reform can stall, but policymakers have more slack for bargaining, promoting special interests, or even rent seeking. Alternatively, high volumes of coverage can provide space for public debate and deliberation in the unusual circumstances that a proposed policy is fully explored, and press monitoring can raise the costs of bestowing privileges on personal or group interests over the public welfare.

Juan Carlos Cortázar Velarde (2002) attributes the demise of state administrative reform in Peru to an opposition congressman's use of press denunciations to change the balance during cabinet negotiations, eventually convincing President Alberto Fujimori to abandon the reform altogether. Coverage of the proposal in the mostly subordinated Peruvian press had been positive until the opponent leaked a cabinet minister's estimate that 200,000 jobs would be cut as a result of the reform. Negative coverage of the proposal surpassed positive coverage for the first time in Lima's main newspapers, according to Cortázar Velarde's content analysis. The coverage emboldened cabinet ministers who opposed the reform because of the prerogatives it would strip away. More importantly, President Fujimori was paying close attention to his popularity ratings as he forced a law through congress that would allow him to hold a third term in office. While in the midst of a severe economic crisis, Peruvians had supported tough economic measures and authoritarian political machinations, but seven years into Fujimori's rule their patience had worn thin. Fujimori killed the reform as his approval rating plummeted. Cortázar Velarde notes, "The public opinion domain had been the decisive space for consolidation of the (Fujimori) regime outside of formal political institutions. So Fujimori was very sensitive to the changes that occurred in it, abandoning everything that might deepen the turn in public opinion toward criticism of the regime. Administrative modernization was among the things that were pushed aside" (pp. 45–46).

The job loss estimate immediately grabbed journalists' attention in what otherwise seemed like tedious bureaucratic reform, and Cortázar Velarde documented a spike in articles on the reform after the statement was leaked. The cases of administrative reform in Uruguay and Brazil also support the notion that media are less interested in covering the adoption phase of policymaking unless something in the event itself fulfills news narrative needs of drama or personalization. A frame that highlighted conflict and pitted state bureaucrats against a neoliberal technocrat was an easy and compelling logic around which to structure the coverage of efforts at administrative reform in Brazil. It took great effort by reform supporters to transform this frame. In Uruguay, the "reform without losers" packaging of the administrative reform sought to avoid conflict and confrontation in public arenas. Coverage of parliament during the adoption phase centered on unrelated budget disputes, not the administrative reform.

In addition to covering the adoption process, there is another way that news media can influence the adoption process. This is as an interest group rather than as news producers. In these circumstances, media outlets openly support coalitions during the policy adoption process. This especially seems to be the case when policy issues affect the media's business or professional interests, such as when legislatures take up telecommunications reform or issues related to journalism professionalization.

Direct media participation in the negotiations surrounding policy adoption can amount to the defense of corporate or personal privileges. News reports suggest that lobbying by media owners' associations and large commercial networks have derailed attempts to open Mexico's radio and television concession process to greater competition. A senator who sponsored the reform said: "They have spoken to practically all of the legislators. To our legislative whip, the president of our party, the chairmen of all of the Senate committees…They have told us that the politician who approves of the proposal is burned with the industry, that this isn't in his best interest, that businessmen know how to return a favor."[10] Similarly, in Brazil, new market entrants helped push legislation to decentralize cable television through parliament in the

---

[10] Miryam Audiffred, "El reality show de concesionarios," *La Revista/El Universal*, February 21, 2005, pp. 23–29.

mid-1990s against the entrenched interests of open-air broadcasters (Galperín, 2000).

Sometimes media outlets decide to openly support reforms that have positive implications for journalistic professionalism and democratic consolidation, such as the decriminalization of libel or codification of shield laws protecting journalists' confidential sources.[11] The new access-to-government information law in Mexico offers an impressive case of media policy advocacy on behalf of democratizing reform. Major newspaper outlets worked in tandem with academic specialists to write and lobby for their own version of the law, which they believed had better enforcement provisions than a more restrictive executive branch proposal. At various points in the legislative process, the coalition—known as the "Oaxaca Group," for the city in which they first met—used the news pages to frame public perceptions and pressure government negotiators. One particularly important juncture occurred when the executive's more restrictive version of the bill was leaked. As the Vicente Fox administration pushed for public hearings on the executive branch bill, the newspaper *Reforma* dedicated an entire page of coverage under the headline "No to the Government Hearings" (November 24, 2001, p. 1A). Meanwhile, the capital's largest newspaper *El Universal* published on its front page: "The press rejects state regulation. The Mexican Editors Association... expressed its 'public condemnation before the evident signs that the government seeks to chill citizen enthusiasm for learning on what and how the government spends the public's money'" (November 24, 2001, p. 1A). As the coalition gained the support of opposition party lawmakers, hearings were not held and the bill passed essentially as the coalition had written it.[12]

Policy Implementation

By this stage, certain tendencies in news coverage have emerged that continue to shape the role media play during the implementation phase of the policymaking process. Similar to coverage traits during policy

---

[11] The Inter-American Press Association and the Organization of American States Ombudsman for Freedom of Expression have worked on these reforms regionally.

[12] For a more extended account of the formation and tactics of the Oaxaca Group, see Escobedo (2003) and Gill and Hughes (2005).

adoption, which is the province of congress, news coverage is sporadic during the period of policy implementation by state bureaucracies. News coverage about the implementation of policies usually is focused on high-impact policies that can be fragmented into particular incidents or a few connected stories, personalized through the portrayal of villains, victims, or heroes, and dramatized through conflict or moral transgression. The daily *El Mercurio* in Santiago, Chile covered the construction of housing for the poor when the housing minister responded vociferously to a presidential candidate who had criticized their design.[13] More in a watchdog role, *El Universal* in Mexico pointed out that a subsidized food basket for the rural poor was cheaper to buy in Mexico City grocery stores and that government supply warehouses were filling up because competitors offered cheaper prices.[14]

Increasingly in Latin America, coverage focuses on policy failures involving corruption. For example, investigative reporting in Brazil in the years after the end of the military dictatorship touched on corruption in a large number of policy arenas: bidding for public works contracts, advertising contracts for state companies, the implementation of the *Plan Cruzado*, the privatization of state-owned companies, and antitrust rules in public transportation, among others (Waisbord, 2000, pp. 39–40). This is the classic monitoring function of the news media in democratic press theory. While not always in relation to policy failure, media scandals were the origin of each of seven cases of presidential crises analyzed by Pérez-Liñán in Latin America between 1990 and 1997. In three of those crises, presidents were forced from office (Pérez-Liñán, 2003b).

Like reports during the policy formulation stage, coverage suggesting policy success or failure can be misleading. News media can report positive outcomes when results are poor, or suggest a policy failure when the policy is essentially working.

Implications

What implications does this review of media influences hold for the creation of sustainable, coherent, and public-regarding policy in Latin

---

[13] Uziel Gómez, "Lavín-Tschorne: Dura pelea política por las viviendas sociales," *El Mercurio,* Santiago, Chile, February 25, 2005. Available online at http://diario.elmercurio.com/.

[14] G. Guillén, "La 'Canasta Contigo' es más barata en la Ciudad de México." *El Universal,* Mexico City, February 22, 2005. Available online at www.eluniversal.com.mx.

America? Spiller, Stein, and Tommasi (2008) identify the characteristics of optimal policy as: stability over sufficient time to encourage institutionalization of the new rules; flexibility to make necessary adjustments as new information or conditions emerge; coherence or coordination among different policy actors in varying stages of the policymaking process; investment in bureaucrats' policy implementation capacities; and a public focus promoting the general welfare rather than benefits for individuals, factions, or regions. These authors argue that the creation of optimal public policies requires the creation of intertemporal pacts of cooperation between politicians, administrators, and interest groups during the policymaking process. The pacts over time can be supported by: payoffs for long-term cooperation among policymaking players, greater observability of moves during negotiations and implementation, a smaller and more compact group of policymaking players, and the delegation of operations and enforcement to neutral authorities.

The analysis and review in this chapter suggest a set of propositions about how the media may affect these determinants.

1. Negative coverage focusing on policy costs, corruption, conflict, or future losers increases the short-term costs of cooperation and thus increases the incentives for defection from intertemporal pacts.
2. Positive coverage focusing on policy benefits, beneficiaries, or proponents increases incentives for long-term cooperation.
3. News coverage can confer legitimacy on or withhold it from governmental and nongovernmental actors, influencing the number of actors that must be considered in a negotiation, as well as the balance of power in negotiations.
4. News coverage can expose secret actors or moves during policy negotiations and implementation, including who benefits and what motives they have.
5. When media play a monitoring role, they increase the visibility of player moves and decrease payoffs for secrecy.
6. However, when media companies act as policy players and not only as news producers, they can hide moves by omission or distortion.
7. Media monitoring can promote appropriate design of policy enforcement, or the search for such mechanisms.
8. Demands for quick, high-profile responses to events framed as crises can lead to symbolic action or poorly designed policy.

Conclusion and Future Study

This chapter has presented a first approximation of the role of the news media in the policymaking process in Latin America, based on empirical comparative literature on media and policymaking and observations of media behavior in Latin America. These roles include influence on the policy agenda, the pace and level of decision making, the symbolic or substantive nature of policy responses, the incentives for rent seeking, the legitimacy of the direct players and policy options considered, and the nature of evaluation of policies in operation. A number of propositions about the media's role in policymaking were then generated using the intertemporal transactions framework of Spiller, Stein, and Tommasi (2008). What remains to be done is an empirical research project to test these hypotheses in a more systematic manner within Latin America. Studies in the United States suggest that the best method would combine in-depth interviews of policymakers with case studies involving systematic media content analysis.

References

Abuelafia, E., S. Berenstein, M. Braun, and L. di Grezia. 2009. Who Decides on Public Expenditures? The Importance of the Informal Budget Process in Argentina. In M. Hallerberg, C. Scartascini, and E. Stein, eds., *Who Decides the Budget? A Political Economy Analysis of the Budget Process in Latin America*. Washington, DC and Cambridge, MA: Inter-American Development Bank and David Rockefeller Center for Latin American Studies, Harvard University.

Acuña, C.H., and W.C. Smith. 1994. The Political Economy of Structural Adjustment: The Logic of Support and Opposition to Neoliberal Reform. In W.C. Smith, C.H. Acuña, and E.A. Gamarra, eds., *Latin American Political Economy in the Age of Neoliberal Reform*. New Brunswick and London: Transaction Publishers.

Acuña, C., S. Galiani, and M. Tommasi. 2007. Understanding the Political Economy of Structural Reform: The Case of Argentina. In J. Fanelli, ed., *Understanding Reform in Latin America: Similar Reforms, Diverse Constituencies, Varied Results*. New York: Palgrave Macmillan.

Agosin, Manuel, Eduardo Fernández-Arias, and Fidel Jaramillo, eds. 2009. *Growing Pains: Binding Constraints to Productive Investments in Latin America*. Washington, DC: Inter-American Development Bank.

Aisen, A., and F.J. Veiga. 2006. *Political Instability and Inflation Volatility*. Washington, DC: Asia and Pacific Department, International Monetary Fund.

Alcántara Sáez, Manuel, ed. 2008. *Politicians and Politics in Latin America*. Boulder, CO: Lynne Rienner Publishers.

Alcántara Sáez, Manuel, and Flavia Freidenberg, eds. 2001. *Partidos Políticos de América Latina* (three volumes). Salamanca, Spain: Ediciones Universidad Salamanca.

Alemán, Eduardo, and Thomas Schwartz. 2006. Presidential Vetoes in Latin American Constitutions. *Journal of Theoretical Politics* 18(1): 98–120.

Alesina, A., S. Ozler, N. Roubini, and P. Swagel. 1992. *Political Instability and Economic Growth.* Cambridge, MA: National Bureau of Economic Research.

Alivizatos, Nicos. 1995. Judges as Veto Players. In H. Doering, ed., *Parliaments and Majority Rule in Western Europe.* New York: St. Martin's Press.

Alston, Lee, Bernardo Mueller, and Gary D. Libecap. 2005. How Interest Groups with Limited Resources Can Influence Political Outcomes: Information Control and the Landless Peasant Movement in Brazil. ICER Working Paper Series No. 15. Available at SSRN: http://ssrn.com/abstract=761750.

Alston, Lee, Marcus Melo, Bernardo Mueller, and Carlos Pereira. 2008. On the Road to Good Governance: Recovering from Economic and Political Shocks in Brazil. In E. Stein and M. Tommasi, with P. Spiller and C. Scartascini, eds., *Policymaking in Latin America: How Politics Shapes Policies.* Washington, DC and Cambridge, MA: Inter-American Development Bank and David Rockefeller Center for Latin American Studies, Harvard University.

————. 2009. Presidential Power, Fiscal Responsibility Laws, and the Allocation of Spending: The Case of Brazil. In M. Hallerberg, C. Scartascini, and E. Stein, eds., *Who Decides the Budget? A Political Economy Analysis of the Budget Process in Latin America.* Washington, DC and Cambridge, MA: Inter-American Development Bank and David Rockefeller Center for Latin American Studies, Harvard University.

Alt, James, and David Lassen. 2005. Political and Judicial Checks on Corruption: Evidence from American State Governments. Economic Policy Research Unit Working Paper 2005–12. Department of Economics, University of Copenhagen.

Alt, J., J. Frieden, M. Gilligan, D. Rodrik, and R. Rogowski. 1996. The Political Economy of International Trade: Enduring Puzzles and an Agenda for Inquiry. *Comparative Political Studies* 29(6): 689–717.

Altheide, David. 1996. *Qualitative Media Analysis.* Thousand Oaks, CA: Sage Publications.

Alves Maciel, Débora, and Andrei Koerner. 2002. Sentidos da Judicialização da Política: Duas Análises. *Lua Nova-Revista de Cultura e Política* 57: 113–33.

Amaro, Roberto. 2001. Cambios en Comunicación y Cultura. El desconcierto llega a la Moneda. *El Sur en internet.* Accessed February 18, 2005 at http://www.elsur.cl/archivo/2001/mayo2001/6mayo2001/elsur/reportajes/reportajes.php3?n=4.

Amorim Neto, Octavio. 2002. Presidential Cabinets, Electoral Cycles, and Coalition Discipline in Brazil. In Scott Morgenstern and Benito Nacif, eds., *Legislative Politics in Latin America.* New York: Cambridge University Press.

———. 2006. The Presidential Calculus: Executive Policy Making and Cabinet Formation in the Americas. *Comparative Political Studies* 39: 415–40.

Amorim Neto, Octavio, and Hugo Borsani. 2004. Presidents and Cabinets: The Political Determinants of Fiscal Behavior in Latin America. *Studies in Comparative International Development* 39(1): 3–27.

Amorim Neto, Octavio, Gary W. Cox, and Mathew McCubbins. 2003. Agenda Power in Brazil's Cámara dos Deputados, 1989–98. *World Politics* 55: 550–78.

Andeweg, R. 2000. Ministers as Double Agents? The Delegation Process between Cabinet and Ministers. *European Journal of Political Research* 37(3): 377–95.

Aninat, Cristóbal, John Londregan, Patricio Navia, and Joaquín Vial. 2008. Political Institutions, Policymaking Processes, and Policy Outcomes in Chile. In E. Stein and M. Tommasi, with P. Spiller and C. Scartascini, eds., *Policymaking in Latin America: How Politics Shapes Policies.* Washington, DC and Cambridge, MA: Inter-American Development Bank and David Rockefeller Center for Latin American Studies, Harvard University.

Anner, Mark. 2002. Between Economic Nationalism and Transnational Solidarity: Labor Responses to Internationalization and Industrial Restructuring in the Americas. Paper presented at the annual meeting of the American Political Science Association, August 28–31. Boston, MA.

Arantes, Rogério. 1999. Direito e Política: o Ministério Público e a Defesa dos Direitos Coletivos. *Revista Brasileira de Ciências Sociais* 14(39): 83–102.

———. 2003. The Brazilian 'Ministério Público' and Political Corruption in Brazil. Working Paper CBS-50-04. Center for Brazilian Studies, Oxford University.

Araujo, L., C. Pereira, and E. Raile. 2008. Executive-Legislative Exchanges in Coalition-based Presidential Systems: Ideology and Transfers. Paper presented at the annual conference of the Midwest Political Science Association, April 3–6, Chicago.

Ardanaz, M., M. Leiras, and M. Tommasi. 2009. The Foundations of Ineffective Policies and Weak Accountability: Federalism Argentine Style. Universidad de San Andrés. Unpublished.

Armijo, Leslie Elliot, and Philippe Faucher. 2002. We Have a Consensus: Explaining Political Support for Market Reforms in Latin America. *Latin American Politics and Society* 44(2): 1–40.

Axelrod, R. 1970. *Conflict of Interest: A Theory of Divergent Goals with Applications to Politics.* Chicago: Markham Publishing Co.

Baldez, Lisa, and John Carey. 2002. Budget Procedure and Fiscal Restraint in Post-Transition Chile. In Stephan Haggard and Mathew McCubbins, eds., *Presidents, Parliaments, and Policy.* New York: Cambridge University Press.

Ballard, Mega. 1999. The Clash between Local Courts and Global Economics: The Politics of Judicial Reform in Brazil. *Berkeley Journal of International Law* 17: 230–76.

Bambaci, Juliana, Pablo Spiller, and Mariano Tommasi. 2007. The Bureaucracy. In P. Spiller and M. Tommasi, eds., *The Institutional Foundations of Public Policy in Argentina.* New York: Cambridge University Press.

Baron, David P. 1994. Electoral Competition with Informed and Uninformed Voters. *American Political Science Review* 88(1) March: 33–47.

Barrett, Patrick. 2001. Labour Policy, Labour-Business Relations and the Transition to Democracy in Chile. *Journal of Latin American Studies* 33(3): 561–97.

Bartolini, Stefano, and Peter Mair. 1990. *Identity, Competition and Electoral Availability: The Stabilization of European Electorates, 1885–1985.* Cambridge, England: Cambridge University Press.

Bates, R.H., and A. Krueger, eds. 1993. *Political and Economic Interactions in Economic Policy Reform: Evidence from Eight Countries.* Oxford, England: Basil Blackwell.

Beer, C. 2004. Electoral Competition and Fiscal Decentralization in Mexico. In A. Montero and D. Samuels, eds., *Decentralization and*

Democracy in Latin America. South Bend, IN: University of Notre Dame Press.

Bennett, W. Lance. 2003. *News: The Politics of Illusion.* New York: Addison Wesley Longman.

Bennett, Robert. 1983. The Burger Court and the Poor. In Vincent Blasi, ed., *The Burger Court: The Counter-Revolution That Wasn't.* New Haven, CT: Yale University Press.

Bergara, M., A. Pereyra, R. Tansini, A. Garcé, D. Chasquetti, D. Buquet, and J.A. Moraes. 2006. Political Institutions, Policymaking Processes, and Policy Outcomes: The Case of Uruguay. Working Paper No. R-510. Latin American Research Network, Inter-American Development Bank, Washington, DC.

Berkman, H., C. Scartascini, E. Stein, and M. Tommasi. 2009. Political Institutions, State Capabilities, and Public Policy: An International Dataset. Inter-American Development Bank, Washington, DC. Available at: http://www.iadb.org/RES/pub_List.cfm?pub_topic_id=DBA&type=pub_type&pub_type_id=DBA&pub_type_id1=DBA&language=english.

Blanchflower, David. 2006. A Cross-Country Study of Union Membership. Institute for Labor Studies/IZA Discussion Paper 2016. Institute for the Study of Labor (IZA), Bonn, Germany.

Blondel, J. 1985. *Government Ministers in the Contemporary World.* London: Sage Publications.

Blondel, J., and F. Müller-Rommel. 1993. *Governing Together: The Extent of Joint Decision-Making in Western European Cabinets.* New York: St. Martin's Press.

Borg, Ingwer, and Patrick Groenen. 2005. *Modern Multidimensional Scaling: Theory and Applications (2nd edition).* New York: Springer-Verlag.

Bouzas, Roberto, and Enrique Avogadro. 2002. Trade Policy-Making and the Private Sector: A Memorandum on Argentina. In Inter-American Development Bank, ed., *The Trade Policymaking Process, Level One of the Two Level Game: Country Studies in the Western Hemisphere.* INTAL-ITD-STA Occasional Paper 13. Buenos Aires: Inter-American Development Bank.

Brachet-Márquez, Viviane. 1992. Explaining Sociopolitical Change in Latin America: The Case of Mexico. *Latin American Research Review* 27(3): 91–123.

Bresser-Pereira, Luiz Carlos. 2003. The 1995 Public Management Reform in Brazil: Reflections of a Reformer. In Ben Ross Schneider and Blanca Heredia, eds., *Reinventing Leviathan: The Politics of Administrative Reform in Developing Countries*. Coral Gables, FL: North-South Center Press/University of Miami.

Brewer-Carías, Allan R. 1997. La jurisdicción constitucional en América Latina. In Domingo García Belaúnde and D. Fernández Salgado, eds., *La jurisdicción constitucional en Iberoamérica*. 119–61, Discussion. Madrid: Dykinson.

Bronstein, Arturo. 1995. Societal Change and Industrial Relations in Latin America: Trends and Prospects. *International Labour Review* 134(2): 163–86.

———. 1997. Labour Law Reform in Latin America: Between State Protection and Flexibility. *International Labour Review* 136(1): 5–27.

Burgess, Katrina. 1998a. Is the Party Over? Economic Reform and Party-Union Relations in Venezuela. Paper presented at the 1998 meeting of the Latin American Studies Association, September 24–26, Chicago.

———. 1998b. Loyalty Dilemmas and Market Reform: Party-Union Alliances under Stress in Mexico, Spain, and Venezuela. *World Politics* 52(1): 105–34.

Buscaglia, Edgardo, and Maria Dakolias. 1999. An Analysis of the Causes of Corruption in the Judiciary. *Law and Policy in International Business* 30: 95–116.

Calmfors, Lars, and John Driffill. 1988. Bargaining Structure, Corporatism and Macroeconomic Performance. *Economic Policy* 3(6): 13–51.

Calvo, E., and J.P. Micozzi. 2005. The Governor's Backyard: A Seat-Vote Model of Electoral Reform for Subnational Multiparty Races. *The Journal of Politics* 67: 1050–74.

Calvo, Ernesto, and María Victoria Murillo. 2005. The New Iron Law of Argentine Politics? Partisanship, Clientelism, and Governability in Contemporary Argentina. In Steven Levitsky and María Victoria Murillo, eds., *Argentine Democracy: The Politics of Institutional Weakness*. University Park, PA: Penn State University Press.

Cameron, David. 1978. The Expansion of the Public Economy: A Comparative Analysis. *American Political Science Review* 72(4): 1243–61.

Camp, Roderic. 1989. *Entrepreneurs and Politics in Twentieth-Century Mexico*. New York: Oxford University Press.

————. 2002. *Mexico's Mandarins: Crafting a Power Elite for the Twenty-First Century*. Berkeley, CA: University of California Press.

Campos, José, and Hilton Root. 1996. *The Key to the Asian Miracle: Making Shared Growth Credible*. Washington, DC: Brookings Institution Press.

Caraway, Teri. 2006. Freedom of Association: Battering Ram or Trojan Horse? *Review of International Political Economy* 13(2): 210–32.

Cárdenas, M., R. Junguito, and M. Pachón. 2008. Political Institutions and Policy Outcomes in Colombia: The Effects of the 1991 Constitution. In E. Stein and M. Tommasi, with P. Spiller and C. Scartascini, eds., *Policymaking in Latin America: How Politics Shapes Policies*. Washington, DC and Cambridge, MA: Inter-American Development Bank and David Rockefeller Center for Latin American Studies, Harvard University.

Cardoso, F.H., and E. Falletto. 1979. *Dependency and Development in Latin America*. Berkeley, CA: University of California Press (first published in Spanish in 1971).

Carey, John M. 2003. Presidentialism and Representative Institutions. In J. Domínguez and M. Shifter, eds., *Constructing Democratic Governance in Latin America*. Baltimore, MD: Johns Hopkins University Press.

Carey, John M., and John Polga-Hecimovich. 2004. Primary Elections and Candidate Strength in Latin America. Dartmouth College, Hanover, New Hampshire. Unpublished.

Carey, John M., and Matthew Soberg Shugart. 1995. Incentives to Cultivate a Personal Vote: A Rank Ordering of Electoral Formulas. *Electoral Studies* 14(4): 417–39.

————. 1998. *Executive Decree Authority*. Cambridge, England and New York: Cambridge University Press.

Casar, Maria Aparo. 1998. Executive-Legislative Relations: The Case of Mexico. Working Paper No. 84. Centro de Investigación y Docencia Económicas, Mexico City.

————. 2002. Executive-Legislative Relations: The Case of Mexico (1946–1997). In Scott Morgenstern and Benito Nacif, eds., *Legislative Politics in Latin America*. New York: Cambridge University Press.

Cassels, Jamie. 1989. Judicial Activism and Public Interest Litigation in India: Attempting the Impossible? *American Journal of Comparative Law* 37(3): 495–519.

Castañeda, Jorge. 2006. Latin America's Left Turn. *Foreign Affairs* 85(3): 28–43.

CBO (U.S. Congressional Budget Office). 1997. CBO Memorandum: Promoting Worker Rights in Developing Countries: U.S. Policies and Their Rationale. CBO, Washington, DC.

CCE (Consejo Coordinador Empresarial). 1987. Informe de Labores que el Ing. Claudio X. González, Presidente del CCE, Presenta al Consejo Directivo de Dicha Institución por el Período 1985–87. Mexico City: Consejo Coordinador Empresarial.

Centeno, Miguel. 1994. *Democracy within Reason: Technocratic Revolution in Mexico*. University Park, PA: Penn State University Press.

Centeno, M.A., and P. Silva. 1998. *The Politics of Expertise in Latin America*. New York: St. Martin's Press.

Chang, K., D. Lewis, and N. McCarty. 2000. Turnover among Political Appointees. Paper presented at the annual meeting of the American Political Science Association, September, Washington, DC.

Chasquetti, Daniel. 2001. Democracia, Multipartidismo y Coaliciones en América Latina: Evaluando la Difícil Combinación. In Jorge Lanzaro, ed., *Tipos de Presidencialismo y Coaliciones en América Latina*. Buenos Aires, Argentina: CLACSO.

Chau, Nancy, and Ravi Kanbur. 2002. The Adoption of International Labor Standards Conventions: Who, When and Why? In Susan M. Collins and Dani Rodrik, eds., *Brookings Trade Forum: 2001*. Washington, DC: Brookings Institution Press.

Cheibub, José Antonio, Argelina Figueiredo, and Fernando Limongi. 2009. Political Parties and Governors as Determinants of the Behavior of Brazilian Legislators. *Latin American Politics and Society* 51(1): 1–30.

Cheibub, José Antonio, Adam Przeworski, and Sebastian Saiegh. 2004. Government Coalitions and Legislative Success under Presidentialism and Parliamentarism. *British Journal of Political Science* 34: 565–87.

CLAD (Centro Latinoamericano de Administración para el Desarrollo). 2003. Carta Iberoamericana de la Función Pública. Key Documents: Estado, Administración Pública y Sociedad; 9. Available at http://www.clad.org.ve/documentos/declaraciones/cartaibero.pdf/ view.

Clark, Mary. 2001. *Gradual Economic Reform in Latin America: The Costa Rican Experience.* Albany, NY: State University of New York Press.

Collier, Ruth Berins, and David Collier. 1979. Inducements versus Constraints: Disaggregating "Corporatism". *American Political Science Review* 73(4): 967–86.

———. 1991. *Shaping the Political Arena: Critical Junctures, the Labor Movement, and Regime Dynamics in Latin America.* Princeton, NJ: Princeton University Press.

Committee to Protect Journalists. 2003. *Argentina: Attacks on the Press in 2003.* New York: The Committee to Protect Journalists.

Conaghan, Catherine M. 2002. Cashing in on Authoritarianism: Media Collusion in Fujimori's Peru. *Harvard International Journal of Press/ Politics* 7(1): 115–25.

Conaghan, Catherine, and Carlos de la Torre. 2008. The Permanent Campaign of Rafael Correa: Making Ecuador's Plebiscitary Presidency. *International Journal of Press/Politics* 13(3): 267–84.

Cook, María Lorena. 1998. Toward Flexible Industrial Relations? Neo-Liberalism, Democracy, and Labor Reform in Latin America. *Industrial Relations* 27(3): 311–36.

———. 2002. Labor Reform and Dual Transitions in Brazil and the Southern Cone. *Latin American Politics and Society* 44(1): 1–35.

Cook, Timothy E. 1998. *Governing with the News: The News Media as a Political Institution.* Chicago: University of Chicago Press.

Coppedge, Michael. 2003. *Venezuela: Popular Sovereignty versus Liberal Democracy.* Baltimore, MD: Johns Hopkins University Press.

Corrales, Javier. 2002. *Presidents without Parties: The Politics of Economic Reform in Argentina and Venezuela in the 1990s.* University Park, PA: Penn State University Press.

———. 2004. Multiple Preferences, Variable Strengths: The Politics of Education Reforms in Argentina. In Robert R. Kaufman and Joan M. Nelson, eds., *Crucial Needs, Weak Incentives: Social Sector Reform, Democratization, and Globalization in Latin America.* Washington, DC: Woodrow Wilson Center Press.

Correa Sutil, Jorge. 1999. Judicial Reforms in Latin America: Good News for the Underprivileged? In Juan E. Méndez and Paulo Sérgio

Pinheiro, eds., *The (Un)Rule of Law and the Unprivileged in Latin America*. South Bend, IN: University of Notre Dame Press.

Cortázar Velarde, Juan Carlos. 2002. *La reforma de la administración pública peruana (1990–1997). Conflicto y estrategias divergentes en la elaboración de políticas de gestión pública.* Washington, DC: Inter-American Development Bank.

Costa, Silvio, and Jayme Brener. 1997. Dossiê das concessões de TV: Coronelismo eletrônico. *Observatório da Imprensa.* Available at *www.observatoriodaimprensa.com.br.*

Cox, Gary. 1999. Electoral Rules and Electoral Coordination. *Annual Review of Political Science* 2: 145–61.

Cox, Gary, and Mathew McCubbins. 2001. The Institutional Determinants of Economic Policy Outcomes. In Stephan Haggard and Mathew McCubbins, eds., *Presidents, Parliaments, and Policy.* Cambridge, England: Cambridge University Press.

Cox, Gary W., and Scott Morgenstern. 2002. Epilogue: Latin America's Reactive Assemblies and Proactive Presidents. In Scott Morgenstern and Benito Nacif, eds., *Legislative Politics in Latin America.* Cambridge, England: Cambridge University Press.

Crisp, Brian F. 2000. *Democratic Institutional Design: The Powers and Incentives of Venezuelan Politicians and Pressure Groups.* Palo Alto, CA: Stanford University Press.

Crisp, B.F., and R.E. Ingall. 2002. Institutional Engineering and the Nature of Representation: Mapping the Effects of Electoral Reform in Colombia. *American Journal of Political Science* 46(4): 733–48.

Cukierman, A., S. Edwards, and G. Tabellini. 1992. Seigniorage and Political Instability. *American Economic Review* 82(June): 537–55.

Cukierman, Alex, and Mariano Tommasi. 1998. When Does It Take a Nixon to Go to China? *American Economic Review* 88(1): 180–97.

Dakolias, Maria, Luis Sprovieri, Giuseppe Di Federico, Roberto de Michele, Marcela Rodríguez, Roberto Saba, Daniel Sabsay, Beth Dabak, and Cristina Motta. 2001. *Argentina: Legal and Judicial Sector Assessment.* Washington, DC: The World Bank.

Damiani, Octavio. 2003. Effects on Employment, Wages, and Labor Standards of Non-traditional Export Crops in Northeast Brazil. *Latin American Research Review* 38(1): 83–112.

Daughters, R., and L. Harper. 2007. Fiscal and Political Decentralization Reforms. In E. Lora, ed., *The State of State Reform in Latin America.*

Washington, DC and Palo Alto, CA: Inter-American Development Bank and Stanford University Press.

Deheza, G.I. 1998. Gobiernos de coalición en el sistema presidencial: América del Sur. In D. Nohlen and M. Fernández, eds., *El presidencialismo renovado: institucionalismo y cambio político en América Latina*. Caracas: Nueva Sociedad.

De Luca, M., M. Jones, and M.I. Tula. 2002. Back Rooms or Ballot Boxes? Candidate Nomination in Argentina. *Comparative Political Studies* 35(4): 413–36.

de Melo, Jaime, Jean-Marie Grether, and Marcelo Olarreaga. 1999. Who Determines Mexican Trade Policy? Discussion Paper 2176. Center for Economic and Policy Research, London.

de Riz, Liliana, and Catalina Smulovitz. 1990. Instituciones y dinámica política: el presidencialismo argentino. CEDES Working paper. Centro de Estudios de Estado y Sociedad, Buenos Aires.

De Swann, A. 1973. *Coalition Theories and Cabinet Formation*. Amsterdam: Elsevier.

Dewan, T., and K. Dowding. 2005. The Corrective Effect of Ministerial Resignations on Government Popularity. *American Journal of Political Science* 49(February): 46–56.

Díaz-Cayeros, A. 2004. Do Federal Institutions Matter? Rules and Political Practices in Resource Allocation in Mexico. In E. Gibson, ed., *Federalism and Democracy in Latin America*. Baltimore, MD: Johns Hopkins University Press.

Diermeier, D., and A. Merlo. 2000. Government Turnover in Parliamentary Democracies. *Journal of Economic Theory* 94(1): 46–79.

Diermeier, D., and R. Stevenson. 2000. Cabinet Terminations and Critical Events. *American Political Science Review* 94(3): 627–40.

Diniz, Eli, and Renato Boschi. 2004. *Empresários, Interesses e Mercado: Dilemas do Desenvolvimento no Brasil*. Belo Horizonte, Brazil: Editora UFMG.

Dix, Robert. 1989. Cleavage Structures and Party Systems in Latin America. *Comparative Politics* 22(1): 23–37.

Doctor, Mahrukh. 2000. The Politics of Port Reform in Brazil: Business Lobbying and the Legacy of Corporatism (1990–98). Ph.D. dissertation, Oxford University.

Dodd, L. 1976. *Coalitions in Parliamentary Government*. Princeton, NJ: Princeton University Press.

Domingo, Pilar. 2000. The Politics of the Mexican Supreme Court. *Journal of Latin American Studies* 32(3) October: 705–35.

———. 2004. Judicialization of Politics or Politicization of the Judiciary? Recent Trends in Latin America. *Democratization* 11(1): 104–26.

Doner, Richard, and Ben Ross Schneider. 2000. Business Associations and Development: Why Some Associations Contribute More Than Others. *Business and Politics* 2(3) November: 261–88.

Douglas, William, John-Paul Ferguson, and Erin Klett. 2004. An Effective Confluence of Forces in Support of Workers' Rights: ILO Standards, U.S. Trade Laws, and NGOs. *Human Rights Quarterly* 26: 273–99.

Dresser, Denise. 2003. Mexico: From PRI Predominance to Divided Democracy. In J. Domínguez and M. Shifter, eds., *Constructing Democratic Governance in Latin America*. Baltimore, MD: Johns Hopkins University Press.

Duncan, Raymond. 1976. *Latin American Politics: A Developmental Approach*. New York: Praeger.

Durand, Francisco, and Eduardo Silva. 1998. *Organized Business, Economic Change, and Democracy in Latin America*. Miami, FL: University of Miami, North-South Center Press.

Eaton, Kent. 2002. *Politicians and Economic Reform in New Democracies: Argentina and the Philippines in the 1990s*. University Park, PA: Penn State University Press.

———. 2004a. The Link between Political and Fiscal Decentralization in South America. In A. Montero and D. Samuels, eds., *Decentralization and Democracy in Latin America*. South Bend, IN: University of Notre Dame Press.

———. 2004b. Risky Business: Decentralization from Above in Chile and Uruguay. *Comparative Politics* 37(1): 1–22.

Echebarría, Koldo, ed. 2006. *Informe sobre la situación del servicio civil en América Latina*. Washington, DC: Regional Policy Dialogue, Public Policy and Transparency Network, Inter-American Development Bank.

Eckstein, Susan. 2004. Globalization and Mobilization in the Neoliberal Era in Latin America. Department of Sociology, Boston University. Unpublished.

Ely, John. 1980. *Democracy and Distrust: A Theory of Judicial Review*. Cambridge, MA: Harvard University Press.

Entman, Robert M. 2000. Declarations of Independence. The Growth of Media Power after the Cold War. In B.L. Nacos, R.Y. Shapiro, and P. Isernia, eds., *Decision-Making in a Glass House: Mass Media, Public Opinion, and American and European Foreign Policy in the 21st Century*. Lanham, MD: Rowman & Littlefield.

———. 2004. *Projections of Power: Framing News, Public Opinion, and U.S. Foreign Policy*. Chicago: University of Chicago Press.

Epp, Charles. 1998. *The Rights Revolution: Lawyers, Activists and Supreme Courts in Comparative Perspective*. Chicago: University of Chicago Press.

Epstein, D., and S. O'Halloran. 1999. *Delegating Powers: A Transaction Cost Politics Approach to Policymaking under Separate Powers*. Cambridge, England: Cambridge University Press.

Escobar-Lemmon, Maria C. 2006. Executives, Legislatures, and Decentralization. *Policy Studies Journal* 34(2): 245–63.

Escobar-Lemmon, Maria C., and Michelle M. Taylor-Robinson. 2005. Women Ministers in Latin American Government: When, Where, and Why? *American Journal of Political Science* 49(4): 829–44.

Escobedo, Juan Francisco. 2003. Movilización de opinión pública en México: el caso del Grupo Oaxaca y de la Ley Federal de Acceso a la Información Pública. *Diálogos de la Comunicación* 66: 16–28.

Etchemendy, Sebastián. 2001. Constructing Reform Coalitions: The Politics of Compensations in Argentina's Economic Liberalization. *Latin American Politics and Society* 43(3): 1–35.

———. 2009. *Models of Economic Liberalization: Regime, Power and Compensation in the Iberian-American Region*. Universidad Di Tella. Unpublished.

Etchemendy, Sebastián, and Ruth Collier. 2007. Down but Not Out: Union Resurgence and Segmented Neocorporatism in Argentina. *Politics & Society* 35(3): 363–401.

Evans, Peter. 1992. The State as Problem and Solution: Predation, Embedded Autonomy, and Structural Change. In Stephan Haggard and Robert Kaufman, eds., *The Politics of Economic Adjustment: International Constraints, Distributive Conflicts, and the State*. Princeton, NJ: Princeton University Press.

Fairfield, Tasha. Forthcoming. Business Power and Tax Reform: Taxing Income and Profits in Chile and Argentina. *Latin American Politics and Society*.

Faletti, T. 1999. New Fiscal Federalism and the Political Dynamics of Decentralization in Latin America. Northwestern University, Evanston, IL.. Unpublished.

————. 2004. Federalism and Decentralization in Argentina. In J. Tulchin and A. Selee, eds., *Decentralization and Democratic Governance in Latin America*. Woodrow Wilson Center Report on the Americas No. 12. Washington, DC: Woodrow Wilson Center.

Feld, Lars, and Stefan Voigt. 2003. Economic Growth and Judicial Independence: Cross-Country Evidence Using a New Set of Indicators. *European Journal of Political Economy* 19(3): 497–527.

Ferejohn, John. 2002. Judicializing Politics, Politicizing Law. *Law and Contemporary Problems* 41 (Summer). Available at http://www.law.duke.edu/journals/lcp/articles/lcp65dSummer2002p41.htm.

Fleischer, David. 2002. Financiamento de Campanhas Políticas: Brasil Tenta Regulamentação e Melhor Fiscalização. In Gerardo Caetano, ed., *Dinero y Política*. Montevideo: Ediciones de la Banda Oriental.

Fleishman-Hillard International Communication. 2003. *Análisis de Posicionamiento, Lineamientos Estratégicos y Plan Táctico Recomendado: Estrategia Nacional de Desarrollo*. Fleishman-Hillard International Communication, Miami, FL. Unpublished.

Foweraker, Joe. 1998. Institutional Design, Party Systems, and Governability—Differentiating the Presidential Regimes of Latin America. *British Journal of Political Science* 28: 651–76.

Freidenberg, Flavia, and Francisco Sánchez López. 2002. ¿Cómo se elige un candidato a presidente? Reglas y prácticas en los partidos políticos en América Latina. *Revista de Estudios Políticos* 118: 321–61.

Frieden, Jeffry. 1991. *Debt, Development, and Democracy*. Princeton, NJ: Princeton University Press.

Frieden, Jeffry, and Lisa Martin. 2002. International Political Economy: Global and Domestic Interactions. In Ira Katznelson and Helen Milner, eds., *Political Science: The State of the Discipline*. New York: Norton.

Frundt, Henry. 1998. *Trade Conditions and Labor Rights: U.S. Initiatives, Dominican and Central American Responses*. Gainesville, FL: University Press of Florida.

————. 2002. Central American Unions in the Era of Globalization. *Latin American Research Review* 37(3): 7–53.

Galhardi, Regina. 2002. Financing Training: Innovative Approaches in Latin America. Working Paper 12. International Labour Organization, Geneva.

Gallart, María. 2001. La articulación entre el sector público y la empresa privada en la formación profesional de América Latina. In G. Labarca, ed., *Formación para el trabajo: ¿pública o privada?* Montevideo: Cinterfor.

Galperín, Hernán. 2000. Regulatory Reform in the Broadcasting Industries in Brazil and Argentina in the 1990s. *Journal of Communication* 50(4): 176–91.

Gamboa, Juan Carlos. 1999. Presidential Popularity in Mexico and Peru: Traditional Approaches, News Perspectives. Ph.D. dissertation, Department of Political Science, Tulane University, New Orleans.

Gamson, William A., and A. Modigliani. 1989. Media Discourse and Public Opinion on Nuclear Power: A Constructionist Approach. *The American Journal of Sociology* 95(1): 1–37.

García, Fátima, and Araceli Mateos. 2000. Elites Parlamentarias en América Latina. *Revista Española de Ciencia Política* 5: 173–94.

García Montero, Mercedes. 2008. Instituciones y actividad legislativa en América Latina. Documentos CIDOB (Centro de Estudios Internacionales de Barcelona), Serie América Latina, Número 23, Barcelona, Spain.

Gargarella, Roberto. 2003. *La justicia frente al gobierno: sobre el carácter contramayoritario del poder judicial.* Barcelona, Spain: Editorial Ariel.

Garman, C., S. Haggard, and E. Willis. 2001. Fiscal Decentralization: A Political Theory with Latin American Cases. *World Politics* 53(2): 205–36.

Garrett, Geoffrey, and Christopher Way. 1995. The Sectoral Composition of Trade Unions, Corporatism, and Economic Performance. In Barry Eichengreen, Jeffry Frieden, and Jurgen von Hagen, eds., *Monetary and Fiscal Policy in an Integrated Europe.* Berlin: Springer-Verlag.

Geddes, Barbara. 1994. *Politician's Dilemma: Building State Capacity in Latin America.* Berkeley, CA: University of California Press.

————. 1995. The Politics of Economic Liberalization. *Latin American Research Review* 30(2): 194–214.

————. 2002. The Great Transformation in the Study of Politics in Developing Countries. In I. Katznelson and H. Milner, eds., *Political Science: State of the Discipline*. New York: W.W. Norton & Co.

Geddes, B., and A. Benton. 1997. Federalism and Party Systems. University of California at Los Angeles (UCLA). Unpublished.

Gibson, E. 2004. Federalism and Democracy: Theoretical Connections and Cautionary Insights. In E. Gibson, ed., *Federalism and Democracy in Latin America*. Baltimore, MD: Johns Hopkins University Press.

Gibson, E., E. Calvo, and T. Falleti. 2004. Reallocative Federalism: Legislative Overrepresentation and Public Spending in the Western Hemisphere. In E. Gibson, ed., *Federalism and Democracy in Latin America*. Baltimore, MD: Johns Hopkins University Press.

Gibson, E., and T. Falleti. 2004. Unity by the Stick: Regional Conflict and the Origins of Argentine Federalism. In E. Gibson, ed., *Federalism and Democracy in Latin America*. Baltimore, MD: Johns Hopkins University Press.

Gibson, James, Gregory Caldeira, and Vanessa Baird. 1998. On the Legitimacy of National High Courts. *American Political Science Review* 92 (June): 343–58.

Gill, Juliet, and Sallie Hughes. 2005. Bureaucratic Incentives in Mexico's New Access to Government Information Law. *Critical Studies in Mass Communication* 22(2): 121–37.

Ginsberg, Benjamin, and Martin Shefter. 2002. *Politics by Other Means: Politicians, Prosecutors, and the Press from Watergate to Whitewater*. New York: W.W. Norton & Company.

Gloppen, Siri, Roberto Gargarella, and Elin Skaar. 2004. *Democratization and the Judiciary: The Accountability Function of Courts in New Democracies*. Portland, OR: Frank Cass Publishers.

González, R., and C. Mascareño. 2004. Decentralization and Restructuring of Politics in Venezuela. In J. Tulchin and A. Selee, eds., *Decentralization and Democratic Governance in Latin America*. Woodrow Wilson Center Report on the Americas No. 12. Washington, DC: Woodrow Wilson Center for Scholars.

Government of Argentina. 2003. *Memoria Detallada del Estado de la Nación 2003*. Buenos Aires: Government of Argentina.

Grindle, Merilee. 1997. *Getting Good Government: Capacity Building in the Public Sectors of Developing Countries.* Cambridge, MA: Harvard University Press.

Griner, Steve, and Daniel Zovatto, eds. 2004. *De las Normas a las Buenas Prácticas. El Desafío del Financiamiento Político en América Latina.* San José, Costa Rica: Organization of American States/IDEA.

Guasch, J. Luis, and Sarath Rajapatirana. 1998. Antidumping and Competition Policies in Latin America and the Caribbean: Total Strangers or Soul Mates? World Bank Policy Research Working Paper Series No. 1958. World Bank, Washington, DC.

Guillén, Mauro. 2000. Business Groups in Emerging Economies: A Resource-Based View. *Academy of Management Journal* 43(3) June: 362–80.

———. 2001.*The Limits of Convergence: Globalization and Organizational Change in Argentina, South Korea, and Spain.* Princeton, NJ: Princeton University Press.

Haggard, S., and R. Kaufman. 1992. *The Politics of Economic Adjustment: International Constraints, Distributive Conflicts, and the State.* Princeton, NJ: Princeton University Press.

Haggard, S., S. Maxfield, and B.R. Schneider. 1997. Alternative Theories of Business and Business-State Relations. In Sylvia Maxfield and Ben Ross Schneider, eds., *Business and the State in Developing Countries.* Ithaca, NY: Cornell University Press.

Haggard, S., and M.D. McCubbins. 2001. *Presidents, Parliaments, and Policy.* Cambridge, England: Cambridge University Press.

Haggard, S., and S. Webb, eds. 1994. *Voting for Reform: Democracy, Political Liberalization, and Economic Adjustment.* Washington, DC: World Bank.

———. 2004. Political Incentives and Intergovernmental Fiscal Relations: Argentina, Brazil, and Mexico Compared. In A. Montero and D. Samuels, eds., *Decentralization and Democracy in Latin America.* South Bend, IN: University of Notre Dame Press.

Hagopian, F., and S. Mainwaring. 2005. *The Third Wave of Democratization in Latin America: Advances and Setbacks.* Cambridge, England and New York: Cambridge University Press.

Hall, Peter, and David Soskice. 2001. An Introduction to Varieties of Capitalism. In Peter Hall and David Soskice, eds., *Varieties of Capitalism.* New York: Oxford University Press.

Hallerberg, Mark, and Patrik Marier. 2004. Executive Authority, the Personal Vote, and Budget Discipline in Latin American and Caribbean Countries. *American Journal of Political Science* 48(3): 571–87.

Hallerberg, Mark, Carlos Scartascini, and Ernesto Stein. *Who Decides the Budget? A Political Economy Analysis of the Budget Process in Latin America.* Washington, DC and Cambridge, MA: Inter-American Development Bank and David Rockefeller Center for Latin American Studies, Harvard University.

Hallin, Daniel C., and Paolo Mancini. 2004. Americanization, Globalization, and Secularization: Understanding the Convergence of Media Systems and Political Communication. In Frank Esser and Barbara Pfetsch, eds., *Comparing Political Communication: Theories, Cases and Challenges.* New York: Cambridge University Press.

Hammergren, Linn. 2002. Fifteen Years of Judicial Reform in Latin America: Where We Are and Why We Haven't Made More Progress. USAID Global Center for Democracy and Governance, Washington, DC. Available at http://undp-pogar.org/publications/judiciary linn2/index.html#intro.

Hammond, John L. 2004. The MST and the Media: Competing Images of the Brazilian Landless Farmworkers' Movement. *Latin American Politics and Society* 46(4): 61–90.

Hawkins, Carroll. 1967. Reflections on Labor's Relation to Government and Politics in Latin America. *Western Political Quarterly* 20(4): 930–40.

Heath, Roseanna Michelle, Leslie A. Schwindt-Bayer, and Michelle M. Taylor-Robinson. 2005. Women on the Sidelines: Women's Representation on Committees in Latin American Legislatures. *American Journal of Political Science* 49(2): 420–36.

Helmke, Gretchen. 2002. The Logic of Strategic Defection: Court-Executive Relations in Argentina under Dictatorship and Democracy. *American Political Science Review* 96(2): 291–303.

Helpman, Elhanan, and Gene M. Grossman. 1996. Electoral Competition and Special Interest Politics. *Review of Economic Studies* 63: 265–86.

Heredia, Blanca. 2002. *La economía política de la reforma de sistemas de administración de personal público en América Latina: un marco de análisis.* Paper prepared for the Public Policy and Transparency

Network, II Meeting, Regional Policy Dialogue (RPD), Inter-American Development Bank, April, Washington, DC.

Heredia, Blanca, and Ben Ross Schneider. 2003. The Political Economy of Administrative Reform. In Ben Ross Schneider and Blanca Heredia, eds., *Reinventing Leviathan: The Politics of Administrative Reform in Developing Countries.* Coral Gables, FL: North-South Center Press, University of Miami.

Hicken, Allen, and Heather Stoll. Forthcoming. How Presidential Elections Shape Coordination in Legislative Elections. *Comparative Political Studies* 44(8).

Hochstetler, Kathryn. 2003. Fading Green? Environmental Politics in the Mercosur Free Trade Agreement. *Latin American Politics and Society* 45(4): 1–32.

———. 2006. Rethinking Presidentialism: Challenges and Presidential Falls in South America. *Comparative Politics* 38(4): 401–18.

Horowitz, Robert. 1994. Judicial Review of Regulatory Decisions: The Changing Criteria. *Political Science Quarterly* 109 (Spring): 133–69.

Houtzager, Peter. 2001. Collective Action and Political Authority: Rural Workers, Church, and State in Brazil. *Politics and Society* 30(1): 1–45.

Huber, J. 1998. How Does Cabinet Instability Affect Political Performance? Credible Commitment, Information, and Health Care Cost Containment in Parliamentary Politics. *American Political Science Review* 92: 577–92.

Huber, J., and C. Martínez-Gallardo. 2003. Cabinet Turnover in Parliamentary Democracies. Paper prepared for delivery at the annual meeting of the American Political Science Association, September, Philadelphia, PA.

———. 2004. Cabinet Instability and the Accumulation of Experience: The French Fourth and Fifth Republics in Comparative Perspective. *British Journal of Political Science* 34: 27–48.

Huber, J., and N. McCarty. 2001. Cabinet Decision Rules and Political Uncertainty in Parliamentary Bargaining. *American Political Science Review* 95(2): 345–61.

Huber, J., and C.R. Shipan. 2002. *Deliberate Discretion? The Institutional Foundations of Bureaucratic Autonomy.* Cambridge, England: Cambridge University Press.

Hughes, Sallie. 2000. Government, Political Parties and the Mexican News Media: Tentative Findings on a Crucial Relationship. La Jolla, CA: Center for U.S.-Mexico Studies, University of California, San Diego.

————. 2005. The Role of the News Media in the Policymaking Process. Paper prepared for the Inter-American Development Bank Workshop on State Reform, Public Policies, and Policymaking Processes, February 28–March 2. Washington, DC. Available at: http://www.iadb.org/research/pub_desc.cfm?pub_id=S-303.

————. 2006. *Newsrooms in Conflict: Journalism and the Democratization of Mexico*. Pittsburgh, PA: University of Pittsburgh Press.

————. 2009. The Evolution of Network News in Mexico. Capturing the Communications Regulatory Regime. In M. Chávez and M. Guerrero, eds., *Information, Entertainment and Citizenship in Latin America*. East Lansing, MI, Mexico City, and Miami, FL: Michigan State University, Universidad Iberoamericana, and University of Miami.

Hughes, Sallie, and Manuel Alejandro Guerrero. 2009. The Disenchanted Voter: Emotional Attachment, Social Stratification, and Mediated Politics in Mexico's 2006 Presidential Election. *International Journal of Press/Politics* 14(3): 353–75.

Hughes, Sallie, and Chappell Lawson. 2004. Propaganda and Crony Capitalism: Partisan Bias in Mexican News Coverage. *Latin American Research Review* 39(3): 81–105.

————. 2005. The Barriers to Media Opening in Latin America. *Political Communication* 22(1): 9–25.

Hughes, Sallie, and Paola Prado. Forthcoming. Media Diversity and Societal Inequality in Latin America. In Merike Blofield, ed., *The Great Gap. The Politics of Social Inequality in Latin America*. University Park, PA: Penn State University Press.

Human Rights Watch. 1999. Systemic Injustice: Torture, Disappearance, and Extra-Judicial Execution in Mexico. Available at http://hrw.org/reports/1999/mexico/.

Humphries, Martha Anne, and Donald R. Songer. 1999. Law and Politics in Judicial Oversight of Federal Administrative Agencies. *The Journal of Politics* 61(1): 207–20.

Huntington, S. 1992. *The Third Wave: Democratization in the Late Twentieth Century*. Norman, OK: University of Oklahoma Press.

Iacoviello, Mercedes. 2006. Análisis comparativo por subsistemas. In Koldo Echebarría, ed., *Informe sobre la situación del servicio civil en América Latina*. Washington, DC: Regional Policy Dialogue, Public Policy and Transparency Network, Inter-American Development Bank.

Iacoviello, Mercedes, and Laura Zuvanic. 2006. Desarrollo e integración de la gestión de recursos humanos en los estados latinoamericanos. In *Revista Documentos y Aportes en Administración Pública y Gestión Estatal. Año 6, Nº 7*. Santa Fe, Argentina: Facultad de Ciencias Económicas and Universidad Nacional del Litoral.

Iaryczower, Matías, Pablo Spiller, and Mariano Tommasi. 2002. Judicial Independence in Unstable Environments, Argentina 1935–1998. *American Journal of Political Science* 46(4) October: 699–716.

IDB (Inter-American Development Bank). 2002. *The Trade Policymaking Process, Level One of the Two Level Game: Country Studies in the Western Hemisphere*. INTAL-ITD-STA Occasional Paper 13. Buenos Aires: Inter-American Development Bank.

———. 2003. *Good Jobs Wanted: Labor Markets in Latin America*. Economic and Social Progress in Latin America: 2004 Report. Washington, DC: Inter-American Development Bank.

———. 2005. *The Politics of Policies*. Economic and Social Progress in Latin America: 2006 Report. Washington, DC: Inter-American Development Bank. Available at http://www.iadb.org/res/ipes/2006/index.cfm?language=english.

———. 2008. *Policymaking in Latin America: How Politics Shapes Policies*. Washington, DC and Cambridge, MA: Inter-American Development Bank and David Rockefeller Center for Latin American Studies, Harvard University.

ILO (International Labour Organization). 2002. *2002 Labour Overview: Latin America and the Caribbean*. Lima: International Labour Organization.

———. 2003. *Fundamental Principles and Rights at Work: A Labour Law Study (Central America)*. Geneva: ILO.

———. 2004. *Fundamental Principles and Rights at Work: A Labour Law Study (Dominican Republic)*. Geneva: ILO.

———. 2006. ILOLEX: Database of international labor standards. Available at http://www.ilo.org/ilolex/english/newcountryframeE.htm.

Ingham, Geoffrey. 1974. *Strikes and Industrial Conflict*. London: Macmillan.

Inter-American Press Association. 2005. Report of the Committee on Freedom of the Press and Information, Country-by-Country. Prepared for the Inter-American Press Association, Mid-Year Meeting, March 11–14, Panama City, Panama.

Jackson, Donald, and C. Neal Tate. 1992. *Comparative Judicial Review and Public Policy*. Westport, CT: Greenwood Press.

Jacobs, Lawrence R., and Robert Y. Shapiro. 1996. Towards an Integrated Study of Political Communication, Public Opinion, and the Policymaking Process. *PS: Political Science and Politics* 29(1): 10–13.

Johnson, D.E. Forthcoming. The Mass Media's Dual Role: "Watchdog" and Guardian of Their Own Interests. *Journal of Public Affairs, Special Issue: Interests, Interest Groups and Lobbying in Latin America: A New Era or More of the Same?*

Jones, Mark P. 2005. The Role of Parties and Party Systems in the Policymaking Process. Prepared for the Inter-American Development Bank Workshop on State Reform, Public Policies, and Policymaking Processes, February 28–March 2, Washington, DC.

Jones, Mark P., and Scott Mainwaring. 2003. The Nationalization of Parties and Party Systems: An Empirical Indicator and an Application to the Americas. *Party Politics* 9: 139–66.

Jones, M., O. Meloni, and M. Tommasi. 2009. Voters as Fiscal Liberals: Incentives and Accountability in Federal Systems. Universidad de San Andrés, Buenos Aires. Unpublished.

Jones, Mark P., Sebastian M. Saiegh, Pablo T. Spiller, and Mariano Tommasi. 2001. Keeping a Seat in Congress: Provincial Party Bosses and the Survival of Argentine Legislators. Paper prepared for the annual meeting of the Latin American Studies Association, September 6–8, Washington, DC.

———. 2002. Amateur Legislators–Professional Politicians: The Consequences of Party-Centered Electoral Rules in a Federal System. *American Journal of Political Science* 46(3): 656–69.

Juárez, Carlos. 1995. The Political Economy of Economic Policy Reform in Colombia: Technocratic Bureaucracy and Business-Government Relations, 1966–92. Ph.D. dissertation, University of California at Los Angeles (UCLA).

Karl, T. 1990. Dilemmas of Democratization in Latin America. *Comparative Politics* 23(1): 1–21.

Katzenstein, Peter. 1985. *Small States in World Markets: Industrial Policy in Europe.* Ithaca, NY: Cornell University Press.

Katzmann, Robert. 1997. *Courts and Congress.* Washington, DC: The Brookings Institution Press.

Kaufman, Robert, Carlos Bazdresch, and Blanca Heredia. 1994. Mexico: Radical Reform in a Dominant Party System. In Stephan Haggard and Steven Webb, eds., *Voting for Reform.* New York: Oxford University Press.

Kaufman, Robert, and Joan Nelson, eds. 2004a. *Crucial Needs, Weak Incentives: Social Sector Reform, Democratization, and Globalization in Latin America.* Baltimore, MD: Johns Hopkins University Press.

————. 2004b. Conclusions: The Political Dynamics of Reform. In Robert Kaufman and Joan Nelson, eds., *Crucial Needs, Weak Incentives: Social Sector Reform, Democratization, and Globalization in Latin America.* Baltimore, MD: Johns Hopkins University Press.

Kaufmann, Daniel, Aart Kraay, and Massimo Mastruzzi. 2003. Governance Matters III: Governance Indicators for 1996–2002. World Bank Policy Research Working Paper No. 3106. World Bank, Washington, DC.

Keefer, Philip. 2001. When Do Special Interests Run Rampant? Disentangling the Role in Banking Crises of Elections, Incomplete Information, and Checks and Balances in Banking Crises. Policy Research Working Paper No. 2543. World Bank, Washington, DC.

Kellam, Marisa Andrea. 2007. Parties for Hire: The Instability of Presidential Coalitions in Latin America. Ph.D. dissertation, Department of Political Science, University of California at Los Angeles (UCLA).

Kernell, Sam. 1997. *Going Public: New Strategies of Presidential Leadership.* Washington, DC: Congressional Quarterly Press.

Kikeri, Sunita. 1998. Privatization and Labor: What Happens to Workers When Governments Divest? World Bank Technical Paper 396. World Bank, Washington, DC.

King, G., J. Alt, N. Burns, and M. Laver. 1990. A Unified Model of Cabinet Dissolution in Parliamentary Democracies. *American Journal of Political Science* 34 (August): 846–71.

Kitschelt, Herbert. 2000. Linkages between Citizens and Politicians in Democratic Polities. *Comparative Political Studies* 33: 845–79.

Kitschelt, Herbert, Kirk A. Hawkins, Juan Pablo Luna, Guillermo Rosas, and Elizabeth J. Zechmeister. Forthcoming. *Latin American Party Systems.* New York: Cambridge University Press.

Klingner, D.E., and V. Pallavicini Campos. 2001. Strengthening Personnel Management in Developing Countries: Lessons Learned, Lessons Forgotten, and an Agenda for Action. *Public Personnel Management* 30(1) Spring: 1–15.

Knudson, Jerry W. 1998. Rebellion in Chiapas: Insurrection by Internet and Public Relations. *Media, Culture & Society* 20(3): 507–18.

Knutsen, Oddbjørn. 1998. The Strength of the Partisan Component of Left-Right Identity: A Comparative Longitudinal Study of Left-Right Party Polarization in Eight West European Countries. *Party Politics* 4: 5–31.

Kraemer, M. 1997. Intergovernmental Transfers and Political Representation: Empirical Evidence from Argentina, Brazil, and Mexico. Working Paper 345. Office of the Chief Economist, Inter-American Development Bank, Washington, DC.

Kriesi, H. 2004. Strategic Political Communication: Mobilizing Public Opinion in "Audience Democracies". In F. Esser and B. Pfetsch, eds., *Comparing Political Communication: Theories, Cases and Challenges.* Cambridge, England: Cambridge University Press.

Kurtz, Marcus. 1999. Chile's Neo-Liberal Revolution: Incremental Decisions and Structural Transformation, 1973–89. *Journal of Latin American Studies* 31(2): 399–427.

———. 2004. The Dilemmas of Democracy in the Open Economy: Lessons from Latin America. *World Politics* 56: 262–302.

Laakso, Markku, and Rein Taagepera. 1979. Effective Number of Parties: A Measure with Application to Western Europe. *Comparative Political Studies* 12: 3–27.

Lagos, Marta. 2003. Public Opinion. In Jorge Domínguez and Michael Shifter, eds., *Constructing Democratic Governance in Latin America.* Baltimore, MD: Johns Hopkins University Press.

Laver, M., and K.A. Shepsle. 1994. *Cabinet Ministers and Parliamentary Government.* Cambridge, England: Cambridge University Press.

————. 1996. *Making and Breaking Governments: Cabinets and Legislatures in Parliamentary Democracies.* Cambridge, England: Cambridge University Press.

Lawson, C., A. Baker, K. Bruhn, R. Camp, W. Cornelius, J. Domínguez, K. Greene, J. Klesner, B. Magaloni, J. McCann, A. Moreno, A. Poiré, and D. Shirk. 2007. The Mexico 2006 Panel Study. Wave X. Available at http://web.mit.edu/polisci/research/mexico06.

LB (Latinobarometer). Various years. Latinobarometer: Latin American Public Opinion. Available at www.latinobarometro.org.

Lehne, Richard. 2006. *Government and Business: American Political Economy in Comparative Perspective.* Washington, DC: Congressional Quarterly Press.

Lehoucq, Fabrice. 2005. Policymaking and Institutions in Democratic Costa Rica. Paper presented at the Conference on Reform of the State and the Policymaking Process, Inter-American Development Bank, February, Washington, DC. Available at: http://www.iadb. org/res/publications/pubfiles/pubS-306.pdf.

Lehoucq, F., G. Negretto, F. Aparicio, B. Nacif, and A. Benton. 2008. Policymaking in Mexico under One-Party Hegemony and Divided Government. In E. Stein and M. Tommasi, with P. Spiller and C. Scartascini, eds., *Policymaking in Latin America: How Politics Shapes Policies.* Washington, DC and Cambridge, MA: Inter-American Development Bank and David Rockefeller Center for Latin American Studies, Harvard University.

Leiras, Marcelo. 2006. Parties, Provinces and Electoral Coordination: A Study on the Determinants of Party and Party System Aggregation in Argentina, 1983–2005. Ph.D. dissertation, University of Notre Dame, South Bend, IN.

LeoGrande, William. 2005. From the Red Menace to Radical Populism: U.S. Insecurity in Latin America. *World Policy Journal* 22(4): 25–35.

Levitsky, Steven, and Maxwell A. Cameron. 2003. Democracy without Parties? Political Parties and Regime Change in Fujimori's Peru. *Latin American Politics and Society* 45(3): 1–33.

Levitsky, Steven, and Lucan Way. 1998. Between a Shock and a Hard Place: The Dynamics of Labor-Backed Adjustment in Poland and Argentina. *Comparative Politics* 30(2): 171–92.

Linsky, Martin. 1986. *Impact: How the Press Affects Federal Policymaking.* New York: W.W. Norton.

Linz, J., and A. Stepan. 1996. *Problems of Democratic Transition and Consolidation.* Baltimore, MD: Johns Hopkins University Press.

Lipset, S.M. 1960. *Political Man: The Social Bases of Politics.* Garden City, NY: Doubleday.

Llanos, Mariana, and Detlef Nolte. 2003. Bicameralism in the Americas: Around the Extremes of Symmetry and Incongruence. *Journal of Legislative Studies* 9(3): 54–86.

Longo, Francisco. 2002. Marco analítico para el diagnóstico institucional de sistemas de servicio civil. Report prepared for the Regional Policy Dialogue, Inter-American Development Bank, April 4–5, Washington, DC.

———. 2004. *Mérito y flexibilidad. La gestión de las personas en las organizaciones del sector público.* Barcelona, Spain: Editorial Paidós.

López, Humberto. 2003. Errores de comunicación del Presidente Uribe en el referendo. *Revista Chasqui* 84 (December). Available at http://chasqui.comunica.org/content/view/138/61/.

Lora, Eduardo, and Ugo Panizza. 2003. The Future of Structural Reform. *Journal of Democracy* 14(2): 123–37.

Lupia, Arthur, and Mathew McCubbins. 1994. Learning from Oversight: Fire Alarms and Police Patrols Reconstructed. *Journal of Law, Economics and Organization* 10(1): 86–125.

Lyne, Mona. 2008. *The Voter's Dilemma and Democratic Accountability: Latin America and Beyond.* University Park, PA: Penn State University Press.

Macleod, Dag. 1998. Privatization and Bureaucratic Transformation in Mexico: The Strategy and Structure of a Neo-Liberal Transformation. Paper presented at the 1998 meeting of the Latin American Studies Association, September 24–26, Chicago.

Madrid, Raúl. 2003a. Labouring against Neoliberalism: Unions and Patterns of Reform in Latin America. *Journal of Latin American Studies* 35(1): 53–89.

———. 2003b. *Retiring the State: The Politics of Pension Privatization in Latin America and Beyond.* Palo Alto, CA: Stanford University Press.

Mahon, James. 1996. *Mobile Capital and Latin American Development.* University Park, PA: Penn State University Press.

Mainwaring, Scott. 1998. Rethinking Party Systems Theory in the Third Wave of Democratization: The Importance of Party System Institutionalization. Kellogg Institute Working Paper No. 260. University of Notre Dame, South Bend, IN.

———. 1999. *Rethinking Party Systems in the Third Wave of Democratization: The Case of Brazil*. Palo Alto, CA: Stanford University Press.

Mainwaring, S., G. O'Donnell, and A. Valenzuela, eds. 1992. *Issues in Democratic Consolidation*. South Bend, IN: University of Notre Dame Press.

Mainwaring, S., and T. Scully, eds. 1995. *Building Democratic Institutions: Party Systems in Latin America*. Palo Alto, CA: Stanford University Press.

Mainwaring, S., and M. Shugart, eds. 1997. *Presidentialism and Democracy in Latin America*. Cambridge, England and New York: Cambridge University Press.

Manzano, O., F. Monaldi, J.M. Puente, and S. Vitale. 2009. Oil-Fueled Centralization: The Case of Venezuela. Forum on Federations, Ottawa. Unpublished.

Manzetti, Luigi. 1999. *Privatization South American Style*. Oxford, England: Oxford University Press.

Martin, Cathie Jo. 1991. *Shifting the Burden: The Struggle over Growth and Corporate Taxation*. Chicago: University of Chicago Press.

Martin, L. 2004. The Government Agenda in Parliamentary Democracies. *American Journal of Political Science* 48(3): 445–61.

Martínez-Gallardo, C. 2005. *Presidents, Posts and Policy: Ministerial Appointments and Political Strategy in Presidential Systems*. Ph.D. dissertation, Columbia University, New York.

———. 2008. Coalition Duration in Presidential Systems. Paper prepared for presentation at the American Political Science Association meeting, August 28, Boston.

Martínez Nogueira, Roberto. 2002. Las administraciones públicas paralelas y la construcción de capacidades institucionales: la gestión por proyectos y las unidades ejecutoras. In *Revista del CLAD Reforma y Democracia*, 24 (October). Caracas.

Maxfield, Sylvia. 1997. *Gatekeepers of Growth: The International Political Economy of Central Banking in Developing Countries*. Princeton, NJ: Princeton University Press.

————. 1998. Understanding the Political Implications of Financial Internationalization in Emerging Market Countries. *World Development* 26(7): 1201–19.

McCann, Michael. 1994. *Rights at Work: Pay Equity Reform and the Politics of Legal Mobilization*. Chicago: University of Chicago Press.

McCubbins, Mathew, and Thomas Schwartz. 1984. Congressional Oversight Overlooked: Police Patrols versus Fire Alarms. *American Journal of Political Science* 28(1) February: 165–79.

McGuire, James. 1997. *Peronism without Perón: Unions, Parties, and Democracy in Argentina*. Palo Alto, CA: Stanford University Press.

Mehrez, Gil, and Daniel Kaufmann. 1999. Transparency, Liberalization and Banking Crises. The World Bank Institute, Washington, DC. Unpublished.

Mejía Acosta, A., M.C. Araujo, A. Pérez-Liñán, and S. Saiegh. 2008. Veto Players, Fickle Institutions, and Low-Quality Policies: The Policymaking Process in Ecuador. In E. Stein and M. Tommasi, with P. Spiller and C. Scartascini, eds., *Policymaking in Latin America: How Politics Shapes Policies*. Washington, DC and Cambridge, MA: Inter-American Development Bank and David Rockefeller Center for Latin American Studies, Harvard University.

Méndez, José. 1993. The Development of the Colombian Cut Flower Industry. In J. Michael Finger, ed., *Antidumping*. Ann Arbor, MI: University of Michigan Press.

Méndez, Juan E., Guillermo O'Donnell, and Paulo Sérgio Pinheiro, eds. 1999. *The (Un)Rule of Law & the Unprivileged in Latin America*. South Bend, IN: University of Notre Dame Press.

Merryman, John Henry. 1985. *The Civil Law Tradition: An Introduction to the Legal Systems of Western Europe and Latin America*. Palo Alto, CA: Stanford University Press.

Mizrahi, Y. 2004. Mexico: Decentralization from Above. In J. Tulchin and A. Selee, eds., *Decentralization and Democratic Governance in Latin America*. Woodrow Wilson Center Report on the Americas No. 12. Princeton University, NJ.

Modesto, Paulo. 1997. Reforma Administrativa e Marco Legal das Organizações Sociais no Brasil. *Revista do Serviço Público* 48(2): 27–58.

Molotch, Harvey, David L. Protess, and Margaret T. Gordon. 1987. The Media-Policy Connection: Ecology of News. In David L. Paletz, ed., *Political Communication Research: Approaches, Studies, Assessments.* Norwood, NJ: Ablex Publishing Corporation.

Monaldi, F., R. González, R. Obuchi, and M. Penfold. 2008. Political Institutions and Policymaking in Venezuela: The Rise and Collapse of Political Cooperation. In E. Stein and M. Tommasi, with P. Spiller and C. Scartascini, eds., *Policymaking in Latin America: How Politics Shapes Policies.* Washington, DC and Cambridge, MA: Inter-American Development Bank and David Rockefeller Center for Latin American Studies, Harvard University.

Montero, Alfred. 1998. State Interests and the New Industrial Policy in Brazil: The Privatization of Steel, 1990–1994. *Journal of Interamerican Studies and World Affairs* 40(3): 29–62.

———. 2001. Making and Remaking "Good Government" in Brazil: Subnational Industrial Policy in Minas Gerais. *Latin American Politics and Society* 43(2) Summer: 49–80.

Montero, A., and D. Samuels. 2004. The Political Determinants of Decentralization in Latin America: Causes and Consequences. In A. Montero and D. Samuels, eds., *Decentralization and Democracy in Latin America.* South Bend, IN: University of Notre Dame Press.

Moreno, Alejandro. 1996. The Political Use of Public Opinion Polls: Building Popular Support in Mexico under Salinas. In Roderic A. Camp, ed., *Polling for Democracy: Public Opinion and Political Liberalization in Mexico.* Wilmington, DE: Scholarly Resources.

Moreno, Francisco José. 1970. Justice and Law in Latin America: A Cuban Example. *Journal of Interamerican Studies and World Affairs* 12(3): 367–78.

Morgenstern, Scott. 2002. Towards a Model of Latin American Legislatures. In Scott Morgenstern and Benito Nacif, eds., *Legislative Politics in Latin America.* Cambridge, England: Cambridge University Press.

Morgenstern, S., and B. Nacif, eds. 2002. *Legislative Politics in Latin America.* Cambridge, England and New York: Cambridge University Press.

Mosley, Layna. 2003. *Global Capital and National Governments.* New York: Cambridge University Press.

Motta Veiga, Pedro da. 2002. Trade Policy-Making in Brazil: Transition Paths. In S. Ostry, ed., *The Trade Policy-Making Process, Level One of the Two Level Game: Case Studies in the Western Hemisphere*. INTAL-ITD-STA Occasional Paper 13. Buenos Aires: Inter-American Development Bank.

Muñoz, Oscar, ed. 2000. *El Estado y el Sector Privado*. Santiago: Dolmen.

Murillo, M. Victoria. 1997a. Union Politics, Market-Oriented Reforms and the Reshaping of Argentine Corporatism. In Douglas Chalmers, Katherine Robert Hite, and Carlos Vilas, eds., *The New Politics of Inequality in Latin America: Rethinking Participation and Representation*. Oxford, England: Oxford University Press.

———. 1997b. A Strained Alliance: Continuity and Change in Mexican Labor Politics. In Monica Serrano, ed., *Mexico: Assessing Neoliberal Reform*. London: The Institute of Latin American Studies, University of London.

———. 2000. From Populism to Neoliberalism: Labor Unions and Market Reforms in Latin America. *World Politics* 52 (January): 135–74.

———. 2001. *Labor Unions, Partisan Coalitions and Market Reforms in Latin America*. Cambridge, England: Cambridge University Press.

———. 2005. Partisanship amidst Convergence: The Politics of Labor Reform in Latin America. *Comparative Politics* 37(4): 441–58.

Murillo, M. Victoria, and Andrew Schrank. 2005. With a Little Help from My Friends: Partisan Politics, Transnational Alliances, and Labor Rights in Latin America. *Comparative Political Studies* 38(8): 971–99.

Mustapic, Ana Maria. 2002. Oscillating Relations: President and Congress in Argentina. In Scott Morgenstern and Benito Nacif, eds., *Legislative Politics in Latin America*. Cambridge, England: Cambridge University Press.

Naím, Moisés. 1993. *Paper Tigers and Minotaurs: The Politics of Venezuela's Economic Reforms*. Washington, DC: Carnegie Endowment.

Nash, June. 1979. *We Eat the Mines and the Mines Eat Us: Dependency and Exploitation in Bolivian Tin Mines*. New York: Columbia University Press.

Navia, Patricio, and Julio Ríos-Figueroa. 2005. The Constitutional Adjudication Mosaic of Latin America. *Comparative Political Studies* 38(2): 189–217.

Negretto, G. 2006. Minority Presidents and Democratic Performance in Latin America. *Latin American Politics and Society* 48(3): 63–92.

Nelson, J. 1990. *Economic Crisis and Policy Choice: The Politics of Adjustment in Less Developed Countries*. Princeton, NJ: Princeton University Press.

Nickson, R. Andrew. 1995. *Local Government in Latin America*. Boulder, CO: Lynne Rienner.

Njaim, Humberto. 2004. Financiamiento Político en los Países Andinos: Bolivia, Colombia, Ecuador, Perú y Venezuela. In Steve Griner and Daniel Zovatto, eds., *De las Normas a las Buenas Prácticas*. San José, Costa Rica: OAS/IDEA.

Norris, Pippa. 2004. *Electoral Engineering: Voting Rules and Political Behavior*. New York: Cambridge University Press.

Ochoa-Reza, E. 2004. Multiple Arenas of Struggle: Mexico's Transition to Democracy. In E. Gibson, ed., *Federalism and Democracy in Latin America*. Baltimore, MD: Johns Hopkins University Press.

O'Donnell, Guillermo. 1972. *Modernization and Authoritarianism*. Berkeley, CA: Institute of International Studies, University of California.

———. 1999. Horizontal Accountability in New Democracies. In Andreas Schedler, Larry Diamond, and Marc Plattner, eds., *Self-Restraining State: Power and Accountability in New Democracies*. Boulder, CO: Lynne Rienner Publishers.

O'Donnell, G., P. Schmitter, and L. Whitehead, eds. 1986. *Transitions from Authoritarian Rule: Latin America*. Baltimore, MD: Johns Hopkins University Press.

O'Heffernan, Patrick. 1991. *Mass Media and American Foreign Policy: Insider Perspectives on Global Journalism and the Foreign Policy Process*. Norwood, NJ: Ablex Publishing Corporation.

———. 1994. A Mutual Exploitation Model of Media Influence in U.S. Foreign Policy. In W. Lance Bennett and David L. Paletz, eds., *Taken by Storm: The Media, Public Opinion, and U.S. Foreign Policy in the Gulf Crisis*. Chicago: University of Chicago Press.

Olarreaga, Marcelo, and Isidoro Soloaga. 1998. Endogenous Tariff Formation: The Case of MERCOSUR. *World Bank Economic Review* 12(2): 297–320.

Oliveira, Vanessa Elias. 2005. Judiciário e Privatizações no Brasil: Existe uma Judicialização da Política? *DADOS Revista de Ciências Sociais* 48(3): 559–87.

Olson, Mancur. 1965. *The Logic of Collective Action*. Cambridge, MA: Harvard University Press.

———. 1982. *The Rise and Decline of Nations*. New Haven, CT: Yale University Press.

O'Neill, K. 2003. Decentralization as an Electoral Strategy. *Comparative Political Studies* 36(9): 1068–91.

———. 2005. *Decentralizing the State: Elections, Parties and Local Power in the Andes*. Cambridge, England: Cambridge University Press.

Oppenheimer, Andrés. 1998. *Bordering on Chaos: Mexico's Roller-Coaster Journey toward Prosperity*. Boston: Little, Brown, & Co.

Ortega, Juan Manuel. 2002. Institutions and Economic Reform in Mexico: The Case of Economic Pacts, 1987–1997. Ph.D. dissertation, Boston University.

Oszlak, O. 2002. Redemocratization and the Modernization of the State: The Alfonsin Era in Argentina. In R. Baker, ed., *Transitions from Authoritarianism: The Role of the Bureaucracy*. Westport, CT: Praeger.

Oxhorn, Phillip. 2005. Neopluralism and the Challenges for Citizenship in Latin America. Paper presented at the conference, After Neo-liberalism? Consequences for Citizenship, November 4–5, Montreal.

Ozler, S., and G. Tabellini. 1991. *External Debt and Political Instability*. Cambridge, MA: National Bureau of Economic Research.

Pagés, Carmen. 2004. A Cost-Benefit Approach to Labor Market Reform. *Economic Review* 89(2): 67–85.

Paletz, David L. 1998. The Media and Policymaking. In Doris Graber, Denis McQuail, and Pippa Norris, eds., *The Politics of the News: The News of Politics*. Washington, DC: Congressional Quarterly Press.

Paletz, David L., and W. Lance Bennett, eds. 1994. *Taken by Storm: The Media, Public Opinion, and U.S. Foreign Policy in the Gulf Crisis*. Chicago: University of Chicago Press.

Panizza, Francisco. 2004. A Reform without Losers: The Symbolic Economy of Civil Service Reform in Uruguay, 1995–96. *Latin American Politics and Society* 46(3): 1–28.

Payne, J. Mark, Daniel Zovatto, and Mercedes Mateo Díaz. 2007. *Democracies in Development: Politics and Reform in Latin America* (revised edition). Washington, DC: Inter-American Development Bank.

Pedersen, Mogens N. 1983. Changing Patterns of Electoral Volatility in European Party Systems, 1948–1977: Explorations in Explanation. In Hans Daalder and Peter Mair, eds., *Western European Party Systems: Continuity and Change.* London: Sage.

PELA (Proyecto de Elites Latinoamericanas). Various years. Proyecto de Elites Latinoamericanas, 1994–2005. Salamanca, Spain: Universidad de Salamanca.

Penfold-Becerra, M. 2004a. Electoral Dynamics and Decentralization in Venezuela. In A. Montero and D. Samuels, eds., *Decentralization and Democracy in Latin America.* South Bend, IN: University of Notre Dame Press.

———. 2004b. Federalism and Institutional Change in Venezuela. In E. Gibson, ed., *Federalism and Democracy in Latin America.* Baltimore, MD: Johns Hopkins University Press.

Pérez-Liñán, Aníbal. 2003a. Presidential Crises and Democratic Accountability in Latin America, 1990–1999. In S.E. Eckstein and T.P. Wickham-Crowley, eds., *What Justice? Whose Justice? Fighting for Fairness in Latin America.* Berkeley, CA: University of California Press.

———. 2003b. Pugna de poderes y crisis de gobernabilidad: ¿hacia un nuevo presidencialismo? *Latin American Research Review* 38(3): 149–64.

———. 2005. Democratization and Constitutional Crises in Presidential Regimes. *Comparative Political Studies* 38(1): 51–74.

Perrone, Luca, Erik Olin Wright, and Larry Griffin. 1984. Positional Power, Strikes, and Wages. *American Sociological Review* 49(3): 412–26.

Persson, T., and G.E. Tabellini. 2000. *Political Economics: Explaining Economic Policy.* Cambridge, MA: MIT Press.

Peruzzotti, Enrique, and Catalina Smulovitz. 2006. *Enforcing the Rule of Law: Social Accountability in the New Latin American Democracies.* Pittsburgh, PA: University of Pittsburgh Press.

Pinto, Juliet. 2009a. Diffusing and Translating Watchdog Journalism. *Media History* 15(1): 1–16.

———. 2009b. Muzzling the Watchdog: The Case of Disappearing Watchdog Journalism from Argentine Mainstream News. *Journalism* 9(6): 750–74.

Piore, Michael, and Andrew Schrank. 2006. Trading Up? *Boston Review* 31(5): 11–4.

Pires, Roberto. 2008. Promoting Sustainable Compliance: Styles of Labour Inspection and Compliance Outcomes in Brazil. *International Labour Review* 147(2–3): 199–229.

Plasser, Fritz. 2000. American Campaign Techniques Worldwide. *Harvard International Journal of Press/Politics* 5(4): 33–54.

———. 2001. Parties' Diminishing Relevance for Campaign Professionals. *Harvard International Journal of Press/Politics* 6(4): 44–59.

Polanyi, Karl. 1944. *The Great Transformation: The Political and Economic Origins of Our Time.* Boston, MA: Beacon.

Popkin, Margaret. 2002. Efforts to Enhance Judicial Independence in Latin America: A Comparative Perspective. In Due Process of Law Foundation and U.S. Agency for International Development, Office for Democracy and Governance, eds., *Guidance for Promoting Judicial Independence and Impartiality* (revised edition). Washington, DC. Available at http://www.dplf.org/uploads/1192572321.pdf.

Porto, Mauro. 2007. Frame Diversity and Citizen Competence: Towards a Critical Approach to News Quality. *Critical Studies in Media Communication* 24(4): 303–21.

Powell, G. 1982. *Contemporary Democracies: Participation, Stability, and Violence.* Cambridge, MA: Harvard University Press.

Prats i Català, Joan. 2003. Reinventar la burocracia y construir la nueva gerencia pública. Virtual Library of the Instituto Internacional de Gobernabilidad de Cataluña, Spain.

Prevost, Gary. 1996. The Nicaraguan Revolution—Six Years after the Sandinista Electoral Defeat. *Third World Quarterly* 17(2): 307–27.

Pritchard, David. 1992. The News Media and Public Policy Agendas. In J.D. Kennamer, ed., *Public Opinion, the Press, and Public Policy.* Westport, CT: Praeger.

Protess, David, Fay Lomax Cook, Jack C. Doppelt, James S. Ettma, Margaret T. Gordon, Donna R. Leff, and Peter Miller. 1991. *The Journalism of Outrage: Investigative Reporting and Agenda Building in America.* New York: The Guilford Press.

Przeworski, A., M.E. Alvarez, J.A. Cheibub, and F. Limongi. 2000. *Democracy and Development: Political Institutions and Well-Being in the World, 1950–1990.* Cambridge, England: Cambridge University Press.

Przeworski, Adam, and José María Maravall. 2003. *Democracy and the Rule of Law*. Cambridge, England: Cambridge University Press.

Pulido, Alberto. 2001. Chile: New Chilean Labor Law. *Mondaq Business Briefing*, October 15. Available at http://www.mondaq.com/article.asp?articleid=13704.

Remington, Thomas F., Steven S. Smith, and Moshe Haspel. 1998. Decrees, Laws, and Inter-Branch Relations in the Russian Federation. *Post-Soviet Affairs* 14: 287–322.

Remmer, Karen. 1980. Political Demobilization in Chile, 1973–1978. *Comparative Politics* 12(3): 275–301.

Repetto, F., and F. Potenza. 2005. Trayectorias institucionales y políticas frente a la pobreza: los casos de Argentina, Chile y México. *Revista del CLAD Reforma y Democracia* 31: 103–46. Caracas.

Riker, W. 1964. *Federalism: Origin, Operation, Significance*. Boston, MA: Little, Brown.

Rinne, Jeffrey. 2003. The Politics of Administrative Reform in Menem's Argentina: The Illusion of Isolation. In Ben Ross Schneider and Blanca Heredia, eds., *Reinventing Leviathan: The Politics of Administrative Reform in Developing Countries*. Coral Gables, FL: North-South Center Press/University of Miami.

Roberts, Kenneth. 2002. Social Inequalities without Class Cleavages in Latin America's Neoliberal Era. *Studies in Comparative International Development* 36(4): 3–33.

Rockwell, Rick, and Noreen Janus. 2003. *Media Power in Central America*. Urbana, IL: University of Illinois Press.

Rodden, J. 2004. Comparative Federalism and Decentralization: On Meaning and Measurement. *Comparative Politics* 36(4): 481–99.

———. 2006. *Hamilton's Paradox: The Promise and Peril of Fiscal Federalism*. New York: Cambridge University Press.

Rodrigues de Carvalho, Ernani. 2004. Em Busca da Judicialização da Política no Brasil: Apontamentos para uma Nova Abordagem. *Revista de Sociologia e Política* 23: 115–26.

Rodrik, Dani. 1995. Political Economy of Trade Policy. In G.M. Grossman and K. Rogoff, eds., *Handbook of International Economics*, Volume 3. Amsterdam: Elsevier.

———. 1996. Understanding Economic Policy Reform. *Journal of Economic Literature* 34(1): 9–41.

————. 2004. Industrial Policy for the Twenty-First Century. Working Paper Series rwp04-047. John F. Kennedy School of Government, Harvard University, Cambridge, MA.

————. 2007. *One Economics, Many Recipes: Globalization, Institutions, and Economic Growth.* Princeton, NJ: Princeton University Press.

Romer, Daniel, Sean Aday, and Kathleen Hall Jamieson. 2003. Television News and the Cultivation of Fear of Crime. *Journal of Communication* 53(1): 88–104.

Roxborough, Ian. 1992. Inflation and Social Pacts in Brazil and Mexico. *Journal of Latin American Studies* 24(3): 639–64.

Ruiz-Tagle, Pablo. 2005. El segundo piso de la Moneda, el pato volador, el pato cojo, y los desafíos de la constitución gatopardo. Santiago, Chile. Unpublished. Available at http://www.pabloruiz-tagle.cl/docs/constituciongatopardo-chilexxi.pdf.

Rundquist, Paul S., and Clay H. Wellborn. 1994. Building Legislatures in Latin America. In Lawrence D. Longley, ed., *Working Papers on Comparative Legislative Studies.* Appleton, WI: Research Committee of Legislative Specialists of the IPSA.

Saiegh, Sebastian M. 2005. The Role of Legislatures in the Policymaking Process. Paper prepared for the Inter-American Development Bank Workshop on State Reform, Public Policies, and Policymaking Processes, February 28–March 2, Washington, DC.

Samuels, D. 2003. *Ambition, Federalism, and Legislative Politics in Brazil.* Cambridge, England: Cambridge University Press.

————. 2004. The Political Logic of Decentralization in Brazil. In A. Montero and D. Samuels, eds., *Decentralization and Democracy in Latin America.* South Bend, IN: University of Notre Dame Press.

Samuels, D., and S. Mainwaring. 2004. Strong Federalism, Constraints on Central Government, and Economic Reform in Brazil. In E. Gibson, ed., *Federalism and Democracy in Latin America.* Baltimore, MD: Johns Hopkins University Press.

Sanabria, Harry. 2000. Resistance and the Arts of Domination: Miners and the Bolivian State. *Latin American Perspectives* 27(1): 56–81.

Sandbrook, Richard, Marc Edelman, Patrick Heller, and Judith Teichman. 2006. Can Social Democracies Survive in the Global South? *Dissent* 53(2): 76–83.

Santín Del Río, L. 2004. Decentralization and Democratic Governance in Mexico. In J. Tulchin and A. Selee, eds., *Decentralization and Democratic Governance in Latin America*. Woodrow Wilson Center Report on the Americas No. 12. Princeton University, NJ.

Santiso, Carlos. 2003. Insulated Economic Policymaking and Democratic Governance: The Paradox of Second Generation Reforms in Argentina and Brazil. School of Advanced International Studies (SAIS) Working Paper Series 02/03. Johns Hopkins University, Washington, DC.

Scarpetta, Stefano, and Thierry Tressel. 2002. Productivity and Convergence in a Panel of OECD Countries: Do Regulations and Institutions Matter? Working Paper No. 342. Economic Department, Organisation for Economic Co-operation and Development (OECD), Paris.

Scartascini, Carlos. 2008. Who's Who in the PMP. In E. Stein and M. Tommasi, with P. Spiller and C. Scartascini, eds., *Policymaking in Latin America: How Politics Shapes Policies*. Washington, DC and Cambridge, MA: Inter-American Development Bank and David Rockefeller Center for Latin American Studies, Harvard University.

Scartascini, Carlos, Ernesto Stein, and Mariano Tommasi. 2008. Political Institutions, State Capabilities, and Public Policy: International Evidence. Working Paper No. 661. Research Department, Inter-American Development Bank, Washington, DC.

Scavino, Julio. 2005. *Panorama de organizaciones de profesionales y trabajadores de la salud en las Américas*. Montevideo: Pan American Health Organization.

Schamis, Hector. 2002. *Re-Forming the State: The Politics of Privatization in Latin America and Europe*. Ann Arbor, MI: University of Michigan Press.

Schattschneider, E.E. 1960. *The Semi-Sovereign People: A Realist's View of Democracy in America*. New York: Holt, Rinehart & Winston.

Schneider, Ben Ross. 1997–98. Organized Business Politics in Democratic Brazil. *Journal of Interamerican Studies and World Affairs* 39(4) Winter: 95–127.

———. 2001. Business Politics and Regional Integration: The Advantages of Organization in NAFTA and MERCOSUR. In Victor Bulmer-Thomas, ed., *Regional Integration in Latin America and the Caribbean: The Political Economy of Open Regionalism*. London: Institute for Latin American Studies.

————. 2004a. *Business Politics and the State in Twentieth-Century Latin America*. Cambridge, England: Cambridge University Press.

————. 2004b. Organizing Interests and Coalitions in the Politics of Market Reform in Latin America. *World Politics* 56(3): 456–79.

————. 2005. Business Politics and Policy Making in Contemporary Latin America. Paper prepared for the Inter-American Development Bank Workshop on State Reform, Public Policies, and Policy-making Processes, February 28–March 2, Washington, DC. Available at http://www.iadb.org/research/pub_desc.cfm?pub_id= S-304.

————. Forthcoming. Business Politics in Latin America: Patterns of Fragmentation and Centralization. In David Coen, Wyn Grant, and Graham Wilson, eds., *The Oxford Handbook of Business and Government*. Oxford, England: Oxford University Press.

Schrank, Andrew. 2009. Professionalization and Probity in a Patrimonial State. *Latin American Politics & Society* 51(1): 91–115.

Schrank, Andrew, and Marcus Kurtz. 2005. Credit Where Credit Is Due: Open Economy Industrial Policy and Export Diversification in Latin America and the Caribbean. *Politics and Society* 33(4): 671–702.

Schurman, Rachel. 1996. Chile's New Entrepreneurs and the "Economic Miracle": The Invisible Hand or a Hand from the State? *Studies in Comparative International Development* 31(2): 83–109.

Schwartz, Frank. 1992. Of Fairy Cloaks and Familiar Talks: The Politics of Consultation. In Gary Allinson and Yasunori Sone, eds., *Political Dynamics in Contemporary Japan*. Ithaca, NY: Cornell University Press.

Seddon Wallack, Jessica, Alejandro Gaviria, Ugo Panizza, and Ernesto Stein. 2003. Particularism around the World. *The World Bank Economic Review* 17(1): 133–43.

Seers, Dudley. 1982. Inflation: The Latin American Experience. *Bulletin of Latin American Research* 1(2): 79–88.

Shadlen, Kenneth. 2004. *Democratization without Representation: The Politics of Small Industry in Mexico*. University Park, PA: Penn State University Press.

Shafer, D. Michael. 1994. *Winners and Losers: How Sectors Shape the Developmental Prospects of States*. Ithaca, NY: Cornell University Press.

Shapiro, Martin, and Alec Stone Sweet. 2002. *On Law, Politics, and Judicialization.* Oxford, England: Oxford University Press.

Shetreet, Shimon. 1985. Judicial Independence: New Conceptual Dimensions and Contemporary Challenges. In Shimon Shetreet and Jules Deschenes, eds., *Judicial Independence: The Contemporary Debate.* Dordrecht, The Netherlands: Martinus Nijhoff.

Shugart, M.S., and J.M. Carey. 1992. *Presidents and Assemblies: Constitutional Design and Electoral Dynamics.* Cambridge, England: Cambridge University Press.

Shugart, Matthew Soberg, and Scott Mainwaring. 1997. Presidentialism and Democracy in Latin America: Rethinking the Terms of the Debate. In Scott Mainwaring and Matthew Soberg Shugart, eds., *Presidentialism and Democracy in Latin America.* New York: Cambridge University Press.

Siavelis, Peter. 2000. *The President and Congress in Postauthoritarian Chile: Institutional Constraints to Democratic Consolidation.* University Park, PA: Penn State University Press.

Sieder, Rachel. 2007. The Judiciary and Indigenous Rights in Guatemala. *International Journal of Constitutional Law* 5(2): 211–41.

Sieder, Rachel, Line Schjolden, and Alan Angell, eds. 2005. *The Judicialization of Politics in Latin America.* New York: Palgrave Macmillan.

Silva, Eduardo. 1996. *The State and Capital in Chile: Business Elites, Technocrats, and Market Economics.* Boulder, CO: Westview.

Singh, Anoop, Agnès Belaisch, Charles Collyns, Paula De Masi, Reva Krieger, Guy Meredith, and Robert Rennhack, eds. 2005. *Stabilization and Reform in Latin America: A Macroeconomic Perspective on the Experience since the Early 1990s.* Washington, DC: International Monetary Fund.

Skidmore, Thomas. 2004. Brazil's Persistent Income Inequality: Lessons from History. *Latin American Politics and Society* 4(2): 13–51.

Smith, Peter. 1969. *Politics and Beef in Argentina.* New York: Columbia University Press.

———. 1979. *Labyrinths of Power: Political Recruitment in Twentieth Century Mexico.* Princeton, NJ: Princeton University Press.

Smithey, Shannon, and John Ishiyama. 2002. Judicial Activism in Post-Communist Politics. *Law and Society Review* 36(4): 719–42.

Snyder, Richard. 2001. *Politics after Neoliberalism: Reregulation in Mexico.* New York: Cambridge University Press.

Snyder, R., and D. Samuels. 2004. Legislative Malapportionment in Latin America. In E. Gibson, ed., *Federalism and Democracy in Latin America*. Baltimore, MD: Johns Hopkins University Press.

Sosa Plata, G., and R. Gómez García. 2008. Reforma a la legislación de radio, televisión y telecomunicaciones en México (2005–2007). In A. Vega Montiel, M. Portillo, and J. Repoll, eds., *Las claves necesarias de una comunicación para la democracia*. Mexico City and Villahermosa, Tabasco: Asociación Mexicana de Investigadores de la Comunicación and Universidad Juárez Autónoma de Tabasco.

Sousa, Mariana. 2007. A Brief Overview of Judicial Reform in Latin America: Objectives, Challenges, and Accomplishments. In Eduardo Lora, ed., *The State of State Reform in Latin America*. Washington, DC and Palo Alto, CA: Inter-American Development Bank and Stanford University Press.

Spiller, Pablo, Ernesto Stein, and Mariano Tommasi. 2008. Political Institutions, Policymaking, and Policy: An Introduction. In E. Stein and M. Tommasi, with P. Spiller and C. Scartascini, eds., *Policymaking in Latin America: How Politics Shapes Policies*. Washington, DC and Cambridge, MA: Inter-American Development Bank and David Rockefeller Center for Latin American Studies, Harvard University.

Spiller, Pablo, and Mariano Tommasi. 2003. The Institutional Foundations of Public Policy: A Transactions Approach with Application to Argentina. *Journal of Law, Economics and Organization* 19(2): 281–306.

———. 2007. *The Institutional Foundations of Public Policy in Argentina*. New York: Cambridge University Press.

Spitzer, Robert J. 1993. Introduction: Defining the Media-Policy Link. In Robert J. Spitzer, ed., *Media and Public Policy*. Westport, CT: Praeger.

Stahler-Sholk, Richard. 1995. The Dog That Didn't Bark: Labor Autonomy and Economic Adjustment under the Sandinista and UNO Governments. *Comparative Politics* 28(1): 77–102.

Stallings, B., and R. Kaufman. 1989. *Debt and Democracy in Latin America*. Boulder, CO: Westview.

Stein, Ernesto. 1999. Fiscal Decentralization and Government Size in Latin America. *Journal of Applied Economics* 2(2): 357–91.

Stein, Ernesto, and Mariano Tommasi. 2007. The Institutional Determinants of State Capabilities in Latin America. In F. Bourguignon and B. Pleskovic, eds., *Annual World Bank Conference on Development*

Economics 2007, Regional: Beyond Transition. Washington, DC: World Bank.

Stepan, A. 2004a. Electorally Generated Veto Players in Unitary and Federal Systems. In E. Gibson, ed., *Federalism and Democracy in Latin America.* Baltimore, MD: Johns Hopkins University Press.

————. 2004b. Toward a New Comparative Politics of Federalism, Multinationalism, and Democracy: Beyond Rikerian Federalism. In E. Gibson, ed., *Federalism and Democracy in Latin America.* Baltimore, MD: Johns Hopkins University Press.

Stokes, S. 2001. *Mandates and Democracy: Neoliberalism by Surprise in Latin America.* Cambridge, England: Cambridge University Press.

Stone Sweet, Alec. 1992. *The Birth of Judicial Politics in France: The Constitutional Council in Comparative Perspective.* New York: Oxford University Press.

————. 2000. *Governing with Judges: Constitutional Politics in Europe.* New York: Oxford University Press.

Strøm, K., and S. Swindle. 2002. Strategic Parliamentary Dissolution. *American Political Science Review* 96(3): 575–91.

Sturzenegger, F., and M. Tommasi, eds. 1998. *The Political Economy of Reform.* Cambridge, MA: MIT Press.

Suchyta IV, Joseph F. 1997. This Is Not Independence: The Mexican Judiciary and President Ernesto Zedillo's Reforms of 1994. *Legal Brief* L.J. 4. Available at www.LegalBrief.com/suchyta.html.

Swanson, David L. 2004. Transnational Trends in Political Communication: Conventional Views and New Realities. In F. Esser and B. Pfetsch, eds., *Comparing Political Communication: Theories, Cases, and Challenges.* New York: Cambridge University Press.

Tarr, Alan. 2002. *Judicial Process and Judicial Policymaking.* Belmont, CA: Wadsworth/Thomson Learning.

Tarrow, Sidney. 1998. *Power in Movement: Social Movements and Contentious Politics.* New York: Cambridge University Press.

Tate, C. Neal, and Torbjörn Vallinder, eds. 1995. *The Global Expansion of Judicial Power.* New York: New York University Press.

Taylor, Matthew MacLeod. 2004. Activating Judges: Courts, Institutional Structure, and the Judicialization of Policy Reform in Brazil, 1988–2002. Ph.D. dissertation, Georgetown University, Washington, DC.

Taylor, Michael. 1997. Why No Rule of Law in Mexico? Explaining the Weakness of Mexico's Judicial Branch. *New Mexico Law Review* 27(1): 141–66.

Taylor, Michael, and Valentine Herman. 1971. Party Systems and Government Stability. *American Political Science Review* 65: 28–37.

Taylor, Michelle M. 1996. When Electoral and Party Institutions Interact to Produce Caudillo Politics. *Electoral Studies* 15: 327–37.

Taylor-Robinson, Michelle M. 1999. Who Gets Legislation Passed in a Marginal Legislature and Is the Label Marginal Legislature Still Appropriate? A Study of the Honduran Congress. *Comparative Political Studies* 32(5): 589–625.

————. 2009. Selección de Candidatos al Congreso Nacional de Honduras por los Partidos Tradicionales. In Flavia Freidenberg and Manuel Alcántara Sáez, eds., *Selección de Candidatos, Política Partidista y Rendimiento Democrático*. Mexico City: Tribunal Electoral del Distrito Federal de México.

Teichman, Judith. 2001. *The Politics of Freeing Markets in Latin America: Chile, Argentina, and Mexico*. Chapel Hill, NC: University of North Carolina Press.

Tendler, Judith. 2002. The Fear of Education. Paper presented at meetings of Banco do Nordeste, July 19, Fortaleza, Brazil. Available at: http://www.oecd.org/dataoecd/43/40/2489865.pdf.

Thacker, Strom. 2000. *Big Business, the State, and Free Trade: Constructing Coalitions in Mexico*. Cambridge, England: Cambridge University Press.

Thomassen, Jacques. 1999. Political Communication between Political Elites and Mass Publics: The Role of Belief Systems. In Warren E. Miller, ed., *Policy Representation in Western Democracies*. New York: Oxford University Press.

Thorp, Rosemary. 1991. *Economic Management and Economic Development in Peru and Colombia*. Pittsburgh, PA: University of Pittsburgh Press.

Tilson, Donn J. 2004. Privatization and Government Campaigning in Ecuador. In D.J. Tilson and E.C. Alozie, eds., *Toward the Common Good: Perspectives in International Public Relations*. Boston, MA: Pearson.

Timmermans, A. 2006. Standing Apart and Sitting Together: Enforcing Coalition Agreements in Multiparty Systems. *European Journal of Political Research* 45(2): 263–83.

Tommasi, Mariano. 2004. Crisis, Political Institutions, and Policy Reform: The Good, the Bad, and the Ugly. In B. Tungodden, N. Stern, and I. Kolstad, eds., *Toward Pro-Poor Policies: Aid, Institutions, and Globalization,* Annual World Bank Conference on Development Economics–Europe 2003. Washington, DC: World Bank.

———. 2006. Federalism in Argentina and the Reforms of the 1990s. In J. Wallack and T.N. Srinivasan, eds., *Federalism and Economic Reform: International Perspectives.* Cambridge, England: Cambridge University Press.

Tommasi, M., and A. Velasco. 1996. Where Are We in the Political Economy of Reform? *Journal of Policy Reform* 1 (April): 187–238.

Treisman, D. 2000. Decentralization and Inflation: Commitment, Collective Action, or Continuity? *American Political Science Review* 94(4): 837–57.

Tsebelis, George. 1995. Decisionmaking in Political Systems: Veto Players in Presidentialism, Parliamentarism, Multicameralism, Multipartyism. *British Journal of Political Science* 25(3): 289–325.

———. 2002. *Veto Players: How Political Institutions Work.* Cambridge, England: Cambridge University Press.

Uggla, Fredrik. 2004. The *Ombudsman* in Latin America. *Journal of Latin American Studies* 36: 423–50.

UNDP (United Nations Development Programme). 2004. *La democracia en América Latina: hacia una democracia de ciudadanas y ciudadanos.* New York: UNDP. Available at http://www.undp.org/spanish/proddal/idal_completo.pdf.

———. 2005. *Democracy in Latin America: Towards a Citizens Democracy.* Buenos Aires: Aguilar.

Urrutia, Miguel. 1983. *Gremios, Política Económica y Democracia.* Bogotá: Fondo Cultural Cafetero.

Valadés, D. 2005. Cabinet Government and Latin American Neopresidentialism. *Mexican Law Review* [Instituto de Investigaciones Jurídicas] 4 (July–December).

Valenzuela, Arturo. 2006. Is Latin America Moving Left? In Klaus Schwab, ed., *Latin American Competitiveness Review 2006: Paving the Way to Regional Prosperity.* Geneva: World Economic Forum.

Vallinder, Torbjörn. 1994. The Judicialization of Politics: A World-Wide Phenomenon. *International Political Science Review* 15(2): 91–100 (Introduction).

Verner, Joel. 1984. The Independence of Supreme Courts in Latin America: A Review of the Literature. *Journal of Latin American Studies* 16(2): 463–506.

Villasmil, R., F. Monaldi, G. Ríos, and M. González. 2007. The Difficulties of Reforming an Oil Dependent Economy: The Case of Venezuela. In J.M. Fanelli, ed., *Understanding Market Reforms in Latin America: Similar Reforms, Diverse Constituencies, Varied Results*. New York: Palgrave Macmillan.

Waisbord, Silvio R. 1996. Investigative Reporting and Political Accountability in South America. *Critical Studies in Mass Communication* 13: 343–63.

———. 2000. *Watchdog Journalism in South America: News, Accountability and Democracy*. New York: Columbia University Press.

Waltman, Jerold, and Kenneth Holland, eds. 1988. *The Political Role of Law Courts in Modern Democracies*. New York: St. Martin's Press.

Wampler, Brian. 2004. Expanding Accountability through Participatory Institutions: Mayors, Citizens, and Budgeting in Three Brazilian Municipalities. *Latin American Politics and Society* 46(2): 73–99.

Warwick, P. 1979. The Durability of Coalition Governments in Parliamentary Democracies. *Comparative Political Studies* 11: 465–98.

———. 1992. Rising Hazards: An Underlying Dynamic of Parliamentary Government. *American Journal of Political Science* 36 (November): 857–76.

———. 1994. *Government Survival in Parliamentary Democracies*. Cambridge, England: Cambridge University Press.

Wehner, J. 2009. Cabinet Structure and Fiscal Policy Outcomes. Paper presented at the Midwest Political Science Association's 67th Annual National Conference, April 2–5, Chicago.

Weingast, B. 2005. The Performance and Stability of Federalism. In C. Menard and M. Shirley, eds., *Handbook of New Institutional Economics*. New York: Springer.

Weyland, Kurt. 1997. "Growth with Equity" in Chile's New Democracy? *Latin American Research Review* 32(1): 37–68.

Wibbels, E. 2005. *Federalism and the Market: Intergovernmental Conflict and Economic Reform in the Developing World.* Cambridge, England: Cambridge University Press.

Willis, E., C. Garman, and S. Haggard. 1999. The Politics of Decentralization in Latin America. *Latin American Research Review* 34(1): 7–56.

Wise, Carol. 1999. Latin American Trade Strategy at Century's End. *Business and Politics* 1(2) August: 117–54.

Wolfe, Christopher. 1997. *Judicial Activism: Bulwark of Freedom or Precarious Security?* Lanham, MD: Rowman & Littlefield Publishers.

World Bank. 2005. *World Development Indicators.* Washington, DC: World Bank.

World Economic Forum. 2004. *The Global Competitiveness Report 2003–2004.* New York: Oxford University Press.

———. 2005. *The Global Competitiveness Report 2004–2005.* New York: Oxford University Press.

———. Various years. *The Global Competitiveness Report*–Executive Opinion Survey. Available at www.weforum.org.

Wright, Erik Olin. 2000. Working-Class Power, Capitalist-Class Interests, and Class Compromise. *American Journal of Sociology* 105(4): 957–1002.

Wright, Thomas. 1982. *Landowners and Reform in Chile: The Sociedad Nacional de Agricultura 1919–40.* Urbana, IL: University of Illinois Press.

Zaller, John. 1994. Strategic Politicians, Public Opinion and the Gulf Crisis. In W. Lance Bennett and David L. Paletz, eds., *Taken by Storm: The Media, Public Opinion, and U.S. Foreign Policy in the Gulf Crisis.* Chicago: The University of Chicago Press.

Zemans, Frances Kahn. 1983. Legal Mobilization: The Neglected Role of the Law in the Political System. *American Political Science Review* 77(3): 690–703.

Zuvanic, Laura, and Mercedes Iacoviello. 2005. El rol de la burocracia en el PMP en América Latina. Paper prepared for the Inter-American Development Bank Workshop on State Reform, Public Policies and Policymaking Processes, February 28–March 2, Washington, DC.